Salud

Medical Spanish Dictionary and Phrase Book

This book is intended to assist the health professional to better communicate and understand the medical and health needs of the Spanish speaking community. It is not meant to replace language instruction.

Bonifacio Contreras
Educational News Service, Inc.

Salud Medical Spanish
Dictionary and Phrase Book

Copyright © 2003 by Educational News Service, Inc.

Publisher	Educational News Service, Inc.
Managing Editor	Rose Marie Anaya
Translation	Dr. Silvia Berger Smith College
	Emma Rivera-Rábago Mt. Holyoke College
Publication Design	Dog House Graphics
Front Cover Art	Pamela DiMauro
Back Cover Art	"Sky" Deborah Lusko
Marketing	University of New Mexico Press Educational News Service, Inc.

Educational News Service, Inc.
600 Central Avenue SE Suite 233
e-mail: info@ednews.com
www.ednews.com
1-800-600-4494

Library of Congress Cataloging–in-Publication Data
Contreras, Bonifacio,
Salud Medical Spanish Dictionary and Phrase Book
ISBN 1-881050-07-6
1. Dictionary, Spanish 2. Spanish medical phrases
3. medical terms 4. Spanish grammar

Second Edition 2003
Printed in the United States of America
Starline Printing
7111 Pan American Hwy. NE
Albuquerque, NM 87109
www.starlineprinting.com

This book is dedicated to my nephew Karl Anaya who passed away from cancer while this book was being prepared fo printing.

TABLE OF CONTENTS

Spanish Grammar at a Glance

Copyright © 2002 by Educational News Service, Inc.

PRONUNCIATION

The Spanish vowel consists of one short, crisp sound that basically never changes in pronunciation.

■ The Spanish **a** is pronounced like the *a* of the English word **father**.
casa *(house)*   parte *(part)*   vamos *(let's go)*   mañana *(tomorrow)*

■ The Spanish **e** is pronounced like the **e** in the word **met**. **Do not** pronounce a Spanish *e* as the *a* in m**a**y. (mesa is pronounced meh-sa — not **may**-sa).
mesa *(table)*   me *(me)*   este *(this)*   tela *(cloth)*

■ The Spanish **i** is pronounced like the *e* in the English word *me*.
Fino *(fine)*   libro *(book)*   sí *(yes)*   chico *(little)*

■ The Spanish **o** is pronounced like the *o* in the English n**o**te.
mucho *(much)*   todo *(all)*   corte *(court)*

■ The Spanish **u** is pronounced like the English *oo* in b**oo**t.
puro *(pure)*   tú *(you)*   uno *(one)*

■ The Spanish **qu** is pronounced like the English *k* or *'hard c'* in the words **k**ettle or **c**andy.
Que *(that)*   queso *(cheese)*

■ The Spanish **ñ** is pronounced like the *ni* in English onion.
año *(year)*   niño *(boy)*   niña *(girl)*

■ The Spanish **h** is always silent. 'Hacienda' is pronounced 'Ah-see-en-da.'
hermano *(brother)*   hambre *(hunger)*   hasta *(until)*

■ The Spanish **ll** is pronounced like the English *y* in **y**es. The word **llamar** *(to be named)* is pronounced 'ya-mar.'
calle *(street)*   ella *(her)*   milla *(mile)*

The Spanish **g** has two pronunciations. The most common is like the English *g* in **g**et.
gato *(cat)*   grito *(scream)*   golfo *(gulf)*

The Spanish **g** is also pronounced like the English *h* in **h**e.
gente *(people)*   gira *(tour)*   gitano *(gypsy)*

The Spanish **j** is pronounced similar to the English *h* in **h**oe. Junta *(meeting)* is pronounced 'hun-ta.'
jornada *(working day)*   jabón *(soap)*   jalar *(to pull)*

NOUNS AND ARTICLES

Spanish nouns have a gender: either **masculine** or **feminine**. Nouns that specifically refer to males (*father, brother, man* etc.) are masculine. Nouns that refer to females (*mother, sister, woman* etc.) are feminine. The same is true for animals. For all other nouns, it is necessary to learn the gender of the noun.

1. Nouns ending in **-o** are usually masculine. Thus:

el tí**o**	the uncle
el niñ**o**	the boy
el gat**o**	the cat
el centr**o**	the center

2. Nouns ending in **-a** are usually feminine. Thus:

la tí**a**	the aunt
la niñ**a**	the girl
la herman**a**	the sister
la puert**a**	the door

3. Nouns have **definite** and **indefinite** articles; both have four forms. The definite articles are: **el, la, los, las.**

el niño	the boy
la niña	the girl
los niños	the boys
las niñas	the girls

The indefinite articles are: **un, una, unos, unas.**

un libro	a book
una casa	a house
unos libros	some books
unas casas	some houses

4. Un, *(a, one)* is used before a masculine noun; una, *(a, one)*, is used before a feminine noun. Unos, *some,* is used before a masculine plural noun; unas, *some,* is used before a feminine plural noun.

5. To form the plural of nouns ending in **-o** or **-a**, an **-s** is added. Note that the plural of **el** is **los**, and the plural of **la** is **las**.

el herman**o**	**los** herman**os**
el cuart**o**	**los** cuart**os**
la herman**a**	**las** herman**as**
la cas**a**	**las** cas**as**

Add **-es** to nouns ending in a consonant.

la lecci**ón**	**las** lecci**ones**
el profesor	**los** profesor**es**
el mineral	**los** mineral**es**

6. All nouns ending in **-dad, -tad, -tud, -ción, -umbre, -sión** are feminine.

la ciu**dad**	the city
la universi**dad**	the university
la dificul**tad**	the difficulty
la acti**tud**	the attitude
la na**ción**	the nation
la c**umbre**	the summit
la transfu**sión**	the transfusion

THE DEFINITE ARTICLE

In Spanish the definite article must be used in certain situations:

1. The definite article is used with general or abstract nouns.
La leche es buena para la salud.
Milk is good for you.
El azúcar es dulce. Sugar is sweet.
El amor es una cosa divina.
Love is a divine thing.

2. Use the definite article before titles when talking about a person.
El doctor Rodríguez es dentista.
Doctor Rodriguez is a dentist.
La señora López es abogada.
Mrs. Lopez is a lawyer.

3. Use the definite article with parts of the body or with clothing.
Charlotte tiene los ojos verdes.
Charlotte has green eyes.
Juan tiene el pelo negro.
John has black hair.
María se puso la chaqueta.
Mary put on her coat.

4. Use the definite article before the name of a language.
El francés es un idioma muy bonito.
French is a beautiful language.
El inglés es la lengua de Estados Unidos.
English is the language of the United States.

5. Use the definite article with the days of the week when it means on a certain day.
Vamos de compras el lunes.
We are going shopping on Monday.
No estudio los domingos.
I do not study on Sundays.

6. Omit the definite article in direct discourse.
"Buenos días, profesor López?".
"Good morning, professor Lopez."
"¿Cómo está usted, señorita García"?
"How are you, Miss Garcia?"

7. Do not use the definite article before a language if the language is used immediately after **hablar** or after **en** or **de**.
El señor López no habla inglés.
Mr. Lopez does not speak English.
El libro está escrito en español.
The book is written in Spanish.
Hablo inglés.   I speak English.

8. Do not use the definite article before an unmodified noun denoting occupation, rank or nationality.
Es estadounidense. She is an American.
Es médico.   He is a doctor.
Es abogada.   She is a lawyer.

CONTRACTED ARTICLES

The masculine definite article **el** is contracted when it appears with the prepositions **a** or **de**. Note that such a contraction does not exist with the feminine article **la** nor with the plural article **los** or **las**.

1. The preposition **de** contracts with the article **el** to form **del** (of, from the).
¿Dónde está el libro del alumno.
Where is the student's book?
La mayoría del grupo está aquí.
The majority of the group is here.
El diccionario es del profesor, ¿no?
The dictionary is the teacher's, isn't it?

2. The preposition **a** (to) contracts with the article **el** to form **al** (to the).
Vamos al cine.
We are going to the movies.
María va al mercado.
Mary is going to the market.

3. No other forms of articles contract with **de** or **a**.
Juan y Carlos van a la escuela.
Juan and Carlos go to school.
La madre de los niños está aquí.
The children's mother is here.
Van a las montañas.
They are going to the mountains.

THE NEUTER ARTICLE "LO"

The neuter article lo is used before a masculine singular adjective. It is also used before a past participle or a possessive to express their value in an abstract sense. In addition, it forms abstract nouns.

1. Here are a few adjectives which may be combined with lo.

lo bello	the beautiful
lo bueno	the good
lo difícil	what is difficult
lo justo	that which is just
lo mejor	the best
lo necesario	the necessary
lo útil	what is useful

Es lo mejor que tenemos.
It is the best that we have.
Quiero lo justo. I want what is just.

2. Here are a few past participles used together with lo.

lo inesperado	the unexpected
lo ocurrido	what happened

3. Possesives such as mío and suyo can be used together with lo.

lo mío	what is mine
lo suyo	what is yours

Defiendo lo mío. I defend what is mine.

ADJECTIVES

In Spanish, adjectives agree in gender and number with the nouns or pronouns they modify.

1. Most adjectives in Spanish end in -o and have four forms. The forms are -o, -os, -a, -as. To form the plural of an adjective ending in -o, add an -s.

el carro moderno	the modern car
los carros modernos	the modern cars
la casa moderna	the modern house
las casas modernas	the modern houses

2. Adjectives that end in -e do not change the -e ending in the feminine. To form the plural, add an -s.

el carro grande	the large car
los carros grandes	the large cars
la casa grande	the large house
las casas grandes	the large houses

3. Adjectives that end with a consonant do not change for feminine nouns, either. To form the plural, add -es.

el auto azul	the blue car
la casa azul	the blue house
los autos azules	the blue cars
las casas azules	the blue houses
la niña bella	the pretty girl
las niñas bellas	the pretty girls

SHORT FORMS OF ADJECTIVES

Some adjectives have a shortened form before masculine singular nouns; they drop the -o. These adjectives are:

bueno	good
un buen hombre	a good man
malo	bad
un mal hombre	a bad man
primero	first
el primer capítulo	the first chapter
tercero	third
el tercer capítulo	the third chapter
alguno	some
algún* día	some day
ninguno	no one
ningún* hombre	no man

*NOTE: algún and ningún carry a written accent in this shortened form. The adjective grande has a shortened form in both the masculine and the feminine. However, it means *famous* or *great* instead of *big* or *large*.

un gran hombre	a great man
una gran mujer	a great woman

COMPARATIVE ADJECTIVES

To form the comparative of adjectives in Spanish, the construction más...que is used. This is equivalent to the comparative in English more ... than.

Juan es más alto que Carlos.
John is taller than Carl.
Tengo más dinero que él.
I have more money than he (has).

When a comparative is followed by a number, use más de instead of más ... que.

Tengo más de veinte dólares.
I have more than twenty dollars.

When the sentence is negative, más que and not más de is used with numbers.

No tengo más que diez dólares.
I have no more than ten dollars.

SUPERLATIVE ADJECTIVES

Form the superlative by using the word más and the appropriate article.

1. Superlatives are followed by the preposition de (más de). The article goes before the person or thing being compared.

Nueva York es la ciudad más grande de EE UU.
New York is the largest city in the US.
Ana es la niña más alta de la clase.
Ana is the tallest girl in the class.
Juan y Carlos son los más altos del grupo.
John and Carl are the tallest of the group.

2. The adjectives bueno, malo, grande, and pequeño have irregular forms in the comparative and the superlative. Note that each irregular form ends with the letters "or."

bueno	mejor
malo	peor
grande	mayor
pequeño	menor

3. The four irregular adjectives noted above take no articles in the comparative. Use a definite article to form the superlative.

Este auto es mejor que el otro.
This car is better than the other one.
Este auto es el mejor de todos.
This car is the best of all.

POSSESSIVE ADJECTIVES

Possesive adjectives are used to denote ownership or possession. They are placed before nouns and agree in number and in gender with the thing possessed, and not with the possessor.

mi profesor	mis profesores
tu profesor	tus profesores
su profesor	sus profesores
nuestro profesor	nuestros profesores
nuestra profesora	nuestras profesoras

1. Because su and sus can have several meanings, the definite article may be used with the following forms:

de usted	de ustedes
de él	de ellos
de ella	de ellas

Es el libro de él. It's his book.
Es la casa de ellos. It's their house.

2. The possessive adjective **nuestro** (our) has four forms: **nuestro, nuestros, nuestra** and **nuestras.**
Es nuestro coche. It's our car.
Son nuestros coches. They are our cars.
Es nuestra casa. It's our house.
Son nuestras casas. They are our houses.

DEMONSTRATIVE ADJECTIVES

Demonstrative adjectives agree in gender and number with the noun or pronoun they modify.

1. The demonstrative adjective **este** (this) has four forms:
Este libro es interesante.
This book is interesting.
Estos libros son interesantes.
These books are interesting.
Esta casa es bonita.
This house is pretty.
Estas casas son bonitas.
These houses are pretty.

2. In Spanish there are two ways to express the demonstrative adjective *that*. One of them is **ese**. It is used when the object is near to the person spoken to, but not to the speaker. **Ese** has four forms.
Ese niño es español.
That child (boy) is Spanish.
Esa niña es española.
That child (girl) is Spanish.
Esos niños son españoles.
Those children (boys) are Spanish.
Esas niñas son españolas.
Those children (girls) are Spanish.

3. **Aquel** is used when the object is far from both the speaker and the person spoken to. **Aquel** also has four forms.
Aquel señor es médico.
That man is a doctor.
Aquella señora es abogada.
That woman is a lawyer.
Aquellos señores son chilenos.
Those men are Chilean.
Aquellas señoras son españolas.
Those women are Spanish.

PERSONAL PRONOUNS

A personal pronoun can be used as either the subject or object of a verb. Personal pronouns may also be the object of a preposition, or a reflexive pronoun object. Since the verb ending in Spanish indicates the subject, it is most common to eliminate the subject pronoun. This is particularly true with **yo, tú, nosotros,** and **nosotras.**

1. The subject pronouns in Spanish are:

SINGULAR		PLURAL	
yo	I	**nosotros/as**	we
tú	you	**ustedes**	you
usted	you	**ustedes**	you
él	he	**ellos**	they
ella	she	**ellas**	they

*NOTE: In Latin America **vosotros/as** has been replaced by the pronoun **ustedes. Vosotros/as** is used mainly in Spain.

2. Direct object pronouns receive the action of the verb. The direct object pronouns in Spanish are:

SINGULAR		PLURAL	
me	me	**nos**	us
te	you	**los**	you, them
lo	you, him	**las**	you, them
la	you, her, it	**lo**	it

Jean me ve. Jean sees me.
Juan te ve. John sees you.
Rosa lo ve. Rosa sees you.
Yo lo veo. I see him.
Juan la ve. John sees her.
Tomás nos ve. Thomas sees us.
Sofía los ve. Sofia sees them.
Ana lee el libro. Ana reads the book.
Ana lo lee. Ana reads it.

3. The indirect object pronoun denotes the person *to, for, or from whom* any thing is given, told, sent, etc.

SINGULAR		PLURAL	
me	to me	**nos**	to us (m/f)
te	to you	**les**	to you (m/f)
le	to you	**les**	to them (m/f)
le	to him, to her		

Juan me mandó dinero.
John sent me some money.
Ella te compró un regalo.
She bought you a gift.
Yo le hablo en inglés.
I speak to him (to her) in English.
Pablo nos habla. Paul is talking to us.
Ella les habla. She is talking to them.

4. When using both direct and indirect object pronouns in the same sentence, the indirect object pronoun always comes first.
¿Cuándo me pagas el dinero? Te lo pago mañana.
When are you paying me the money? I'll pay (it to) you tomorrow.

5. When the main verb is an infinitive, attach both object pronouns to the end of the infinitive. The indirect object comes before the direct object.
José quiere mandármelo por correo.
Joe wants to send it to me by mail.

6. If the main verb is **poder, saber,** or **querer,** the two object pronouns may be placed in front of the verb.
María me lo quiere comprar.
Mary wants to buy it for me.

REFLEXIVE PRONOUNS

A reflexive verb is one whose subject and object are the same. The subject acts upon itself. A reflexive verb is indicated by the pronoun **se** attached to the infinitive.

1. The singular reflexive pronouns are:

me	myself; to (for) myself
te	yourself; to (for) yourself
se	himself; to (for) himself herself; to (for) herself yourself; to (for) yourself itself; to (for) itself themselves; to (for) themselves

Yo me visto. I dress myself.
Tú te vistes. You dress yourself.
Él se viste. He dresses himself.
Ella se viste. She dresses herself.

2. The plural reflexive pronouns are:

nos	ourselves; to (for) ourselves
se	yourselves; to (for) yourselves

Nos vestimos. We dress ourselves.
Se visten. They dress themselves.

*NOTE: In order to make these sentences negative, place **no** in front of the reflexive pronoun.

No se levanten todavía. Don't get up yet.

PRONOUNS AS OBJECTS OF A PREPOSITION

Some prepositions require a pronoun, called a prepositonal pronoun.

mí	me	**nosotros/as**	us
ti	you	**ustedes**	you
usted	you	**usted**	you
él	him	**ellos**	them
ella	her	**ellas**	them
ello	it		

sí (singular) yourself, himself, herself
sí (plural) yourselves, themselves

Esos libros son para mí.
Those books are for me.
Las flores son para ti.
The flowers are for you.
Hablamos de él. We're talking about him.
Su padre insistió en ello.
Her father insisted on it.

NOTE: The preposition **con** combines with **mí**, **ti**, and **sí** to form the words **conmigo**, *with me*, **contigo** *with you*, and **consigo** *with yourself, with himself, with herself, with yourselves, with themselves.*

Charlotte va conmigo.
Charlotte is going with me.
Iré contigo. I'll go with you.
No voy contigo. Voy con ellos.
I'm not going with you. I'm going with them.

RELATIVE PRONOUNS

A relative pronoun refers to something previously mentioned in the sentence. It may serve as the subject or object of a verb, or as the object of a preposition. **Que** and **quien** are the relatives most commonly used.

1. The relative pronoun **que** can be used to replace either a person or a thing, and can function as either the subject or object of the clause.
   La muchacha que habla con Juan es mi hermana.
   The girl who is talking to John is my sister.
   El libro que está en la mesa es mío.
   The book that is on the table is mine.
   La casa en que viven es grande.
   The house in which they live is large.

2. The relative pronoun **quien** (**quienes**), *who/whom*, can replace the pronoun **que**.
   Hablé con Ana, quien es su tía.
   I spoke with Ana, who is his aunt.
   El señor Molina, quien es profesor, conoce a mi padre.
   Mr. Molina, who is a teacher, knows my father.

3. **Quien** and **quienes**, when used with a preposition, means *whom*.
   El médico, a quien llamamos, vino enseguida.
   The doctor, whom we called, came right away.
   Los amigos, a quienes espero, no han llegado.
   The friends, whom I am waiting for, have not arrived.

4. **Lo que**, *what* or *that which*, is used as a neuter relative pronoun when referring to an abstract or general idea.
   Lo que necesita es más dinero.
   What he needs is more money.
   Lo que él pide es imposible.
   What he asks is impossible.

5. **Lo cual** is used in supplementary clauses when the antecedent is a clause, phrase or an idea.

María estudia todos los días, lo cual es bueno.
Mary studies every day, which is good.
Ella se negó a recibirme, lo cual lamento mucho.
She refused to see me, which I regret.

6. **El cual, la cual, los cuales, las cuales,** *who, that, who, which, the one's which, the one's who,* may be used in place of **que**, to clarify number and gender.
   Los libros, los cuales están sobre la mesa, son míos.
   The books, which are on the table, are mine.

VERBS

Verbs are classified according to their infinitive ending: **-ar, -er,** or **-ir.** The three classes are called the first, second, and third conjugation.

THE PRESENT TENSE

1. The **FIRST CONJUGATION** is the **-ar** conjugation. To form the present tense, replace the **-ar** ending with **-o, -as, -a, -amos, -an.**

NOTE: In Spain, **vosotros(as)** is the plural form of **tú** and is used when addressing two or more relatives, intimate friends, small children, or animals. In the south of Spain and in Latin America, **vosotros** has been replaced by **ustedes.** We will omit the **vosotros** form in these conjugations.

yo hablo	I speak
tú hablas	you speak
él habla	he speaks
ella habla	she speaks
usted habla	you speak
nosotros/as hablamos	we speak
ustedes hablan	you speak
ellos hablan	they speak
ellas hablan	they speak

Yo hablo español. I speak Spanish.
Tú hablas inglés. You speak English.
Ella habla árabe. She speaks Arabic.
Nosotros hablamos español.
We speak Spanish.
¿Hablan ustedes inglés?
Do you speak English?
Ellos hablan alemán. They speak German.

NOTE: Omit subject pronouns except when needed for clarity and emphasis.
Hablo español. I speak Spanish.
Hablan inglés. They speak English.

COMMON 1st CONJUGATION VERBS

buscar	to look for	**cambiar**	to change
gastar	to spend	**hablar**	to talk
cantar	to sing	**invitar**	to invite
enseñar	to teach	**lavar**	to wash
esperar	to wait	**pagar**	to pay
estudiar	to study	**viajar**	to travel

2. The **SECOND CONJUGATION** is referred to as the **-er** conjugation. The personal endings **-o, -es, -e, -emos, -en** are added to the stem.

yo como	I eat
tú comes	you eat
él come	he eats
ella come	she eats
usted come	you eat
nosotros/as comemos	we eat
ustedes comen	you eat
ellos comen	they eat
ellas comen	they eat

Nosotros comemos carne. We eat meat.
¿Comen ustedes carne? Do you eat meat?

COMMON 2ᴺᴰ CONJUGATION VERBS

aprender	to learn	**esconder**	to hide
beber	to drink	**leer**	to read
comer	to eat	**meter**	to insert
correr	to run	**vender**	to sell

3. The **THIRD CONJUGATION** is referred to as the -ir conjugation. The personal endings for the -ir verbs are -o, -es, -e, -imos, -en. Note that most of the personal endings are the same for both the -er and -ir verbs.

yo vivo	I live
tú vives	you live
él vive	he lives
ella vive	she lives
usted vive	you live
nosotros/as vivimos	we live
ustedes viven	you live
ellos viven	they live
ellas viven	they live

Yo vivo en Tejas. I live in Texas.
¿Dónde vives tú? Where do you live?
Nosotros vivimos en México.
We live in Mexico.

COMMON 3ᴿᴰ CONJUGATION VERBS

abrir	to open	**admitir**	to admit
asistir	to attend	**cubrir**	to cover
subir	to go up	**sufrir**	to suffer
vivir	to live		

THE IMPERFECT

There are two past tenses in Spanish. One is the **imperfect** and the other is the **preterite**. Their uses vary. The imperfect tense is used for events that *used* to happen or *repeated* or habitual events in the past. The translation of the imperfect into English depends on the context.

1. In order to form the imperfect tense of regular -ar verbs, drop the infinitive ending -ar and add the following endings: -aba, -abas, -aba, -ábamos, -aban.

hablaba { I used to speak; talk
I was speaking; talking
I spoke; talked

hablaba	hablábamos
hablabas	
hablaba	hablaban

María hablaba de su viaje.
Mary was talking about her trip. Mary used to talk about her trip. Mary talked about her trip.

Yo nadaba cada verano.
I used to swim every summer. I swam every summer.

Ella cenaba en aquel restaurante todos los viernes.
She used to eat dinner in that restaurant every Friday. She ate dinner in that restaurant every Friday.

Tú cantabas muy bien. You used to sing very well. You sang very well.

2. The imperfect tense of regular -er and -ir verbs is the same. To form the imperfect tense, drop the infinitive ending and add the following to the stem: -ía, ías, -ía, -íamos, -ían.

comía { I was eating
I used to eat
I ate

vivía { I was living
I used to live
I lived

comía	comíamos
comías	
comía	comían
vivía	vivíamos
vivías	
vivía	vivían

Comíamos en ese restaurante.
We used to eat in that restaurant.
Yo leía mucho cuando era niño.
I used to read a lot when I was young.
Ustedes vivían en Madrid.
You used to live in Madrid.

THE PRETERITE

The **preterite** is the past tense used to express an action completed at a definite time in the past. The English auxiliary **did** is always understood.

1. The preterite of the regular -ar verbs is formed by dropping the infinitive ending and adding the following endings: -é, -aste, -ó, -amos, -aron.

hablé	hablamos
hablaste	
habló	hablaron

Tú hablaste con él ayer.
You spoke with him yesterday.
El halló el dinero la semana pasada.
He found the money last week.
Ellos compraron una casa pequeña.
They bought a small house.

2. The preterite of regular -er and -ir verbs is formed by dropping the infinitive ending and adding the following personal endings: -í, -iste, -ió, -imos, -ieron.

comí	comimos
comiste	
comió	comieron
viví	vivimos
viviste	
vivió	vivieron

Viví en España tres años.
I lived in Spain for three years.
Ellos comieron aquí ayer.
They ate here yesterday.
Recibió la carta esta tarde.
He received the letter this afternoon.
Carlos no asistió ayer a la clase.
Carlos didn't attend class yesterday.

THE FUTURE

The future tense in Spanish has only one set of endings for all three conjugations.

1. Add the following endings to the infinitive: -é, -ás, -á, -emos, -án.

hablaré	hablaremos
hablarás	
hablará	hablarán
comeré	comeremos
comerás	
comerá	comerán
viviré	viviremos
vivirás	
vivirá	vivirán

Hablaré con él mañana.
I'll speak with him tomorrow.

Comerán a las seis. They will eat at six.
Ana escribirá la carta.
Ana will write the letter.

2. In spoken Spanish, the future is often formed by using **ir a** + infinitive. This is equivalent to the English "going to."

Voy a trabajar allí.
I'm going to work there.
Vamos a comer en casa.
We are going to eat at home.

THE CONDITIONAL

The conditional tense expresses an idea dependent on a condition which is either expressed or understood.

1. The conditional is formed by adding the endings -ía, -ías, -ía, -íamos, -ían to the entire infinitive, not just the stem. These endings are the same for all three conjugations. Note that they are also the same personal endings as those used for the imperfect of -er and -ir verbs.

hablaría	**hablaríamos**
hablarías	
hablaría	**hablarían**

comería	**comeríamos**
comerías	
comería	**comerían**

viviría	**viviríamos**
vivirías	
viviría	**vivirían**

2. Use the conditional to express conjecture or probability, referring to the past.
María estaría enferma.
Mary was probably ill.
Llegarían anoche.
They probably arrived last night.

REFLEXIVE VERBS

A reflexive verb is one whose subject and object are the same. The subject acts upon itself. The verb is always used with some form of the reflexive pronoun. In Spanish a reflexive verb is indicated by the pronoun **se** *(singular:* oneself, yourself, himself, herself, itself; *plural:* yourselves, themselves) attached to the infinitive.

1. The reflexive verb **lavarse** (to wash oneself) is often used as the model reflexive verb. Here we conjugate it in the present tense.

me lavo	I wash myself
te lavas	you wash yourself
se lava	you wash yourself he washes himself she washes herself it washes itself
nos lavamos	we wash ourselves
se lavan	you wash yourselves they wash themselves

NOTE: Reflexives, like other object pronouns, often precede the verb. When used with the infinitive, they follow the verb and are attached to it.

Quiero lavarme. I want to wash myself.
¿Quieres lavarte?
Do you want to wash yourself?
Voy a acostarme. I'm going to bed.

2. A reflexive verb is called a reciprocal when the action passes from one person or thing to another, or from one group to another. It is only used in the first and third persons plural.

Se miran. They look at each other.
Nos ayudamos. We help each other.

THE SUBJUNCTIVE

There are four tenses of the subjunctive in common use. The present subjunctive and the past subjunctive are by far the most common.

1. The **present subjunctive** of all three verb types (-ar, -er, -ir) is formed by adding the endings to the stem of the present indicative first person singular. Drop the final -o and add the following endings:

-ar verbs **-e, -es, -e, -emos, -en**
-er verbs **-a, -as, -a, -amos, -an**
-ir verbs **-a, -as, -a, -amos, -an**

hablar (and regular -ar verbs)	
hable	**hablemos**
hables	
hable	**hablen**

comer (and regular -er verbs)	
coma	**comamos**
comas	
coma	**coman**

vivir (and regular -ir verbs)	
viva	**vivamos**
vivas	
viva	**vivan**

A few common verbs often used with the subjunctive:

querer	**estar contento**	**esperar**
preferir	**temer**	**sentir**

Yo quiero que ustedes hablen inglés.
I want you to speak English.
Ella prefiere que comamos en casa.
She prefers that we eat at home.

NOTE: The present subjunctive can be translated in many ways according to how it is used. Many times it is translated as *may...,* expressing possibility or uncertainty. The present subjunctive is also used in commands with **usted** and **ustedes**. With **tú**, it is used only in negative commands.

Hable usted español. Speak Spanish.
No hables tú. (Negative) Don't talk.
Quizas me escriba.
Perhaps he'll write to me.

2. The past subjunctive is formed on the stem of the preterite of the third person plural (ellos). For -ar verbs, add these endings to the stem: -ara, -aras, -ara, -áramos, -aran.

hablara	**habláramos**
hablaras	
hablara	**hablaran**

Te dije que te lavaras las manos.
I told you to wash your hands.
Le di el dinero para que comprara el libro.
I gave him the money so that he might buy the book.

For -er and -ir verbs, find the stem in the same way (the preterite of the third person plural [ellos]) and add the following endings: -iera, -ieras, -iera, -iéramos, -ieran.

comiera	**comiéramos**
comieras	
comiera	**comieran**

viviera	**viviéramos**
vivieras	
viviera	**vivieran**

Si recibiera el dinero, yo pagaría la cuenta.
If I should receive the money, I would pay the bill.

Esperábamos que comieran temprano.
We were hoping that they would eat early.

3. The **present perfect subjunctive** is formed with the present subjunctive of the auxiliary verb **haber** and the past participle of the main verb.

haya hablado	haya comido
hayas hablado	hayas comido
haya hablado	haya comido
hayamos hablado	hayamos comido
hayan hablado	hayan comido

haya vivido
hayas vivido
haya vivido
hayamos vivido
hayan vivido

No creo que hayamos pagado la cuenta todavía.
I don't think we have paid the bill yet.

Espero que por lo menos su ayudante los haya visto. I hope at least that your assistant has seen them.

4. The **past perfect subjunctive** is formed with the imperfect subjunctive of **haber** plus a past participle.

hubiera hablado	hubiera comido
hubieras hablado	hubieras comido
hubiera hablado	hubiera comido
hubiéramos hablado	hubiéramos comido
hubieran hablado	hubieran comido

hubiera vivido
hubieras vivido
hubiera vivido
hubiéramos vivido
hubieran vivido

Yo temía que Carlos no hubiera hablado con ella.
I feared that Carlos might not have spoken with her.

Ellos querían que hubiéramos llegado antes.
They wanted us to have arrived earlier.

USES OF THE SUBJUNCTIVE

In Spanish the subjunctive mood is used almost always in subordinate clauses to designate events that the speaker sees as not part of reality or not part of his or her own experience. It is used to express doubt, uncertainty, or when a contrary-to-fact supposition is made. It is also used in the following situations:

1. The present subjunctive is used in direct and implied commands, both affirmative and negative.

Hable usted
Hablen ustedes } Speak.

No hable usted
No hablen ustedes } Do not speak.
No hables tú.

2. The subjunctive is used with verbs of volition: some common volition verbs are querer, aconsejar, sugerir, preferir recomendar, etc.
Te aconsejo que estudies.
I advise you to study.
Ella quiere que yo le escriba.
She wants me to write to her.
Yo les sugiero que no se muden hasta fines de junio.

I suggest that you don't move until the end of June.

3. The subjunctive is also required after many impersonal expressions that denote an element of subjectivity.

es necesario	
es preciso }	it is necessary
es menester	
es posible	it is possible
es imposible	it is impossible
es probable	it is probable
es bueno	it is good
es malo	it is bad
es mejor	it is better
es una lástima	it is a pity
es raro	it is rare
es importante	it is important
es fácil	it is easy
es difícil	it is difficult
es triste	it is sad
puede ser que	it may be that

Es necesario que llegues a tiempo.
It is necessary that you arrive on time.
Es importante que ella lo prepare.
It is important that she prepare it.
Es una lástima que estés enfermo.
It's a pity that you are ill.
Quiero que se lave las manos.
I want him to wash his hands.

4. Use the subjunctive with expressions of doubt.

no creer	not to believe
dudar	to doubt
es dudoso	it is doubtful
es incierto	it is uncertain
no es cierto	it is not certain

No creo que ella pueda venir.
I don't believe she will be able to come.
Es dudoso que Juan escriba.
It is doubtful that John will write.

5. The subjunctive is used when one person tells (**decir**) or asks (**pedir**) another person to do something.
Dígale que lo escriba.
Tell him to write it.
Me dijo que lo escribiera.
He told me to write it.
Nos piden que salgamos.
They are asking us to leave.

THE PROGRESSIVE TENSES

The progressive tenses in Spanish show that the action of the verb is in the process of taking place. The progressive forms are most commonly used with the present and the imperfect. It is on occasion also used with the future. **Estar, seguir, ir,** or **andar** are used along with the present participle to form the progressive tenses. You will find that the most commonly used auxiliary is **estar**.

1. The **present progressive** describes an action that is taking place at the moment that we are talking. In Spanish, it is formed with the present tense of **estar** and the equivalent of the *-ing* form of the conjugated verb. The *-ing* form endings in Spanish are -ando for the -ar (**hablar**) verbs and -iendo for the -er (**comer**) and -ir (**vivir**) verbs.

hablar (FIRST CONJUGATION VERB)
estoy hablando
estás hablando
está hablando
estamos hablando
están hablando

comer (SECOND CONJUGATION VERB)
estoy comiendo
estás comiendo
está comiendo
estamos comiendo
están comiendo

vivir (THIRD CONJUGATION VERB)
estoy viviendo
estás viviendo
está viviendo
estamos viviendo
están viviendo

Estoy estudiando mi lección.
I am studying my lesson.
María está comiendo. Mary is eating.
¿Qué estás tomando?
What are you drinking?
¿Dónde estás viviendo?
Where are you living? (Where do you live?)

NOTE: The present progressive is never used in Spanish to refer to a future action:

Salgo mañana.
I'm leaving tomorrow. (I leave tomorrow.)

2. The **past (imperfect) progressive** indicates an action in progress in the past. It is formed with the imperfect (simple past) tense of the verb **estar** and the -ando, or -iendo form of the verb.

estaba hablando
estabas hablando
estaba hablando
estábamos hablando
estaban hablando

estaba comiendo
estabas comiendo
estaba comiendo
estábamos comiendo
estaban comiendo

estaba viviendo
estabas viviendo
estaba viviendo
estábamos viviendo
estaban viviendo

¿En qué estabas pensando?
What were you thinking about?
¿Qué estabas haciendo?
What were you doing?

3. **Seguir** (instead of **estar**) is often used to form a progressive tense to imply that an action is continuing (not yet finished).

Ellos siguen trabajando.
They are still working.

IRREGULAR VERBS
1. The verbs **ir, dar,** and **estar** are considered irregular in the present tense. Note, however, that the only irregularity exists in the first person singular (**yo**). All other forms are the same as those for a regular -ar verb.

IR	DAR	ESTAR
voy	doy	estoy
vas	das	estás
va	da	está
vamos	damos	estamos
van	dan	están

2. **Poner, hacer, valer, traer** and **salir** are considered irregular in the present tense. Again, the only irregular form is the first person singular **yo**.

PONER	HACER	VALER
pongo	hago	valgo
pones	haces	vales
pone	hace	vale
ponemos	hacemos	valemos
ponen	hacen	valen

TRAER	SALIR
traigo	salgo
traes	sales
trae	sale
traemos	salimos
traen	salen

3. Most verbs that end in **-cer** or **-cir** are also irregular in the present tense. Again, they are irregular only in the first person singular.

APARECER	CONOCER
aparezco	conozco
apareces	conoces
aparece	conoce
aparecemos	conocemos
aparecen	conocen

CONDUCIR	DECIR
conduzco	digo
conduces	dices
conduce	dice
conducimos	decimos
conducen	dicen

4. **Saber** is also irregular in the present tense. The only irregularity is the first person singular, (**yo**):**sé, sabes, sabe, sabemos, saben.**

IRREGULAR VERBS:

PAST TENSE
Some verbs are irregular in the preterite (simple past) tense.

ANDAR	CAER	DAR
anduve	caí	di
anduviste	caíste	diste
anduvo	cayó	dio
anduvimos	caímos	dimos
anduvieron	cayeron	dieron

SER AND ESTAR
There are two verbs in Spanish which have the English meaning *to be*: ser and estar.

1. **Ser** is used to express origin, possession and material. The preposition **de** is added.

Es de España. He is from Spain.
Es el libro de Rosa. It is Rosa's book.
La casa es de madera.
The house is made of wood.

2. **Ser** is used for description.
El auto es rojo. The car is red.
La casa es grande. The house is big.

Use **ser** with expressions of time.

Es la una. It is one o'clock.
Hoy es martes. Today is Tuesday.

3. **Ser** is used with marital status.
¿Es usted casada? Are you married?

4. **Estar** is used to express location or position. Note that the verb estar is always used whether the location is permanent or temporary.

Ellos están en Los Ángeles.
They are in Los Angeles.

Madrid está en España.
Madrid is in Spain.
El hotel está en la Avenida Colón.
The hotel is on Columbus Avenue.

5. **Estar** is used to describe a current condition.
¿Cómo está su esposa?

13

How is your wife?
María está enferma. Mary is ill.

6. Estar is used to form the progressive tenses.
Estoy escribiendo. I am writing.
Estamos jugando al béisbol.
We are playing baseball.

PEDIR AND PREGUNTAR
The verbs **pedir** and **preguntar** mean *to ask*.

1. Pedir means to ask for or to request something:
¿Qué le piden los muchachos?
What do the boys ask you for?
¿Vas a pedirle dinero a Juan?
Are you going to ask Juan for money?

2. Preguntar means to ask a question:
¿Qué vas a preguntarle a María?
What are you going to ask Mary?
Le voy a preguntar a María si quiere ir al cine.
I'm going to ask Mary if she wants to go to the movies.

CARDINAL NUMBERS

0	cero
1	uno
2	dos
3	tres
4	cuatro
5	cinco
6	seis
7	siete
8	ocho
9	nueve
10	diez
11	once
12	doce
13	trece
14	catorce
15	quince
16	dieciséis
17	diecisiete
18	dieciocho
19	diecinueve
20	veinte
21	veintiuno
22	ventidós
30	treinta
31	treinta y uno

40	cuarenta
50	cincuenta
60	sesenta
70	setenta
80	ochenta
90	noventa
100	cien(to)
101	ciento uno
110	ciento diez
200	doscientos
300	tescientos
400	cuatrocientos
500	quinientos
600	seiscientos
700	setecientos
800	ochocientos
900	novecientos
1000	mil
1.000.000	un millón
2.000.000	dos millones

ORDINAL NUMBERS
Ordinal numbers in Spanish agree with the noun in number & gender: **primero/a, primeros/as**, etc.

1 primero	first
2 segundo	second
3 tercero	third
4 cuarto	fourth
5 quinto	fifth
6 sexto	sixth
7 séptimo	seventh
8 octavo	eighth
9 noveno	ninth
10 décimo	tenth
11 undécimo	eleventh
12 duodécimo	twelfth
13 decimotercero	thirteenth
14 decimocuarto	fourteenth
15 decimoquinto	fifteenth
16 decimosexto	sixteenth
17 decimoséptimo	seventeenth
18 decimoctavo	eighteenth
19 decimonoveno	nineteenth
20 vigésimo	twentieth
30 trigésimo	thirtieth

CAREERS & OCCUPATIONS
A selection of common occupations & titles.

abogado/a	lawyer
actor, actriz	actor, actress
aduanero/a	customs officer
agente de relaciones públicas	public relations agent
agente de bolsas	stockbroker
agente de inmigración	immigration agent
agente de viajes	travel agent
agente de la migra	INS agent
agente secreto	secret agent
agricultor	farmer
alcalde	mayor
ama de casa	housewife
analista de finanzas	financial analyst

analista de sistemas	systems analyst
artesano	craftsman
asistente social (manejador/a de casos)	caseworker
autónomo que trabaja por cuenta propia	self employed
auxiliar de vuelo	flight attendant
azafata	flight attendant
bibliotecario/a	librarian
bolsista	stockbroker
cajero/a	cashier; bank teller
camarera/o	waitress, waiter
camionero	truck driver
camionero	teamster
camionista	truck driver
carpintero	carpenter
cartero/a	mail carrier
cervecero	brewer
chófer de autobús	bus driver (Spain)
científico/a	scientist
cineasta	film director
cocinero	cook
comprador/a	buyer
conductor/a	driver
conductor/a de autobús	bus driver (Lat Am)
consejero/a	counselor
conserje	caretaker
contador/a	accountant
contratista	contractor
corredor de bienes raíces	realtor
corredor de bolsas	stockbrocker
corredor de fincas	realtor
dentista	dentist
dependiente	clerk
dibujante	draftsman
dibujante de chistes	cartoonist
director/a	curator (museum)
doble agente	double agent
doctor/a	doctor (title)
director/a de reparto	casting director
economista	economist
electricista	electrician
empresario/a	businessman/woman
enfermero/a	nurse
entrenador/a	coach
estudiante	student
experto en computadoras	computer expert
fontanero	plumber
gerente	manager
granjero	farmer (Lat Am)
higienista dental	dental hygienist
hombre de la limpieza	cleaning man
humorista	cartoonist
informático/a	computer scientist
ingeniero/a agrónomo	agronomist
ingeniero/a de minas	mining engineer

ingeniero/a forestal	forestry expert
ingeniero/a técnico	engineeering technician
inspector/a de fábricas	factory inspector
intérprete	interpreter
jefe de cocina	chef
jubilado/a	retired
juez/a	judge
librero/a	bookseller
locutor/a	announcer
maestro/a	teacher (elem school)
mampostero	mason
mandadero/a	messenger
matemático/a	mathmatician
médico/a	physician
mensajero/a	messenger
meteorólogo	weatherman
miembro de un grupo de presión	lobbyist
monja	nun
mozo	waiter
mujer de la limpieza	cleaning woman
músico/a	musician
niñera	nanny
obrero/a de construcción	construction worker
óptico/a	optician
optometrista	optometrist
panadero	baker
peluquero/a	hairdresser
periodista	journalist
piloto	pilot
plomero	plumber
policía	policeman
policía femenino (agente de policía)	policewoman
político/a	politician
portero/a	janitor
profesor/a	teacher (high school)
profesor/a	professor (Univ)
programador	programmer
reportero/a	reporter
sacerdote	priest
sastre	tailor
tenedor/a de libros	bookkeeper
terapista físico	physical therapist
trabajador social	social worker
vendedor/a	seller
veterinario/a	veterinary surgeon; vet
viajante de comercio	traveling salesman

SPANISH-ENGLISH
DICTIONARY

A

a principios de at the beginning of
a prueba de niños childproof
abajo; de abajo (under) beneath; **el piso de abajo** the floor beneath; **el abajo firmante** the undersigned; **los abajo firmantes** the undersigned
abajofirmante: el abajofirmante the undersigned; **la abajofirmante** the undersigned
abandono infantil child neglect
abatido depressed
abatimiento depression
abdomen agudo acute abdomen
abortar miscarry
aborto abortion
aborto cervical cervical abortion
aborto espontáneo miscarriage
aborto inducido induced abortion
aborto no provocado miscarriage
aborto provocado induced abortion
aborto terapéutico therapeutic abortion
abotagado (body) bloated; (eyes, face) swollen
abotagarse (body) become bloated; (eyes, face) swell up
abotonar button
abrasador burning
abrigo coat
abril April (see enero)
abrochar button
absceso abscess
absceso crónico chronic abscess
absorbente absorbent
absorbifaciente absorbifacient
absorción absorption
abstenerse abstain
abstenerse de las relaciones sexuales abstain from sexual relations
abstracción abstraction
abuela grandmother
abuelita grandmother; granny
abuelito grandfather
abuelo gramps; grandfather; grandad; grandaddy
abuelos grandparents; **tus abuelos** your grandparents
abulia extreme apathy; abulia
abusar abuse; molest
abusar sexualmente de molest sexually
abuso abuse
abuso de sustancias drug abuse
abusos deshonestos (sexually) molestation; sexual abuse
ácaros mites
accidente accident
aceite de hígado de bacalao cod-liver oil
aceite de ricino castor oil
aceite mineral mineral oil
acetaminofén acetaminophen
acetato de celulosa cellulose acetate
achaques aches and pains; ailments
ácido acid
ácido acético acetic acid
ácido arsénico arsenic acid
ácido ascórbico ascorbic acid

ácido bórico boric acid
ácido ciánico cyanic acid
ácido fólico folic acid
acné acne
acoso sexual sexual harassment
acostarse get into bed; go to bed; lie down
acrílico acrylic
acta de nacimiento birth certificate
activo active
acto sexual coitus
actual present
actualidad present; present day; now
acuchillar to stab
acupuntura acupuncture
adelgazar grow thin; slim down
adicción addiction; **causar adicción** cause addiction; **que crea adicción** addictive (drugs); **que crea dependencia** addictive (drugs)
adicción a la heroína heroin addiction
adicto addict (drugs); addicted
adicto a addicted to (drugs)
¡adiós! bye; bye-bye
aditivos alimentarios food additives
administración del hospital hospital administration
administrar administer
administrar medicación administer medication
ADN DNA
adrenalina adrenalin
adulteración adulteration
adultez adulthood
adulto adult
afasia infantil childhood aphasia
afectado affected
afeitar shave
afeitarse to shave oneself
aflicción distress
afonía aphonia; loss of voice
afta canker
afta dolorosa canker sore
agacharse bend down
agarrarse un resfriado catch a cold
agitado agitated; anxious
agitar shake; **agite bien antes de usar** shake well before use
agosto August (see enero)
agotado exhausted; **estar agotado** be exhausted; **tener cara de estar agotado** look exhausted
agotador backbreaking; exhausting
agotamiento exhaustion; **sufrir de agotamiento** suffer from exhaustion
agotar exhaust
agotarse exhaust oneself
agregar add
agresión sexual sexual assault
agrupamiento por edades age group
agua del baño bathwater
agua tibia lukewarm water
aguantar bear
agudo (pain) acute; intense; (eyesight) sharp
ahogado drowning
ahogamiento drowning
ahogamiento accidental accidental drowning
ahogamiento producido por accidente accidental drowning

ahogar to choke; to drown
ahogarse to drown; be drowned
al revés (in reverse order) backward
albaricoque apricot
alcanfor camphor
alcohol alcohol
alcohol para fricciones rubbing alcohol
alcohólico alcoholic; liquor
Alcohólicos Anónimos (AA) Alcoholics
    Anonymous (AA)
alcoholismo alcoholism
alcoholismo crónico chronic alcoholism
alergia allergy
alergia alimentaria food allergy
alergia alimenticia food allergy
alérgico allergic
algodón cotton
algodón estéril sterile cotton
algodón hidrófilo absorbent cotton
aliento breath; tener mal aliento have bad
    breath
alimentación diet; una alimentación rica en
    proteínas a protein-rich diet; a diet rich in
    protein
alimentación con biberón bottle feeding
alimentación del lactante infant feeding
alimentación forzada forced feeding
alimentación integral health food
alimentación intravenosa intravenous feeding
alimentador de lactantes infant feeder
alimentar feed; nourish; ¿cuántos hijos tiene
    que alimentar? how many children do you
    have to feed?
alimentar con biberón bottlefeed
alimentar por la fuerza force-feed
alimenticio nourishing
alimento food; nourishment
alimentos de bajo contenido vitamínico food
    deficient in vitamins
alimento dietético dietetic food
alimentos naturales health food
alimento rico en hierro iron-rich food
aliño (culinary) dressing
aliño para ensaladas a base de aceite, vinagre
    y mostaza French dressing
aliviar alleviate
aliviar el dolor alleviate the pain
alguien anybody; anyone
almidón starch
almohada pillow
almohadilla para callos corn pad
alrededor around
alrededor de around; envolver el vendaje
    alrededor de wrap the bandage around
alta temperatura high temperature
alto high
alto riesgo de infección high risk for infection
altura height
alubia bean
alumbramiento birth
alvéolos alveoli (also: alveolos)
ama de cría baby nurse; wet nurse
ama de leche wet nurse
amalgama amalgam
amamantar breastfeed
amarrar bind
ambulancia ambulance
ambulatorio outpatient

amenorrea amenorrhea
amígdalas tonsils
amigdalitis tonsillitis
aminoácidos amino acids
amoníaco ammonia (also: amoniaco)
amonio ammonium
amnesia amnesia
amniocentesis amniocentesis
amplio broad
ampolla blister; ampule; me ha salido una
    ampolla en el pie I got a blister on my
    foot; I have a blister on my foot; hacer
    ampollas give blisters
ampolla en los labios fever blister
ampolla de sangre blood blister
ampollarse blister; se me ampollaron los pies
    I have blisters on my feet; my feet blistered
ampolleta ampule
amputación amputation; practicar una
    amputación perform an amputation
amputar amputate
analgésico (noun) painkiller; (adj) painkilling
análisis analysis; llevar a cabo un análisis
    perform an analysis; hacer un análisis to
    do an analysis
ancho broad
ancho de espaldas broad-shouldered
ancho de hombros broad-shouldered
anciano/a elderly; los ancianos the elderly;
    una anciana an elderly lady; un anciano
    an elderly man; muchos de los pacientes
    son ancianos many of the patients are
    elderly; (patient) geriatric
andar walk
anemia anemia
anemia drepanocítica sickle cell anemia
anemia ferropénica iron deficiency anemia
anemia perniciosa pernicious anemia
anémico (noun) anemic; (adj) anemic
anestesia anesthesia
anestesia en silla de montar saddle block
    anesthesia
anestesia epidural epidural anesthesia
anestesia espinal spinal anesthesia
anestesia general general anesthesia
anestesia local local anesthesia
anestesia regional regional anesthesia
anestesiar anesthetize
anestésico anesthetic
anestesiólogo/a anesthesiologist
aneurisma aneurysm
aneurisma disecante dissecting aneurysm
anfetaminas amphetamines
angina angina
angina de pecho angina pectoris
angioplastia angioplasty
angioplastia con balón balloon angioplasty
angiosarcoma angiosarcoma
angustia anguish; distress
angustiado anguished; worried; anxious
animal animal
ano anus
anomalía deviance; anomaly
anorexia anorexia
anorexia nerviosa anorexia nervosa
anormal abnormal; deviant
anquilosamiento (of joints) stiffness
ansiedad anxiety

ansioso anxious
anteayer the day before yesterday
anteojos eyeglasses
antes before
antes de before
antes de que before
antes y después before and after
antiácido antacid
antibacteriano antibacterial
antibiótico antibiotic
antibiótico de alcance amplio broad-spectrum
    antibiotic
antibiótico de espectro amplio broad-
    spectrum antibiotic
anticarcinógeno anticarcinogenic
anticoagulante anticoagulant
anticonceptivo contraceptive
anticongestivo (noun) decongestant; (adj)
    decongestant
anticuerpo antibody
antidepresivo antidepressant
antídoto antidote
antiespasmódico antispasmodic
antigripal flu remedy; remedy for the flu
antihistamínico antihistamine
antiinflamatorio anti-inflammatory
antioxidante antioxidant
antiséptico antiseptic
antisocial antisocial
antitoxina antitoxin
ántrax anthrax
añadir add
año year; tener _____ años be _____ years
    old
aorta aorta
apalear (victim) batter
aparato circulatorio circulatory system
aparato de fijación attachment apparatus
aparato de rayos x X-ray machine
aparato digestivo digestive system
aparato ortopédico brace
aparato respiratorio respiratory system
aparatos (dental) braces
apatía apathy
apellido family name; surname
apenado ashamed
apenas hardly; barely
apendectomía appendectomy
apéndice (anat) appendix
apendicitis appendicitis
apendicitis crónica chronic appendicitis
apepsia indigestion; apepsia
apetito appetite; tener buen apetito have a
    good appetite; perder el apetito lose one's
    appetite; pérdida de apetito loss of
    appetite
aplicación application
aplicar apply; aplicar el ungüento apply
    ointment; aplicar el ungüento a la zona
    afectada apply ointment to the affected
    area
apoplejía (stroke) apoplexy
aporrear (person) beat
aporte dietético dietary allowances
apósito dressing; le pusieron un apósito en la
    herida they put a dressing on his wound
apósito absorbente absorbent dressing
apoyo emocional emotional support

aprobar el tratamiento authorize treatment
aptitud aptitude; ability
apuñalar stab
árbol bronquial bronchial tree
ardiente burning
ardor burn; burning sensation
ardor de estómago acid reflux
arrodillarse (act) to kneel
arroz rice
arroz blanco white rice
arroz con leche rice pudding
arroz integral brown rice
arruga wrinkle
arrugado wrinkled
arrugar to wrinkle
arteria artery
arterias coronarias coronary arteries
arterial arterial
arteriosclerosis hardening of the arteries;
    arteriosclerosis
articulación joint; articulation
articulación del hombro shoulder joint
articulación de la rodilla knee joint
articulación del tobillo ankle joint
articulación esférica ball-and-socket joint
articulado jointed; articulated
artificial artificial
artritis arthritis
artritis reumatoide rheumatoid arthritis
artrosis degenerative osteoarthritis
asesoría familiar family counseling
asfixia asphyxia
asfixiar choke; asphyxiate
asfixiarse asphyxiate
aseo personal personal cleanliness
asiento chair; seat; tome asiento take a seat
    please
asignación familiar child benefit
asintomático asymptomatic
asistencia cardíaca de urgencias (ACE)
    emergency cardiac care (ECC)
asistencia de catástrofes catastrophic care
asistencia durante la convalecencia aftercare
asistencia médica medical care; medical
    attention
asistencia post-operatoria aftercare
asistencia sanitaria medical care
asma asthma
asma bronquial bronchial asthma
asma en niños asthma in children
asma infantil asthma in children
asmático/a asthma sufferer
aspirar take a breath
aspirina aspirin
aspirina para niños children's aspirin
astigmatismo astigmatism
astilla (wood) splinter
astringente astringent
asustado frightened
asustar frighten
ataque attack
ataque al corazón heart attack
ataque asmático asthmatic attack
ataque cardíaco heart attack
ataque de apoplejía stroke
ataque de asma asthma attack
ataque epiléptico epileptic seizure

atar bind
atención care
atención a largo plazo long-term care
atención al enfermo care of the sick
atención al enfermo crónico care of the chronically ill
atención centrada en la familia family-centered care
atención crónica chronic care
atención dirigida managed care
atención domiciliaria home care
atención emocional al moribundo emotional care of the dying patient
atención holística holistic health care
atención integral comprehensive care
atención intermedia intermediate care
atención médica medical care
atención postalta aftercare
atención prenatal prenatal care
atención preventiva preventive care
atención primaria primary care
atención sanitaria primaria primary health care
atención sanitaria secundaria secondary health care
atender to nurse
atender un parto (action performed by a doctor) deliver; **El doctor Smith atendió el parto de los gemelos** Doctor Smith delivered the twins
atrás de behind
atrofia atrophy
aturdido dazed
aturdimiento daze; bewilderment
aturdir daze
audición hearing
audífono hearing aid
aún yet; still
auto exploración de las mamas self-breast examination
autoestima self esteem
autorización authorization
autorizar authorize; **autorizar el tratamiento** authorize treatment
auxiliar certificado de odontología certified dental assistant
avance advance
avena oatmeal
avergonzado ashamed; embarrased
avisar notify
axila armpit
ayuda aid; help
ayudar aid; assist; help
ayunas empty stomach; fasting; **en ayunas** on an empty stomach; **debe tomarse en ayunas** it should be taken on an empty stomach
ayuno fast
azúcar sugar
azúcar sanguínea blood-sugar
azul blue

B

bacalao cod
bacteria bacterium
bacterial bacterial
bajar (stairs) to go down; to lower

bajar de peso slim down; lose weight
bajo (under) beneath
bajo vientre lower abdomen
bala bullet
balanza (apparatus) balance
balbucear babble
balbuceo babbling
bálsamo (soothing agent) balm; balsam
banco de sangre blood bank
banda (cloth) swath; (people) gang
bañadera bathtub
bañarse have a bath; take a bath
bañera bathtub
baño bath; bathroom; **darse un baño**; take a bath; **ir al baño** go to the bathroom
baño con manta blanket bath
baño de almidón starch bath
baño de asiento sitz bath
baño de burbujas bubble bath
baño de esponja sponge bath
baño de espuma foam bath
baño de harina de avena oatmeal bath
baño de leche milk bath
baño de mostaza mustard bath
baño de salvado bran bath
baño de sodio sodium bath
baño emoliente emollient bath
baño salino saline bath
barandilla de la cama bedrail
barba beard; **con barba** bearded; **de barba** bearded
barbado bearded
barbilla chin
barbitúrico barbiturate
barbudo bearded
bario barium
barriga (colloquial) belly; paunch; **dolor de barriga** bellyache
barrigón, barrigona pudgy; **volverse barrigón** get a bit of a tummy
barrillo blackhead; pimple
base del cráneo base of the cranium
básico basic; **servicios básicos de salud** basic health services; **necesidades básicas** basic human needs; **soporte vital básico** basic life support
bastante enough
bastón cane
bastón de paseo walking cane
bastoncillo cotton swab
bastoncillo de algodón Q-Tip®
bata gown; **póngase esta bata** put on this gown
bata de baño bathrobe
bebé baby
bebé azul blue baby
bebé maltratado battered baby
bebé que viene de nalgas breech baby
beber drink
bebida drink; booze
bebidas alcohólicas liquor
bencedrina benzedrine
beneficiar benefit
beneficio benefit
benigno benign; **tumor benigno** benign tumor
bicarbonato de soda bicarbonate of soda
bicarbonato de sodio bicarbonate of soda
bíceps biceps

bien well
bilirrubina bilirubin
bilis bile
bisturí surgical knife
bizco cross-eyed
blanqueador (noun) bleach
blanquear to bleach
bloqueador blocker; beta bloqueador beta blocker
blusa blouse
boca mouth
boca abajo face down
boca arriba face up
bocado bite; snack; comer un bocado have a bite to eat
bocado de Adán Adam's apple
bolsa bag; tener bolsas en los ojos have bags under one's eyes
bolsa amniótica amniotic sac
bolsa de agua caliente hot-water bag; hot-water bottle
bolsa de aguas bag of waters
bolsa para el mareo sick bag
bomba corazón-pulmón heart-lung machine
bomba intravenosa intravenous pump
boquera cold sore
borrachera drinking binge
borracho drunk; estar borracho be drunk
borroso blurred
bota boot
bote can
botella bottle
botica drug store
botiquín de primeros auxilios first-aid kit
botón button
brazo arm; brazo roto broken arm; brazo izquierdo left arm; brazo derecho right arm
breve brief
brisa breeze
bromuro bromide
bronquial bronchial
bronquios bronchial tubes
bronquitis bronchitis
bronquitis crónica chronic bronchitis
bulimia bulimia
bulímico bulimic
bulto (on the head) bump
bursitis bursitis
buscar to look for; to search
buscatoques addict in search of a fix

cabello hair; lavarse el cabello to wash one's hair
cabestrillo sling; to have one's arm in a sling llevar el brazo en cabestrillo
cabeza head
cácara acne
cacaraña pockmark
cacarizo pockmarked
cachete cheek
cadáver dead body
cadena alimentaria food chain
caer fall
caerse fall

café coffee
cafeína caffeine
cafetería cafeteria
caída fall
caja de las costillas ribcage
caja de dientes dentures
caja torácica rib cage
cajero/a cashier
calcio calcium
calambres cramps; darle un calambre get a cramp
cálculo calculation
cálculo de la dosis para niños calculation for children's dosage
caldo broth
calendario calendar
caliente (food, water) hot
calistenia calisthenics
callarse be quiet
calle principal main street
Calle Mayor main street
callo callus; (on toe) corn
calma (of behavior) sedateness
calmante painkiller; sedative
calmar el dolor alleviate the pain
calmarse calm down
caloría calorie; una dieta baja en calorías a calorie controlled diet; alimentos de bajo contenido calórico food with low calorie content
calórico caloric
caluroso (weather, day) hot
calvicie baldness
calvo bald; baldheaded; es calvo he's bald; quedarse calvo go bald; está calvo he's gone bald; se ha quedado calvo he's gone bald
cama bed; meterse en la cama get into bed; lavar a alguien en la cama give somebody a bedbath
cama del paciente hospital bed
cambiar to change
cambiarse (clothes) to change; to get changed
cambiarse de ropa change one's clothes
cambiarse de zapatos change one's shoes
caminar walk
camisa de noche bedgown
cambio change
cambio de vida change of life
camilla stretcher
caminar dormido sleepwalk
camiseta blouse
camisón nightgown
canal (anat) canal
canal alimentario alimentary canal
camita de niño crib
camita con barandillas para niño crib
canal del parto birth canal
cancelación cancellation
cancelar cancel
cáncer cervical cervical cancer
cáncer colorrectal colorectal cancer
cáncer cutáneo skin cancer
cáncer de cuello del útero cancer of the uterus
cáncer de escroto scrotal cancer
cáncer de hígado cancer of the liver
cáncer de intestino delgado cancer of the small intestine

cáncer de laringe laryngeal cancer
cáncer de mama breast cancer
cáncer de páncreas pancreatic cancer
cáncer de pene penile cancer
cáncer de piel skin cancer
cáncer de próstata prostate cancer
cáncer de pulmón lung cancer
cáncer de recto rectal cancer
cáncer de vesícula biliar gall bladder cancer
cáncer óseo bone cancer
cáncer ovárico ovarian cancer
cáncer terminal terminal cancer
cáncer testicular testicular cancer
cáncer uterino uterine cancer
cáncer vaginal vaginal cancer
canceroso cancerous
canilla shin
capacidad capability; ability
capilar capillary
capilares sanguíneos blood capillaries
capuchón cervical cervical cap
cápsula capsule
cara face; lavarse la cara wash one's face
carbón activado activated charcoal
carcinógeno carcinogen
carcinoma de células claras clear cell
     carcinoma
cardíaco (condition) cardiac
cardiógrafo cardiograph
cardiograma cardiogram
cardiólogo/a cardiologist; heart specialist
cardiopulmonar cardiopulmonary
cardiorespiratorio cardiorespiratory
cardiovascular (surgery) cardiac
caries caries; cavities
carne meat
carne de cerdo pork
carne de gallina goose pimples; gooseflesh;
     ponerse la carne de gallina to break out in
     goose pimples
carne de puerco pork
carne de res beef
casa house
carta de examen visual eye chart
cartílago cartilage
casa de convalecencia convalescent home
casado married; están casados they are
     married
caso case
caspa dandruff
castración castration
catarata cataract
catarro cold; catarrh
catarro de pecho chest cold
catártico cathartic
catéter catheter
cátodo cathode
causa cause; causa de la muerte cause of
     death; causarle problemas a alguien cause
     somebody problems; las pastillas le
     causaron una reacción cutánea the pills
     caused a skin reaction
cautela caution; actuar con cautela act with
     caution
cautelosamente cautiously
cauteloso cautious
cauto cautious
cavidad (hole) cavity

cefalea en racimos cluster headache
ceguera nocturna night blindness
ceja eyebrow
célula cell
célula ósea bone cell
célula sanguínea blood cell
celulosa cellulose
celular cellular
centro de cuidado diurno para adultos adult
     day-care center
centro de formación de imágenes imaging
     center
centro de preparación al parto childbirth
     center
centro de quemados burn center
centro de salud mental de la comunidad
     community mental health center
centro médico medical center
cereal cereal
cerebelo cerebellum
cerebro brain
cerrar close
cerrar la boca close one's mouth
cerrar los ojos close one's eyes
certificado de muerte death certificate
certificado de nacimiento birth certificate
certificado de salud health certificate
certificado médico medical certificate
cerveza beer
cervical cervical
cérvix cervix
cesárea cesarean section; c-section
chabacano apricot
champú shampoo
champú de hierbas herbal shampoo
champú anti-caspa dandruff shampoo
chata bedpan
¡chao! bye
¡chau! bye
chequeo medical; check up; hacerse un
     chequeo have a medical; have a check up
chichón (lump on the surface) bump
chica girl
chico boy
chinche (biting insect) bug; bedbug
chiquita (woman) petite
chofer de ambulancia ambulance driver
chuleta de cerdo pork chop
chupete pacifier
chupón pacifier
cicatrizar (wound) to heal
ciclo vital life cycle
ciega blind woman
ciego blind; blind man
cigarrillos cigarettes
cigarros cigars
cinta band
cinta adhesiva adhesive tape
cinto belt
cintura waistline; waist; binder
cinturón belt
circulación (blood) circulation; tener mala
     circulación have bad circulation; tener
     buena circulación have good circulation;
     circulación de la sangre circulation of the
     blood
circulación sanguínea blood circulation
circuncisión circumcision

circuncisión femenina female circumcision
circuncidar circumcise
cirrosis del hígado cirrhosis of the liver
cirrosis hepática cirrhosis of the liver
ciruela seca prune
cirugía surgery
cirugía abdominal abdominal surgery
cirugía cardíaca heart surgery
cirugía de bypass bypass surgery
cirugía exploratoria exploratory surgery
cirugía mayor major surgery
cirugía menor minor surgery
cirujano surgeon
cirujano dental dental surgeon
cirujano jefe chief surgeon
cita appointment; concertar una cita make an
    appointment; pedir una cita make an
    appointment; ¿tiene cita? do you have an
    appointment?
ciudadano de Estados Unidos U.S. citizen
clara de huevo egg white
clavícula collarbone
clima climate
clínica clinic
clínica de reposo convalescent home
clínicamente muerto brain-dead
clínico clinical
clítoris clitoris; del clítoris clitoral
cloruro mercúrico bichloride of mercury
coagulación clotting
coagulación sanguínea blood clot; blood
    clotting
coagularse to clot
coágulo (blood) clot
coágulo de sangre blood clot
cobija blanket
cobijas bedcovers
cocaína cocaine
cocainómano/a cocaine addict
coche car
cochecito baby carriage
cocido (ham) boiled
codeína codeine
código de la zona area code
código genético genetic code
codo elbow
codo de tenis tennis elbow
cognitivo cognitive
coito coitus
coitus interruptus coitus interruptus
cojear to limp
cojo lame; estar cojo be lame
colación light meal
colapso collapse
colapso físico physical collapse
colapso pulmonar collapse of the lung;
    collapsed lung
colcha bedcover; bedspread
colchón mattress
colchón de muelles spring mattress
colchoncillo para la cama bedpad
cólera anger
colesterol cholesterol
cólico colic
cólico hepático biliary colic
cólico renal renal colic
colirio eyewash

collar collar
collar ortopédico surgical collar; cervical
    collar
collarín surgical collar; cervical collar
colmillo canine tooth
colon colon
colonoscopia colonoscopy
color color; ¿de qué color es ...? what color is
    ...?
columna vertebral (anatomy) backbone
coma coma
comadrona midwife
Comadrona Diplomada Certified-Nurse-
    Midwife
comatoso comatose
comedón blackhead
comenzar begin
comer eat; comer un bocado have a bite to
    eat; comer algo have a bite to eat; comer
    carne to eat meat; no comer carne not eat
    meat
comida food; meal
comida basura junk food
comida principal main meal
comida rápida fast food
comida y bebida food and drink
comienzo beginning
complejo de madre mother complex
complejo de padre father complex
cómodo comfortable
comodidad comfort
comportamiento behavior
comportarse behave
comprar buy
compresa fría cold compress; cold pack
comprimido recubierto coated tablet
comprometer (lung, liver) affect
comunidad community
con anticipación before
con la cabeza descubierta bareheaded
condón condom
conducta behavior
conducta anormal abnormal behavior
conducta desviada deviated behavior
conducto canal; duct
conducto biliar bile duct
conducto cervical cervical canal
conducto radicular root canal
confinar confine; estar confinado a una silla
    de ruedas confined to a wheel chair
confort comfort
confortable comfortable
congelación (anatomy) exposure;
    (extremities) frostbite; tener síntomas de
    congelación to be suffering from exposure;
    exposición a sustancias químicas tóxicas
    exposure to toxic chemicals
congelado frostbitten
congestión ocular bloodshot eye
congénito congenital
congestión nasal nasal congestion
congoja anguish; distress; sorrow; grief
conmoción cerebral concussion
conocimiento consciousness; perder el
    conocimiento lose consciousness; recobrar
    el conocimiento regain consciousness;
    volver en sí regain consciousness

consecuencia consequence; **ser consecuencia de** be a consequence of; **tener consecuencias** have consequences; **traer consecuencias** have consequences

consejería counseling

consejero counselor

constantes vitales vital signs

constantemente constantly; **observar constantemente** constantly monitor; **seguir constantemente** constantly monitor; **controlar constantemente** constantly control; **se seguirá constantemente muy de cerca** will be constantly monitored

consulta consultation

consulta médica medical consultation

consultar consult; **si los síntomas continúan, consulte a su médico** if symptoms persist, consult a doctor

consumidor de drogas drug user

contacto contact; **evite contacto con los ojos** avoid contact with the eyes; **evite contacto con la piel** avoid contact with the skin

contagiarse (become infected with) catch; **contagiarse el sarampión** catch the measles

contagioso contagious; infectious; **no es contagioso** it isn't contagious; **es contagioso** it is contagious

contaminación contamination

contaminantes alimentarios food contaminants

contenido controlled

contestar answer

contigo with you

continuar continue

contra against

contra criterio médico against medical advice

contracciones contractions

contraer (become infected with) catch

control control

control del estrés stress management

control de la natalidad birth control

controlado controlled; **dieta controlada** controlled diet

controlar el consumo de azúcar to control the intake of sugar

contusión contusion; bruise

contusionar (body, arm, skin) bruise

convalecer convalesce

convencer persuade

coraje anger

corazón heart

córnea cornea

corona crown

coronario coronary

coronariopatía coronary artery disease

corpulento burly

corpúsculo sanguíneo blood corpuscle

cortada cut

cortarse cut oneself; **se cortó pero no le salió sangre** he cut himself but he didn't bleed

cortarse el dedo cut one's finger

corte cut; gash

corte profundo deep gash; deep cut

cortisona cortisone

corto de vista nearsighted

costilla (anat) rib

costilla de cerdo pork chop

coyuntura articulation; joint

cráneo skull

crecear to speak with a lisp

creceo (noun) lisp

crecer grow; **dejarse crecer la barba** grow a beard; **ha crecido mucho** he's grown a lot

creer believe; **creo que** I believe that

crema (milk) cream; (lotion) cream

crema de mano hand cream

crema para la cara face cream

crema para las manos hand cream

criarse grow up

criatura baby; child

crimen crime

crisis crisis

crisis de ansiedad anxiety attack

crisis de los cuarenta midlife crisis

crisis de la edad madura midlife crisis

crisis nerviosa nervous breakdown

crisis respiratoria respiratory failure

crónico chronic

cruce cross

cuarto room

cuarto de baño bathroom

cuarto de dormir bedroom

cubierta cover

cubrir cover; **cubra la herida** cover the wound

cubre cama bedcover; bedspread

cuchillada (with a knife) cut

cuello neck

cuello del útero cervical opening; neck of the womb; uterus

cuello uterino cervix

cuerpo body

cuerpo celular cell body

cuerpo extraño foreign body

cuerpos cancerígenos cancer bodies

cuidado care

cuidador/a de niños child care provider

cuidados agudos acute care

cuidado del cutis skin care

cuidado de los niños childcare

cuidado de la piel skin care

cuidados coronarios de enfermería coronary care nursing

cuidado crítico critical care

cuidados de enfermería centrados en la familia family-centered nursing care

cuidados de maternidad centrados en la familia family-centered maternity care

cuidados intensivos intensive care

cuidador caregiver

cuidar to look after; to take care of; to nurse

cuidarse to take care of oneself

culebrilla shingles

cultivo celular cell culture

cumpleaños birthday

cuna (child) cot; crib

cuña bedpan

cura cure; **que tiene cura** curable

cura de sueño sleep therapy

curable curable

curalotodo cure-all

curandero/a folk healer

curar to cure; to heal

curita® Band-Aide®

cutáneo cutaneous

cutis (of face and quality) skin

D

daltonismo color blindness
daltónico color blind
dar a luz (obstetrics) give birth
dar de alta (from hospital) discharge; **fue dado de alta del hospital** he was discharged from the hospital
dar náuseas to nauseate
darle de mamar a breastfeed
darle el pecho a breastfeed
darse un golpe en la cabeza to bang one's head
dañar to damage
daño damage; **causar daño** cause damage; **grandes daños** a lot of damage; **hacerse daño** to hurt oneself; **¿te hiciste daño?** did you hurt yourself?; **no te voy a hacer daño** I'm not going to hurt you
dar a luz (obstetrics) deliver
de alto contenido proteínico high protein
de antemano before
de aquí a between now and; **de aquí al jueves** between now and Thursday
de habla inglesa English-speaking
de raza blanca Caucasian
debido a because of
débil weak
debilidad (of body) weakness
debilitar weaken
decisión decision; **tomar una decisión** make a decision; **llegar a una decisión** reach a decision; **es tu decisión** it's your decision
declaración previa advance declaration
defecación defecation
defecar defacate
defecto de nacimiento birth defect
defectuoso defective
deficiencia de hierro iron deficiency
deficiencia mineral mineral deficiency
deficiente deficient
déficit auditivo hearing impairment
degenerativo degenerative
delantal apron
delgado (person) slim
delirio delirium; suffer from delirium **delirar**
delirio alcohólico crónico chronic alcohol delirium
delirium tremens delirium tremens
delito crime
demanda complaint
demorar delay
dentadura postiza dentures; **una dentadura postiza** a set of dentures
dental dental; a dental appoinment **una cita dental**
dentista dentist
departamento de oído, nariz y garganta ear, nose and throat department
deposición intestinal bowel movement
depresión depression; **sufrir depresiones** suffer from depression
deprimido (person) depressed; **anda un poco diprimida** she's a bit depressed
derivación coronaria coronary bypass
dermatólogo dermatologist

derrame cerebral stroke; **tener un derrame cerebral** have a stroke; **sufrir un derrame cerebral** have a stroke
desacuerdo disagreement; **estar en desacuerdo con** be in disagreement with
desangrar bleed
desangrarse bleed to death
desarrollo development
desarrollo cognitivo cognitive development
desarrollo infantil child development
desarrollo retardado delayed development
desayunar have breakfast
desayuno breakfast; **tomar el desayuno** have breakfast; **hora del desayuno** breakfast time
descalzo (foot) bare; barefoot
descongestionante (noun) decongestant; (adj) **anticongestivo**
descoyuntarse (joint) become dislocated
descubierto (head) bare
descubrimiento detection; discovery
desesperado desperate; **estar desesperado** be desperate
deshecho (marriage, home, etc) broken; **hogar deshecho** broken home
deshidratación dehydration
deshidratado dehydrated
deshidratarse become dehydrated
deshincharse (feet, ankles) swelling is going down; **se le van deshinchando los tobillos** the swelling in the ankles is going down
desinfectante disinfectant
desmayarse to faint
desmayo faint; blackout; **sufrir un desmayo** to faint
desnudo (body; flesh, shoulder, etc) bare; **desnudo hasta la cintura** bare from the waist up; **con el torso desnudo** bare from the waist up
desnudo de la cintura para arriba barechested
desesperación anxiety; desperation; despair
desodorante deodorant
despertar arouse (from sleep); to wake; to wake up
despertarse wake up
después after
después de after
después de que after
destreza dexterity
desvanecimiento (loss of consciousness) blackout; **sufrir un desvanecimiento** have a blackout; **tener un desvanecimiento** have a blackout
desvestirse disrobe
desviación deviance
desviado deviant
detección detection
detección precoz early detection
detergente detergent
determinadas horas set times; **las comidas son a determinadas horas** meals are at set times
detrás de behind
detrimento detriment
devolver vomit
devolver la salud to heal
día day; **cada dos días** every other day; **el día anterior** the day before; **el día siguiente** the following day; **todos los días** every day

diabetes diabetes

diabetes del adulto adult-onset diabetes

diabético diabetic

diafragma (contraceptive) diaphragm

diagnosticar diagnose

diagnóstico diagnosis; make a diagnosis **hacer un diagnóstico**; give a diagnosis **dar un diagnóstico**

diagnóstico clínico clinical diagnosis

diagnóstico médico medical diagnosis

diagnóstico precoz early diagnosis

diálisis dialysis

dializador dialysis machine

diario daily; **a diario** on a daily basis

diarrea diarrhea

diciembre December (see enero)

diente cariado bad tooth

diente canino canine tooth

dientes de conejo buckteeth

diente de leche milk tooth

diente incrustado embedded tooth

diente permanente permanent tooth

dientes postizos false teeth

diente primario primary tooth

dientes salidos buckteeth; **tener los dientes salidos** have buckteeth; **con los dientes salidos** bucktoothed

dientudo bucktoothed

dieta diet; a fat free diet **una dieta sin grasas**

dieta blanda bland diet

dieta equilibrada balanced diet

dieta hídrica liquid diet

dieta ligera light diet

dieta para diabéticos diabetic diet

dieta sin grasas fat free diet

dietista dietician

difícil (task, problem) difficult

dificultad difficulty; **tiene dificultad para entender el inglés** she has difficulty understanding English; **caminaba con mucha dificultad** she had great difficulty walking; **dificultades de aprendizaje** learning difficulties

difteria diptheria

difunto (person) late; deceased

digestible digestible

digerir (food) digest; **fácil de digerir** easily digestible

digestión digestion

dinero cash; money

dirección address

dirección permanente permanent address

discapacidad disability; handicap

discapacitado disabled; **los discapacitados** the disabled

disentería amebiana amoebic dysentery

dislocarse dislocate

distrofia muscular muscular dystrophy

diurético (noun and adj) diuretic

divorciado divorced; **estar divorciado** be divorced

divorcio divorce

doblar (arm; back; leg) bend; **doble la rodilla** bend your knee; **dóblese** bend over; **dóblese** bend down

doctor; doctora doctor

dolencia ailment; illness; complaint; **falleció tras una larga dolencia** he died after a long illness

doler hurt; **no duele nada** it doesn't hurt at all; **le duele una muela** he has a toothache; **le duele la cabeza** she has a headache; **me duele la garganta** I have a sore throat; **me duelen los pies** my feet ache; my feet hurt; **¿dónde le duele?** where does it hurt?; **me duele todo el cuerpo** I ache all over

dolor ache; pain; **¿siente mucho dolor?** are you in much pain? does it hurt much?; **¿es una punzada o un dolor sordo?** is it a sharp pain or a dull ache?; **sentir dolor permanentemente** constant pain; **gritar en dolor** cry out in pain; **calmar el dolor** ease the pain; **no causar dolor** painless; **sin dolor** painlessly

dolor abdominal abdominal pain (stomachache)

dolor ardiente burning pain

dolor cardíaco cardiac pain

dolor crónico chronic pain

dolor de apendicitis appendicitis pain

dolor de barriga bellyache

dolor de cabeza headache; **tener dolor de cabeza** have a headache

dolor de pecho chest pain

dolor de espalda backache

dolor de garganta sore throat

dolor de guata bellyache

dolor de oído earache

dolor de parto labor pain

dolor de tripa bellyache

dolor torácico chest pain

dolor urente burning pain

dolores de crecimiento growing pains

dolores de parto labor pains; birth pains

dolores por gas gas pains

doloroso painful

doméstico (of the house, persons, problems) domestic; **violencia en el hogar** domestic violence

domingo Sunday

dormido asleep; **estar dormido** be asleep; **se quedó dormido** he fell asleep

dormir to sleep; **sin poder dormir** sleepless; **trata de dormir un poco** try to get some sleep

dormirse fall asleep; go to sleep; **no podía dormirme** I couldn't go to sleep

dorso (of hand) back

dosis dose; **dosis recomendada** recommended dose; **no sobrepasar la dosis recomendada** do not exceed the recommended dose

dosis permisible permissable dose

drenaje drainage

drenaje bronquial bronchial drainage

depranocitosis sickle cell anemia

droga drug; dope

droga que crea adicción addictive drug

drogadependencia drug dependence

drogadicción drug addiction; drug habit

drogar to drug

drogarse to be on drugs; I don't do drugs **yo no me drogo**

drogas blandas soft drugs

drogas duras hard drugs

droguería drug store

ducha vaginal douche

E

echar (head) bend; **echa la cabeza hacia atrás** bend your head back; **echa la cabeza hacia adelante** bend your head forward

edad age; **¿qué edad tiene?** how old is he?; **quince años de edad** fifteen years old; **a la edad de** at the age of

edad adulta adulthood

edad cronológica chronological age

edad de desarrollo development age

edad emocional emotional age

edad mental mental age

edad senil advanced age

educación sanitaria health education

efectivo cash; pay in cash **pagar en efectivo**

efecto secundario aftereffect; side effect

ejercicio exercise

ejote green bean

elección (option) choice

electrocardiograma electrocardiogram

elegir make one's choice; to choose

emborracharse to get drunk

emergencia emergency; it's an emergency **es una situación de emergencia**; in case of emergency **en caso de emergencia**

emoción emotion

empezar begin

empatía empathy

emplasto dressing

emplasto adhesivo adhesive plaster

empujar (in childbirth) bear down; push

en alma y cuerpo body and soul

encéfalo brain

encías gums

endoscopia endoscopy

enema enema

enema de bario barium enema

enema de limpieza cleansing enema

energía calórica caloric energy

enero January; **el primero de enero; el uno de enero** the first of January; **a principios de enero** at the beginning of January; **a fines de enero** at the end of January

enfadado annoyed; angry

enfadar annoy; anger

enfadarse get angry; get mad

enfado anger; annoyance

enfermedad disease; illness

enfermedad aguda acute disease

enfermedad articular degeneretiva degenerative joint disease

enfermedad autoinmune autoimmune disease

enfermedad bipolar bipolar disorder

enfermedad cardiovascular cardiovascular disease

enfermedad catastrófica catastrophic illness

enfermedad clínica clinical disease

enfermedad congénita congenital disease

enfermedad contagiosa contagious disease

enfermedad crónica chronic disease

enfermedad de Chagas Chagas disease

enfermedad degenerativa degenerative disease

enfermedad del pulmón negro black lung disease

enfermedad del sueño sleeping sickness

enfermedad de transmisión sexual sexually transmitted disease

enfermedad emocional emotional illness

enfermedad infantil childhood disease

enfermedad infecciosa infectious disease

enfermedad mental mental illness

enfermedad nerviosa nervous disorder

enfermedad por arañazo de gato cat scratch disease

enfermedad provocada por el estrés stress related illness

enfermedad pulmonar pulmonary disease

enfermedad que no tiene cura an incurable disease

enfermedad social social disease

enfermedad transmisible communicable disease

enfermedad venérea venereal disease

enfermera clínica especialista clinical nurse specialist

enfermera del turno diurno day nurse

enfermera del turno nocturno night nurse

enfermería sick bay; infirmary; (school) sickroom

enfermería de maternidad maternity nursing

enfermería de salud comunitaria community health nursing

enfermería de urgencias emergency nursing

enfermería individualizada case nursing

enfermero, enfermera nurse

enfermero de adultos adult nurse practitioner

enfermero práctico nurse practitioner

enfermero práctico de familia family nurse practitioner

enfermizo (person, unhealthy) sickly

enfermo; enferma sick; to get sick (about to vomit) **tener ganas de vomitar**; sick to my stomach **me da ganas de vomitar**

enfermo crónico chronically ill

enfermo de cáncer cancer patient

enfermera diplomada registered nurse

enfermera titulada registered nurse

enfermero diplomado registered nurse

enfermero titulado registered nurse

enfisema emphysema

engordar fatten

engripado (adj) **estar engripado** to have the flu

engriparse to catch the flu

enjuage bucal mouthwash

enojado angry; mad

enojarse get angry

enojo anger; annoyance

entero; entire

enterrar bury

entre between; between meals **entre comidas**; between now and Thursday **de aquí al jueves**

entrepiernas (genital area) crotch

enuresis nocturna bedwetting

envenenamiento poisoning; **el envenenamiento fue un accidente** accidental poisoning

envenenar (make ill) **intoxicar**

envenenarse take poison

enviudar to be widowed

entablillar put a spint on; **le entablillaron la pierna** they put a splint on his leg; **tiene el brazo entablillado** his arm is in splints

envejecido aged
envenenamiento poisoning
envenenamiento accidental accidental poisoning
envenenamiento producido por accidente accidental poisoning
envenenamiento de la sangre blood poisoning
envoltura fría cold pack
epilepsia epilepsy
equilibrio (equilibrium) balance; **mantener el equilibrio** keep one's balance; **perder el equilibrio** lose one's balance
equipo de mantenimiento de vida life-support system; the patient is on a life-support system **el paciente está conectado a una máquina que mantiene a sus constantes vitales**
equivocado mistaken
error mistake; **un grave error** a serious mistake
eructar belch
eructo belch
erupción rash
esbelto (person) slim
escalofríos chills; shivers; **tener escalofríos** have the shivers
escáner (noun) scan; **hacer un escáner** do a scan
escoger make one's choice; choose; **escoja su médico** choose your doctor
escorbuto scurvy
escorbuto del lactante infantile scurvy
escuchar listen
escupidera emesis basin
escurrimiento de la nariz runny nose
espalda (anatomy of human) back
esparadrapo adhesive plaster; Band-Aid®; adhesive tape
espasmos musculares muscle spasms
especialista clínico clinical specialist
especialista de corazón heart specialist
especialista de las vías respiratorias chest specialist
especialista en geriatría geriatrician
especialista en medicina interna internist
espéculo speculum
espejo vaginal speculum
esperar (baby) carry; wait; wait for; expect; **cuando esperaba mi primer hijo** when I was carrying my first baby; **cuando esperaba mi segundo hijo** when I was carrying my second baby; **está esperando** she's expecting
esperanza de vida life expectancy
esperma semen; sperm
espermatozoide sperm
espina bífida spina bifida
espina dorsal spinal column; spine; backbone
espinacas (culinary) spinach
espinilla blackhead; shin
espinilla de cabeza negra blackhead
espinillas acne
espirar (breathe out) exhale; breathe in deeply and then exhale **inspire profundamente y después espire**
esponja sponge
esponja de gasa sponge gauze
esposa wife
esposo husband

esputo sanguinolento bloody sputum
esquirla (of glass, bone) splinter
estable stable
establecido set; **hay horas de visitas establecidas** there are set times for visiting; **un procedimiento establecido** a set procedure
estacionario stable; **el estado del paciente es estacionario** the patient's condition is stable
estado de alerta alertness
estado de ánimo mood
estar de rodillas (state) kneel down
estar en edad fértil be of childbearing age
estar en estado (pregnant) to be expecting
estatura body size
esternón (anat) breastbone
estevado bowlegged
estilo de vida lifestyle
estimulación erótica previa al acto sexual foreplay
estiramiento facial face lift
estirar stretch; **estirar las piernas** stretch one's legs
estofado stew
estofar to stew
estómago stomach; **estar mal del estómago** have an upset stomach
estrangular choke
estreñido constipated
estreñimiento constipation
estructura familiar family structure
estudio de salud health screening
estupefaciente drug
evacuación bowel movement
evacuar defecate
evitar avoid; **evitar comida grasosa** avoid fatty foods; **evite contacto con los ojos** avoid contact with the eyes; **evite contacto con la piel** avoid contact with the skin
examen examination
examen cardiovascular cardiovascular assessment
examen de mama breast examination
examen de salud health assessment
examen médico medical exam
examinar examine
exantema de pañal (formal) diaper rash
excitado excited
excitar (sexually) arouse
exhalar exhale
excrementos feces
expectativas de vida life expectancy
experto en dietética dietician
explicar explain; **explicar el tratamiento** explain the treatment; **explicarse** to explain oneself; **por favor explíquese más claramente** please explain yourself more clearly
exposición a sustancias químicas tóxicas exposure to toxic chemicals
extender to stretch
extirpación (organ, tumor) removal
extracción de nalgas breech extraction removal
extremidad limb
extremidad artificial artificial limb
eyaculación precoz premature ejaculation

F

faja band; belt; bandage; binder
fajar bandage
fallecer to die; to pass away
fallecido deceased
fallecimiento death
falta de aire shortness of breath
familia family; **la familia Lunas** the Lunas family; **un amigo de la familia** a friend of the family; **tiene familia en California**; he has family in California; **tiene familiares en California** he has family in California; **son una familia muy unida** they are a very close family; **estar esperando** to be in the family way; **estar en estado** to be in the family way
familiares family; **tiene familiares en California** he has family in California
fantasía sexual sexual fantasy
farmacéutico pharmacist
farmacia drug store
fármaco medicine; drug; **este fármaco puede provocar somnolencia** this drug may cause drowsiness
fármaco de prescripción prescription drug
fastidiar bother; pester; annoy
fastidio annoyance
fatiga fatigue
fatiga física physical fatigue
fatiga mental mental fatigue
fatiga visual eyestrain
febrero February (see enero)
febrícula low-grade fever
fecha date
fecha de nacimiento date of birth
felicitaciones congratulations
fertilización cruzada cross fertilization
fertilización externa external fertilization
fibrosis cística cystic fibrosis
fibra dietética dietary fiber
fiebre fever; **tener mucha fiebre** have a high fever; **tener fiebre** run a fever
fiebre amarilla yellow fever
fiebre del heno hay fever
fiebre del parto childbed fever
fiebre inducida induced fever
fiebre leve low-grade fever
fiebre por arañazo de gato cat scratch fever
fiebre por mordisco de gato cat-bite fever
fierros (dental) braces
fijación fixation; obsession
flaco skinny
flexión de piernas kneebend
flexionar bend
flexura flexure; **flexura del brazo** bend of the arm
flujo sanguíneo blood flow
fórceps forceps
forma shape; **estar en muy buena forma** to be in great shape; **mantenerse en forma** to keep in shape; to stay in shape
formación (education) background
formación de tipo práctico que capacita para desenvolverse en la vida diaria lifeskills
formulario de entrada admittance form
formulario médico prescription
fornido burly

forúnculo (anat) boil
forzar force
fractura break
fractura de fatiga stress fracture
fractura doble double fracture
fractura en ojal buttonhole fracture
fractura por sobre carga stress fracture
frágil (bones, etc) brittle
fragmentar (tooth) chip
frasco (medicine) bottle
frazada blanket; bedcover
frazada eléctrica electric blanket
frecuencia cardíaca heart rate
frenos para los dientes braces
frente brow
fresco (weather) cool; (vegetables, fruits) fresh
frijol bean
frío cold; **tener frío** be cold; **morir de frío** to die from exposure
frotis cervical cervical smear
fruta fruit
fruta seca dried fruit
fuertes dolores de estómago severe stomach pains
fuerza force; strength; **le fallaron las fuerzas** his strength failed him; **ahora tienes que descansar para recobrar las fuerzas** you must rest now to get your strength back
funcionamiento behavior
funda de almohada pillow case
fundamental main

gafas eyeglasses
gammagrafía cerebral brain scan
ganglio (lymph node) gland
garrapata tick
gasa gauze; dressing
gasa absorbente absorbent gauze
gasa esterilizada surgical gauze
gases (flatulence) gas; **eliminar los gases** to pass gas
gástrico gastric
gato cat
gen gene
gen dominante dominant gene
género gender
genio temper; **tiene muy mal genio** he has a violent temper
genital genital
genitales genitalia
geriatra geriatrician
geriatría geriatric medicine; geriatrics
germen germ
gestación gestation
ginecología gynecology
ginecológico gynecological
ginecólogo; ginecóloga gynecologist
glándula (organ) gland
glándula linfática lymph gland
gándula mamaria mammary gland
globo ocular eyeball
golpe blow; **darse un golpe en la cabeza** to bang one's head; **pegarse un golpe** to hurt oneself

golpear beat
golpiza beating
gonorrea (slang) clap
gordo fat
gorra cap
gotas drops
gotas nasales nose drops
gotas oculares eye drops
gotas para la nariz nose drops
gotas para los oídos eardrops
gotas para los ojos eye drops
grado degree; quemaduras de primer grado first degree burns; quemaduras de segundo grado second degree burns; quemaduras de tercer grado third degree burns
gráfico chart
grano pimple
grasa fat; este queso contiene un 30 por ciento de materia grasa this cheese contains 30 percent fat
grasa animal animal fat
gripe flu; tener gripe catch the flu; tiene gripe he's got the flu; estar con gripe have the flu
grupo de edades age group
grupo de los aminoácidos amino acid group
grupo dominante dominant group
grupo etario age group
grupo sanguíneo blood group
guagua baby
guardar cama confined to bed; remain in bed
guardería infantil day-care center
guarderías childcare facilities
guisar to stew
guiso stew
gusto taste

habichuela bean
habilidad dexterity
habitación room
habitación individual single room
habitación doble double room
hacer de vientre bowel movement
hacerse + profession become
hacerse un chequeo have a medical
hacia toward; towards
hacia atrás (movement) backward
hambre hunger
hambre repentino sudden hunger
heces feces
hemorragia hemorrhage; bleeding; sufrió una hemorragia interna she suffered internal bleeding
hemorragia arterial arterial bleeding
hemorragia nasal bloody nose
hemorroide hemorrhoid
hemorroides piles; hemorrhoids
hendidura cleft
herida wound
herida de bala bullet wound
herida en la cabeza head wound
herida en el pecho chest wound
herida profunda deep wound
herida punzante puncture wound

hermana sister; una hermana mayor an older sister; una hermana menor a younger sister
hermanita baby sister
hermanito baby brother
hermano brother; hermanos brothers and sisters; tener hermanos have brothers and sisters; un hermano mayor an older brother; un hermano menor a younger brother
hernia hernia
herpes cold sore; fever blister
hervir (water) to boil
hervido (potatoes, rice, etc) boiled
hidrato de carbono carbohydrate
hiel bile
hierro iron
hígado liver
higienista dental dental hygienist
hija daughter
hija adoptiva adopted daughter
hija política daughter-in-law
hijo son; tener un hijo have a son; have a child; espera un hijo she's expecting a baby; (boys only) mis hijos my sons; (boys and girls) mis hijos my children
hijo adoptivo adopted son
hijo de madre adicta infant of addicted mother
hijo político son-in-law
hijo único, hija única only child
hilo dental dental floss
hincarse de rodillas kneel down
hinchado (body, face) bloated; (leg, ankle) swollen
hincharse swell up; se le han hinchado mucho las piernas his legs have really swollen up; se le empezó a hinchar la cara her face began to swell
hinchazón abscess; swelling
hipermétrope far-sighted
hipermetropía far-sightedness
hirviendo boiling; añada agua hirviendo add boiling water
hisopo swab
hisopo de algodón cotton swab; Q-Tip®
histerectomía con cesárea cesarean hysterectomy
historia clínica health history
historia de la enfermedad actual history of present illness
historia familiar family history
historia personal y familiar case history
historia sexual sexual history
historial clínico medical history
historial médico (of patient) medical history
hogar de ancianos geriatric home
hombre man
hombro shoulder
hondo deep
hora de acostarse bedtime
hora de comer mealtime
hora de irse a la cama bedtime
hora del desayuno breakfast time
horas de visitas establecidas set visiting hours
hospital hospital; estar en el hospital be in the hospital; estar hospitalizado be in the hospital; estar internado be in the hospital
hospital de la comunidad community hospital

hospital del condado county hospital
hospital general general hospital
hospital para veteranos Veteran's Hospital
hospital privado private hospital
hospital público public hospital
hoy today
hoyo pockmark
hueso bone; de huesos grandes big boned
hueso de la pechuga (culinary) breastbone
hueso del tobillo anklebone
huevo egg; huevo frito fried egg; huevo
    estrellado scrambled egg; huevo pasado
    por agua boiled egg; huevos escalfados
    poached eggs; huevos revueltos scrambled
    eggs
huevos (vulgar) balls
humor acuoso aqueous humor

impartir asistencia médica give medical
    assistance
incapacitado disabled
inclinar (head) bend; inclina la cabeza hacia
    atrás bend your head back; inclina la
    cabeza hacia adelante bend your head
    forward
indiferencia apathy; indifference
índice de materias table of contents
índice de natalidad birthrate
indigestión indigestion; producir indigestión
    give indigestion
individuo de conducta desviada deviant
indoloro (causing no pain) painless
inducir (sleep, labor) induce
infancia childhood
infección infection; infección de garganta
    throat infection
infeccioso (disease) infectious
infectar infect
informar notify; inform
infusión intravenosa intravenous infusion
inglés English; hablar inglés to speak English
iniciar begin
injertar to graft
injerto graft
injerto cutáneo skin graft
injerto óseo bone graft
inodoro toilet
inquieto anxious; worried; estar inquieto be
    worried
insolación heat stroke
inspirar take a breath
instrucciones previas advance directive
insuficiencia cardíaca heart failure
insuficiencia circulatoria circulatory failure
insuficiente deficient
interacciones entre alimentos y fármacos food
    and drug interactions
internado internship
internista internist
intervención de crisis crisis intervention
intervención quirúrgica de menor importancia
    minor surgery
intervenir operate
intestino intestinal tract
intestino ciego cecum; blindgut
intestino delgado small intestine

intestino grueso large intestine; large bowel
intoxicación alimentaria food poisoning
intoxicación alimentaria bacteriana bacterial
    food poisoning
intoxicación por cáusticos caustic poisoning
invalidez disability; disablement
invalidez permanente permanent disability
inválido disabled; handicapped; quedar
    inválido be disabled
invierno winter
inyección injection; darle una inyección a
    alguien give someone an injection; ponerle
    una inyección a alguien give someone an
    injection
ir to go
ir a pie walk; go by foot
ir y venir come and go; ¿Le va y le viene el
    dolor? does the pain come and go?
ira anger; rage; descargar su ira en vent one's
    anger on
irreparable (damage) permanent
irrigación colónica colonic irrigation
irrigador vaginal (syringe) douche
irritación annoyance; irritation; (Med)
    inflamation
irritación en las nalgas de un bebé
    (colloquial) diaper rash
IV = intravenosa intravenous
IV inyección intravenous injection

jabón en polvo detergent
jabón mineral mineral soap
jacueca migraine
jalea anticonceptiva contraceptive jelly
jamón ham
jarabe para la tos cough syrup
jefe de residentes chief resident
joven (noun) young person; young man;
    young woman; (adj) young
juanete bunion
judía verde green bean
juego play; (of plates, tools, etc.) set
juego activo active play
juego amoroso foreplay
juego cooperativo cooperative play
juego de dramatización dramatic play
juego de habilidad skill play
juego pasivo passive play
jueves Thursday
jugo de manzana apple juice
jugo de toronja grapefruit juice
jugo de uva grape juice
jugo gástrico gastric juice
jugo intestinal intestinal juices
julio July (see enero)
junio June (see enero)
junto a next to; together with
junto con together with
junto a la cabecera at one's bedside

K

L

la sobredosis fue un accidente accidental overdose
labio lip
labio hendido cleft lip
lactancia materna breastfeeding
lácteos dairy products
lado de la cama bedside
lámpara para llamar a call light
langosta (culinary) lobster
laringitis laryngitis
lata (of soup, beer, etc) can; **lata de tomates** can of tomatoes
latir (heart) to beat; (vein) to pulsate
lavabo washstand; washbowl
lavamanos washbowl
lavar wash; (eyes; wound) bathe
lavar a alguien en la cama give somebody a bedbath
lavarse wash oneself
lavarse las manos wash one's hands
lavarse el pelo wash one's hair
lavativa enema
lavoratorio washstand
laxante laxative
leche milk
leche con garantía sanitaria certified milk
leche de magnesia milk of magnesia
leche descremada skim milk
leche desnatada skim milk
leche materna breast milk
lecho de enfermo sickbed
lecho de muerte deathbed
lejía bleach
lengua (anat) tongue; (linguistic) language; **moderse la lengua** to bite one's lip
lengua hendida cleft tongue
lengua saburral coated tongue
lenguaje afónico aphonic speech
lenguaje corporal body language
lenguaje infantil baby talk
lentes eyewear
lentes de contacto contact lens
lentes protectoras protective eyewear
lesión injury
lesión cerebral brain damage; **con lesión cerebral** brain-damaged
lesión de parto birth injury
lesión en la cabeza head injury
leucemia leukemia
levadura yeast
levadura de cerveza brewer's yeast
leve mild
ligadura ligature
ligadura de trompas sterilization; tubal ligation; **le hicieron una ligadura de trompas** she was sterilized
ligamento ligament; **tiene rotura de lgamentos** he has torn ligaments
ligamento ancho broad ligament
ligamento ancho del hígado broad ligament of the liver
limpieza cleanliness
limpiar to clean
limpiar una herida to swab down a wound; to clean a wound

limpio clean; **manos limpias** clean hands
lipoma de células grasas fat cell lipoma
líquido liquid
líquido amniótico amniotic fluid
líquido corporal body fluid
lisiado (noun) cripple; (adj) cripple
llaga sore; ulcer
llaga de cama bedsore
llagarse get a sore; get sores; **se le llagó la boca** she got a mouth ulcer
llamada call
llamada de larga distancia long distance call
llamada interurbana long distance call
llamada urbana local call
llamar call
llamar más tarde call back
llamar por teléfono make a call
llanto cry
llegar a ser + profession become
lleno de manchas (skin) blotchy
lleno de vida cheerful
llevar bring; take; wear
llevar puesto wear
llevar al hijo en brazos carry the baby
llevar a la hija en brazos carry the baby
llorar to cry
lo fundamental the main thing
lo más importante the main thing
lo principal the main thing
lobotamía lobotomy
lóbulo lobe
loco deranged; crazy
lugar de nacimiento birthplace
lunar (on skin) mole
lunes Monday; **lunes por la manana** Monday morning

M

macho male
machucadura bruise
madre mother
madre de nacimiento birth mother
magullado bruised
magulladura bruise
magullar; magullarse (person) bruise
maíz (cereal) corn
mal; malo; mala; malos; malas bad
mal aliento bad breath; **tener mal aliento** have bad breath
mal enfocado blurred
malentendido misunderstanding
malestar discomfort
malnutrido malnourished
malo para la salud bad for one's health
malos tratos abuse
malos tratos al anciano abuse of the elderly
malos tratos a menores child abuse
malos tratos sexuales sexual abuse
maltratado (woman, child) battered; **bebé maltratado** battered baby
maltratos abuse
maltratar (child, wife) batter; beat
mamá mom; mommy; mother
mama breast
mamar (baby) to feed
mamario mammary

mamografía mammography
mamograma mammogram
mancha (on skin) blotch; (on clothes) stain
mancha de nacimiento birthmark
mancha de sangre bloodstain
manchado stained
manchado de sangre blood-stained
manchar to stain
manco have one arm; ser manco de una mano have only one hand; quedar manco to lose one arm
mandíbula jaw; jawbone
mano hand; darse la mano; to shake hands; darle la mano a alguien to shake hands with somebody; estrecharle la mano a alguien to shake hands with somebody
mano en garra clawhand
mano zamba clubhand
manojo de nervios (colloquial) nervous wreck; es un manojo de nervios she's a nervous wreck
manta blanket
manta de baño bath blanket
mantas (bedclothes) covers
mantenimiento de la salud health maintenance
mantenimiento de vida life support
mantequilla butter
manzana apple
manzana de Adán (anat) Adam's apple
mañana morning; en la mañana in the morning; por la mañana in the morning
máquina corazón-pulmón life-support system
marca de nacimiento birthmark
marca de vieruela pockmark
marcapasos pacemaker
marcapasos externo external pacemaker
mareado sick; queasy; (dizzy; unwell) estar meareado feel sick
mareado por viajar en coche carsick
mareo dizziness; dizzy spell
mareo por viajar en coche carsickness
marido husband; son marido y mujer they are husband and wife
marzo March (see enero)
más sano; más sana better; la fruta es más sana que los caramelos fruit's better for you than candy
mascar chew
masticar chew
matarratas rat poison
matar a golpes beat to death; lo mataron a golpes they beat him to death
maternidad childbearing
matrona midwife
Matrona Diplomada Certified-Nurse-Midwife
maxilar inferior lower jaw
maxilar superior upper jaw
mayo May (see enero)
medicación (drugs); medication
medicamento medicine; medicament; drug; tomar medicamentos para el corarzón take drugs for the heart
medicina medicine
medicina de familia family medicine
médico; médica doctor; physician; ir al médico to see a doctor; Dr. Jones el doctor Jones; Which doctor are you under? ¿Qué médico le atiende?

médico de familia family practice physician
medir (length, waist) measure
médula espinal spinal cord
médula ósea bone marrow
mejilla cheek
mejor better; estar mejor be better; sentirse mejor feel better; aún mejor even better
mejorarse (person) get better; que te mejores get well soon
mejoría improvement
membrana celular cell membrane
membrana mucosa mucus membrane
memoria a corto plazo short-term memory
mendigar beg
menopausia menopause
menor minor
mensual month
mente mind
mentón chin
menuda (woman) petite
menudo (person) small; slight
mes month; el mes de junio the month of June; a principios de mes at the beginning of the month; a fines de mes at the end of the month
mesita de noche bedside table
microbio germ
miedo afraid; tener miedo be afraid; tener miedo a algo be frightened about something; tener miedo a alguien be frightened about someone
miembro (anatomy) limb
miembro viril (colloquial) penis
miércoles Wednesday
migraña migraine
mineral mineral
minusvalía disability; physical handicap
minusválido (person) physically handicapped person (adj) physically handicapped; los minusválidos the disabled
miopo nearsighted
moco mucus
mocoso brat
modo de pensar mind-set
moho (on wall, fabric) mildew
mohoso moldy
moisés (cradle) bassinet
molde cast; un molde de yeso de la huella a plaster cast of the footprint
molestar bother; ¿le molesta el cuello? is your neck bothering you?
morder bite
molestar annoy; bother
molestarse get upset
molestia discomfort; annoyance alguna molestia; some discomfort
morder (nails, etc) chew; bite
mordida bite
mordisca bite
moreno (person) brunette, dark
morir to die
morir de frío to die from exposure
moretón bruise; con moretones bruised
movimiento corporal body movement
mortalidad infantil infant mortality
muela molar
muela cariada bad tooth

muerte death; **no hubo muertes** no lives were lost
muerte cerebral brain death
muerte clínica brain death
muerte de cuna cot death
muerte infantil infant death
muerte natural natural death
muerte prematura early death
muerte repentina sudden death
muerte temprana early death
muerte senil death at an advanced age
muertes súbitas de recién nacidos (MSRN) sudden infant death syndrome (SIDS
muerto dead
muestra de excremento stool specimen
muestra de orina urine sample
muestra de sangre blood sample
mujer woman
muletas crutches
músculo (anatomy) muscle
musculoso burly

nacer be born; **al nacer** at birth
nacido born; **nacido muerto** stillborn
nacimiento birth; **ser ciego de nacimiento** be born blind
nacimiento del pelo hairline
nacimiento natural natural birth
nacimiento prematuro premature birth
nalgas butt; buttocks
nariz nose; **sonarse la nariz** blow one's nose; (adult) **le sale sangre de la nariz**; your nose is bleeding; (child) **te sale sangre de la nariz** your nose is bleeding
náuseas heaves; nausca; sickness
náuseas matutinas morning sickness
navajazos stab
necesidades básicas basic human needs
necesidad emocional emotional need
negro black
nena baby girl
nene baby boy
nervio nerve
nerviosidad nervousness
neurona nerve cell
noche night; **por la noche** at night
niña baby girl
niña de pecho young girl
niña de pañales small baby girl
niñera baby nurse; nursemaid
niñez childhood
niño baby; boy; child; **de niño** as a child; **esperar un niño** expect a baby
niño amamantado breastfed baby
niño de pañales small baby boy
niño de pecho young boy
niño mimado brat
nitrocelulosa cellulose nitrate
nivel degree; level
nivel de vida standard of living
niveles de atención levels of care
nivel de azúcar en la sangre the blood-sugar level
nivel de vida standard of living
nivel sanguíneo blood level

nivel sanguíneo de glucosa blood level of glucose
no causar dolor painless
no hay por qué preocuparse there's no cause for concern
nocivo para la salud bad for one's health
nodriza baby nurse; wet nurse
nombre de pila first name; given name; Christian name
notificar notify
noviembre November (see enero)
nuca back of the neck
nuera daughter-in-law
nuez de Adán Adam's apple
número number
número de casos (atendidos por un médico) case load
nutrir nourish
nutritivo nourishing

O

obligar force; **¿tiene que obligarse a comer?** do you have to force yourself to eat?
observación observation; **bajo observación** monitoring
obstrucción crónica de las vías respiratorias chronic airway obstruction
octubre October (see enero)
ocupado busy
oído (organ) ear; hearing
oído externo outer ear
oído interno inner ear
oído medio middle ear
ojal buttonhole
ojeras bags under the eyes; dark circles under the eyes
ojeroso: estar ojeroso have bags under one's eyes
ojo eye; **tener los ojos azules** have blue eyes
ojo de latón brassy eye
ojo inyectado de sangre bloodshot eye
ojo morado (bruise) black eye
oler mal smell bad; **huele mal** it smells bad (oler is an irregular verb)
olor corporal body odor
olor a transpiración body odor
ombligo bellybutton
omóplato shoulder blade; scapula
onda cerebral brain wave
operar operate
oreja (outer part) ear
oreja deformada cauliflower ear
oreja en coliflor cauliflower ear
órganos críticos critical organs
orientación sexual sexual orientation
origen (of person) background
oscuro (room, street) dark
otoño autumn; fall
otro; otra; otros; otras another
ovario ovary

paciente patient
paciente de corazón heart patient
paciente externo outpatient

padres reales birth parents
pagos únicamente al contado cash only
pagos únicamente en efectivo cash only
país country
país de nacimiento country of birth
palabra word
palabras de consuelo words of comfort
paladar hendido cleft palate
paliza beating
palito de algodón Q-Tip®
palpitar (heart) palpitate
páncreas pancreas
pandilla (of youths and criminals) gang; **estar relacionado con la pandilla** gang related
pañuelo bandana
pantalones vaqueros blue jeans
pantorrilla (anat) calf
panza (colloquial) belly; **tener panza** have a belly
papá dad
papada double chin
Papanicolau cervical smear; Pap smear
papas fritas French fries
papi daddy
papila gustativa taste bud
papilla de bario barium meal
parálisis cerebral cerebral palsy
parálisis del parto birth paralysis
parche en el ojo eyepatch; **llevar un parche en el ojo** wear an eyepatch
pared celular cell wall
parientes family; **tiene parientes en California** he has family in California
parientes cercanos immediate family
paro (medical) arrest
paro cardíaco cardiac arrest
paro cardiopulmonar cardiopulmonary arrest
párpado eyelid
parte de muerte death certificate
partera midwife
partería midwifery
parto (childbirth) birth; delivery; **un parto difícil** a difficult birth; **estar de parto** be in labor; **entrar en trabajo de parto** go into labor
parto con fórceps forceps delivery
parto de nalgas breech birth
parto en el que el niño nace muerto stillbirth
parto natural natural birth
parto repentino emergency childbirth
pasado mañana the day after tomorrow
pasado por agua (egg) boiled
paseo walk
pastilla pill
pastillas anticonceptivas contraceptive pills
pastillas para dormir sleeping pills
pastillas para la tos cough drops; cough lozenges
patatas fritas French fries
patatas a la francesa French fries
patizambo bowlegged
pato (Andes, Mex) bedpan
patrón de sueño sleep pattern
pecho breast; chest
pedazo (fragment, scrap) bit
pedir (request) ask; ask for
pegar (inflict blows on) beat
pegarle a batter; beat

pegarse un golpe to hurt oneself
peinarse comb oneself; comb one's hair
peine comb
pelea brawl
peligro danger; **no hay ningún peligro** there's no danger; **su vida está en peligro** her life is in danger; **estar fuera de peligro** be out of danger
peligroso dangerous
pelo hair
pena sad; **tenía mucha pena** he was very sad; **tenía mucha pena** he felt very sad
pene penis
penoso bashful; shy
pensamiento thought
pensamiento abstracto abstract thinking
pequeño (size) small; (age) young; **de pequeño** when I was young/when he was young/when she was young etc.
perder el niño miscarry
pérdida loss
pérdida de cabello hair loss
pérdida del apetito loss of appetite
pérdida de peso weight loss
periodo crítico critical period
periodo de fecundidad childbearing period
periodo de gestación gestation period
perjudicar to damage; **fumar perjudica seriamente la salud** smoking can seriously damage your health
perjudicial detrimental
perjuicio damage; detriment; **sin perjuicio para su salud** without detriment to his health
permanente (address, job) permanent
permiso permission; **con mi permiso** with my permission; **sin mi permiso** without my permission; **necesita un permiso escrito** you'll need written permission; **dar permiso** give permission
persistente (cough, virus) persistent
persona que somete a un niño a abusos deshonestos child molester
persona que se aparta de la norma deviant
personal médico medical staff
personal sanitario allied health personnel
personalidad personality; **personalidad múltiple** split personality
pesadilla nightmare
pescado fish
pescado frito con papas fish and chips
peso weight; body weight; **subir de peso** put on weight; gain weight; **bajar de peso** slim down; lose weight
peso al nacimiento birth weight
peso al nacer birth weight
pestaña eyelash
peste bubónica bubonic plague
pezón (on breast of women) nipple
pH sanguíneo blood pH
picadura de abeja bee sting
picadura por ciempiés centipede bite
picar to prick; **picar con una alfiler** to prick with a needle
pie foot
pie deforme clubfoot; **con el pie deforme** clubfooted
pie en garra clawfoot
pie hendido cleft foot

pie zambo clubfoot
piel (of person) skin
pierna ortopédica artificial leg
pigmentación cutánea skin pigment
píldora pill; tomar la píldora go on the pill
píldora anticonceptiva birth control pill
píldora del día siguiente morning after pill
píldoras para dormir sleeping pill
pinchar to prick
pirámide de alimentos food pyramid
placenta afterbirth
plan de atención médica medical care plan
planificación familiar family planning
plasma sanguíneo blood plasma
plato principal (meal) main course
poder (noun) power; (verb) can; able to; ven
    al hospital en cuanto pueda come to the
    hospital as soon as you can
pólipo cervical cervical polyp
política sanitaria health policy
pollo chicken; pollo asado roast chicken
pomelo grapefruit
pómulo cheekbone
ponerse de rodillas to kneel
por motivos familiares for domestic reasons
por poco tiempo briefly
por razones de salud on medical grounds
porque because
portabustos (brassiere) bra
portador carrier
portar carry
portarse behave
portarse muy bien behave very well
portarse muy mal behave very badly
postrado en cama bedridden
precoz early; premature; detección precoz del
    cáncer early detection of cancer
prefijo local area code
preguntar (inquire) ask
prematuro premature
preocupación anxiety; worry
preocupado worried; estar preocupado por be
    worried about
prescripción prescription; preparar una
    prescripción fill a prescription
presente present; estar presente con su esposa
    be present with your wife
presión alta high blood pessure
presión arterial blood pressure; bajar la
    presión arterial lower the blood pressure
presión baja low blood pressure
presión crítica critical pressure
primavera (season) spring
primeros auxilios first aid
principal main
principio beginning
problema problem; disability; consiguió
    superar su problema she managed to
    overcome her disability
problemas auditivos hearing difficulties
problemas de audición hearing difficulties
problema del que se orina durante la noche
    bedwetting
procedimiento procedure
procedimiento establecido set procedure
procedimiento invasivo invasive procedure
profesional de enfermería comunitaria
    community nurse practitioner

profesional de la salud health professional
profundo deep; herida profunda deep wound
progreso avanzado advance
pronóstico prognosis
próstata prostate gland
protección a la infancia child welfare
proteínico protein; de alto contenido
    proteínico high protein
proveedor de salud health provider
provocar bring on; to cause; las pastillas le
    provocaron una reacción cutánea; the
    pills brought on a skin reaction
provocar el parto induce labor
prueba calórica caloric test
prueba cutánea skin test
prueba de aptitud aptitude test
pruebas de alergia allergy testing
prueba del alcohol breath test; Breathalyzer®
    test; no pasar la prueba del alcohol fail the
    Breathalyzer® test; pasar la prueba del
    alcohol pass the Breathalyzer® test
prueba de estrés stress test
prueba del sexo gender testing
psicología del desarrollo developmental
    psychology
psicología infantil child psychology
pubiano (region, bone) pubic
púbico pubic hair
puente dental bridgework
puericultura childcare
puerta door
puesto de primeros auxilios first-aid station
pujar (in childbirth) bear down
pulga de mar sand flea
pulmón (plural drops the accent) lung
pulmón artificial artificial lung
pulmón perforado punctured lung
pulmonar lung
pulmonía pneumonia
pulso pulse; tomar el pulso take someone's
    pulse
punción puncture
puncionar puncture
punto stitch
punto de ebullición boiling point
puñalada stab; matar a puñaladas to stab to
    death
puño fist; cierre el puño make a fist
puro cigar
pus pus

que crea adicción addictive (drugs)
que crea dependencia addictive (drugs)
quebradizo (bones, etc) brittle
queja complaint
queja principal chief complaint
quejarse complain; quejarse de complain of;
    se quejó de dolor de cabeza she
    complained of a headache
quemadura burn; sufrir quemaduras leves en
    la cara suffer minor burns on the face;
    sufrir quemaduras graves en la cara suffer
    severe burns on the face; una quemadura
    de cigarrillo a cigarette burn
quemaduras de primer grado first degree
    burns

quemaduras de segundo grado second degree
  burns
quemaduras de tercer grado third degree
  burns
quemadura solar sunburn
quemar burn
quemarse burn oneself
queso cheese
queso azul blue cheese
queso de Cheddar cheddar cheese
quimioterapia chemotherapy
quirófano operating room; el paciente está en
  el quirófano the patient is in surgery
quirúgicamente surgically; hay que
  eliminarlos quirúrgicamente they have to
  be surgically removed
quirúrgico surgical
quiste cyst
quiste cervical cervical cyst
quiste óseo bone cyst

R

rabia anger
radioterapia externa external radiation
  therapy
raquitismo del adulto adult rickets
rasgo dominante dominant trait
rasguño graze; scratch; no es más que un
  rasguño it's just a scratch
raspado scrape; curettage
raspadura scrape; abrasion
raspar to scrape
raspaje curettage
raspón abrasion; scratch; graze
rasurar to shave
rasurarse to shave oneself
rayo catódico cathode ray
rayos x X-ray
reacción alérgica allergic reaction
rebozado (culinary for fried fish, fried
  chicken) batter
recaída relapse; tener una recaída have a
  relapse; sufrir una recaída suffer a relapse
recidiva relapse
recién nacido newborn
recobrar recover
reconocimiento examination
recto anus
recuento globular blood count
recuento sanguíneo blood count
recuperar recover
recuperarse convalesce; recover
reflejo del tendón de Aquiles Achilles tendon
  reflex
reflujo reflux
reflujo gastroesofágico acid reflux
régimen (special food) diet; hacer régimen to
  diet
registrar gráficamente chart
registrar los episodios gráficamente chart the
  episodes
regurgitar belch; regurgitate
relaciones sexuales intercourse; tener
  relaciones sexuales con alguien; have
  intercourse with somebody
reloj clock

remedio cure
reposo en cama bed rest
reproducción sexual sexual reproduction
respuesta answer
refrescarse cool off
resfriado cold; pescar un resfriado catch a
  cold; agarrarse un resfriado catch a cold
resfriado común common cold
resfriarse catch a cold
residencia para enfermos desahuciados (for
  the dying) hospice
resistir bear; (pain) withsstand
resolución de la crisis crisis resolution
respiración respiration
respiración artificial artificial respiration
respiración asmática asthmatic breathing
respiración boca a boca mouth-to-mouth
  resuscitation
respiración pesada heavy breathing
respiración regular regular breathing
respiración superficial shallow breathing
respirar breathe
respirar con dificultad breathe with difficulty;
  gasp for breath
respirar por la boca breathe through one's
  mouth
respirar por la nariz breathe through one's
  nose
respirar hondo take a deep breath; breathe
  deeply
respuesta emocional emotional response
restringir confine
resuello wheeze
resuello asmático asthmatic wheeze
resultados adversos adverse results
retrasar delay
retorcerse (pain) bend; se retorcía de dolor he
  was bent double with pain
retorcijón sharp pain
retorcijones de estómago stomach cramps
retorcijones de tripa stomach cramps
retraso delay; tener retraso be late
retraso mental mental retardation
revisar examine
revisión médica medical; medical check up
reyerta brawl
rico en proteínas high protein; high in protein
riesgo risk
riesgo de contagio risk of infection
riesgo de infección risk of infection
riesgo para la salud health risk
riesgo sanitario health hazard
rigidez (of muscles) stiffness
rigidez matutina morning stiffness
riñón kidney
riñón artificial artificial kidney
ritmo cardíaco heart rate
RM resonancia magnética MRI magnetic
  resonance imaging
roce chafing; rubbing
rodilla knee
rogar beg
romper; romperse break; romperse el brazo
  break an arm; romperse un diente break a
  tooth; chip a tooth; romperse una uña
  break a nail; se rompió la muñeca he
  broke his wrist

ronchas hives
ronco hoarse
ronquera aphonia; hoarseness
ropa clothes; clothing; **mudarse de ropa** change one's clothes; **cambiarse de ropa** change one's clothes; **ponerse la ropa** put on one's clothes; **quitarse la ropa** take off one's clothes
ropa de cama bed linen; bedding
rostro face
rotavirus del adulto adult rotavirus
roto (arm, leg, etc) broken; **brazo roto**; broken arm
rótula kneecap
rotura break
rozadura scratch; chafing
rubio blond; fair
ruido respiratorio bronquial bronchial breath sound

S

sábado Saturday
sábana sheet; bedsheet
sabañón chilblain
saber know; taste; **sabe muy dulce** it tastes sweet
saber mal taste bad
sabor (flavor) taste
sal salt
sal biliar bile salt
sala de guardia emergency; **la ambulancia lo llevó a la sala de guardia** the ambulance rushed him to emergency
sala de operaciones operating room; **el paciente está en la sala de operaciones** the patient is in surgery
sala de partos delivery room
sala de recuperación recovery room
sala de urgencias (SU) emergency room (ER)
salchicha sausage
salpullido hives; rash; diaper rash
salud health; **no estar bien de salud** failing health; **no está bien de salud** his health is failing; **devolver la salud** to heal; **estar bien de salud** be in good health; **estar mal de salud** be in bad health
salud actual present health
salud familiar family health
salud mental de la comunidad community mental health
salud sexual sexual health
salvado bran
sanar heal
sangrado por la nariz bloody nose
sangrar bleed; **me sale sangre de la nariz** my nose is bleeding
sangre blood; **donar sangre** give blood; **dar sangre** give blood; **una transfusión de sangre** a blood transfusion;
sano (in good health) healthy; **sano y fuerte** healthy and strong
sarampión measles; **contagiarse el sarampión** catch the measles
sarna scabies
sarpullido rash; hives; diaper rash
seco dry; **mantenga la herida seca** keep the wound dry; **guardar en lugar fresco y seco** store in a cool, dry place

secreción discharge
sed thirsty; **tener sed** be thirsty
seda dental dental floss
sedación sedation
sedante sedated; **estar bajo los efectos de los sedantes** be under sedation; **le habían administrado un fuerte sedante** she was heavily sedated
seguimiento monitoring
seguir continue; **siga haciendo ejercicios** continue exercising
segundo parto afterbirth
seguro safe; **guarde la medicina en un lugar seguro** keep the medicine in a safe place
seguro de asistencia sanitaria ante catástrofes catastrophic health insurance
seguro de enfermedad health insurance
seguro médico health insurance
seguro de vida life insurance
semen semen; sperm
seno breast
sentarse sit; **por favor, siéntese** please sit down; please take a seat
sentido común common sense
septiembre September (see enero)
sepultar to bury
ser be; **llegar a ser + profession** become + profession
ser ciego de nacimiento be born blind
ser común be common
ser de come from; be from
ser parientes (of same family) to be related
servicios restroom; washroom
servicios básicos de salud basic health services
servicio de guardería infantil day care
servicio de urgencias emergency department
Servicio de Urgencia Médica (SMU) Emergency Medical Service (EMS)
servicios relacionados con la salud health-related services
sextillizo/a sextuplet
sexualidad sexuality
shock shock; **estar en estado de shock** suffer from shock; be in shock
sicópata psychopath
sicoterapia psychotherapy
sicótico psychotic
sida AIDS
siempre always
signos vitales vital signs
silbidos wheezing
silencio quiet
silencioso quiet
silla chair; **silla de dentista** dentist's chair
silla con orinal (for invalid) commode
silla de parto birthing chair
silla de ruedas wheelchair
silla orinal pottychair
silla plegable folding chair
sin aliento breathless
sin camisa barechested
sin demora without delay
sin dolor painlessly
sin hijos (couple) childless
sin sombrero bareheaded
sin tardanza without delay
sin vida (body, dead) lifeless
sin zapatos barefoot

síndrome cerebral crónico chronic brain syndrome

síndrome de abstinencia alcohólica alcohol withdrawal syndrome

síndrome de dificultad respiratoria del adulto (SDRA) adult respiratory distress syndrome (ARDS)

síndrome de fatiga crónica chronic fatigue syndrome

síndrome de muerte súbita del lactante (SMSL) sudden infant death syndrome SIDS

síndrome de la mujer maltratada battered woman syndrome

síndrome del niño maltratado shaken baby syndrome

síndrome del pie urente burning feet syndrome

síndrome del pie ardiente burning feet syndrome

sistema circulatorio circulatory system

sistema de asistencia sanitaria health care system

sistema inmunitario immune system

sistema inmunológico immune system

sistema nervioso central (SNC) central nervous system (CNS)

síndrome de muerte súbita del lactante (SMSL) sudden infant death syndrome SIDS

sobaco armpit

sobre cama bedspread

sobredosis overdose; **tomar una sobredosis** take an overdose

sobredosis accidental accidental overdose

sobredosis producida por accidente accidental overdose

socorro help; **pedir socorro** ask for help; **un pedido de socorro** a call for help

sofocos hot flashes; **le dan sofocos** she keeps getting hot flashes

solución oftálmica eyewash

sombra de ojos eye shadow

someterse a una revisión médica have a medical

someterse a un examen médico have a medical

somnolencia drowsiness; sleepiness; **este fármaco puede provocar somnolencia** this drug may cause drowsiness

somnoliento sleepy

sonámbulo/a sleepwalker; somnambulist

sonar wipe; **suénale la nariz** wipe her nose

sonarse blow; **sonarse la nariz** blow one's nose

sonda catheter; probe

sonografía sonogram

sonograma sonogram

soñar to dream; **soñar con** have a dream about

soñolencia sleepiness; drowsiness **este fármaco puede provocar soñolencia** this drug may cause drowsiness

soñoliento sleepy

soplo murmur; heart murmur

soplo cardíaco heart murmur

soplo cardiopulmonar cardiopulmonary murmur

soplo venoso venous hum

sopor drowsiness

soporte para el arco del pie arch support

soporte vital básico basic life support

soporte vital cardíaco avanzado (SVCA) advanced cardiac life support (ACLS)

sordera deafness

sordo deaf; **estar sordo** be deaf; **estar sordo de un oído** be deaf in one ear

sordomudo; sordomuda deaf-mute

sostén (brassiere) bra

sostenedor (brassiere) bra

sótano basement

sucio dirty; **usted tiene las manos sucias** your hands are dirty

sudaciones nocturnas night sweats

sudores nocturnos night sweats

sueño (state) sleep; (representation) dream; **conciliar el sueño** to get to sleep; **tener sueño** be sleepy; feel sleepy

suero (to nourish) saline solution; (to immunize) serum

suero de la leche buttermilk; whey

suficiente enough; **dormir lo suficiente** get enough sleep; **no dormir lo suficiente** not get enough sleep

sumario abstract; contents; table of contents

supositorio suppository

supurar discharge; discharge pus

suspiro sigh

suturar to stitch

tabla chart

tabla para la cama bedboard

tablilla splint

tajo gash

talle waist

también also

tapa cover

tapar cover

tardanza delay

tarde late; **llegar tarde** arrive late

tasa de natalidad birthrate

taza cup; **una taza de café** a cup of coffee; **taza de medir** measuring cup

té de manzanilla camomile tea

tejanos blue jeans

tejido óseo bone tissue

tela adhesiva adhesive tape

teleadicto/a couch potato

temblar shake

temperatura corporal body temperature

temperatura crítica critical temperature

temprano early

tendón de Aquiles Achilles tendon

tener náuseas vomit

tener relaciones sexuales sleep together

tener un aborto miscarry

tensión alta high blood pressure

tensión baja low blood pressure

terapeuta sexual sexual therapist

terapia de divorcio divorce therapy

terapia de familia family therapy

terapia de pareja marriage counselling

terapia genética gene therapy

terapia sexual sexual therapy

termómetro thermometer; **poner un termómetro en la boca** put a thermometer in your mouth
terrores nocturnos night terrors
testículos testicles; (vulgar) balls
testigo ocular eyewitness
testigo presencial eyewitness
tétano(s) lockjaw; tetanus
tetilla (on breast of men) nipple
tía aunt
tibia shinbone
tibio lukewarm; **agua tibia** lukewarm water
tiempo de recuperación recovery time
tijeras scissors
tijeras de vendaje bandage shears
timbre buzzer
timidez bashfulness
tímido bashful; shy; timid
tímpano eardrum
tina bathtub; tub; **me di un baño de tina** I took a bath
tío uncle
tipo corporal body type
tipo somático body type
toalla de baño bath towel
toalla de manos hand towel
toalla de papel paper towel
toallita para lavarse facecloth; washrag; washcloth
tobillera ankle support
tobillo ankle
tocino bacon
todavía still
todo entire; **todo el cuerpo** entire body
todos los días every day
tomar drink
tomar decisiones difíciles make hard choices; **los médicos a veces tienen que tomar decisiones difíciles** doctors have to make hard choices sometimes
tomar las medidas (length, waist) measure
toronja grapefruit
torrente sanguíneo bloodstream
tos cough
tos asmática asthmatic cough
tos convulsa whooping cough
tos de fumador smoker's cough
tos ferina whooping cough
tos métalica brassy cough
toser cough
trabajo de asistencia social individual casework
tracto respiratorio respiratory tract
traer bring
trabajo de menores child labor
tracto respiratorio respiratory tract
traficante de drogas drug dealer
tragar to swallow; **¿le duele al tragar?** do you find it painful to swallow?
tragar a duras penas (swallow) force down
trago booze
tranquilidad (person) calmness
tranquilo calm
tranquilizante calming
transmisible communicable
trasplante de corazón heart transplant
trastornado deranged
trastorno agudo acute illness

trastorno alérgico allergic reaction
trastorno de la conducta behavior disorder
trastornos de ansiedad anxiety disorders
trastorno de pánico panic disorder
trastornos del estado de ánimo mood disorders
trastorno del patrón de sueño sleep pattern disorder
trastornos profundos del desarrollo de inicio en la infancia childhood-onset pervasive development disorders
tratamiento treatment
tratamiento de la diabetes diabetic treatment
tratamiento de quemados burn therapy
traumatismo del parto birth trauma
triste (person) sad; **estar triste** feel sad; **sentirse triste** feel sad
tronco de encéfalo brainstem
tubo alimentario alimentary canal
tubo auditivo auditory tube
tubo capilar capillary tube
tubo digestivo alimentary canal
tullido cripple; **un brazo tullido** a crippled arm
tumefacción cerebral brain swelling
tumor benigno benign tumor
tumor cerebral brain tumor
tumor maligno malignant tumor
túnel carpiano carpal tunnel
turnio cross-eyed; **ser turnio** be cross-eyed

úlcera canker
úlcera de decúbito bedsore
úlcera de estómago gastric ulcer
úlcera de estrés stress ulcer
úlcera gástrica gastric ulcer
úlcera por decúbito bedsore
ulceroso cankerous
ungüento ointment; balsam; **aplicar el ungüento** apply ointment; **aplicar el ungüento a la zona afectada** apply ointment to the affected area
unidad de cuidados coronarios (UCC) coronary care unit (CCU)
unidad de cuidados intensivos intensive care unit
unidad de intervención de crisis crisis-intervention unit
unidad de vigilancia intensiva intensive care unit
urgencia emergency; **la ambulancia lo llevó a urgencias** the ambulance rushed him to emergency
urticaria hives
uva grape

vacuna vaccine
vacuna de refuerzo booster shot
vacuna de recuerdo booster shot
vacunación vaccination
vacunar vaccinate
valeroso brave
valiente brave

varicela chickenpox
varón male
vaso cup; **orine en este vaso de plástico** urinate in this plastic cup
vaso capilar capillaries
vegetaciones adenoides adenoids
vegetal vegetable; **grasa vegetal** vegetable fat
vejiga bladder
vello body hair; pubic hair
velocidad de circulación circulation rate
vena vein
venda (strip of cloth) bandage
venda en mariposa butterfly bandage
vendaje bandage; **el vendaje del señor Mata está sucio** Mr. Mata's bandage is dirty; **usted necesita un nuevo vendaje** you need a new bandage
vendaje abdominal binder
vendaje elástico elastic bandage
vendar to bandage
veneno poison
venir come
venir de come from
venir al mundo be born into the world
ventaja advantage
verano summer
verdura vegetable
verduras green vegetables; greens
vergonzoso bashful; shy
vértigo vertigo; dizziness; **padecer de vértigo** suffer from vertigo; have vertigo
vesícula gall bladder
vesícula biliar gall bladder
vestido (noun) dress
vestir to dress
vestirse get dressed; dress oneself
vida life; lifetime; **una cuestión de vida o muerte** a matter of life and death; **una decisión de vida o muerte** a life-and-death decision; **de toda la vida** lifelong; **durante toda su vida** lifelong
vieja old woman
viejo aged; old; old man
vientre abdomen; **hacer de vientre** have a bowel movement
vientre bajo lower abdomen
viernes Friday
vinculación afectiva bonding
vinculación emocional bonding
vínculo bond; **vínculo afectivo entre madre e hijo** bond between mother and child
violencia en el hogar domestic violence
violento violent; **tuvo una muerte violenta** he met a violent death
visión doble double vision
vista eyesight; **tener buena vista** have good eyesight; **tener mala vista** have bad eyesight; **la vista ya no es lo que era** failing eyesight; **su vista ya no es lo que era** your eyesight is failing
vista borrosa blurry vision
vista cansada eyestrain
vitaminas del complejo B B complex vitamins
viuda widow; **quedar viuda** to be widowed
viudo widower
viveza alertness; liveliness
vivienda housing
viviente living

vivo alive
volver en sí regain consciousness
vomitar vomit; **tener ganas de vomitar** (about to vomit) to get sick
vomitar sin nada que expulsar dry heaves
vómito inducido induced vomiting

yema de huevo egg yolk
yerno son-in-law
yeso cast; gypsum; plaster
yeso bivalvo bivalve cast
yeso cilíndrico de pierna leg cylinder cast
yeso de antebrazo short-arm cast
yeso de brazo completo long-arm cast
yeso de marcha walking cast
yeso de pierna short-leg cast
yeso de pierna completa long-leg cast
yeso de pierna con andador short-leg cast with walker
yeso de pierna con tacón long-leg cast with walker

zona afectada affected area
zumbido buzz
zumbido de oídos buzzing in the ear

ENGLISH-SPANISH
DICTIONARY

A

abdomen abdomen; vientre; (colloquial) panza

abdominal pain (stomachache) dolor abdominal

abdominal surgery cirugía abdominal

ability aptitud; capacidad

ability to walk movimiento

abnormal anormal

abnormal behavior conducta anormal

abortion aborto (see induced; spontaneous; therapeutic; threatened)

abrasion raspón; rozadura

abscess absceso; hinchazón

absorbent absorbente

absorbent cotton algodón hidrófilo

absorbent dressing apósito absorbente

absorbent gauze gasa absorbente

absorbifacient absorbifaciente

absorption absorción

abstain abstenerse

abstain from sexual relations abstenerse de las relaciones sexuales

abstract sumario

abstract thinking pensamiento abstracto

abstraction abstracción

abuse (noun) abuso; malos tratos; maltratos (verb) abusar

abuse of the elderly malos tratos al anciano

accident accidente

accidental overdose sobredosis accidental; sobredosis producida por accidente

accidental poisoning envenenamiento accidental; envenenamiento producido por accidente

accidental drowning ahogamiento accidental; ahogamiento producido por accidente

acetaminophen acetaminofén

acetic acid ácido acético

ache (noun) dolor; (verb) doler; **does your head ache?** ¿le duele la cabeza?; **aches and pains** achaques

Achilles tendon tendón de Aquiles

Achilles tendon reflex reflejo del tendón de Aquiles

acid ácido

acid reflux reflujo gastroesofágico; ardor de estómago

acne acné; espinillas; cácara

acrylic acrílico

activated charcoal carbón activado

active activo

acupuncture acupuntura

acute agudo

acute abdomen abdomen agudo

acute care cuidados agudos

acute disease enfermedad aguda

acute illness trastorno agudo

Adam's apple bocado de Adán; manzana de Adán; nuez de Adán

add agregar; añadir

addict (to drugs) adicto, adicta; **addict in search of a fix** buscatoques; adicto en busca de una cura

addicted adicto; adicta

addiction adicción; **cause addiction** causar adicción

addictive (drugs) que crea adicción; que crea dependencia

addictive drug droga que crea adicción; droga que crea dependencia

address dirección; **permanent address** dirección permanente

adenoids vegetaciones adenoides

adhesive plaster esparadrapo; emplasto adhesivo

adhesive tape esparadrapo; cinta adhesiva; tela adhesiva

administer administrar

administer medication administrar medicación

admittance form formulario de entrada

adopted daughter hija adoptiva

adopted son hijo adoptivo

adrenalin adrenalina

adult adulto, adulta

adult day-care center centro de cuidado diurno para adultos

adult nurse practitioner enfermero de adultos; enfermera de adultos

adult-onset diabetes diabetes del adulto

adult respiratory distress syndrome (ARDS) síndrome de dificultad respiratoria del adulto (SDRA)

adult rickets raquitismo del adulto

adult rotavirus (ADRV) rotavirus del adulto (RVAD)

adulteration adulteración

adulthood edad adulta; adultez

advance avance; progreso avanzado

advance declaration declaración previa

advance directive instrucciones previas

advanced age edad senil

advanced cardiac life support (ACLS) soporte vital cardíaco avanzado (SVCA)

advantage ventaja

adverse results resultados adversos

affect (lung, liver) comprometer; afectar a

affected afectado

affected area zona afectada

afraid miedo; **be afraid** tener miedo

after después; después de; después de que; tras

afterbirth placenta; segundo parto

aftercare asistencia post-operatoria; asistencia durante la convalecencia; atención postalta

aftereffect efecto secundario

against contra

against medical advice contra criterio médico

age edad; **at the age of** a la edad de; **fifteen years of age** quince años de edad

age group agrupamiento por edades; grupo de edades; (formal) grupo etario

aged envejecido; viejo; anciano

agitated agitado

aid (noun) ayuda; (verb) ayudar

AIDS sida

ailment dolencia

ailments achaques

alcohol alcohol

alcohol abuse alcoholismo

alcohol withdrawal syndrome síndrome de abstinencia alcohólica

alcoholic alcohólico; alcohólica

Alcoholics Anonymous (AA) Alcohólicos Anónimos (AA)

alcoholism alcoholismo

alertness estado de alerta; viveza; en alerta

alive vivo

allergic alérgico

allergic reaction reacción alérgica; trastorno alérgico

allergy alergia

allergy testing pruebas de alergia

alleviate aliviar; alleviate the pain aliviar el dolor; calmar el dolor

allied health personnel personal sanitario

also también

alveoli alvéolos

always siempre

amalgam amalgama

ambulance ambulancia

ambulance driver chofer de ambulancia

amenorrhea amenorrea

amino acids aminoácidos

amino acid group grupo de los aminoácidos

ammonia amoníaco; amoniaco (note that it may also be written without an accent)

ammonium amonio

amnesia amnesia

amniocentesis amniocentesis

amniotic fluid líquido amniótico

amniotic sac bolsa amniótica

amoebic dysentery disentería amebiana; amebiasis

amphetamines anfetaminas

ampule ampolleta

amputate amputar; perform an amputation practicar una amputación

amputation amputación

analgesic analgésico

analysis análisis; perform an analysis hacer un análisis; llevar a cabo un análisis

anemia anemia

anemic anémico

anemic person anémico; anémica

anesthesia anestesia; general anesthesia anestesia general; local anesthesia anestesia local; regional anesthesia anestesia regional

anesthesiologist anestesiólogo; anestesióloga

anesthetic anestésico

anesthetize anestesiar

aneurysm aneurisma; dissecting aneurysm aneurisma disecante

anger cólera; coraje; rabia; ira; enojo

angry (get angry) enojarse; enfadarse

angina angina

angina pectoris angina de pecho

angioplasty angioplastia

angiosarcoma angiosarcoma

anguish angustia; congoja

animal animal

animal fat grasa animal

ankle tobillo

ankle support tobillera

anklebone hueso del tobillo

ankle joint articulación del tobillo

annoy (verb) molestar; fastidiar; enfadar

annoyance irritación; fastidio; (anger) enojo; molestia

annoyed enfadado; enojado

anorexia anorexia

anorexia nervosa anorexia nerviosa

another otro; otra; otros; otras at one time or another en algún momento

answer (noun) respuesta; (verb) contestar; responder

antacid antiácido

anthrax ántrax

antibacterial antibacteriano

antibiotic antibiótico

antibody anticuerpo

anticarcinogenic anticarcinógeno

anticoagulant anticoagulante

antidepressant antidepresivo

antidote antídoto

antigen antígeno

antihistamine antihistamínico

anti-inflammatory antiinflamatorio

antioxidant antioxidante

antiseptic antiséptico

antisocial antisocial

antispasmodic antiespasmódico

antitoxin antitoxina

anus recto; ano

anxiety (distress, concern) ansiedad; desesperación; preocupación; angustia

anxiety attack crisis de ansiedad

anxiety disorders trastornos de ansiedad

anxious ansioso; preocupado; inquieto; agitado

anybody alguien

anyone alguien

aorta aorta

apathy apatía; indiferencia; extreme apathy abulia

aphonia (hoarseness) afonía; ronquera

aphonic speech lenguaje afónico

apoplexy (stroke) apoplejía

appendectomy apendectomía

appendicitis apendicitis

appendicitis pain dolor de apendicitis

appendix (anatomy) apéndice

appetite apetito; have a good appetite tener buen apetito; lose one's appetite perder el apetito; loss of appetite pérdida de apetito

apple manzana

apple juice jugo de manzana

application aplicación

apply aplicar; solicitar; apply ointment aplicar el ungüento; apply ointment to the affected area aplicar el ungüento a la zona afectada

appointment cita; make an appointment concertar una cita; pedir una cita; do you have an appointment? ¿tiene cita?

apricot albaricoque; chabacano

April abril (see January)

apron delantal

aptitude aptitud

aptitude test prueba de aptitud

arch supports soportes para el arco del pie
area code código de la zona; prefijo local
arm brazo; **broken arm** brazo roto; **left arm** brazo izquierdo; **right arm** brazo derecho
armpit axila; sobaco
around alrededor; alrededor de; **wrap a bandage around** envolver un vendaje alrededor de
arouse (from sleep) despertar; (sexually) excitar
arrest (medical) paro; **cardiac arrest** paro cardíaco
arsenic acid ácido arsénico
arterial arterial
arterial bleeding hemorragia arterial
arteriosclerosis arteriosclerosis
artery arteria
arthritic artrítico
arthritis artritis; **rheumatoid arthritis** artrosis
articulated articulado
articulation articulación; coyuntura
artificial artificial
artificial kidney riñón artificial
artificial leg pierna ortopédica
artificial limb extremidad artificial
artificial lung pulmón artificial
artificial respiration respiración artificial
ascorbic acid ácido ascórbico
ashamed avergonzado; apenado; **be ashamed** tener vergüenza
ask (request) pedir; (inquire) preguntar
asleep dormido; **fall asleep** dormirse; **be asleep** estar dormido
asphyxia asfixia
asphyxiate asfixiar; asfixiarse
aspirin aspirina
assist ayudar
asthma asma
asthma attack ataque de asma
asthma sufferer asmático
asthma in children asma en niños; asma infantil
asthmatic attack ataque asmático
asthmatic breathing respiración asmática
asthmatic cough tos asmática
asthmatic wheeze resuello asmático
astigmatism astigmatismo
astringent astringente
asymptomatic asintomático
atrophy atrofia
attachment (fondness) cariño
attachment apparatus aparato de fijación
attack ataque; **heart attack** ataque al corazón; ataque cardíaco
attack of nerves crisis nerviosa
auditory tube tubo auditivo
August agosto (see January)
aunt tía
authorization autorización
authorize autorizar; **authorize treatment** autorizar el tratamiento; aprobar el tratamiento
autoimmune disease enfermedad autoinmune
autumn otoño

avoid evitar; **avoid fatty foods** evite comida grasosa; **avoid contact with the eyes** evite contacto con los ojos; **avoid contact with the skin** evite contacto con la piel

B complex vitamins vitaminas del complejo B
babble balbucear
babbling balbuceo
baby bebé; niño; criatura; guagua; **have a baby** estar embarazada; tener un hijo; tener un niño
baby boy niño; nene
baby brother hermanito
baby carriage cochecito
baby sister hermanita
baby girl niña; nena
baby nurse nodriza; niñera; ama de cría
baby talk lenguaje infantil
back (anatomy of human) espalda; (of hand) dorso
backache dolor de espalda
backbone (anatomy) columna vertebral; espina dorsal
backbreaking agotador
background (of person) origen; (education) formación
bacteria (plural of bacterium)
bacterium bacteria
backward (movement) hacia atrás; (in reverse order) al revés
bacon tocino
bacteria bacteria; **bacteria cause disease** las bacterias causan enfermedades
bacterial bacterial
bacterial food poisoning intoxicación alimentaria bacteriana
bad mal; malo; mala; malos; malas; **taste bad** saber mal; **smell bad** oler mal; **it smells bad** huele mal (oler is an irregular verb); **salt is bad for you** la sal le hace mal; **a bad cold** un resfriado fuerte; **bad for one's health** malo para la salud; nocivo para la salud; **she's got a bad leg** está mal de la pierna; **this is his bad leg** esta es su mala pierna; **you've got a bad tooth** tiene un diente cariado; tiene una muela cariada
bad breath mal aliento; **have bad breath** tener mal aliento
bag bolsa
bag of waters bolsa de aguas
bags under the eyes ojeras; **have bags under one's eyes** tener bolsas en los ojos; estar ojeroso
balance (apparatus) balanza; (equilibrium) equilibrio; **keep one's balance** mantener el equilibrio; **lose one's balance** perder el equilibrio
balanced diet dieta equilibrada
bald calvo; **he's bald** es calvo; **go bald** quedarse calvo; **he's gone bald** está calvo; se ha quedado calvo
baldheaded calvo
baldness calvicie

ball-and-socket joint articulación esférica

balloon angioplasty angioplastia con balón

balls (vulgar) testículos; huevos; cojones

balm (soothing agent) bálsamo

balsam bálsamo; ungüento

band cinta; faja

bandage vendaje; (strip of cloth) venda; **Mr. Mata's bandage is dirty** el vendaje del señor Mata está sucio; **you need a new bandage** usted necesita un nuevo vendaje

bandage (verb) vendar; fajar

Band-Aide® curita®

bandage shears tijeras de vendaje

bandana pañuelo

barbiturate barbitúrico

bare (body, flesh, shoulder, etc) desnudo; (head) descubierto; (foot) descalzo; **bare from the waist up** desnudo hasta la cintura; con el torso desnudo

barechested desnudo de la cintura para arriba; sin camisa

barefoot descalzo; sin zapatos

bareheaded sin sombrero; con la cabeza descubierta

barium bario

barium enema enema de bario

barium meal papilla de bario

base of the cranium base del cráneo

basement sótano

bashful tímido; vergonzoso; penoso

bashfulness timidez

basic básico; **basic health services** servicios básicos de salud; **basic human needs** necesidades básicas; **basic life support** soporte vital básico

bassinet (cradle) moisés

bath baño; **take a bath** bañarse; darse un baño; **have a bath** bañarse; darse un baño

bath blanket manta de baño

bath towel toalla de baño

bathe (eyes; wound) lavar; (baby) bañar; **take a bath** bañarse

bathrobe bata de baño

bathroom baño; cuarto de baño; **go to the bathroom** ir al baño

bathtub bañera; bañadera

bathwater agua del baño

batter (victim) apalear; aporear; (child, wife) maltratar; pegarle a; (culinary for fried fish, fried chicken) rebozado

battered (woman, child) maltratado; **battered baby** bebé maltratado

battered woman syndrome síndrome de la mujer maltratada

bean habichuela; frijol; alubia

bear aguantar; resistir

bear down (in childbirth) empujar; pujar

beard barba

bearded con barba; de barba; barbudo; barbado

beat (heart) latir; (inflict blows on) golpear; pegar; maltratar; **beat to death** matar a golpes; **they beat him to death** lo mataron a golpes

beating golpiza; paliza

because porque; **because of** debido a; por

become llegar a ser + profession; hacerse + profession

become bloated abotagarse

bed cama; **get into bed** acostarse; meterse en la cama; **go to bed** acostarse

bed linen ropa de cama

bed rest reposo en cama

bedbath lavar en la cama; **give somebody a bedbath** lavar a alguien en la cama

bedboard tabla para la cama

bedbug chinche

bedclothes ropa de cama

bedcover cubre cama; colcha

bedcovers cobijas; frazadas

bedding ropa de cama

bedpad colchoncillo para la cama

bedpan cuña; chata; (Andes, Mex) pato

bedrail barandilla de la cama

bedridden postrado en cama

bedroom cuarto de dormir

bedsheet sábana

bedside junto a la cabecera; lado de la cama

bedside table mesita de noche

bedsore llaga de cama; úlcera por decúbito; úlcera de decúbito

bedspread sobre cama; cubre cama; colcha

bedtime hora de acostarse; hora de irse a la cama

bedwetting enuresis nocturna; problema del que se orina durante la noche

bee sting picadura de abeja

beef carne de res

beer cerveza

before antes; antes de; antes de que; de antemano; con anticipación

before and after antes y después

beg rogar; pedir; mendigar

begin comenzar; empezar; iniciar

beginning principio; comienzo; **at the beginning of** a principios de

behave comportarse; portarse; **behave very badly** portarse muy mal; **behave very well** portarse muy bien

behavior conducta; comportamiento; funcionamiento

behavior disorder trastorno de la conducta

behind detrás de; atrás de

belch (noun) eructo; (verb) eructar; regurgitar

believe creer

belly (colloquial) panza; barriga

bellyache dolor de barriga; dolor de tripa

bellybutton ombligo

belt cinto; cinturón; faja

bend (arm; back; leg) doblar; flexionar; inclinar; echar; **bend your knee** doble la rodilla; **bend your head back** inclina la cabeza hacia atrás; echa la cabeza hacia atrás; **bend your head forward** inclina la cabeza hacia adelante; echa la cabeza hacia adelante; **bend over** dóblese; **bend down** dóblese; **he was bent double with pain** se retorcía de dolor

bend down agacharse

bend of the arm flexura del brazo

beneath (under) bajo; de abajo; **the floor beneath** el piso de abajo

benefit (noun) beneficio; (verb) beneficiar
benign benigno
benign tumor tumor benigno
benzedrine bencedrina
better mejor; **be better** estar mejor; **feel better** sentirse mejor; (person) **get better** mejorarse; recuperarse; (healthy) más sano; más sana; **fruit's better for you than candy** la fruta es más sana que los caramelos; **even better** aún mejor
between entre; **between meals** entre comidas; **between now and Thursday** de aquí al jueves
bicarbonate of soda bicarbonato de soda; bicarbonato de sodio
biceps bíceps
bichloride of mercury cloruro mercúrico
big boned de huesos grandes
bile bilis; hiel
bile duct conducto biliar
bile salt sal biliar
biliary colic cólico hepático
bilirubin bilirrubina
bind amarrar; atar
binder cintura; faja; vendaje abdominal
binge borrachera
bipolar disorder enfermedad bipolar
birth nacimiento; (childbirth) parto; alumbramiento; **a difficult birth** un parto difícil; **at birth** al nacer; **give birth** dar a luz; **date of birth** fecha de nacimiento; **country of birth** país de nacimiento; **by birth** de nacimiento; **he's Argentinian by birth** es argentino de nacimiento
birth canal canal del parto
birth certificate acta de nacimiento; certificado de nacimiento
birth control control de la natalidad
birth control pill píldora anticonceptiva
birth defect defecto de nacimiento
birth injury lesión de parto
birth mother madre de nacimiento
birth pains dolores de parto
birth paralysis parálisis del parto
birth parents padres reales; padres de nacimiento
birth trauma traumatismo del parto
birth weight peso al nacimiento; peso al nacer
birthday cumpleaños
birthing chair silla de parto
birthmark mancha de nacimiento; marca de nacimiento
birthplace lugar de nacimiento
birthrate índice de natalidad; tasa de natalidad
bit (fragment, scrap) pedazo; trozo; (small amount) poquito; **a bit of** un poco de; **hurt a bit** doler un poco; doler poquito; **hurt quite a bit** doler bastante
bite (noun) mordida; mordisca; (verb) morder; **have a bite to eat** comer un bocado; comer algo
bivalve cast yeso bivalvo
black negro
black eye (bruise) ojo morado

black lung disease enfermedad del pulmón negro
blackhead espinilla; comedón; barrillo; espinilla de cabeza negra
blackout (loss of consciousness) desvanecimiento; desmayo; **have a blackout** sufrir un desvanecimiento; tener un desvanecimiento
bladder vejiga
bland diet dieta blanda
blanket frazada; manta; cobija
blanket bath baño con manta
bleach (noun) lejía; blanqueador; (verb) blanquear
bleed sangrar; desangrar; **bleed to death** desangrarse; **my nose is bleeding** me sale sangre de la nariz; **he cut himself but he didn't bleed** se cortó pero no le salió sangre
bleeding hemorragia
blind ciego
blind man ciego
blind woman ciega
blindgut intestino ciego
blister (noun) ampolla; **give blisters** hacer ampollas; (verb) ampollarse; **I got blisters on my feet** se me ampollaron los pies; **my feet blistered** se me ampollaron los pies
bloated (body, face) hinchado; abotagado; **feel bloated** sentirse hinchado
blocker bloqueador; **beta blocker** beta bloqueador
blond rubio (see fair)
blood sangre; **give blood** donar sangre; dar sangre; **a blood transfusion** una transfusión de sangre
blood bank banco de sangre
blood blister ampolla de sangre
blood capillaries capilares sanguíneos
blood cell célula sanguínea
blood circulation circulación sanguínea
blood clot coagulación sanguínea; coágulo de sangre
blood clotting coagulación sanguínea
blood corpuscle corpúsculo sanguíneo
blood count recuento sanguíneo; recuento globular
blood flow flujo sanguíneo
blood group grupo sanguíneo
blood level nivel sanguíneo
blood level of glucose nivel sanguíneo de glucosa
blood pH pH sanguíneo
blood plasma plasma sanguíneo
blood poisoning envenenamiento de la sangre
blood pressure presión arterial; **lower the blood pressure** bajar la presión arterial
blood sample muestra de sangre
blood stain mancha de sangre
blood-stained manchado de sangre
bloodstream torrente sanguíneo
blood-sugar azúcar sanguínea
blood-sugar level nivel de azúcar en sangre; nivel de azúcar sanguínea
blood test prueba sanguínea; análisis de sangre

blood transfusion transfusión de sangre
blood type grupo sanguíneo
blood vessel vaso sanguíneo
bloodshot eye ojo inyectado de sangre; congestión ocular
bloody nose sangrado por la nariz; hemorragia nasal
bloody sputum esputo sanguinolento
blotch (on skin) mancha
blotchy (on skin) lleno de manchas
blouse blusa; camiseta
blow (noun) golpe; (verb) sonar; sonarse; **blow one's nose** sonarse la nariz
blue azul
blue baby bebé azul
blue jeans pantalones vaqueros; tejanos
blurred borroso; mal enfocado
blurry vision vista borrosa
body cuerpo; **a dead body** un cadáver; **foreign body** cuerpo extraño
body and soul en alma y cuerpo
body fluid líquido corporal
body hair vello
body language lenguaje corporal
body movement movimiento corporal
body odor olor corporal; olor a transpiración
body size estatura
body temperature temperatura corporal
body type tipo corporal; tipo somático
body weight peso
boil (noun) furúnculo; forúnculo; (verb) hervir
boiled (potatoes, rice, etc) hervido; (ham) cocido; (egg) pasado por agua
boiling hirviendo; **add boiling water** añada agua hirviendo
boiling point punto de ebullición
bond vínculo; **bond between mother and child** vínculo afectivo entre madre e hijo
bonding vinculación afectiva; vinculación emocional
bone hueso; **big boned** de huesos grandes
bone cancer cáncer óseo
bone cell célula ósea
bone cyst quiste óseo
bone graft injerto óseo
bone marrow médula ósea
bone tissue tejido óseo
booster shot vacuna de refuerzo; vacuna de recuerdo
boot bota
booze bebida; trago
boric acid ácido bórico
born nacido; **be born** nacer; **be born blind** ser ciego de nacimiento; ser ciega de nacimiento; **be born into the world** venir al mundo
bother molestar; **is your neck bothering you?** ¿le molesta el cuello?
bottle botella; (medicine) frasco; **hot-water bottle** bolsa de agua caliente
bottle feeding alimentación con biberón
bottlefeed (verb) alimentar con biberón
bow legged patizambo; estevado
bowel vientre; **have a bowel movement** hacer de vientre; **large bowel** intestino grueso

bowel movement evacuación; deposición intestinal; hacer de vientre
boy niño; chico
bra (brassiere) sostén; sostenedor; portabustos
brace aparato ortopédico
braces (dental) aparatos; frenos para los dientes; fierros
brain cerebro; encéfalo
brain damage lesión cerebral
brain-damaged con lesión cerebral
brain-dead clínicamente muerto
brain death muerte clínica; muerte cerebral
brain scan gammagrafía cerebral
brain swelling tumefacción cerebral
brain tumor tumor cerebral
brain wave onda cerebral
brainstem tronco de encéfalo
bran salvado
bran bath baño de salvado
brassy cough tos metálica
brassy eye ojo de latón
brat mocoso; niño mimado
brave valiente; valeroso
brawl pelea; reyerta
break (noun) fractura; rotura; (verb) romper; romperse; **break an arm** romperse un brazo; **break a tooth** romperse un diente; **break a nail** romperse una uña; **he broke his wrist** se rompió la muñeca
breakfast desayuno; **have breakfast** desayunar; tomar el desayuno
breakfast time hora del desayuno
breast pecho; mama; seno
breast cancer cáncer de mama
breast examination examen de mama
breast milk leche materna
breast self examination auto exploración de las mamas
breastbone (anatomy) esternón; (culinary) hueso de la pechuga
breastfeed darle el pecho a; darle de mamar a; amamantar
breastfed baby niño amamantado
breastfeeding lactancia materna
breast milk leche materna
breath aliento; **have bad breath** tener mal aliento; **take a deep breath** respirar hondo
breath test prueba del alcohol
Breathalyzer® test prueba del alcohol; **fail the Breathalyzer® test** no pasar la prueba del alcohol; **pass the Breathalyzer® test** pasar la prueba del alcohol
breathe respirar
breathe deeply respirar hondo
breathe in aspirar
breathe out espirar
breathe through one's mouth respirar por la boca
breathe through one's nose respirar por la nariz
breathe with difficulty respirar con difficultad

breathing respiración; **heavy breathing** respiración pesada; **regular breathing** respiración regular

breathless sin aliento

breech baby bebé que viene de nalgas

breech birth parto de nalgas

breech extraction extracción de nalgas

breeze brisa

brewer's yeast levadura de cerveza

bridgework puente dental

brief breve

briefly por poco tiempo

bring traer; llevar; **bring ... with you** traer ... consigo

bring on provocar; **the pills brought on a skin reaction** las pastillas le provocaron una reacción cutánea

brittle (bones, etc) quebradizo; frágil

broad ancho; amplio

broad ligament ligamento ancho

broad ligament of the liver ligamento ancho del hígado

broad-shouldered ancho de hombros; ancho de espaldas

broad-spectrum antibiotic antibiótico de alcance amplio; antibiótico de espectro amplio

broken (arm, leg, etc) roto; **broken arm** brazo roto; (marriage, home, etc) deshecho; **broken home** hogar deshecho

bromide bromuro

bronchial bronquial

bronchial asthma asma bronquial

bronchial breath sound ruido respiratorio bronquial

bronchial drainage drenaje bronquial

bronchial tree árbol bronquial

bronchial tubes bronquios

bronchitis bronquitis

broth caldo

brother hermano; **brothers and sisters** hermanos; **have brothers and sisters** tener hermanos

brow frente

brown marrón; café

brown rice arroz integral

bruise (noun) moretón; magulladura; machucadura; contusión; (verb: body, arm, skin) contusionar; magullar; (verb: person) magullarse

bruised con moretones; magullado

brunette (hair) moreno

bubble bath baño de burbujas; baño de espuma

bubonic plague peste bubónica

buckteeth dientes salidos; dientes de conejo; **have buckteeth** tener los dientes salidos

bucktoothed con los dientes salidos; dientudo

bug (biting insect) chinche

bulimia bulimia

bulimic bulímico

bullet bala

bullet wound herida de bala

bump (on the head) chichón; (lump on the surface) bulto

bunion juanete

burly fornido; corpulento; musculoso

burn (noun) quemadura; ardor; (verb) quemar; **burn oneself** quemarse; **suffer minor burns on the face** sufrir quemaduras leves en la cara; **suffer severe burns on the face** sufrir quemaduras graves en la cara; **first degree burns** quemaduras de primer grado; **second degree burns** quemaduras de segundo grado; **third degree burns** quemaduras de tercer grado; **a cigarette burn** una quemadura de cigarrillo

burn center centro de quemados

burn therapy tratamiento de quemados

burning ardiente; abrasador

burning feet syndrome síndrome del pie urente; síndrome del pie ardiente

burning pain dolor urente; dolor ardiente

burning sensation ardor

burp (noun) eructo; (verb) eructar

bursitis bursitis

bury enterrar; sepultar

busy ocupado

butt nalgas

buttocks nalgas

butter mantequilla

butterfly bandage venda en mariposa

buttermilk suero de la leche

buttock nalga; **buttocks** nalgas

button (noun) botón; (verb) abotonar; abrochar

buttonhole ojal; **buttonhole fracture** fractura en ojal

buy comprar

buzz zumbido

buzzer timbre

buzzing in the ear zumbido de oídos

bye ¡adiós!; ¡chao!; ¡chau!

bye-bye ¡adiós!

bypass surgery cirugía de bypass

cafeteria cafetería

caffeine cafeína

calcium calcio

calculation cálculo; **calculation for children's dosage** cálculo de la dosis para niños

calendar calendario

calf (anatomy) pantorrilla

calisthenics calistenia

call llamar; **a call for help** un pedido de socorro; **call back** llamar más tarde; **local call** llamada urbana; **long distance call** llamada interurbana; llamada de larga distancia; **make a call** llamar por teléfono

call light lámpara para llamar a

callus callo

calm tranquilo; calma; **calm down** ¡tranquilízate! ¡tranquilo!; ¡no te pongas así! **keep calm** ¡tranquilo!; ¡calma!; **remain calm** no perder la calma; **calm yourself** tranquilízate; cálmate

calm down calmarse

calming tranquilizante

calmness (person) calma; tranquilidad

caloric calórico; **caloric energy** energía calórica; **caloric test** prueba calórica

calorie caloría; **a calorie controlled diet** una dieta baja en calorías; **food with low calorie content** alimentos de bajo contenido calórico

camomile tea té de manzanilla

camphor alcanfor

can (noun) lata; bote; **can of tomatoes** lata de tomates; (verb) poder; (know) saber

canal (anatomy) canal; tubo; conducto; **alimentary canal** tubo alimentario; canal alimentario; **birth canal** canal del parto

cancel cancelar

cancellation cancelación

cancer cáncer

cancer bodies cuerpos cancerígenos

cancer patient enfermo de cáncer

cancer of the breast cáncer de mama

cancer of the liver cáncer de hígado

cancer of the small intestine cáncer de intestino delgado

cancer of the uterus cáncer de cuello del útero

cancerous canceroso

cane bastón

canine tooth diente canino; colmillo

canker úlcera; afta

canker sore afta dolorosa

cankerous ulceroso

cap gorra

capability capacidad

capillary capilar

capillaries vaso capilar

capillary tube tubo capilar

capsule cápsula

car coche

carbohydrate hidrato de carbono

carcinogen carcinógeno

cardiac (condition) cardíaco; (surgery) cardiovascular

cardiac arrest paro cardíaco

cardiac pain dolor cardíaco

cardiogram cardiograma

cardiologist cardiólogo; cardióloga

cardiopulmonary cardiopulmonar

cardiopulmonary arrest paro cardiopulmonar

cardiopulmonary murmur soplo cardiopulmonar

cardiorespiratory cardiorespiratorio

cardiovascular cardiovascular; **cardiovascular assessment** examen cardiovascular; **cardiovascular disease** enfermedad cardiovascular

care (noun) cuidado; atención; (verb) preocuparse; cuidar; atender, **medical care** atención médica; **care for** cuidar de; cuidar a; atender

care of the chronically ill atención al enfermo crónico

care of the sick atención al enfermo

care plan plan de atención

careful cuidado; **be careful** tener cuidado

caregiver cuidador

caries caries

carpal tunnel túnel carpiano

carrier portador

carry portar; esperar; **when I was carrying my first baby** cuando esperaba mi primer hijo; **when I was carrying my second baby** cuando esperaba mi segundo hijo

carry the baby llevar al hijo en brazos; llevar a la hija en brazos

carsick mareado por viajar en coche

carsickness mareo por viajar en coche

cartilage cartílago

case caso

case history historia personal y familiar

case load número de casos

case nursing enfermería individualizada

casework trabajo de asistencia social individual

cash dinero; efectivo; **pay in cash** pagar en efectivo

cash only pagos únicamente en efectivo; pagos únicamente al contado

cashier cajero; cajera

cast yeso; molde; **a plaster cast of the footprint** un molde de yeso de la huella

castor oil aceite de ricino; aceite de castor

castration castración

cat gato

cat-bite fever fiebre por mordisco de gato

cat scratch disease enfermedad por arañazo de gato

cat scratch fever fiebre por arañazo de gato

cataract catarata

catarrh catarro

catastrophic care asistencia de catástrofes

catastrophic health insurance seguro de asistencia sanitaria ante catástrofes

catastrophic illness enfermedad catastrófica

catch (become infected with) contagiarse; contraer; **catch a cold** resfriarse; pescar un resfriado; agarrarse un resfriado; **catch the flu** tener gripe; **catch the measles** contagiarse el sarampión

cathartic (noun) purgante; (adjective) catártico

catheter catéter; sonda

cathode cátodo

cathode ray rayo catódico

Caucasian de raza blanca

cauliflower ear oreja deformada; oreja en coliflor

cause causa; **cause of death** causa de la muerte; **there's no cause for concern** no hay por qué preocuparse; **cause somebody problems** causarle problemas a alguien; **the pills caused a skin reaction** las pastillas le causaron una reacción cutánea

caustic poisoning intoxicación por cáusticos

caution (noun) cautela; prudencia; advertencia; **act with caution** actuar con cautela; (verb) advertir; instruir; informar

cautious prudente; cauteloso; cauto

cautiously cautelosamente

cavity (hole) cavidad; (dental) caries

cecum intestino ciego

cell célula

cell body cuerpo celular

cell culture cultivo celular

cell membrane membrana celular
cell wall pared celular
cellular celular
cellulose celulosa
cellulose acetate acetato de celulosa
cellulose nitrate nitrocelulosa
centipede bite picadura por ciempiés
central nervous system (CNS) sistema
　nervioso central (SNC)
cereal cereal
cerebellum cerebelo
cerebral palsy parálisis cerebral
certain seguro; make certain that
　asegurarse que; asegurarse de que; be
　certain of estar seguro de; on certain
　days solamente ciertos días; at certain
　times of the day a ciertas horas del día
certified dental assistant auxiliar
　certificado de odontología
certified milk leche con garantía sanitaria
Certified-Nurse-Midwife Matrona
　Diplomada; Comadrona Diplomada
cervical cervical; del cuello del útero
cervical abortion aborto cervical
cervical canal conducto cervical
cervical cancer cáncer cervical
cervical cap capuchón cervical
cervical collar collarín; collar ortopédico
cervical opening cuello del útero
cervical cyst quiste cervical
cervical polyp pólipo cervical
cervical smear Papanicolau; citología
cervix cuello uterino; cérvix
cesarean hysterectomy histerectomía con
　cesárea
cesarean section cesárea
chafing rozadura; roce
Chagas disease enfermedad de Chagas
chair silla; dentist's chair silla de dentista;
　take a chair please tome asiento; please
　sit down por favor siéntese; please take
　a seat por favor siéntese
change (noun) cambio; (verb) cambiar;
　cambiarse; alterar; change one's clothes
　cambiarse de ropa; change one's shoes
　cambiarse de zapatos
change of life cambio de vida
chart (noun) gráfico; tabla; eye chart carta
　de examen visual; (verb) trazar;
　registrar gráficamente; chart the
　episodes registrar los episodios
　gráficamente; the chart shows your
　progress el gráfico muestra su progreso
check-up chequeo
cheek mejilla; cachete
cheekbone pómulo
cheerful lleno de vida
cheese queso; blue cheese queso azul;
　cheddar cheese queso de Cheddar
chemotherapy quimioterapia
chest pecho
chest cold catarro de pecho
chest pain dolor torácico; dolor de pecho
chest specialist especialista de las vías
　respiratorias
chew mascar; masticar; (nails, etc) morder
chicken pollo; roast chicken pollo asado
chickenpox varicela

chief complaint queja principal
chief resident jefe de residentes
chief surgeon cirujano jefe
chilblain sabañón
child (boy) niño, (girl) niña; (boy) hijo;
　only child hijo único; hija única; a child
　of six un niño de seis años
child abuse malos tratos a la infancia;
　malos tratos a menores
child benefit asignación familiar
child care provider cuidador de niños;
　cuidadora de niños
child development desarrollo infantil
child labor trabajo de menores
child molester persona que somete a un
　niño a abusos deshonestos
child neglect abandono infantil
child psychology psicología infantil
child welfare protección a la infancia
childbearing maternidad; be of
　childbearing age estar en edad fértil
childbearing period periodo de fecundidad
childbed fever fiebre del parto
childbirth parto; alumbramiento; die in
　childbirth morir de parto; she died in
　childbirth murió de parto
childbirth center centro de preparación al
　parto
childcare cuidado de los niños;
　puericultura
childcare facilities guarderías
childhood niñez; infancia
childhood aphasia afasia infantil
childhood disease enfermedad infantil
childhood-onset pervasive development
　disorders trastornos profundos del
　desarrollo de inicio en la infancia
childless (couple) sin hijos
childproof a prueba de niños
children's aspirin aspirina para niños
chills escalofríos
chin barbilla; mentón; double chin papada
chip (verb) fragmentar; (tooth) romper
choice (option) elección; make ones choice
　elegir; escoger; doctors have to make
　hard choices sometimes los médicos a
　veces tienen que tomar decisiones
　difíciles
choke estrangular; ahogar; asfixiar
cholesterol colesterol
choose elegir; escoger; decidir; querer;
　choose your doctor escoja su médico;
　because I don't choose to porque no
　quiero
chronic crónico
chronic abscess absceso crónico
chronic airway obstruction obstrucción
　crónica de las vías respiratorias
chronic alcohol delirium delirio alcohólico
　crónico
chronic alcoholism alcoholismo crónico
chronic appendicitis apendicitis crónica
chronic brain syndrome síndrome cerebral
　crónico
chronic bronchitis bronquitis crónica
chronic care atención crónica
chronic disease enfermedad crónica

chronic fatigue syndrome síndrome de
fatiga crónica
chronic pain dolor crónico
chronically ill enfermo crónico
chronological age edad cronológica
cigarettes cigarrillos
cigars puros, cigarros
circulation (blood) circulación; **have bad
circulation** tener mala circulación; **have
good circulation** tener buena circulación
circulation rate velocidad de circulación
circulation time, normal tiempo de
circulación normal
circulatory failure insuficiencia circulatoria
circulatory system sistema circulatorio;
aparato circulatorio
circumcise circuncidar
circumcision circuncisión; **female
circumcision** circuncisión femenina
cirrhosis of the liver cirrosis del hígado;
cirrosis hepática
clap (slang) gonorrea
clawfoot pie en garra
clawhand mano en garra
clean limpio; **clean hands** manos limpias;
(verb) limpiar; lavar; **clean oneself**
limpiarse
cleanliness limpieza; **personal cleanliness**
aseo personal
cleansing enema enema de limpieza
clear cell carcinoma carcinoma de células
claras
cleft hendidura
cleft foot pie hendido
cleft lip labio hendido
cleft palate paladar hendido
cleft tongue lengua hendida
climate clima
clinic clínica
clinical clínico
clinical diagnosis diagnóstico clínico
clinical disease enfermedad clínica
clinical nurse specialist enfermera clínica
especialista
clinical specialist especialista clínico
clinically dead clínicamente muerto
clitoral del clítoris
clitoris clítoris
clock reloj
close (verb) cerrar; **close one's mouth**
cerrar la boca; **close one's eyes** cerrar
los ojos
clot (blood) coágulo; (verb) coagular;
coagularse
clotting coagulación
clothes ropa; **change one's clothes** mudarse
de ropa; cambiarse de ropa; **put on
one's clothes** ponerse la ropa; **take off
one's clothes** quitarse la ropa
clothing ropa
clubfoot pie deforme; pie zambo
clubfooted con el pie deforme
clubhand mano zamba
cluster headache cefalea en racimos
coat abrigo
coated tablet comprimido recubierto
coated tongue lengua saburral
cocaine cocaína

cocaine addict cocainómano; cocainómana
cod bacalao
cod-liver oil aceite de hígado de bacalao
codeine codeína
coffee café
cognitive cognitivo
cognitive development desarrollo cognitivo
coitus coito; acto sexual
coitus interruptus coitus interruptus
cold frío; **be cold** tener frío; **catch a cold**
resfriarse; agarrarse un resfriado; pescar
un resfriado
cold compress compresa fría
cold pack envoltura fría; compresa fría
cold sore herpes; boquera
colic cólico
collapse colapso
collapse of the lung colapso pulmonar
collapsed lung colapso pulmonar
collar collar
collarbone clavícula
colon colon
colonic irrigation irrigación colónica
colonoscopy colonoscopia
color color; **what color is ...?** ¿de qué color
es ...?
color blind daltónico
color blindness daltonismo
colorectal cancer cáncer colorrectal
coma coma
comatose comatoso
comb (for hair) peine; (verb) **comb oneself**
peinarse; **comb one's hair** peinarse
come venir; **come from** venir de; ser de;
come in entrar
come and go ir y venir; **does the pain come
and go?** ¿le va y le viene el dolor?
comfort (noun) comodidad; confort; **words
of comfort** palabras de consuelo; (verb)
consolar; confortar
comfortable cómodo; confortable
commode (for invalid) silla con orinal;
(toilet) inodoro
common cold resfriado común; **be
common** ser común
common sense sentido común
communicable transmisible
communicable disease enfermedad
transmisible
community comunidad
community health nursing enfermería de
salud comunitaria
community hospital hospital de la
comunidad
community mental health salud mental de
la comunidad
community mental health center centro de
salud mental de la comunidad
community nurse practitioner profesional
de enfermería comunitaria
complain quejarse; **complain of** quejarse
de; **she complained of a headace** se
quejó de dolor de cabeza
complaint queja; (court) demanda; **chief
complaint** queja principal
comprehensive care atención integral
concussion conmoción cerebral
condom condón

confine restringir; confinar; **confined to bed** guardar cama; **confined to a wheel chair** estar confinado a una silla de ruedas

congenital congénito

congenital disease enfermedad congénita

congratulations felicitaciones

consciousness conocimiento; **lose consciousness** perder el conocimiento; **regain consciousness** recobrar el conocimiento; volver en sí

consequence consecuencia; resultado; **be a consequence of** ser consecuencia de; ser resultado de; **have consequences** tener consecuencias; traer consecuencias

constantly constantemente; **constantly monitor** observar constantemente; seguir constantemente; controlar constantemente; **will be constantly monitored** se seguirá muy de cerca

constipated estreñido

constipation estreñimiento

consult consultar; **if symptoms persist, consult a doctor** si los síntomas continúan, consulte a su médico

consultation consulta; **in consultation with** en conferencia con

contact contacto; **avoid contact with the eyes** evite contacto con los ojos; **avoid contact with the skin** evite contacto con la piel

contact lens lentes de contacto

contagious contagioso; **it is contagious** es contagioso

contagious disease enfermedad contagiosa

contamination contaminación

continue continuar; seguir; **continue to exercise** seguir haciendo ejercicios

contraceptive anticonceptivo

contraceptive jelly jalea anticonceptiva

contraceptive pill píldora anticonceptiva; pastilla anticonceptiva

contractions contracciones; contracciones de la matriz

control control; controlar; **to control the intake of sugar** controlar el consumo de azúcar

controlled controlado; contenido; **controlled diet** dieta controlada

contusion contusión

convalesce recuperarse; convalecer

convalescent home casa de convalecencia; clínica de reposo

cool fresco; frío

cool off refrescarse; (become calmer) calmarse

corn (cereal) maíz; (on toe) callo

corn pad almohadilla para callos

cornea córnea

coronary coronario

coronary arteries arterias coronarias

coronary artery disease coronariopatía

coronary bypass derivación coronaria

coronary care nursing cuidados coronarios de enfermería

coronary care unit (CCU) unidad de cuidados coronarios (UCC)

cortisone cortisona

cot (child) cuna; cama

cot death muerte de cuna

cotton algodón

cotton swab hisopo de algodón; bastoncillo

couch potato teleadicto; teleadicta

cough (noun) tos; (verb) toser

cough drops pastillas para la tos

cough lozenges pastillas para la tos

cough syrup jarabe para la tos

counseling consejería; terapia

counselor consejero

county hospital hospital del condado

country país; **country of birth** país de nacimiento

cover (noun) cubierta; tapa; (verb) cubrir; tapar; **cover the wound** cubra la herida

covers (bedclothes) mantas; cobijas

cramps calambres; **get a cramp** darle un calambre

crazy loco; loca

cream (milk) crema; (lotion) crema; **face cream** crema para la cara

crib cuna; camita de niño; camita con barandillas para niño

crime delito; crimen

cripple (noun) lisiado; tullido; **a crippled arm** un brazo tullido

crisis crisis

crisis intervention intervención de crisis

crisis-intervention unit unidad de intervención de crisis

crisis resolution resolución de la crisis

critical care cuidado crítico

critical organs órganos críticos

critical period periodo crítico

critical pressure presión crítica

critical temperature temperatura crítica

cross cruce

cross-eyed bizco; turnio; **be cross-eyed** ser turnio

cross fertilization fertilización cruzada

crotch (genital area) entrepiernas

crown corona

crutches muletas

cry (noun) llanto; (verb) llorar

c-section cesárea

cup taza; vaso; **a cup of coffee** una taza de café; **measuring cup** taza de medir; **urinate in this plastic cup** orine en este vaso de plástico

curable curable; que tiene cura

cure (noun) cura; remedio (verb) curar

cure-all curalotodo

curettage raspado; raspaje

cut (noun) cortada; corte; (with a knife) cuchillada; **cut oneself** cortarse; **cut one's finger** cortarse el dedo

cutaneous cutáneo

cyanic acid ácido ciánico

cyst quiste

cystic fibrosis fibrosis cística

dad papá

daddy papi

dental surgeon cirujano dental

daily diario; **on a daily basis** a diario

dairy products lácteos

damage (noun) daño; perjuicio; (verb) dañar; perjudicar; **cause damage** causar daño; **a lot of damage** grandes daños; **smoking can seriously damage your health** fumar perjudica seriamente la salud

dandruff caspa

dandruff shampoo champú anti-caspa

danger peligro; **there's no danger** no hay ningún peligro; **her life is in danger** su vida está en peligro; su vida está en riesgo; **be out of danger** estar fuera de peligro

date fecha

date of birth fecha de nacimiento

dangerous peligroso

dark oscuro; (person) moreno

dark circles under the eyes ojeras

daughter hija

daughter-in-law nuera; hija política

day día; **every other day** cada dos días; **the day before** el día anterior; **the following day** el día siguiente; **every day** todos los días; **the day after tomorrow** pasado mañana; **the day before yesterday** anteayer

day care servicio de guardería infantil

day-care center guardería infantil

day nurse enfermera del turno diurno

daze (noun) aturdimiento; (verb) aturdir

dazed aturdido

dead muerto

deaf sordo; **be deaf** estar sordo; **be deaf in one ear** estar sordo de un oído

deaf-mute sordomudo; sordomuda

deafness sordera

death muerte; fallecimiento

death at an advanced age muerte senil

death certificate certificado de muerte; parte de muerte

deathbed lecho de muerte

deceased fallecido; difunto

December diciembre (see January)

decision decisión; **make a decision** tomar una decisión; **reach a decision** llegar a una decisión; **it's your decision** es tu decisión

decongestant (noun) descongestionante; anticongestivo; (adjective) descongestionante; anticongestivo

deep hondo; profundo; **deep wound** herida profunda; **deep gash** corte profundo

defecate defecar; evacuar

defecation defecación

defective defectuoso

deficient deficiente; insuficiente; **foods deficient in vitamins** alimentos de bajo contenido vitamínico

degenerative degenerativo

degenerative disease enfermedad degenerativa

degenerative joint disease enfermedad articular degenerativa

degree grado; nivel; **first degree burns** quemaduras de primer grado; **second degree burns** quemaduras de segundo

grado; **third degree burns** quemaduras de tercer grado

dehydrated deshidratado; **become dehydrated** deshidratarse

dehydration deshidratación

delay (noun) tardanza; (verb) retrasar; demorar; **delayed development** desarrollo retardado; **without delay** sin tardanza; sin demora

delirium delirio; **suffer from delirium** delirar

delirium tremens delirium tremens

deliver (obstetrics) dar a luz; (action performed by a doctor) atender un parto; **Doctor Smith delivered the twins** el doctor Smith atendió el parto de los gemelos

delivery (of baby) parto; alumbramiento

delivery room sala de partos

dental dental; **a dental appoinment** una cita dental

dental floss seda dental; hilo dental

dental hygienist higienista dental

dental surgeon cirujano dental

dentist dentista

dentures dentadura postiza; caja de dientes; **a set of dentures** una dentadura postiza

deodorant desodorante

depressed (person) deprimido; abatido; **she's a bit depressed** anda un poco deprimida; **become depressed** deprimirse; dejarse abatir

depression depresión; abatimientos; **suffer from depression** sufrir depresiones

deranged trastornado; loco

dermatologist dermatólogo; dermatóloga

desperate desesperado; **be desperate** estar desesperado

detection descubrimiento; detección; **early detection** detección precoz

detergent detergente; jabón en polvo

detriment detrimento; perjuicio; **without detriment to his health** sin perjuicio para su salud

detrimental perjudicial

development desarrollo

development age edad de desarrollo

developmental psychology psicología del desarrollo

deviance desviación; anomalía

deviant (noun) individuo de conducta desviada; (adjective) desviado; anormal; persona que se aparta de la norma

deviated behavior conducta desviada

dexterity destreza; habilidad

diabetes diabetes

diabetic diabético; diabética

diabetic diet dieta para diabéticos

diabetic treatment tratamiento de la diabetes

diagnose diagnosticar

diagnosis diagnóstico; **make a diagnosis** hacer un diagnóstico; **give a diagnosis** dar un diagnóstico

dialysis diálisis

dialysis machine dializador

diaper rash (formal) exantema de pañal; (colloquial) irritación en las nalgas de un bebé; salpullido; sarpullido diaphragm (contraceptive) diafragma

diarrhea diarrea

die fallecer; morir

diet (special food) régimen; dieta; **to diet** hacer régimen; **a fat free diet** una dieta sin grasas

dietary allowances aporte dietético

dietary fiber fibra dietética

dietician dietista; experto en dietética

dietetic food alimento dietético

difficult (task, problem) difícil

difficulty dificultad; problema; **he has difficulty understanding English** tiene dificultad para entender el inglés; **she had great difficulty walking** caminaba con mucha dificultad; **learning difficulties** dificultades de aprendizaje; problemas de aprendizaje

digest (food) digerir

digestible digerible; **easily digestible** fácil de digerir

digestion digestión

diptheria difteria

dirty sucio; manchado; **your hands are dirty** usted tiene las manos sucias

disability invalidez; discapacidad; minusvalía; problema; **she managed to overcome her disability** consiguió superar su problema

disabled discapacitado; incapacitado; minusválido; inválido; **be disabled** quedar inválido; **the disabled** los discapacitados; los minusválidos

disagreement desacuerdo; **be in disagreement with** estar en desacuerdo con

discharge (noun) secreción; flujo; (verb) supurar, (from hospital) dar de alta; **vaginal discharge** flujo vaginal; **discharge pus** supurar; **he was discharged from the hospital** fue dado de alta del hospital

discomfort molestia; malestar; **a little discomfort** alguna molestia; **some discomfort** alguna molestia

disinfectant desinfectante

dislocate (shoulder) dislocarse

dislocated (joint) **to become dislocated** descoyuntarse

disrobe desvestirse

distress congoja; angustia; aflicción

diuretic (noun) diurético; (adjective) diurético

divorce divorcio

divorce therapy terapia de divorcio

divorced divorciado; **be divorced** estar divorciado

dizziness vértigo; mareo

dizzy spell mareo

DNA ADN

doctor médico; médica; doctor; doctora; **see a doctor** ir al médico; **Dr. Jones** el doctor Jones; **which doctor are you under?** ¿qué médico le atiende?

domestic (of the house, persons, problems) doméstico; **for domestic reasons** por motivos familiares; **domestic violence** violencia en el hogar

dominant gene gen dominante

dominant group grupo dominante

dominant trait rasgo dominante

door puerta

dope (slang) droga; (cannabis) hachís; chocolate; **dope dealer** camello

dose dosis; **recommended dose** dosis recomendada; **do not exceed the recommended dose** no sobrepasar la dosis recomendada

double fracture fractura doble

double vision visión doble

douche (syringe) irrigador vaginal; ducha vaginal

drainage drenaje

dream (noun) sueño; (verb) soñar; **have a dream about** soñar con; **a bad dream** una pesadilla

dress (noun) vestido; (verb) vestir; vestirse; **get dressed** vestirse; **dress oneself** vestirse

dressing emplasto; apósito; gasa; (bandage) vendaje; (culinary) aliño

dried fruit fruta seca

drink (noun) bebida; (verb) beber; tomar; **food and drink** comida y bebida

drops gotas (see nose, ears)

dry seco; **keep the wound dry** mantenga la herida seca; **store in a cool, dry place** guardar en lugar fresco y seco

drown ahogar; ahogarse; **be drowned** ahogarse

drowning ahogado

drowsiness somnolencia; sopor

drug (noun) fármaco; droga; estupefaciente; medicamento; (verb) drogar; **this drug may cause drowsiness** este fármaco puede provocar somnolencia; **to be on drugs** drogarse; **I don't do drugs** yo no me drogo; no uso drogas; **to take drugs for the heart** tomar medicamentos para el corazón

drug abuse abuso de sustancias

drug addict adicto a drogas

drug addiction drogadicción; drogadependencia

drug dealer traficante de drogas

drug dependence drogadependencia

drug habit drogadicción

drug store farmacia; botica; droguería

drug user consumidor de drogas; consumidora de drogas

drunk borracho; **be drunk** estar borracho; **to get drunk** emborracharse

dry heaves vomitar sin nada que expulsar

double vision visión doble

E

ear (organ) oído; (outer ear) oreja; **inner ear** oído interno; **middle ear** oído medio; **outer ear** oído externo

ear, nose and throat department departamento de oído, nariz y garganta

earache dolor de oído

eardrops gotas para los oídos

eardrum tímpano

early temprano; precoz

early death muerte temprana; muerta prematura

early detection detección precoz

early diagnosis diagnóstico precoz

eat comer; **to eat meat** comer carne; **to not eat meat** no comer carne

egg huevo; **fried egg** huevo frito; huevo estrellado; **boiled egg** huevo pasado por agua; **poached eggs** huevos escalfados; **scrambled eggs** huevos revueltos

egg white clara de huevo

egg yolk yema de huevo

elastic bandage vendaje elástico

elbow codo; **tennis elbow** codo de tenis

elderly anciano; anciana; **the elderly** los ancianos; **an elderly lady** una anciana; **many of the patients are elderly** muchos de los pacientes son ancianos

electric blanket frazada eléctrica

electrocardiogram electrocardiograma

embedded tooth diente incrustado

emergency urgencia; emergencia; **it's an emergency** es una situación de emergencia; **in case of emergency** en caso de emergencia; **the ambulance rushed him to emergency** la ambulancia lo llevó a urgencias; la ambulancia lo llevó a la sala de guardia; la ambulancia lo llevó a la sala de emergencia

emergency cardiac care (ECC) asistencia cardíaca de urgencias (ACE)

emergency childbirth parto repentino

emergency department servicio de urgencias

emergency nursing enfermería de urgencias

emergency room (ER) sala de urgencias (SU); sala de guardia (SG)

emesis basin escupidera

emollient bath baño emoliente

emotion emoción

emotional emocional

emotional age edad emocional

emotional care of the dying patient atención emocional al moribundo

emotional illness enfermedad emocional

emotional need necesidad emocional

emotional response respuesta emocional

emotional support apoyo emocional

empathy empatía

emphysema enfisema

Emergency Medical Service (EMS) Servicio de Urgencia Médica (SMU)

endoscopy endoscopia

enema enema; lavativa (see barium)

English inglés

English-speaking de habla inglesa

enough bastante; suficiente; **get enough sleep** dormir lo suficiente; **not get enough sleep** no dormir lo suficiente

entire todo; entero; **entire body** todo el cuerpo; el cuerpo entero

epidural anesthesia anestesia epidural

epilepsy epilepsia

epileptic seizure ataque epiléptico

equilibrium equilibrio

esophageal cancer cáncer de esófago

examination examen; reconocimiento

examine examinar; revisar

excited (nervous) agitado; ansioso; (sexual) excitado

exercise ejercicio; **to exercise** hacer ejercicio

exhale (breathe out) espirar; exhalar; aspirar; **breathe in deeply and then exhale** inspire profundamente y después espire

exhaust agotar; **exhaust oneself** agotarse

exhausted agotado; **be exhausted** estar agotado; **look exhausted** tener cara de estar agotado

exhaustion agotamiento; **suffer from exhaustion** sufrir de agotamiento

expect esperar; suponer; **I don't expect any problems** no creo vaya a haber problemas; **she's expecting** está esperando; está en estado

explain explicar; **explain the treatment** explicar el tratamiento; **to explain oneself** explicarse; **please explain yourself more clearly** por favor explíquese más claramente

exploratory surgery cirugía exploratoria

exposure congelación; **to be suffering from exposure** tener síntomas de congelación; **to die from exposure** morir de frío; **exposure to toxic chemicals** exposición a sustancias químicas tóxicas

external ear oído externo

external fertilization fertilización externa

external pacemaker marcapasos externo

external radiation therapy (ERT) radioterapia externa (RTE)

eye ojo; **have blue eyes** tener los ojos azules

eye chart carta de examen visual

eye shadow sombra de ojos

eyeball globo ocular

eyebrow ceja

eyeglasses anteojos; gafas

eyelash pestaña

eyelid párpado

eyepatch parche en el ojo; **wear an eyepatch** llevar un parche en el ojo

eyesight vista; **have good eyesight** tener buena vista; **have bad eyesight** tener mala vista; **your eyesight is failing** su vista ya no es lo que era

eyestrain fatiga visual; vista cansada

eyewash colirio; solución oftálmica

eyewear lentes

eyewitness testigo ocular; testigo presencial

face cara; rostro; **wash one's face** lavarse la cara

face cream crema para la cara

face down boca abajo

face lift estiramiento facial

face up boca arriba

facecloth toallita para lavarse

failing health no estar bien de salud; **his health is failing** no está bien de salud

failing eyesight la vista ya no es lo que era

fair rubio

faint (noun) desmayo; (verb) desmayarse

fall (noun) caída; (season) otoño; (verb) caer; caerse

false teeth dientes postizos

family familia; **the Lunas family** la familia Lunas; **a friend of the family** un amigo de la familia; **he has family in California** tiene familia en California; tiene parientes en California; tiene familiares en California; **immediate family** parientes cercanos; **they are a very close family** son una familia muy unida; **to be in the family way** estar esperando; estar en estado

family counseling asesoría familiar

family health salud familiar

family history historia familiar

family medicine medicina de familia

family name apellido

family nurse practitioner enfermero práctico de familia; enfermera práctica de familia

family planning planificación familiar

family practice physician médico de familia

family therapy terapia de familia

family structure estructura familiar

family-centered care atención centrada en la familia

family-centered maternity care cuidados de maternidad centrados en la familia

family-centered nursing care cuidados de enfermería centrados en la familia

far-sighted hipermétrope

far-sightedness hipermetropía

fast (noun) ayuno; ayunas; (adjective) **fast** rápido; veloz; (verb) ayunar; **you should not eat anything before you come** debe venir en ayunas

fast food comida rápida

fat (noun) grasa; **animal fat** grasa animal; (adjective) gordo; **a fat free diet** una dieta sin grasas; **this cheese contains 30 percent fat** este queso contiene un 30 por ciento de materia grasa

fat cell lipoma; lipoma de células grasas

father complex complejo de padre

fatigue fatiga; **mental fatigue** fatiga mental; **physical fatigue** fatiga física

fatten engordar

February febrero (see January)

feces heces; excrementos

feed alimentar; **how many children do you have to feed?** ¿cuántos hijos tiene que alimentar?

female circumcision circuncisión femenina

fever fiebre; **have a high fever** tener mucha fiebre; **run a fever** tener fiebre

fever blister herpes; boquera; ampolla en los labios

first aid primeros auxilios

first-aid kit botiquín de primeros auxilios

first-aid station puesto de primeros auxilios

first name nombre de pila

fish pescado

fish and chips pescado frito con papas

fist puño; **make a fist** cierre el puño

fixation fijación

flow of blood flujo sanguíneo

flu gripe; **he's got the flu** tiene gripe

flu remedy antigripal

folic acid ácido fólico

folk healer curandero; curandera

food alimento; comida; **food with low calorie content** alimentos de bajo contenido calórico

food additives aditivos alimentarios

food allergy alergia alimenticia; alergia alimentaria

food and drug interactions interacciones entre alimentos y fármacos

food chain cadena alimentaria

food contaminants contaminantes alimentarios

food poisoning intoxicación alimentaria

food pyramid pirámide de alimentos

foot pie

force (noun) **fuerza;** (verb) obligar; forzar; provocar; **do you have to force yourself to eat?** ¿tiene que obligarse a comer?

force down (swallow) tragar a duras penas

force-feed alimentar por la fuerza

forced feeding alimentación forzada

forceps fórceps

forceps delivery parto con fórceps

foreign body cuerpo extraño

foreplay estimulación erótica previa al acto sexual

French dressing aliño para ensaladas a base de aceite; vinagre y mostaza

French fries papas fritas; patatas fritas; patatas a la francesa

Friday viernes

frighten asustar

frightened asustado; **be frightened about something** tener miedo a algo; **be frightened about someone** tenerle miedo a alguien

frostbite congelación

frostbitten congelado

fruit fruta; **dried fruit** fruta seca

gall bladder vesícula; vesícula biliar

gall bladder cancer cáncer de vesícula biliar

gang (of youths and criminals) pandilla; banda; **gang related** estar relacionado con la pandilla

gas (flatulence) gases; **to pass gas** eliminar los gases

gas pains dolores por gas

gash tajo; corte profundo

gasp for breath respirar con dificultad

gastric gástrico

gastric juice jugo gástrico

gastric ulcer úlcera gástrica; úlcera de estómago

gauze gasa

gauze sponge esponja de gasa

gender género

gender testing prueba del sexo

gene gen

gene therapy terapia genética

general anesthesia anestesia general

general hospital hospital general

genetic code código genético**

genital genital
genitalia genitales
genitals genitales
geriatric (patient) anciano
geriatric home hogar de ancianos
geriatric medicine geriatría
geriatrician geriatra; especialista en
geriatría
geriatrics geriatría
germ microbio; germen
gestation gestación
gestation period periodo de gestación
given name nombre de pila
gland (organ) glándula; (lymph node)
ganglio
goose pimples carne de gallina; to break
out in goose pimples ponerse la carne
de gallina
gooseflesh carne de gallina
gown (hospital) bata; put on this gown
póngase esta bata
graft (noun) injerto; (verb) injertar
gramps abuelo
grandad abuelo
grandaddy abuelito
grandfather abuelo; abuelito
grandma abuela
grandmother abuela; abuelita
grandpa abuelo
grandparents abuelos; your grandparents
tus abuelos
granny abuelita
grape uva
grape juice jugo de uva
grapefruit toronja; pomelo
grapefruit juice jugo de toronja
green bean habichuela; judía verde; ejote
green vegetables verduras
greens verduras
grow crecer; grow a beard dejarse crecer la
barba; grow thin adelgazar; grow tired
cansarse; he's grown a lot ha crecido
mucho
grow up criarse
growing pains dolores de crecimiento
gums encías
gynecological ginecológico
gynecologist ginecólogo; ginecóloga
gynecology ginecología

hair pelo; cabello
hair loss pérdida de cabello
hairline nacimiento del pelo
ham jamón
hand mano; manco have one arm; ser
manco de una mano have only one
hand; quedar manco to lose one arm
hand cream crema de mano; crema para
las manos
hand towel toalla de manos
hard drugs drogas duras
hardening of the arteries arteriosclerosis
hay fever fiebre del heno
head cabeza

head injury lesión en la cabeza
head wound herida en la cabeza
headache dolor de cabeza; have a headache
tener dolor de cabeza
heal curar; sanar; devolver la salud;
(wound) cicatrizar
health salud (see family history; see present
history); be in good health estar bien de
salud; be in bad health estar mal de salud
health assessment examen de salud
health care atención médica; asistencia
sanitaria
health care system sistema de asistencia
sanitaria
health certificate certificado de salud
health education educación sanitaria
health food alimentos naturales;
alimentación integral
health hazard riesgo sanitario
health history historia clínica
health insurance seguro médico; seguro de
enfermedad
health maintenance mantenimiento de la
salud
health policy política sanitaria
health professional profesional de la salud
health provider proveedor de salud
health-related services servicios
relacionados con la salud
health risk riesgo para la salud
health screening estudio de salud
healthy (in good health) sano; bien de
salud; de buena salud; (diet, living, etc.)
saludable
healthy and strong sano y fuerte
hearing oído; audición
hearing aid audífono
hearing difficulties problemas de audición;
problemas auditivos
hearing impairment déficit auditivo
heart corazón; he underwent open heart
surgery lo operaron a corazón abierto
heart attack ataque al corazón; ataque
cardíaco
heart failure insuficiencia cardíaca
heart-lung machine bomba corazón-
pulmón
heart murmur soplo cardíaco
heart rate frecuencia cardíaca; ritmo
cardíaco
heart specialist especialista de corazón;
cardiólogo; cardióloga
heart surgery cirugía cardíaca
heart transplant trasplante de corazón
heart trouble padecer del corazón
heartbeat latido del corazón; pulsación; 80
heartbeats per minute 80 pulsaciones
por minuto
heartburn ardor de estómago
heat stroke insolación
heaves náuseas
height altura
hemorrhoid hemorroide
hernia hernia
heroin addiction adicción a la heroína
high alto
high blood pressure presión alta; tensión
alta

high protein de alto contenido proteínico; rico en proteínas

high risk for infection alto riesgo de infección

high temperature alta temperatura

history of present illness historia de la enfermedad actual

hives urticaria; salpullido; ronchas

hoarse ronco

hoarseness ronquera

home care atención domiciliaria

hospice (for the dying) residencia para enfermos desahuciados

hospital hospital; **be in the hospital** estar en el hospital; estar hospitalizado; estar internado

hospital administration administración del hospital

hospital bed cama del paciente

hot (food, water) caliente; (weather, day) caluroso

hot flashes sofocos; **she keeps getting hot flashes** le dan sofocos

hot-water bag bolsa de agua caliente

hot-water bottle bolsa de agua caliente

house casa

housing vivienda

hunger hambre; **sudden hunger** hambre repentina

hungry hambre; **be hungry** tener hambre

hurt (noun) dolor; pena; (verb) doler; **to hurt oneself** hacerse daño; **did you hurt yourself?** ¿te hiciste daño?; **I'm not going to hurt you** no te voy a hacer daño; **I've hurt my back** me he hecho daño en la espalda; **my foot is hurting me** duele el pie; **my feet are hurting me** me duelen los pieses; **I hurt my ankle** me hice daño en el tobillo

husband marido; esposo; **they are husband and wife** están casados; son marido y mujer

I

imaging center centro de formación de imágenes

impacted tooth diente impactado

immune system sistema inmunitario; sistema inmunológico

incurable incurable; que no tiene cura; **an incurable disease** una enfermedad que no tiene cura

indigestion apepsia; indigestión; **give indigestion** producir indigestión; **onions give me indigestion** las cebollas me resultan indigestas; las cebollas me producen indigestión

induce (sleep, labor) inducir; provocar; **induce labor** provocar el parto

induced abortion aborto inducido; aborto provocado

induced fever fiebre inducida

induced vomiting vómito inducido

infant death muerte infantil

infant feeder alimentador de lactantes

infant feeding alimentación del lactante

infant mortality mortalidad infantil

infant of addicted mother hijo de madre adicta

infantile scurvy escorbuto del lactante

infect infectar

infection infección; **a throat infection** infección de garganta; **risk of infection** riesgo de contagio

infectious (disease) infeccioso; contagioso

infectious disease enfermedad infecciosa

injection inyección; **give someone an injection** darle una inyección a alguien; ponerle una inyección a alguien

intensive care cuidados intensivos

intensive care unit unidad de cuidados intensivos; unidad de vigilancia intensiva

intercourse coito; acto sexual; relaciones sexuales; **have intercourse with somebody** tener relaciones sexuales con alguien

intermediate care atención intermedia

internist internista; especialista en medicina interna

internship internado

intestinal tract intestino

intravenous feeding alimentación intravenosa

intravenous infusion infusión intravenosa

intravenous pump bomba intravenosa

invasive procedure procedimiento invasivo

iron hierro

iron deficiency anemia ferropénica; deficiencia de hierro

iron-rich food alimento rico en hierro

IV = intravenous intravenosa

IV injection inyección intravenosa

January enero; **on the first of January** el primero de enero; el uno de enero; **around the middle of January** a mediados de enero; **at the beginning of January** a principios de enero; **at the end of January** a fines de enero

jaw mandíbula; **lower jaw** maxilar inferior; **upper jaw** maxilar superior

jawbone mandíbula

jointed articulado

July julio (see enero)

June junio (see enero)

junk food comida basura

knee rodilla

knee joint articulación de la rodilla

kneebend flexión de piernas

kneecap rótula

kneel ponerse de rodillas; (act) arrodillarse

kneel down hincarse de rodillas

kneel down (state) estar de rodillas

L

labor parto; **a difficult labor** un parto difícil; **be in labor** estar de parto; **go into labor** entrar en trabajo de parto
labor pains dolores de parto
lame cojo; **be lame** estar cojo
large bowel intestino grueso
large intestine intestino grueso
laryngeal cancer cáncer de laringe
laryngitis laringitis
late tarde; **be late** tener retraso; **arrive late** llegar tarde
laxative laxante
leg cylinder cast yeso cilíndrico de pierna
leukemia leucemia
level nivel
levels of care niveles de atención
lie down acostarse
life vida; **no lives were lost** no hubo muertes; **a matter of life and death** una cuestión de vida o muerte; **a life-and-death decision** una decisión de vida o muerte
life cycle ciclo vital
life expectancy esperanza de vida; expectativas de vida
life insurance seguro de vida
life span vida; duración; (of equipment) vida útil
life support mantenimiento de vida
life-support system equipo de mantenimiento de vida; máquina corazón-pulmón; **the patient is on a life-support system** el paciente está conectado a una máquina que mantiene a sus constantes vitales
lifeless (body, dead) sin vida
lifelong de toda la vida; durante toda su vida
lifeskills formación de tipo práctico que capacita para desenvolverse en la vida diaria
lifestyle estilo de vida
lifetime vida
ligature ligadura
ligament ligamento; **he has torn ligaments** tiene rotura de ligamentos
light diet dieta ligera
limb (anatomy) miembro; extremidad
limp cojear
lip labio; **to bite one's lip** morderse la lengua
liquid líquido
liquid diet dieta hídrica
liquor alcohol; bebidas alcohólicas
lisp (noun) creceo; (verb) crecear; **to speak with a lisp** crecear
listen escuchar
liver hígado
liver cancer cáncer de hígado
lobe lóbulo
lobotomy lobotomía
lobster (culinary) langosta
local anesthesia anestesia local
lockjaw tétano; tétanos
long-arm cast yeso de brazo completo
long-leg cast yeso de pierna completa
long-leg cast with walker yeso de pierna con tacón

long-term care atención a largo plazo
loss pérdida
loss of appetite pérdida del apetito
low-grade fever febrícula; fiebre leve
lower abdomen (el) bajo vientre
lukewarm tibio; **lukewarm water** agua tibia
lung (noun) pulmón; (plural drops the accent) pulmones; (adjective) pulmonar
lung cancer cáncer de pulmón
lymph gland glándula linfática

M

main principal; fundamental; más importante; **the main thing** lo principal; lo fundamental; lo más importante
main course (meal) plato principal
main meal comida principal
main street calle principal; la Calle Mayor
major surgery cirugía mayor
male varón; macho
male doctor médico; doctor
male nurse enfermero
malnourished malnutrido
mammary mamario
mammary gland gándula mamaria
mammogram mamograma
mammography mamografía
man hombre; **a young man** un joven; **he's a sick man** está muy enfermo
managed care atención dirigida
March marzo (see January)
marriage counselling terapia de pareja
maternity nursing enfermería de maternidad
mattress colchón
May mayo (see January)
meal comida; **light meal** colación
mealtime hora de comer
measles sarampión; **catch the measles** contagiarse el sarampión
measure (length, waist) medir; **to measure** tomar las medidas
meat carne
medical (noun) revisión médica; examen médico; chequeo; (adjective: care, examination, insurance) médico; médica; **on medical grounds** por razones de salud; **have a medical** someterse a una revisión médica; someterse a un examen médico; hacerse un chequeo
medical assistance asistencia médica; **give medical assistance** impartir asistencia médica
medical care atención médica
medical care plan plan de atención médica
medical center centro médico
medical certificate certificado médico
medical consultation consulta médica
medical diagnosis diagnóstico médico
medical history (of patient) historial médico; historial clínico
medical practitioner médico
medical staff personal médico
medication (drugs) medicación; medicamento; tratamiento
medicine medicina; medicamento

menopause menopausia
mental age edad mental
mental illness enfermedad mental
mental retardation retraso mental
midlife crisis crisis de los cuarenta; crisis de la edad madura
midwife partera; matrona; comadrona
midwifery partería
migraine migraña; jacueca
mild leve
mildew (on wall, fabric) moho
milk leche
milk bath baño de leche
milk of magnesia leche de magnesia
milk tooth diente de leche
mind (noun) mente; (verb) cuidar
mind-set modo de pensar
mineral mineral
mineral deficiency deficiencia mineral
mineral oil aceite mineral
mineral soap jabón mineral
minor menor
minor surgery cirugía menor; intervención quirúrgica de menor importancia
miscarriage aborto espontáneo; aborto no provocado; **have a miscarriage** sufrir un aborto; perder un niño; perder un bebé
miscarry abortar; tener un aborto; perder el niño
mistake error; **a serious mistake** un grave error
mistaken equivocado; falso
misunderstanding malentendido
mite ácaro
molar muela
moldy mohoso
mole (on skin) lunar
molest abusar
molest sexually abusar sexualmente de
molestation (sexually) abusos deshonestos
Monday lunes; **Monday morning** lunes por la mañana
monitoring bajo observación; seguimiento; bajo control
month mes; **the month of June** el mes de junio; **at the beginning of the month** a principios de mes; **at the end of the month** a fines de mes
monthly mensual
mood estado de ánimo
mood disorders trastornos del estado de ánimo
morning mañana; **in the morning** en la mañana; por la mañana
morning after pill píldora del día siguiente
morning sickness náuseas matutinas
morning stiffness rigidez matutina
mother madre
mother complex complejo de madre
mouth boca
mouth-to-mouth resuscitation respiración boca a boca
mouthwash enjuage bucal
MRI = magnetic resonance imaging RM = resonancia magnética
mucus moco
mucus membrane membrana mucosa

murmur soplo; **heart murmur** soplo cardíaco
muscle (anatomy) músculo
muscle spasms espasmos musculares
muscular dystrophy distrofia muscular
mustard bath baño de mostaza

nasal congestion (see sniffle) congestión nasal
natural birth parto natural; nacimiento natural
natural death muerte natural
nausea náusea
nauseate dar náuseas
nearsighted miope; corto de vista
neck cuello; **back of the neck** nuca
neck of the womb cuello del útero
nerve nervio
nerve cell neurona
nervous breakdown crisis nerviosa
nervous disorder enfermedad nerviosa
nervous wreck (colloquial) manojo de nervios; **she's a nervous wreck** es un manojo de nervios
nervousness nerviosidad
newborn recién nacido
night noche; **at night** por la noche
night blindness ceguera nocturna
night nurse enfermera del turno nocturno
night sweats sudaciones nocturnas; sudores nocturnos
night terrors terrores nocturnos
nightgown camisón
nightmare pesadilla
nipple (on breast of women) pezón; (on breast of men) tetilla; (on bottle) tetina; chupón; chupete
nose nariz; **blow one's nose** sonarse la nariz; **your nose is bleeding** le sale sangre de la nariz (adult); te sale sangre de la nariz (child)
nose drops gotas para la nariz
notify avisar; informar; notificar
nourish nutrir; alimentar
nourishing nutritivo; alimenticio
nourishment alimento
November noviembre (see January)
nurse (noun) enfermero; enfermera; (verb) atender; cuidar
nurse practitioner enfermero práctico
nursemaid niñera

oatmeal avena
oatmeal bath baño de avena
obsession fijación; obseción
October octubre (see January)
ointment ungüento; **apply ointment** aplicar el ungüento; **apply ointment to the affected area** aplicar el ungüento a la zona afectada
old viejo

on an empty stomach en ayunas; **it should be taken on an empty stomach** debe tomarse en ayunas

only child hijo único; hija única

operate operar; intervenir

operating room quirófano; sala de operaciones

outpatient ambulatorio; paciente externo

ovarian cancer cáncer ovárico

ovary ovario

overdose sobredosis; **take an overdose** tomar una sobredosis

pacemaker marcapasos

pacifier chupete; chupón

pain (physical) dolor; **constant pain** sentir dolor permanentemente; **cry out in pain** gritar en dolor; **ease the pain** calmar el dolor

painful doloroso

painkiller analgésico; calmante

painkilling analgésico

painless (causing no pain) indoloro; no causar dolor

painlessly sin dolor

palpitate (heart) palpitar

pancreas páncreas

pancreatic cancer cáncer de páncreas

panic disorder trastorno de pánico

paper towel toalla de papel

pass away fallecer

patient paciente

paunch (colloquial) panza; barriga

pay pagar

pay in cash pagar en efectivo

penile cancer cáncer de pene

penis pene; (colloquial) miembro viril

permanent (address, job) permanente; fijo; (damage) irreparable

permanent address dirección permanente

permanent tooth diente permanente

permissable dose dosis permisible

permission permiso; **with my permission** con mi permiso; **without my permission** sin mi permiso; **you'll need written permission** necesita un permiso escrito; **give permission** dar permiso; dar autorización

pernicious anemia anemia perniciosa

persistent (cough, virus) persistente

personal cleanliness aseo personal

personality personalidad; **split personality** personalidad múltiple; (personal appeal) personalidad

persuade convencer

petite (woman) chiquita; menuda; (size) para mujeres menudas

pharmacist farmacéutico

pharmacy farmacia; droguería

physical collapse colapso físico

physical handicap minusvalía

physically handicapped minusválido

physician médico

piles hemorroides

pill píldora; pastilla; **go on the pill** tomar la píldora

pillow almohada

pillow case funda de almohada

pimple barrillo; grano

plaster cast molde de yeso

pneumonia pulmonía

pockmark marca de vieruela; hoyo; cacaraña

poison (noun) veneno; **take poison** envenenarse; **rat poison** matarratas; (verb) envenenar; (make ill) intoxicar

pork carne de cerdo; carne de puerco

pork chop chuleta de cerdo; costilla de cerdo

pottychair silla orinal

premature prematuro; precoz

premature birth nacimiento prematuro

premature ejaculation eyaculación precoz

prenatal care atención prenatal

prescription prescripción; **fill a prescription** preparar una prescripción

prescription drug fármaco de prescripción

present (noun) actualidad; (adjective) actual; **be present with your wife** estar presente con su esposa

present day actualidad

present health salud actual

preventive care atención preventiva

prick (verb) pinchar; picar; picar con una alfiler

primary care atención primaria

primary health care atención sanitaria primaria

primary tooth diente primario

private hospital hospital privado

probe sonda

procedure procedimiento

prognosis pronóstico

prostate cancer cáncer de próstata

prostate gland próstata

prosthetic apparatus aparato prótesis

protective eyewear lentes protectores

prune ciruela seca

psychopath sicópata

psychotic sicótico

psychotherapy sicoterapia

pubic (region, bone) pubiano; púbico

pubic hair púbico; vello púbico

public hospital hospital público

pudgy barrigón, barrigona; **get a bit of a tummy** volverse barrigón

pulmonary disease enfermedad pulmonar

pulsate (vein) latir

pulse pulso; **take someone's pulse** tomar el pulso

puncture (noun) punción; (verb) puncionar

puncture wound herida punzante

punctured lung pulmón perforado

pus pus

Q-Tip® bastoncillo de algodón; palito de algodón; hisopo

quiet silencio; silencioso; tranquilo; **be quiet** callarse

R

rash salpullido; erupción
recover recuperar; recobrar
recovery room sala de recuperación
recovery time tiempo de recuperación
rectal cancer cáncer de recto
reflux reflujo
regional anesthesia anestesia regional
registered nurse enfermero diplomado; enfermera diplomada; enfermero titulado; enfermera titulada
regular (in bowel movement) hacer de vientre con regularidad; (in menstrual cycle) ser regular; **at regular intervals** con regularidad
relapse recaída; recidiva; **have a relapse** tener una recaída; **suffer a relapse** sufrir una recaída
related (of same family) **to be related** ser parientes
removal (organ, tumor) extirpación
renal colic cólico renal; cólico nefrítico
respiration respiración
respiratory failure crisis respiratorio
respiratory system aparato respiratorio
respiratory tract tracto respiratorio
restroom baño; servicios
rheumatoid arthritis artrosis; artrosis reumática
rib (anatomy) costilla
ribcage caja torácica; caja de las costillas
rice arroz; **brown rice** arroz integral; **white rice** arroz blanco; **rice pudding** arroz con leche
rings under the eyes ojeras; **to have rings under one's eyes** estar ojeroso
risk riesgo
risk of infection riesgo de infección
room cuarto; habitación; **single room** habitación individual; **double room** habitación doble
rubbing alcohol alcohol para fricciones
runny nose escurrimiento de la nariz; **I've got a runny nose** me gotea la nariz

S

sad (person) triste; pena; **feel sad** estar triste; sentirse triste; **he was very sad** tenía mucha pena; **he felt very sad** tenía mucha pena
saddle block anesthesia anestesia en silla de montar
safe seguro; **keep the medicine in a safe place** guarde la medicina en un lugar seguro
saline bath baño salino
salt sal
sand flea pulga de mar
Saturday sábado
sausage salchicha
scabies sarna
scan (noun) escáner; scanner; escanograma; (verb) **do a scan** hacer un escáner
scissors tijeras
scrape (noun) raspado; (verb) **raspar**

scratch rasguño; **it's just a scratch** no es más que un rasguño
scrotal cancer cáncer de escroto
scurvy escorbuto
secondary health care atención sanitaria secundaria
sedateness (of behavior) calma
sedation sedación; **be under sedation** estar bajo los efectos de los sedantes
sedative calmante
self-esteem autoestima
semen esperma
September septiembre (see January)
set (of plates, tools, etc.) juego; (adjective) fijo; **meals are at set times** las comidas son a determinadas horas; **there are set times for visiting** hay horas de visitas establecidas; **a set procedure** un procedimiento establecido
sextuplet sextillizo; sextilliza
sexual abuse malos tratos sexuales; abusos deshonestos
sexual assault agresión sexual
sexual fantasy fantasía sexual
sexual harassment acoso sexual
sexual health salud sexual
sexual history historia sexual
sexual intercourse relaciones sexuales
sexual orientation orientación sexual
sexual reproduction reproducción sexual
sexual therapist terapeuta sexual
sexual therapy terapia sexual
sexuality sexualidad
sexually transmitted disease enfermedad de transmisión sexual
shaken baby syndrome síndrome del niño maltratado
shallow breathing respiración superficial
shampoo champú; **herbal shampoo** champú de hierbas
shake temblar; agitar; **shake well before use** agite bien antes de usar; **to shake hands** darse la mano; **to shake hands with somebody** darle la mano a alguien; estrecharle la mano a alguien
shape forma; **to be in good shape** estar bastante bien de salud; **to be in pretty bad shape** estar muy mal; andar muy mal; **to be in great shape** estar en muy buena forma; **to get in shape** ponerse en forma; **to keep in shape** mantenerse en forma; **to stay in shape** mantenerse en forma
sharp (pain, eyesight) agudo; (hearing) fino; agudo
sharp pain; retorcijón; **sharp pain in the stomach**; retorcijones de tripa; retorcijones de estómago
shave afeitar; afeitarse; rasurar
sheet sábana
shin espinilla; canilla
shinbone tibia
shiver (noun) escalofrío; **have the shivers** tener escalofríos
shock shock; **suffer from shock** estar en estado de shock; **be in shock** estar en estado de shock
short-arm cast yeso de antebrazo
short-leg cast yeso de pierna

short-leg cast with walker yeso de pierna con andador

shortness of breath falta de aire

short-term memory memoria a corto plazo

shoulder hombro

shoulder blade omóplato

shoulder joint articulación del hombro

sick enfermo; enferma; **to feel sick** (dizzy; unwell) estar meareado

sick bag bolsa para el mareo

sick bay enfermería

sickbed lecho de enfermo

sickle cell anemia anemia drepanocítica; depranocitosis

sickly (person, unhealthy) enfermizo

side effect efecto secundario

SIDS sudden infant death syndrome (SMSL) síndrome de muerte súbita del lactante

sitz bath baño de asiento

skim mild leche descremada; leche desnatada

skin (of person) piel; (of face and quality) cutis; (in terms of color) tez

skin cancer cáncer cutáneo; cáncer de piel

skin care cuidado de la piel; cuidado del cutis

skin graft injerto cutáneo

skin pigment pigmentación cutánea

skin test prueba cutánea

skinny flaco

skull cráneo

sleep (noun) sueño; (verb) dormir; **go to sleep** dormirse; **to get to sleep** conciliar el sueño; **try to get some sleep** trata de dormir un poco

sleep pattern patrón de sueño

sleep pattern disorder trastorno del patrón de sueño

sleep therapy cura de sueño

sleep together tener relaciones sexuales

sleepiness somnolencia; soñolencia

sleeping pills píldoras para dormir; pastillas para dormir

sleeping sickness enfermedad del sueño

sleepless sin poder dormir

sleepwalk caminar dormido; **he used to sleepwalk as a child** solía caminar dormido cuando pequeño

sleepwalker sonámbulo; sonámbula

sleepy somnilento; soñoliento; **be sleepy** tener sueño; **feel sleepy** tener sueño

slight (person) menudo

slim (person) esbelto; delgado

slim down adelgazar; bajar de peso

sling cabestrillo; **to have one's arm in a sling** llevar el brazo en cabestrillo

small pequeño; menudo

small baby boy niño de pañales

small baby girl niña de pañales

small intestine intestino delgado

smoker's cough tos de fumador

snack bocado; **have a snack** comer algo ligero

sniffle resfriado; resfrío; **to have the sniffles** estar resfriado; tener moquera

social disease enfermedad social

sodium bath baño de sodio

soft drugs drogas blandas

son-in-law yerno; hijo político

sonogram sonograma; sonografía

sore throat dolor de garganta

specialist especialista; **heart specialist** especialista de corazón; cardiólogo

speculum espejo vaginal; espéculo

sperm semen; espermatozoide

spina bifida espina bífida

spinach (culinary) espinacas

spinal anesthesia anestesia espinal

spinal column columna vertebral; espina dorsal

spinal cord médula espinal

splint (noun) tablilla; (verb) put a splint on entablillar; **they put a splint on his leg** le entablillaron la pierna; **his arm is in splints** tiene el brazo entablillado

splinter (wood) astilla; (of glass, bone) esquirla

sponge esponja

sponge bath baño de esponja

sponge gauze esponja de gasa

spontaneous abortion aborto espontáneo

spring (season) primavera

spring mattress colchón de muelles

stab (noun) puñalada; navajazos (verb) apuñalar; acuchillar; **stab to death** matar a puñaladas

stable estable; estacionario; **the patient's condition is stable** el estado del paciente es estacionario

stain (noun) mancha; (verb) manchar

stained manchado

standard of living nivel de vida

starch almidón

starch bath baño de almidón

sterile cotton algodón estéril

sterilization ligadura de trompas; **she was sterilized** le hicieron una ligadura de trompas

stew (noun) estofado; guiso; (verb) estofar; guisar

stiffness (of muscles) rigidez; (of joints) anquilosamiento

still todavía; aún

stillbirth parto en el que el niño nace muerto

stillborn nacido muerto

stimulate (circulation) estimular; provocar; **the antigen stimulates the production of antibodies** el antígeno provoca la formación de anticuerpos

stitch (noun) punto; (verb) suturar

stitches puntos

stomach estómago; barriga; panza; **it should be taken on an empty stomach** debe tomarse en ayunas; **have an upset stomach** estar mal del estómago

stomach cramps retorcijones de tripa; retorcijones de estómago

stomach pump bomba estomacal

stomachache dolor de estómago; dolor de barriga

stool deposición; evacuación del vientre; excremento

stool specimen muestra de excremento

strength (person) fuerza; fuerzas; (health) fortaleza física; **his strength failed him** le fallaron las fuerzas; **you must rest now to get your strength back** ahora tienes que descansar par recuperarte; ahora tienes que descansar para recobrar las fuerzas

stress estrés; tensión; **a stress related illness** una enfermedad provocada por el estrés; una enfermedad relacionada con el estrés; **she's under great stress** está muy estresada

stress fracture fractura de fatiga; fractura por sobre carga

stress management control del estrés

stress test prueba de estrés

stress ulcer úlcera de estrés

stretch estirar; extender; **stretch one's legs** estirar las piernas

stretcher camilla

stroke ataque de apoplejía; derrame cerebral

sudden death muerte repentina

sudden infant death syndrome (SIDS) síndrome de muerte súbita del lactante (SMSL)

sugar azúcar

summer verano

sunburn quemadura solar

Sunday domingo

suppository supositorio

surgeon cirujano

surgery cirugía; **he underwent surgery** fue intervenido quirúrgicamente; fue operado; **he had major surgery** fue sometido a una intervención quirúrgica seria; **he had minor surgery** fue sometido a una intervención quirúrgica de menor importancia; **the patient is in surgery** el paciente está en el quirófano; el paciente está en la sala de operaciones

surgical quirúrgico

surgical collar collarín; collar ortopédico

surgical gauze gasa esterilizada

surgical knife bisturí

surgical room sala de operaciones

surgically quirúrgicamente; **they have to be surgically removed** hay que eliminarlos quirúrgicamente

surname apellido

sigh suspiro

swab (noun) hisopo; bastoncillo de algodón; palito de algodón; (verb) limpiar; lavar; **to swab down a wound** limpiar una herida

swallow tragar; **do you find it painful to swallow?** ¿le duele al tragar?

swath (cloth) banda

swathing bandage faja abdominal

sweat sudor

sweat gland glándula sudorípara

sweating sudores

swell hincharse; **her face began to swell** se le empezó a hinchar la cara

swell up hincharse; **his legs have really swollen up** se le han hinchado mucho las piernas

swelling hinchazón

swelling is going down (feet, ankles) deshincharse; **the swelling in her ankles is going down** se le van deshinchando los tobillos

swollen hinchado

table mesa

table of contents sumario; índice de materias

taste (flavor) sabor; gusto

taste bud papila gustativa

temper genio; humor

temperature temperatura; fiebre; calentura; **take someone's temperature** tomarle la temperatura a alguien; **have a temperature** tener fiebre

terminal cancer cáncer terminal

terminal illness enfermedad terminal

testicle testículo

testicular cancer cáncer testicular

thalassemia anemia talasemia

therapeutic abortion aborto terapéutico

therapy terapia

thermometer termómetro; **put a thermometer in your mouth** poner un termómetro en la boca

thin delgado

thirsty sed; **be thirsty** tener sed

threatened abortion amenaza de aborto

Thursday jueves

tick garrapata

toast pan tostado; tostada; **make toast** hacer tostadas; **a piece of toast** una tostada; un pan tostado; **a slice of toast** una tostada; un pan tostado

today hoy; **a week from today** dentro de una semana; de aquí a una semana

toilet baño; servicio; **go to the toilet** hacer de vientre; ir al baño

tomography tomografía

tomorrow mañana; **see you tomorrow** hasta mañana; **we'll see you a week from tomorrow** te vemos de mañana en ocho días

tomorrow afternoon mañana por la tarde

tomorrow morning mañana por la mañana

tonsillitis amigdalitis

tonsils amígdalas

tooth diente

toothbrush cepillo de dientes

toothpaste pasta dentrífica; pasta de dientes

tourniquet torniquete

treatment tratamiento; **undergo medical treatment** estar bajo tratamiento médico

tubal ligation ligadura de trompas

tube feeding alimentación por sonda

Tuesday martes

tummy panza; barriga; pancita

tummyache dolor de barriga

tummy button ombligo

tumor tumor

twin (brother, sister) mellizo; gemelo; **identical twins** gemelos idénticos

twins mellizos; gemelos

twitch (noun) tic; moverse; temblar; **he has a nervous twitch** tiene un tic nervioso; **his eyelid was twitching** le temblaba el párpado; **I've got a twitch in my eye** me tiembla el párpado

two dos

type tipo; **it's a type of** es una especie de

typhoid fever fiebre tifoida

typical típico

ultrasound ultrasonido

uncle tío

unconscious inconsciente; **be unconscious** estar sin conocimiento; **become unconscious** perder el conocimiento

undersigned abajofirmante: **the undersigned** el abajofirmante; **the undersigned** la abajofirmante

universal recipient receptor universal

upset agitado; disgustado; alterado

upset stomach estar mal del estómago

urgent urgente; **urgent surgery** inmediata invervención quirúrgica; (colloquial) operar urgentemente

urine sample muestra de orina

uterine cancer cáncer uterino

uterus cuello del útero

U.S. citizen ciudadano de Estados Unidos

vaccinate vacunar

vaccination vacunación

vaccine vacuna

vaginal cancer cáncer vaginal

vegetable verdura; vegetal **vegetable fat** grasa vegetal

vein vena

venereal disease enfermedad venérea

Veteran's Hospital hospital para veteranos

violence violencia; **domestic violence** violencia en el hogar

violent violento; **he met a violent death** tuvo una muerte violenta; **he has a violent temper** tiene muy mal genio

vital signs signos vitales; constantes vitales

vomit vomitar; devolver; tener náuseas

wait esperar

waist cintura; talle

waistline cintura

wake up despertar

walk (noun) paseo; (verb) andar; caminar; ir a pie

walking cane bastón de paseo

walking cast yeso de marcha

wash lavar; lavarse

wash one's hair lavarse el pelo

wash one's hands lavarse las manos

wash oneself lavarse

washbowl lavabo; lavamanos

washcloth toallita; toallita para lavarse

washrag toallita; toallita para lavarse

washroom servicios

washstand lavabo; lavoratorio

washtub tina de lavar

weak débil

weaken debilitar

weakness (of body) debilidad

wear llevar; llevar puesto

Wednesday miércoles

weight peso; **lose weight** adelgazar; **put on weight** subir de peso; **gain weight** subir de peso

weight loss pérdida de peso

well bien; mejorarse; **get well soon** que te mejores

wet nurse ama de cría; ama de leche; nodriza

wheelchair silla de ruedas

wheeze resuello

wheezing silbidos

white rice arroz blanco

whooping cough tos ferina; tos convulsa

widow viuda; **to be widowed** enviudar; quedar viuda

widower viudo

wife esposa; mujer; **they are husband and wife** están casados; son marido y mujer

winter invierno

with con

with you contigo

worried preocupado; **be worried about** estar preocupado por

worry preocupación

woman mujer; **she's a sick woman** está muy enferma

word palabra

words of comfort palabras de consuelo

wound herida; **bullet wound** herida de bala; **chest wound** herida en el pecho

wrinkle (noun) arruga; (verb) arrugar

wrinkled arrugado

X-ray rayos x

X-ray machine aparato de rayos x

Y

year año; **be _____ years old** tener _____ años

yellow fever fiebre amarilla

yet aún

young joven; **a younger brother** un hermano menor; **a younger sister** una hermana menor; **this is Patricia, our youngest** ésta es Patricia, la más pequeña; **this is Juan, our youngest** éste es Juan, el más pequeño

young boy niño de pecho

young girl niña de pecho

Z

SPANISH-ENGLISH
IDIOMS FOR HEALTH CARE

A

a cargo de un médico ◊ *being seen by a doctor; under*
¿Está **el** paciente a cargo de un médico a causa de algún problema médico? (m)
¿Está **la** paciente a cargo de un médico a causa de algún problema médico? (f)
Is the patient currently being seen by a doctor for any medical problem?

a intervalos de ... ◊ *at ... intervals*
Le harán una serie de placas a intervalos de cinco minutos cada una.
A series of X-rays will be taken at five-minute intervals.

a la derecha ◊ *to the right*
La fuente de agua potable está a la derecha.
The drinking fountain is to the right.

a la izquierda ◊ *to the left*
El ascensor está a la izquierda.
The elevator is to the left.

a la misma hora ◊ *at the same time*
Tome usted la píldora a la misma hora cada día.
Take the pill at the same time each day.

a la salida ◊ *on the way out*
A la salida coja un folleto.
Pick up a leaflet on the way out.

a menudo ◊ *frequently*
¿Está usted ronco a menudo?
Are you frequently hoarse?

¿a qué edad ...? ◊ *at what age ...?*
¿A qué edad murió su padre?
At what age did your father die?
¿A qué edad empezaron sus reglas?
At what age did your periods start?
¿A qué edad caminó?
At what age did he walk?

a su farmacéutico ◊ *to your pharmacist*
Lleve esta receta a su farmacéutico.
Take this prescription to your pharmacist

a veces ◊ *at times; sometimes*
¿Tiene doble visión a veces?
Do you have double vision at times?
¿Siente a veces como que no puede respirar, como que le falta el aire?
Do you sometimes have difficulty in breathing, such as gasping for air?
¿Tiene tos a veces, o está ronco sin estar resfriado?

Do you sometimes have a cough or are you hoarse, without having a cold?

aborto espóntaneo ◊ *miscarriage*
¿Ha tenido usted algún aborto espóntaneo?
Have you had any miscarriages?

abrir la boca ◊ *open your mouth*
Abra la boca bien grande, por favor.
Open your mouth wide, please.

abrir la ventana ◊ *open the window*
¿Abro la ventana?
Shall I open the window?
La enfermera abrirá la ventana ahora.
The nurse will open the window now.

acabar de + infin ◊ *have just*
Acabo de examinar a su hijo.
I have just examined your son.
Acabo de hablar con tu hermano.
I've just talked to your brother

acalambrarse la pierna ◊ *get a cramp in one's leg*
Se me ha acalambrado la pierna.
I've got a cramp in my leg.
¿Se te ha acalambrado la pierna?
Do you have a cramp in your leg?

acceso de tos ◊ *coughing fit*
Tuvo un acceso de tos.
He had a coughing fit.

acerca de ◊ *about*
¿Tiene usted preguntas acerca de su dieta?
Do you have any questions about your diet?

acompañar a su esposo ◊ *accompany your husband*
Usted puede acompañar a su esposo hasta el cuarto.
You can accompany your husband to the room.

acompañar al cuarto ◊ *accompany to the room*
Su familia puede acompañarle al cuarto.
Your family may accompany you to your room.

adormecimiento de ◊ *numbness of*
¿Ha tenido adormecimiento de los miembros?
Have you had numbness in your arms or legs?

agitar la botella ◊ *shake the bottle*
Es importante no agitar la botella.
It's important not to shake the bottle.
No agite la botella.
Do not shake the bottle.

70

agua caliente ◊ *warm water*
Báñese con agua caliente.
Bathe with warm water.

agua potable ◊ *drinking water*
Esta no es agua potable.
This is not drinking water.

agua tibia ◊ *lukewarm water*
Para cuidarla, lávela con agua tibia.
To care for it, wash it in lukewarm water.

ahora mismo ◊ *right now*
El médico está examinando a su hija ahora mismo.
The doctor is examining your daughter right now.

al descansar ◊ *when you are resting*
¿Le falta la respiración al descansar?
Are you short of breath when you are resting?

al día ◊ *daily*
¿Cuánta mantequilla come usted al día?
How much butter do you eat daily?

al hacer ejercicios ◊ *while exercising; when exercising*
¿Le falta la respiración al hacer ejercicios?
Are you short of breath while exercising?

al ingresar ◊ *on admission*
¿Cuál fue el diagnóstico al ingresar?
What was the diagnosis on admission?

al nacer ◊ *at birth*
¿Cuánto pesó el bebé al nacer?
How much did the baby weigh at birth?

al poco rato ◊ *after a while*
Esta sensación desaparecerá al poco rato.
This feeling will go away after a while.

al toser ◊ *upon coughing; when you cough*
¿Le duele al toser?
Does it hurt you when you cough?
Al toser, ¿arroja usted sangre?
Do you cough up blood?

alcanzar con las manos ◊ *reach*
¿Alcanza con las manos algún objeto?
Does he reach for objects?

alegrarse de ◊ *be glad*
Me alegro de mejorarme.
I am glad to be better.
Me alegro de que usted se mejore.
I am glad that you are getting better.

alérgico a ◊ *allergic to*

Si usted es alérgico al yodo debe informárselo al médico.
If you are allergic to iodine, you should inform the doctor about it.

algo difícil ◊ *somewhat difficult; rather difficult*
La operación es algo difícil.
The operation is rather difficult.

algo más ◊ *anything else*
¿Le duele algo más?
Does anything else hurt you?

alguien de la famila ◊ *anyone in the family*
¿Ha tenido alguien de la familia algún problema con drogas o con alcohol?
Has anyone in the family had a drug or alcohol problem?

alguien puede ◊ *someone can*
Creo que alguien puede ayudarme.
I believe someone can help me.

alguna molestia ◊ *some discomfort*
Le advirtieron que sentiría alguna molestia después de la operación.
He was told to expect some discomfort after the operation.

alguna vez ◊ *ever*
¿Ha tenido usted alguna vez comezón después de recibir penicilina?
Have you ever had itching after getting penicillin?
Mientras tiene dolor de cabeza, ¿siente náuseas alguna vez?
Do you ever feel nauseated while you have a headache?
¿Ha estado embarazada alguna vez?
Have you ever been pregnant?

algunas veces ◊ *sometimes*
¿Le duele algunas veces el estómago después de comer?
Does your stomach hurt sometimes after eating?

alta presión sanguínea ◊ *high blood pressure*
¿Cuánto tiempo ha tenido alta presión sanguínea?
How long has he had high blood pressure?

alterar al paciente ◊ *upset the patient*
Traten de no alterar al paciente.
Try not to upset the patient.

alterar el pulso ◊ *the pulse becomes irregular*
Se le alteró el pulso.
The pulse became irregular.

amanecer con ◊ *to wake up with*

¿Amaneció con fiebre?
Did he wake up with a feve?.

amigo mío, amiga mía ◊ *friend of mine*
La paciente es amiga mía.
The patient is a friend of mine.

análisis de orina ◊ *urine analysis; urine test*
Voy a hacer el análisis de orina.
I am going to do a urine analysis.

análisis de sangre ◊ *blood analysis; blood test*
Vamos a hacer un análisis de sangre.
We are going to do a blood analysis.

análisis de tiroides ◊ *thyroid test*
Para el análisis de tiroides voy a sacarle sangre de la vena.
For the thyroid test I'm going to draw blood from the vein.

andar bien de salud ◊ *to be well*
No anda muy bien de salud.
He's not doing very well.

andar con dificultad ◊ *to walk with difficulty*
Andaba con dificultad.
She was walking with difficulty.

andar mal del estómago ◊ *have trouble with the stomach*
Hace días que ando mal del estómago.
I've been having trouble with my stomach for some days now.

anestesiar la encía ◊ *put your gum to sleep*
Voy a ponerle una inyección para anestesiar la encía.
I am going to give you a shot to put your gum to sleep.

anoche ◊ *last night*
Anoche volvió a casa muy tarde.
Last night she returned home very late.

antes de ◊ *before; by*
Debe estar aquí antes de las ocho.
You must be here before eight.
Debe estar en el hospital antes de las tres.
You must be at the hospital by three.
Antes de darle el pecho a su niño, lávese las manos con agua y jabón.
Before breast feeding your child, wash your hands with soap and water.
Por favor, tómelas antes de comer.
Please take them before eating.

antes de acostarse ◊ *at bedtime; before going to bed*
Tome una píldora antes de acostarse.
Take one pill at bedtime.

72

Take one pill before going to bed.

antes de comer ◊ *before eating*
Tómelas antes de comer.
Take them before eating.

antes de usar ◊ *before use*
Agítese antes de usar.
Shake well before use.

antes de las comidas ◊ *before meals*
Tome la medicina antes de las comidas.
Take the medicine before meals.

antojarse + me/te/le/ etc. ◊ *have cravings for*
Cuando estaba embarazada se le antojaban las cosas más extrañas.
When she was pregnant, she had cravings for the strangest things.

apagar la luz ◊ *turn off the light*
¿Apago la luz?
Shall I turn off the light?

apoyar el mentón ◊ *rest one's chin*
Apoye el mentón aquí.
Rest your chin here.

aprender a ◊ *learn how to*
Usted tiene que aprender a enfrentar el estrés.
You must learn how to cope with stress.
Usted tiene que aprender a enfrentar las tensiones.
You must learn how to cope with stress.

aquí tiene ◊ *here is; here are*
Aquí tiene para enjuagarse la boca.
Here is some mouthwash.

arreglar la cama ◊ *make the bed*
Voy a arreglarle la cama.
I'm going to make the bed.

arrojar flemas ◊ *to cough up phlegm*
Al toser, ¿arroja flema?
When you cough, do you cough up phlegm?
Do you cough up phlegm?

asistir a la escuela ◊ *attend school*
¿Cuántos niños asisten a la escuela?
How many children attend school?

atragantarse con ◊ *choke on*
Él se atragantó con la comida.
He choked on the food.

aún tardará ◊ *it will be a while yet*
Aún tardará en llegar.
It will be a while yet before he gets here.

avisar al médico ◊ *call the doctor*

Tuvieron que avisar al médico.
They had to call the doctor.

avisar enseguida ◊ *notify immediately*
Avíseme usted enseguida si hay un cambio en el color de la piel de los dedos.
Notify me immediately if there is a change in the skin color of the fingers.

avíseme cuando ◊ *let me know when*
Avíseme cuando sienta dolor.
Let me know when you feel pain.

ayuda financiera ◊ *financial assistance*
¿Necesita usted ayuda financiera?
Do you need financial assistance?

baja presión sanguínea ◊ *low blood pressure*
¿Cuánto tiempo ha tenido baja presión sanguínea?
How long has he had low blood pressure?

bajar de peso ◊ *lose weight*
Tiene que bajar de peso porque la obesidad es peligrosa.
He has to lose weight because obesity is dangerous.

bajar la cama ◊ *lower the bed*
Este botón baja la cama.
This button lowers the bed.
¿Bajo la cama?
Shall I lower the bed?
Este botón levanta la cama.
This button raises the bed.

bajo cuidado intensivo ◊ *under intensive care*
Su padre está bajo cuidado intensivo.
Your father is under intensive care.

bajo llave ◊ *locked away; under lock and key*
Siempre guarde las medicinas bajo llave.
Always keep the medicines locked away.

bañarse con ◊ *bathe with*
Báñese con agua caliente.
Bathe with warm water.

bañarse en la bañadera ◊ *take a tub bath*
¿Le gustaría bañarse en la bañadera?
Would you like to take a tub bath?

baño jabonoso caliente ◊ *hot soapy bath*
Tómese una ducha o baño jabonoso caliente usando jabón en abundancia.
Take a shower or hot soapy bath using liberal amounts of soap.

barandillas laterales ◊ *side rails*
La cama no tiene barandillas laterales.
The bed does not have side rails.

bastante alto ◊ *quite high*
Su presión arterial está bastante alta.
Your blood pressure is quite high.

bastante fácil de ◊ *fairly easy to*
Lo que tienes es bastante fácil de curar.
What you have is fairly easy to cure.

bastante fuerte ◊ *well enough*
Usted no está bastante fuerte todavía para levantarse.
You are not well enough yet to get out of bed.

bata del hospital ◊ *hospital gown*
Llevará solamente la bata del hospital.
You'll wear only the hospital gown.

beber muchos líquidos ◊ *drink a lot of liquids*
Usted tiene que beber muchos líquidos.
You have to drink a lot of liquids.

boca abajo ◊ *on one's stomach; face down*
Por favor, acuéstese boca abajo.
Please lie on your stomach.
Duerme boca abajo.
He sleeps on his stomach.
Échate boca abajo.
Lie on your stomach.
Póngase usted boca abajo, por favor.
Please turn face down.

boca arriba ◊ *on one's back; face up*
Duerme boca arriba.
He sleeps on his back.
Póngase usted boca arriba, por favor.
Please turn face up.

boca seca ◊ *dry mouth*
Tenía la boca seca.
He had a dry mouth.

bolsa de aguas ◊ *water; amniotic fluid*
Rompió la bolsa de aguas.
Her water broke.

brazo dolorido ◊ *sore arm*
Tengo el brazo muy dolorido.
I've got a very sore arm.

cabecera de la cama ◊ *head of the bed*
Es para controlar la cabecera de la cama.

73

It's for controlling the head of the bed.

¿cada cuánto ...? ◊ *how often ...?*
¿Cada cuánto evacúa el vientre?
How often do you have a bowel movement?

cada día ◊ *each day*
Tome usted la píldora a la misma hora cada día.
Take the pill at the same time each day.

cada hora ◊ *every hour*
Póngase usted una compresa caliente y húmeda cada hora.
Apply a hot and wet compress every hour.

cada noche ◊ *every evening; each evening*
Póngase uno de estos supositiorios cada noche.
Use one of these suppositories every evening.

caer bien ◊ *(Person) to like*
Me cae bien la enfermera de guardia.
I like the nurse on duty.

caerse al suelo ◊ *fall over*
Tropezó y se cayó al suelo.
She tripped and fell over.

cálculos renales ◊ *kidney stones*
¿Ha tenido alguna vez cálculos renales?
Have you ever had kidney stones?

camas para ◊ *beds for*
Tienen cien camas para los enfermos de cáncer.
They have one hundred beds for people who suffer from cancer.

cambiar de empleo ◊ *change jobs*
¿Por qué cambió usted de empleo?
Why did you change jobs?

cambiar el vendaje ◊ *change the dressing*
Es hora de cambiarle el vendaje.
It's time to change your dressing.

cambiar las sábanas ◊ *change the sheets*
¿Cambio las sábanas?
Shall I change the sheets?
Es hora de cambiar las sábanas.
It's time to change the sheets.

cambiarse la ropa ◊ *to change clothes*
Por favor, cámbiese la ropa.
Please change your clothes.

caminar en el pasillo ◊ *walk in the hall*
¿Quiere caminar en el pasillo?
Do you want to go for a walk in the hall?

cáncer de mama ◊ *breast cancer*
Tiene cáncer de mama.
She has breast cancer.

cáncer de piel ◊ *skin cancer*
¿Hay alguien en su familia que padezca de cáncer de piel?
Does anyone in your family have skin cancer?

cáncer de pulmón ◊ *lung cancer*
Tiene cáncer de pulmón.
She has lung cancer.

cansarse la vista ◊ *the eyes get tired; strain the eyes*
Se le cansa la vista.
It strains her eyes.

cantidad de sal ◊ *amount of salt*
Le aconsejo que elimine o por lo menos disminuya la cantidad de sal que usted usa en la comida.
I advise you to eliminate or at least diminish the amount of salt you use in your diet.

casi dos días ◊ *almost two days*
Tuve fiebre por casi dos días.
I had a fever for almost two days.

causa de la enfermedad ◊ *cause of the illness*
Todavía estamos tratando de saber la causa de su enfermedad.
We are still trying to find the cause of your illness.
Pienso que hemos descubierto la causa de su enfermedad.
I think that we have found the cause of your illness.

causa de la muerte ◊ *cause of death*
Se desconoce la causa de la muerte.
The cause of death is unknown.

causar sarpullido ◊ *cause a rash*
Los problemas de la piel quizás podrán causarle sarpullido.
Your skin problems may cause a rash.

cerrar el puño ◊ *make a fist; clench a fist*
Cierre el puño.
Make a fist.
Clench your fist.
Por favor, cierre el puño.
Please make a fist.

cicatrizar muy bien ◊ *heal up well*
La herida le ha cicatrizado muy bien.
The wound has healed up well.

ciento dos grados ◊ *102°*

La fiebre del niño está a ciento dos grados.
The child's fever is 102°.

ciudadano de Estados Unidos ◊ *U.S. citizen*
¿Es usted ciudadano de Estados Unidos?
Are you a U.S. citizen?

coger sarampión ◊ *get the measles; catch the measles*
El niño cogió sarampión.
The child got (caught) the measles.

coger un folleto ◊ *pick up a leaflet*
A la salida coja un folleto.
Pick up a leaflet on the way out.

colocar un marcapasos ◊ *implant a pacemaker*
Le colocaron un marcapasos.
They implanted a pacemaker in him.

comida basura ◊ *junk food*
No coma comida basura.
Don't eat junk food.

comida de lata ◊ *canned food*
¿Comió comida de lata?
Did you eat canned food?

comida grasosa ◊ *fatty foods*
No coma comida grasosa.
Don't eat fatty foods.

comida grasienta ◊ *fatty foods*
No coma comida grasienta.
Don't eat fatty foods.

cocinar comidas ◊ *cook meals*
Usted tiene que cocinar comidas ricas en minerales.
You have to cook meals rich in minerals.

¿cómo está ...? ◊ *how is ...?*
¿Cómo está su hijo?
How is your son?

¿cómo están ...? ◊ *how are ...?*
¿Cómo están sus hijos?
How are your children?

completamente inmóvil ◊ *perfectly still*
Quédese completamente inmóvil.
Remain perfectly still.

componente de riesgo ◊ *element of risk*
En cualquier operación hay un componente de riesgo.
There's an element of risk in any operation.

comprometer el pulmón ◊ *affect the lung*
La puñalada le comprometió el pulmón.

The stab wound affected the lung.

comprometer el riñon ◊ *affect the liver; spread to the liver*
El cáncer ya le ha comprometido el riñón.
The cancer has spread to the liver.
The cancer has affected the liver.

con agua ◊ *with water*
Tome la medicina con agua.
Take the medicine with water.

con anestesia ◊ *under an anesthetic*
Lo operaron con anestesia.
He was operated under an anesthetic.

con el desayuno ◊ *at breakfast; with breakfast*
Tome una cápsula con el desayuno.
Take one capsule at breakfast.

con esto ◊ *with this*
No tome alcohol con esto.
Don't drink alcohol with this.

con frecuencia ◊ *frequently*
¿Ocurre esto con frecuencia?
Does this occur frequently?
¿Le molesta el estómago con frecuencia?
Does your stomach bother you frequently?

con fuerza ◊ *tightly*
Apriete usted mis manos con fuerza.
Grip my hands tightly.

con las palmas hacia afuera ◊ *with your palms facing out*
Ponga las manos en la cadera con las palmas hacia afuera.
Put your hands on your hips with palms facing out.

con las piernas colgando ◊ *with your legs hanging*
Siéntese en esta mesa con las piernas colgando.
Sit on this table with your legs hanging on the side.

con (mucha) frecuencia ◊ *frequently*
¿Le molesta el estómago con frecuencia?
Does your stomach bother you frequently?
¿Está orinando con mucha frecuencia?
Are you urinating frequently?

¿con qué frecuencia ...? ◊ *how frequently ...?*
¿Con qué frecuencia se baña?
How frequently do you bathe?
¿Con qué frecuencia se ducha?
How frequently do you shower?

con quien ◊ *with whom*

Necesitamos saber el nombre y la dirección del hombre con quien tuvo relaciones sexuales.

We need to know the name and address of the man with whom you had sex.

con sarampión ◊ *with the measles*

Está en cama con sarampión.

He is in bed with the measles.

consultar con ◊ *consult; consult with; talk to; talk with*

Quisiera consultar con mi familia.

I'd like to consult my family.

Tendré que consultar con mi esposa.

I'll have to talk to my wife about it.

¿Por qué no consulta usted con un especialista?

Why don't you consult a specialist?

contestar despacio ◊ *answer slowly*

Por favor, conteste despacio.

Please answer slowly.

contentarse con ◊ *be satisfied with*

Me contento con los resultados de la prueba.

I'm satisfied with the test results.

control de la natalidad ◊ *birth control*

Doctor, estoy interesada en usar la píldora para el control de la natalidad.

Doctor, I'm interested in using the pill for birth control.

cortarse las venas ◊ *cut one's wrists; slash one's wrists*

El paciente se cortó las venas.

The patient cut his wrists.

crippled for life ◊ *lisiado de por vida*

Quedó lisiado de por vida.

He was crippled for life.

¿cuál es ...? ◊ *what is*

¿Cuál es su nombre?

What is your name?

¿Cuál es su dirección?

What is your address?

¿Cuál es el factor Rh suyo?

What is your Rh blood factor?

¿Cuál es su número de teléfono?

What is your telephone number?

cuán alto ◊ *how high*

Vamos a ver cuán alta tiene la presión sanguínea.

Let's see how high your blood pressure is.

Vamos a ver cuán alta tiene la tensión arterial.

Let's see how high your blood pressure is.

cuán bajo ◊ *how low*

Vamos a ver cuán baja tiene la presión sanguínea.

Let's see how low your blood pressure is.

cuando era ◊ *when I/he/she was*

Cuando era niña, sufría de asma.

When she was a child, she suffered from asthma.

cuando se pone de pie ◊ *when you stand*

¿Siente usted dolor cuando se pone de pie?

Do you feel pain when you stand?

cuando suene el timbre ◊ *when the bell rings*

Cuando suene el timbre tiene que salir. (one person)

Cuando suene el timbre tienen que salir. (more than one person)

Cuando suene el timbre tienes que salir. (to a child)

When the bell rings you have to leave.

¿cuándo te dan ...? ◊ *when do you get ...?*

¿Cuándo te dan los resultados?

When do you get the results?

cuando te despiertes ◊ *when you wake up*

Cuando te despiertes, estarás aquí en la cama y quizás sientas un poco de dolor.

When you wake up you will be here in your bed, and you may feel a little pain.

cuando tenga dolor ◊ *when you have pain*

Tome la medicina cuando tenga dolor.

Take the medicine when you have pain.

¿cuántas semanas...? ◊ *how many weeks...?*

¿Cuántas semanas de embarazo tenía su hija cuando tuvo el aborto inducido?

How many weeks pregnant was your daughter when she had the abortion?

¿cuánto de ancho...? ◊ *how wide...?*

¿Cuánto de ancho es el quiste?

How wide is the cyst?

¿cuánto de profundo..? ◊ *how deep...?*

¿Cuánto de profundo es el tajo?

How deep is the cut?

¿cuánto tiempo...? ◊ *how long...?*

¿Cuánto tiempo ha vivido en Nueva York?

How long have you lived in New York?

¿Cuánto tiempo le dura el mareo? (m/f)

¿Cuánto tiempo te dura el mareo? (m/f/c)

How long have you felt dizzy?

¿cuánto tiempo ha tenido...? ◊ *how long have you had...?*
¿Cuánto tiempo ha tenido este dolor?
How long have you had this pain?
¿Cuánto tiempo ha tenido este dolor de cabeza?
How long has he had this headache?

¿cuánto tiempo hace que...? ◊ *how long*
¿Cuánto tiempo hace que tiene estos síntomas?
How long have you had these symptoms?
¿Cuánto tiempo hace que tiene estos dolores?
How long have you had these pains?

¿cuántos días...? ◊ *how many days...?*
¿Cuántos días le duran?
How many days does it last?

cuarto de baño ◊ *bathroom*
El cuarto de baño está en la segunda planta.
The bathroom is on the second floor.

cuarto de rayos X ◊ *X-ray room*
Alguien le llevará al cuarto de rayos X.
Someone will come to take you to the X-ray room.

cuidado intensivo ◊ *intensive care*
Por algún tiempo en el pasado, ¿ha estado enfermo o ha requerido cuidado intensivo?
Have you been ill or required intensive care for any amount of time in the past?

cuidados necesarios ◊ *necessary attention*
UCLA Harbor es el hospital donde recibió los cuidados necesarios.
UCLA Harbor is the hospital where she received the necessary attention.

dar a luz ◊ *give birth*
Usted dio a luz a gemelos.
You gave birth to twins.
Dio a luz a una hermosa niña.
She gave birth to a beautiful girl.

dar de alta ◊ *(from a hospital) be released; be discharged*
A usted le van a dar de alta hoy.
You are going to be released today.

dar esta receta ◊ *fill this prescription*
¿Pudiera usted darme esta receta?
Could you fill this prescription?

dar la información siguiente ◊ *give the following information*
Si tiene trabajo, dé la información siguiente.

If you are employed, give the following information.

dar resoplidos ◊ *to puff and pant*
El paciente llegó dando resoplidos.
The patient arrived puffing and panting.

dar una receta ◊ *give a prescription*
La doctora le dará una receta.
The doctor will give you a prescription.

darle el pecho a ◊ *breastfeed*
Antes de darle el pecho a su niño, lávese las manos con agua y jabón.
Before breast feeding your child, wash your hands with soap and water.

darse un golpe ◊ *hurt oneself*
Te vas a dar un golpe.
You'll hurt yourself.

darse un golpe en la cabeza ◊ *bang one's head (on something)*
Se dio un golpe en la cabeza con el estante.
She banged her head on the shelf.
Me di un golpe en la cabeza.
I banged my head.

¿de dónde ...? ◊ *where ... from*
¿De dónde es usted?
Where are you from?

de él ◊ *his*
Tengo las gotas de él.
I have his drops.

de ellos ◊ *their*
Tengo las gotas de ellos.
I have their drops.

de ella ◊ *her*
Tengo las gotas de ella.
I have her drops.

de lo ordinario ◊ *than usual*
¿Sangró usted más de lo ordinario?
Did you bleed more than usual?

de manera que ◊ *so*
Se sentía mejor de manera que no tomó las aspirinas.
She felt better so she didn't take the aspirins.

de nacimiento ◊ *from birth; since birth*
Es sorda de nacimiento.
She's been deaf from birth.
Es ciego de nacimiento.
He's been blind since birth.

¿de qué ...? ◊ *what...?*
¿De qué enfermedades padece?

What diseases do you have?
¿De qué color es la flema?
What color is the phlegm?
¿De qué color es la orina?
What color is your urine?

de usted ◊ *your*
Tengo las gotas de usted.
I have your drops.

de ustedes ◊ *your*
Tengo las gotas de ustedes.
I have your drops.

debajo de ◊ *under; below*
¿Tiene usted o ha tenido dolor debajo de los ojos?
Do you have or have you ever had pain under your eyes?

deber pasar pronto ◊ *should subside rapidly*
El dolor de su herida debe pasar pronto.
The pain of your injury should subside rapidly.

deber someterse a ◊ *should undergo; must undergo*
Debe someterse a un examen físico completo.
You must undergo a thorough physical exam.

debilitarse mucho ◊ *to become very weak*
Se debilitó mucho con la enfermedad.
The illness made him become very weak.

decir "ah" ◊ *say "ah"*
Favor de sacar la lengua y decir "ah".
Please stick your tongue out and say "ah"

dedo del pie ◊ *toe*
Se rompió un dedo del pie.
He broke a toe.

defectos de nacimiento ◊ *birth defects*
¿Nació el bebé con defectos de nacimiento?
Was your baby born with birth defects?
Los gemelos nacieron con defectos de nacimiento.
The twins were born with birth defects.

dejar una cicatriz ◊ *leave a scar*
La herida le dejó una cicatriz.
The wound left her with a scar.

dejar de + infin ◊ *stop; quit*
Deje de tomar las píldoras por una semana entera antes de comenzar a tomarlas de nuevo.
Stop taking the pills for an entire week before beginning to take them again.
Está resuelto a dejar de fumar.

He is determined to stop smoking.

dejar de fumar ◊ *stop smoking; quit smoking*
Usted tiene que dejar de fumar.
You have to stop smoking.

dejar de tomar el pecho ◊ *stop breastfeeding*
¿A qué edad dejó de tomar el pecho?
At what age did he/she stop breastfeeding?

del hospital ◊ *in the hospital*
Es el mejor anestesiólogo del hospital.
He is the best anesthesiologist in the hospital.

demasiadas visitas ◊ *too many visitors*
Hay demasiadas visitas en el cuarto.
There are too many visitors in the room.

demasiado alto ◊ *too high*
Su presión arterial es demasiado alta.
Your blood pressure is too high.

dentro de poco ◊ *soon; shortly*
El médico llegará dentro de poco.
The doctor will arrive soon.
La enfermera le llamará dentro de poco.
The nurse will call you shortly.

dentro de quince días ◊ *in two weeks*
Regrese dentro de quince días.
Come back in two weeks.

dentro de unos días ◊ *in a few days*
El tubo se lo quitaremos dentro de unos días.
The tube will come out in a few days.

dentro de unos minutos ◊ *shortly*
Le atenderemos dentro de unos minutos.
We'll be with you shortly.

descansar más ◊ *to rest more*
Es necesario descansar más.
It is necessary to rest more.

descanso total ◊ *total rest*
El médico recomienda descanso total.
The doctor recommends complete rest.

descongestionante para la nariz ◊ *decongestant for his nose*
Debemos darle un descongestionante para la nariz.
We'll give him a decongestant for his nose.

desde anoche ◊ *since last night*
No he comido nada desde anoche.
I haven't eaten anything since last night.

¿desde cuándo ...? ◊ *how long ...?; since when ...?*
¿Desde cuándo tiene este salpullido?

How long have you had this rash?
¿Desde cuándo tiene este bulto?
How long have you had this growth?

desde niño ◊ *since I was a child*
La conozco desde niño.
I've known her since I was a child.

descanso total ◊ *total rest*
El médico recomienda el descanso total.
The doctor recommends complete rest.

después de + infin ◊ *after*
¿Le duele algunas veces el estómago después
  de comer?
*Does your stomach hurt sometimes after
  eating?*
¿Ha tenido usted alguna vez ronchas después
  de recibir penicilina?
*Have you ever had welts after getting
  penicillin?*

después de cada comida ◊ *after each meal*
Tome una píldora después de cada comida.
Take one pill after each meal.

después de las comidas ◊ *after meals*
Tome la medicina después de las comidas.
Take the medicine after meals.

después del parto ◊ *after birth*
En los primeros días después del parto,
  saldrá un líquido de los pezones llamado
  calostro.
*During the first days after birth, you will
  produce colostrum.*

después de salir del hospital ◊ *after leaving
  the hospital*
Usted debe descansar por unas doce horas
  después de salir del hospital.
*You should rest for about twelve hours after
  leaving the hospital.*

después de toser ◊ *after you cough*
¿Respira usted mejor después de toser?
Do you breathe easier after you cough?

diente picado ◊ *bad tooth*
Tengo un diente picado.
I have a bad tooth.

diente que le duele ◊ *tooth that hurts you*
Indique cuál es el diente que le duele.
Point to the tooth that hurts you.

dificultades respiratorias ◊ *breathing
  problems*
Sufría dificultades respiratorias.
He was suffering from breathing problems.

dígame cuál ◊ *tell me which*
Dígame cuál de las manos se está moviendo.
Tell me which one of my hands is moving.

dígame cuando ◊ *tell me when*
Dígame cuando usted sienta algo en la piel.
*Tell me when you feel something on your
  skin.*

dirección permanente ◊ *permanent address*
¿Es ésta su dirección permanente?
Is this your permanent address?

doler ◊ *have a pain*
Me duele la pierna.
I've got a pain in my leg.

doler la pancita ◊ *have a bellyache; have a
  tummyache*
Le duele la pancita.
She has a tummyache.

dolor de cabeza ◊ *headache*
¿Cuánto tiempo ha tenido este dolor de
  cabeza?
How long has he had this headache?
¿Tiene usted dolores de cabeza?
Do you have headaches?
Mientras tiene dolor de cabeza, ¿siente
  náuseas alguna vez?
*Do you ever feel nauseated while you have a
  headache?*

dolor de oído ◊ *earache*
Llevo toda la mañana con dolor de oído.
I've had an earache all morning.

dolor sordo ◊ *dull pain*
Es un dolor sordo pero aumenta durante la
  noche.
It's a dull pain but it is very strong at night.

dolores de la cintura ◊ *low back pain*
¿Suele usted tener dolores de la cintura?
Do you ever have low back pain?

dolores de parto ◊ *labor pains*
Ya estaba con dolores de parto.
She was already having labor pains.

dolores en el pecho ◊ *pains in your chest*
¿Tiene usted dolores en el pecho?
Do you have pains in your chest?

dolores fuertes del periodo ◊ *severe menstrual
  cramps*
¿Sufre usted de dolores fuertes del periodo?
Do you have severe menstrual cramps?

dormir; dormirse ◊ *sleep; fall asleep; go to
  sleep*

Usted se dormirá dentro de poco y estará dormido durante la cirugía.
You will fall asleep soon and be asleep during surgery.
Se durmió hacia las tres de la madrugada.
She went to sleep at about three in the morning.
No dormí nada.
I didn't sleep a wink.
Trata de dormir un poco.
Try to get some sleep.
Necesito dormir por lo menos ocho horas.
I need at least eight hours sleep.

dos veces al día ◊ *twice daily*
El médico me deja tomarlas dos veces al día.
The doctor lets me take them twice daily.

drogas recetadas ◊ *prescribed drugs*
¿Usa el paciente drogas no recetadas por el médico?
Does the patient use any drugs not prescribed by the doctor?

dueño de la póliza ◊ *policy holder*
¿Cuál es el nombre completo del dueño de la póliza?
What is the complete name of the policy holder?

durante la cirugía ◊ *during surgery*
Usted se dormirá dentro de poco y estará dormido durante la cirugía.
You will fall asleep soon and be asleep during surgery.

durante las horas de visita ◊ *during visiting hours*
Se admiten visitas solamente durante las horas de visita.
Visitors are only allowed during visiting hours.

durante los últimos cinco años ◊ *within the last five years*
¿Ha estado usted hospitalizado por cualquier razón durante los últimos cinco años?
Have you been hospitalized for any reason within the last five years?

durante los últimos días ◊ *over the last few days*
Su condición ha empeorado durante los últimos días.
His condition has worsened over the last few days.

eczema infantil ◊ *childhood eczema*

¿Ha padecido de asma, fiebre de heno o eczema infantil en el pasado?
Do you have a history of asthma, hay fever, or childhood eczema?

ejercicios físicos ◊ *physical exercise*
Evite ejercicios físicos.
Avoid physical exercise.

el lugar donde trabaja ◊ *where you work*
¿Cuál es el número de teléfono del lugar donde trabaja?
What is the telephone number where you work?

embarazada de 4 meses ◊ *4 months pregnant*
Usted está embarazada de 4 meses.
You are 4 months pregnant.

embarazar a alguien ◊ *make someone pregnant*
¿Sabe si su marido embarazó a alguien antes de casarse con usted?
Do you know if your husband made someone pregnant before marrying you?

embarazo y parto ◊ *pregnancy and delivery*
¿Cómo fue su embarazo y parto?
How was your pregnancy and delivery?

en caso de emergencia ◊ *in case of emergency*
Necesitamos alguna información en caso de emergencia.
We need some information from you in case of emergency.
A quién avisamos en caso de emergencia?
Whom do we notify in case of emergency?

en cualquier farmacia ◊ *at any pharmacy*
La receta se puede preparar en cualquier farmacia.
The prescription can be filled at any pharmacy.

en cualquier operación ◊ *in any operation*
En cualquier operación hay un componente de riesgo.
There's an element of risk in any operation.

en el congelador ◊ *in the freezer*
No lo/los/la/las guarde en el congelador.
Do not keep in the freezer.

en el trabajo ◊ *at work*
¿Se lastimó en el trabajo?
Were you hurt at work?
¿Lo lastimaron en el trabajo?
Were you hurt at work?

en la fecha en que ◊ *on the date that*

Un resultado negativo es válido solamente en la fecha en que la muestra fue obtenida.
A negative test result is negative only on the date that the blood specimen was obtained.

en la nevera ◊ *in the fridge; in the refrigerator*
Guarde la medicina en la nevera.
Keep the medicine in the fridge.

en la cara ◊ *on his/her face*
Tiene varios cortes en la cara.
He has several cuts on his face.

¿en qué lugar ...? ◊ *where...?*
¿En qué lugar ocurrió la herida?
Where did the injury occur?

¿en qué puedo...? ◊ *how can I...?*
¿En qué puedo servirle?
How can I help you?

en quince días ◊ *in two weeks*
Haga usted una cita en la clínica para verme en quince días.
Make an appointment to come back to the clinic to see me in two weeks.

en un sólo lugar ◊ *in one place*
¿Se queda el dolor en un sólo lugar?
Does the pain stay in one place?

encender la luz ◊ *turn on the light*
¿Enciendo la luz?
Shall I turn on the light?

enfermarse de ◊ *fall ill; get ill; get sick; develop*
Se enfermó del estómago.
She developed stomach trouble.

enfermedad de Parkinson ◊ *Parkinson's disease*
¿Ha padecido usted alguna vez de la enfermedad de Parkinson?
Have you ever had Parkinson's disease?

enfermedad mental ◊ *mental illness*
¿Alguna vez ha tenido una enfermedad mental algún miembro de la familia **del** paciente? (m)
¿Alguna vez ha tenido una enfermedad mental algún miembro de la familia de **la** paciente? (f)
Has anyone in the patient's family ever had a mental illness?

enfermedad venérea ◊ *veneral disease*
Me gustaría hablar con un médico porque creo que tengo una enfermedad venérea.
I would like to speak with a doctor because I think I have a venereal disease.

enfermedades de la sangre ◊ *blood disease*
¿Hay alguna historia en su familia de enfermedades de la sangre?
Is there any family history of blood disease?

enfermera ambulante ◊ *visiting nurse*
Soy la enfermera ambulante.
I'm the visiting nurse.

enfermera de guardia ◊ *nurse on duty*
Me cae bien la enfermera de guardia.
I like the nurse on duty.

enfermera de salud pública ◊ *public health nurse*
Soy la enfermera de salud pública.
I'm the public health nurse.

enfermera diurna (female) ◊ *day nurse*
Soy la enfermera diurna.
I am the day nurse.

enfermero diruno (male) ◊ *day nurse*
Soy el enfermero diurno.
I am the day nurse.

entablillar + body part ◊ *put a splint on; put in a splint*
Le entablillaron la pierna.
They put a splint on his leg.

entrar por ◊ *enter through*
Entre por esta puerta.
Enter through this door.

entre las comidas ◊ *between meals*
Tome la medicina entre las comidas.
Take the medicine between meals.

entre las manos ◊ *between the hands*
Haga rodar la botella de insulina entre las manos para mezclarla.
Roll the bottle of insulin between your hands in order to mix it.

erupción en la cara ◊ *rash on your face*
¿Desde cuándo tienes esta erupción en la cara?
How long have you had this rash on your face?

es aconsejable ◊ *be advisable*
Es aconsejable que usted vaya al especialista.
It is advisable for you to go to the specialist.

es necesario + infin ◊ *it is necessary to*
Es necesario ir al hospital.
It is necessary to go to the hospital.

es necesario que + subj ◊ *it is necessary for/to*
Es necerario que su hijo vaya al hospital.

It is necessary for your son to go to the
hospital.

es poco el riesgo de que ◊ *there is little
chance of*
La prueba es muy exacta y es poco el riesgo
de que haya un resultado positivo falso.
*The test is extremely accurate and there is
little chance of a false-positive test result.*

escupir sangre ◊ *spit blood; spit up blood*
¿Escupe el niño sangre?
Does the child spit blood?
¿Escupe usted sangre?
Do you spit up blood?

escurrimiento de la nariz ◊ *runny nose*
Y también ha tenido escurrimiento de la
nariz.
And he has also had a runny nose.

esperar aquí ◊ *wait here*
Tú y él pueden esperar aquí.
You and he can wait here.
Espere aquí hasta que oiga su nombre.
Wait here until you hear your name.

esperar que ◊ *hope that*
Espero que duerma bien esta noche.
I hope that you sleep well tonight.

esperar un niño ◊ *have a child*
Espero un niño para mayo.
I'm having a baby in May.

esta tarde ◊ *this afternoon*
Usted puede levantarse por unos diez
minutos esta tarde.
*You may get up for about ten minutes this
afternoon.*

estado civil ◊ *marital status*
¿Cuál es su estado civil?
What is your marital status?

estar agotado ◊ *be exhausted*
Estoy agotado, voy a tomar un respiro.
I'm exhausted, I'm going to take a break.

estar bajo cuidado intensivo ◊ *to be under
intensive care*
Su padre está bajo cuidado intensivo.
Your father is under intensive care.

estar bien ◊ *be well*
Mi madre está bien pero mi padre no.
My mother is well but my father isn't.

estar casado ◊ *be married*
¿Había estado casado su marido antes de
casarse con usted?

Was your husband married before marrying
you?

estar completamente curado/a ◊ *be
completely cured*
No tome ninguna bebida alcohólica hasta
estar completamente curada.
*Don't drink any alcoholic beverages until you
are completely cured.*

estar con gripe ◊ *have the flu; come down
with the flu*
María está con gripe.
Mary has the flu.
Mary came down with the flu.

estar contento con ◊ *be happy with*
¿Está usted contenta con su esposo?
Are you happy with your husband?
¿Está usted contento con su esposa?
Are you happy with your wife?

estar deprimido ◊ *feel depressed*
He estado deprimido.
I have been depressed. (male)
He estado deprimida.
I have been depressed. (female)

estar durmiendo ◊ *be sleeping*
Su hijo está durmiendo.
Your son is sleeping.

estar embarazada ◊ *be pregnant*
Usted está embarazada de 4 meses.
You are 4 months pregnant.

estar embarazada de ◊ *be pregnant with; she
was expecting*
Estaba embarazada de su segundo hijo.
She was pregnant with her second child.
She was expecting her second child.

estar en cama ◊ *be in bed*
Está en cama con sarampión.
He is in bed with the measles.
No se encuentra bien y está en cama.
She's in bed not feeling well.

estar en tratamiento ◊ *be treated*
Está en tratamiento por una úlcera.
She's being treated for an ulcer.

estar encinta ◊ *be pregnant*
La joven fue violada y ahora está encinta.
*The young girl was raped and now she is
pregnant.*

estar enfermo ◊ *be sick; be ill; suffer with;
have trouble*
No sé por qué está enfermo.
I don't know why you are sick.

Está enferma de los nervios.
She suffers with her nerves.

estar engripado ◊ *have the flu*
Mi hijo está engripado.
My son has the flu.

estar estreñido ◊ *be constipated*
El niño está estreñido.
The child is constipated.
¿Está usted estreñido?
Are you constipated?

estar interesado en ◊ *be interested in*
Doctor, estoy interesada en usar la píldora
    para control de la natalidad.
*Doctor, I'm interested in using the pill for
    birth control.*

estar mejor ◊ *be better*
El paciente está mejor.
The patient is better.

estar mejorando ◊ *be improving*
Usted tiene un poco de fiebre, pero está
    mejorando.
*You have a little fever, but you are
    improving.*

estar muriendo ◊ *be dying*
Su padre está muriendo.
Your father is dying.

estar muy estresado ◊ *be under great stress*
Su esposa está muy estresada.
Your wife is under great stress.

estar quejándose ◊ *be complaining*
¿Desde cuándo se está quejando la niña?
    (girl)
¿Desde cuándo se está quejando el niño?
    (boy)
How long has the child been complaining?

estar resfriado ◊ *have a head cold*
Estoy resfriado.
I have a head cold.

estar resuelto a + infin ◊ *be determined to*
Está resuelto a dejar de fumar.
He is determined to stop smoking.

estar ronco ◊ *be hoarse*
¿Tiene tos a veces, o está ronco sin estar
    resfriado?
*Do you sometimes have a cough or are you
    hoarse, without having a cold?*
¿Está usted ronco a menudo?
Are you frequently hoarse?

estar un poco alto ◊ *be a little high*

La presión está un poco alta.
Your pressure is a little high.

estar un poco bajo ◊ *be a little low*
La presión está un poco baja.
Your pressure is a little low.

este año ◊ *this year*
¿Cómo está su salud este año?
How is your health this year?

esto durará ◊ *this will last; this will take*
Esto durará unos diez minutos.
This will last about ten minutes.

estos síntomas ◊ *these symptoms*
¿Cuánto tiempo hace que tiene estos
    síntomas?
How long have you had these symptoms?

evacuar el vientre ◊ *have a bowel movement*
¿Ha habido sangre alguna vez cuando evacuó
    el vientre?
*Has there ever been blood when you had a
    bowel movement?*

evitar tocar ◊ *refrain from handling*
En todo momento los visitantes deben evitar
    tocar los objetos en su cuarto.
*Your visitors should refrain from handling
    things in your room.*

examen médico ◊ *medical examination*
Se sometió a un examen médico.
He had a medical exam.

examinado a fondo ◊ *thorough medical
    examination*
Será examinado a fondo por el médico.
*He will undergo a thorough medical
    examination.*

examinarle la cabeza ◊ *examine your head*
Voy a examinarle la cabeza.
I am going to examine your head.

examinarle los ojos ◊ *examine your eyes*
Voy a examinarle los ojos.
I'm going to examine your eyes.

explicar brevemente ◊ *to explain briefly*
Brevemente explique la manera en que su
    empleo causó esta incapacidad.
*Briefly explain in what way your condition
    was caused by employment.*

extirpar el apéndice ◊ *remove the appendix*
Le extirparon el apéndice.
She had her appendix removed.

extirpar el seno izquierdo ◊ *remove the left
    breast*

83

Le extirparon el seno izquierdo.
She had her left breast removed.

factor Rh ◊ *Rh blood factor*
¿Cuál es el factor Rh suyo?
What is your Rh blood factor?

falta de ◊ *lack of*
Anuria es la falta de formación de orina por
    los riñones.
*Anuria is the lack of urine formation by the
    kidneys.*

faltar el aire ◊ *short of breath*
¿Le falta el aire?
Are you short of breath?

faltarle a uno ◊ *need*
Al doctor Pérez le falta el termómetro.
Dr. Pérez needs a thermometer.

faltarle a uno el aire ◊ *to gasp for air*
¿Siente a veces como que no puede respirar,
    como que le falta el aire?
*Do you sometimes have difficulty in
    breathing, such as gasping for air?*

fecha de ◊ *date of*
¿Cuál es la fecha de su última menstruación?
What is the date of your last menstruation?

fecha de nacimiento ◊ *date of birth*
¿Cuál es la fecha de nacimiento?
What is the date of birth?

fiebre del heno ◊ *hay fever*
¿Ha tenido fiebre del heno?
Have you ever had hay fever?

fiebre escarlatina ◊ *scarlet fever*
¿Ha tenido fiebre escarlatina?
Have you ever had scarlet fever?

filtro solar ◊ *sunscreen*
¿Usa filtro solar regularmente?
Do you wear sunscreen regularly?

formulario de entrada ◊ *admittance form*
Tiene que llenar un formulario de entrada.
You have to fill out an admittance form.

fractura de peroné ◊ *fractured fibula*
Sufrió fractura de peroné.
He has a fractured fibula.

fracturarse la pierna ◊ *to break a leg*
Usted se ha fracturado la pierna.
You have broken your leg.

frotar la espalda ◊ *give a back rub*
Voy a frotarle la espalda.
I'm going to give you a back rub.

frotarse con ◊ *rub oneself with*
Frótese con alcohol.
Rub yourself with alcohol.

fuente de agua potable ◊ *drinking fountain*
La fuente de agua potable está a la izquierda.
The drinking fountain is to the left.

fuera del alcance de los niños ◊ *away from
    children; out of the reach of children*
Guarde todas las medicinas fuera del alcance
    de los niños.
Keep all medicines away from children.

fuera del calor ◊ *away from the heat*
Guarde la medicina fuera del calor.
Keep the medicine away from the heat.

fuera de peligro ◊ *out of danger*
El médico dijo que estaba fuera de peligro.
The doctor said he was out of danger.

ganarse la vida ◊ *earn a living; do for a
    living; do*
¿Cómo se gana usted la vida?
What do you do?
How do you earn a living?

gastos extraordinarios ◊ *unusual expenses*
¿Tiene usted gastos extraordinarios?
Do you have any unusual expenses?

golpearse la frente ◊ *bang one's forehead*
Se golpeó la frente con el estante.
She banged her forehead on the shelf.

goteo al terminar de orinar ◊ *dribbling after
    urination*
¿Ha notado goteo al terminar de orinar?
Have you noticed dribbling after urination?

gozar de buena salud ◊ *be in good health*
¿Gozan de buena salud sus hijos?
Are your children in good health?

gravemente enfermo ◊ *seriously ill*
Está gravemente enfermo.
He is seriously ill.

grupo sanguíneo ◊ *blood type*
¿A qué grupo sanguíneo pertenece usted?
What is your blood type?

guardar cama ◊ *remain in bed, confine to bed*

Usted debe guardar cama hoy.
You are to remain in bed today.
Tienes que guardar cama.
You have to stay in bed.
El médico le mandó guardar cama.
The doctor told her to stay in bed.
Tuvo que guardar cama varios meses.
He was confined to bed for several months.

guardar las medicinas ◊ *keep the medicine*
Siempre guarde las medicinas bajo llave.
Always keep the medicines locked away.

ha llegado ◊ *has ... arrived*
La ambulancia ha llegado.
The ambulance has arrived.
La ambulancia no ha llegado.
The ambulance has not arrived.

¿ha perdido alguna vez...? ◊ *have you ever lost...?*
¿Ha perdido alguna vez el conocimiento?
Have you ever lost consciousness?

hablar con ◊ *talk to; talk with*
La doctora está hablando con tu tía.
The doctor is talking to your aunt.
Acabo de hablar con tu hermana.
I've just talked to your sister.

hace días que ◊ *for some days now*
Hace días que ando mal del estómago.
I've been having trouble with my stomach for some days now.

hacer daño ◊ *to hurt*
No voy a hacerle daño.
I will not hurt you.
Me he hecho daño en la espalda.
I've hurt my back.

hacer efecto ◊ *take effect*
Tendrá que esperar dos o tres horas para que la inyección haga efecto.
You will have to wait from two to three hours for the injection to take effect.

hacer ejercicios ◊ *exercise*
Mantenga el brazo lastimado levantado y haga ejercicios con los dedos para reducir la hinchazón.
Keep the injured arm elevated and exercise the fingers to reduce the swelling.

hacer falta ◊ *need to*
Le hace falta descansar.
He needs to rest.

hacer una cesárea ◊ *have a cesarean*
Le tuvieron que hacer una cesárea.
She had to have a cesarean.

hacer un lavado de estómago ◊ *pump (someone's) stomach*
No hay nadie que le haga un lavado de estómago.
There is no one who will pump his stomach.

hacer un rato ◊ *a while ago*
Hace un rato que se fue.
He left a while ago.

hacer una prueba de ◊ *take a test (of)*
También vamos a hacer una prueba de tuberculosis.
We are also going to take a tuberculin test.

hacer una radiografía ◊ *take an X-ray*
Voy a tener que hacerle una radiografía.
I will have to take an X-ray.

hacerse un tajo en la mano ◊ *gash one's hand*
Me hice un tajo en la mano con un vidrio.
I gashed my hand on a piece of glass.

hallarse en ◊ *be located on; be located in*
La capilla de los pacientes se halla en el piso principal.
The patient's chapel is located on the main floor.

hallarse situado en ◊ *be situated in; be located in*
El hospital se halla situado en las afueras de la ciudad.
The hospital is located on the outskirts of the city.

hasta ahora ◊ *up to now*
¿Han sido regulares sus reglas hasta ahora?
Have your periods been regular up to now?

hasta que ◊ *until*
Por favor, espere aquí hasta que lo llamemos.
Please wait here until we call you.
Apriete el émbolo suavemente hasta que se haya terminado toda la insulina de la jeringuilla.
Push the plunger slowly until all the insulin is gone from the syringe.
Espere aquí hasta que oiga su nombre.
Wait here until you hear your name.

¿hay alguien ◊ *is there anyone... ?; is anybody ...?*
¿Hay alguien en la familia con los mismos problemas?
Is there anyone in the family with the same problems?

85

¿Hay alguien más en la familia que esté
    afectado?
Is anybody else in the family affected?
¿Hay alguien más en la famlia que tenga
    picazón?
Is anybody else in the family itchy?

¿hay alguna señal ...? ◊ *are there any signs
    ...?*
¿Hay alguna señal antes de que el dolor de
    cabeza empiece?
*Are there any signs before the headache
    starts?*

¿hay algún/alguna...? ◊ *are there any ...?*
¿Hay alguna agencia de la ciudad o religiosa
    que le ayuda a usted o a su familia?
*Are there any city or religious agencies
    helping you or your family?*

hay pastillas para ◊ *there are pills to*
Hay pastillas para detener la picazón.
There are pills to stop the itching.

hinchazón de ◊ *swelling of*
¿Ha tenido hinchazón de los tobillos?
Have you had swelling of the ankles?

horas de visita ◊ *visiting hours*
Las horas de visita son de seis a ocho.
The visiting hours are from 6 to 8.
Se admiten visitantes solamente durante las
    horas de visita.
*Visitors are only allowed during visiting
    hours.*

I

iluminarle los ojos ◊ *shine a light in your eyes*
Voy a iluminarle los ojos con una lámpara.
*I'm going to shine a light in your eyes with a
    lamp.*

indicar dónde le duele ◊ *indicate where it
    hurts you*
Por favor, indique dónde le duele.
Please indicate where it hurts you.

infección de oído ◊ *ear infection*
Para una infección de oído, el niño tendrá
    que seguir un tratamiento con antibióticos
    y medicinas para el dolor y la fiebre.
*For an ear infection, the child must undergo
    treatment with an antibiotic and
    medication for the pain and fever.*
Creo que tiene una infección de oído.
I think he has an ear infection.
Parece tener una infección de oído.
He seems to have an ear infection.

infección en los riñones ◊ *kidney infection*
Tengo una infección en los riñones
I have a kidney infection.

infección urinaria ◊ *urinary infection*
Tengo una infección urinaria.
I have a urinary infection.

inflamación de garganta ◊ *strep throat*
¿Ha tenido alguna vez una inflamación de
    garganta?
Have you ever had strep throat?

insuficiencia respiratoria ◊ *respiratory
    complaint*
Sufre de insuficiencia respiratoria.
He has a respiratory complaint.

interrumpir el embarazo ◊ *terminate the
    pregnancy*
Decidió interrumpir el embarazo.
She decided to terminate the pregnancy.

intervención quirúrgica ◊ *operation*
Fue sometido a una intervención quirúrgica.
He underwent an operation.
He had an operation.

inyección de insulina ◊ *insulin shot; insulin
    injection*
Le puso una inyección de insulina.
She gave him an insulin injection.

ir a + noun ◊ *go to*
Van a la sala de partos.
They are going to the delivery room.

ir al cuarto de baño ◊ *go to the bathroom*
Llame cuando tenga que ir al cuarto de baño.
Call when you have to go to the toilet.

ir al inodoro ◊ *go to the toilet*
Llame cuando tenga que ir al inodoro.
Call when you have to go to the toilet.

ir al médico ◊ *go to the doctor; to see a
    doctor*
Fue al médico porque no quedaba
    embarazada.
*She went to the doctor because she couldn't
    get pregnant.*
Tengo que hacer una cita para ir al médico.
*I have to make an appointment to see the
    doctor.*

ir al servicio ◊ *go to the toilet*
Llame cuando tenga que ir al servicio.
Call when you have to go to the toilet.

ir empeorando ◊ *get worse*

La paciente va empeorando.
The patient is getting worse.

 J

jabón en abundancia ◊ *liberal amounts of soap*
Tómese una ducha o baño jabonoso caliente usando jabón en abundancia.
Take a shower or hot soapy bath using liberal amounts of soap.

junto a su cabecera ◊ *at his/her bedside*
Pasaron toda la noche junto a su cabecera.
They sat at his bedside throughout the night.

 K

 L

la semana que viene ◊ *next week*
Le haremos unos análisis la semana que viene.
We are taking some tests next week.
Usted tiene que regresar la semana que viene.
You have to return next week.

la pierna tiene que estar ◊ *your leg needs to be*
La pierna tiene que estar levantada con almohadas para ayudarle con la circulación.
Your leg needs to be elevated on pillows to help your circulation.

lado derecho ◊ *right side*
Favor de voltearse al lado derecho.
Please turn over on your right side.

lado izquierdo ◊ *left side*
Favor de voltearse al lado izquierdo.
Please turn over on your left side.

lámpara para llamar a la enfermera ◊ *call light*
Ésta es la lámpara para llamar a la enfermera.
This is the call light.

largo periodo de descanso ◊ *long period of rest*
Necesitas un largo periodo de descanso para recuperarte.
You need a long period of rest to convalesce.

lavar el estómago ◊ *pump the stomach*
Le lavaron el estómago.
He had his stomach pumped.

lavarse el pelo ◊ *wash one's hair*
Tengo que lavarme el pelo.
I have to wash my hair.

lavarse la cabeza ◊ *wash one's hair*
Tengo que lavarme la cabeza.
I have to wash my hair.

lavarse las manos ◊ *wash one's hands*
Lávese las manos.
Wash your hands.
Antes de darle el pecho a su niño, lávese las manos con agua y jabón.
Before breast feeding your child, wash your hands with soap and water.

le dirán que ◊ *you'll be asked to*
Ya cerca del final le dirán que orine.
Near the end, you will be asked to urinate.

¿le duele cuando ...? ◊ *does it hurt (you) when...?*
¿Le duele cuando orina?
Does it hurt when you urinate?
¿Le duele cuando come?
Does it hurt when you eat?

le han puesto ◊ *they have given ...; they have given . . . to*
Le han puesto una inyección a su hijo.
They have given your son an injection.
They have given an injection to your son.

levantar la cama ◊ *raise the bed*
Este botón levanta la cama.
This button raises the bed.
¿Levanto la cama?
Shall I raise the bed?

lesión cerebral ◊ *brain-damaged*
Nació con una lesión cerebral.
She was born brain-damaged.

levantar las caderas ◊ *raise one's hips*
Levante las caderas, por favor.
Please raise your hips.

limpiar la nariz ◊ *wipe one's nose*
Le tuve que limpiar la nariz.
I had to wipe his nose.

limpiar la tapa ◊ *wipe off the top*
Limpie la tapa de la botella con algodón mojado en alcohol.
Wipe off the top of the bottle with alcohol and cotton.

limpiarse las manos ◊ *wipe one's hands*
Me limpié las manos en un trapo.
I wiped my hands on a cloth.

llamar a alguien ◊ *call someone*
Llame a alguien para que le ayude.
Call someone to help you.

llegar a ser ◊ *to become*
Mi hijo llegó a ser médico.
My son became a doctor.
Por fin llegó a ser el director del hospital.
He finally became the director of the hospital.

llena de cicatrices ◊ *badly scarred*
Tenía la cara llena de cicatrices.
His face was badly scarred.

llenar el formulario ◊ *fill out the form*
Ahora usted tiene que llenar el formulario y firmar aquí.
Now you must fill out the form and sign here.
Tiene que llenar un formulario de entrada.
You have to fill out an admittance form.

llene este frasco ◊ *fill up this bottle*
Cuando usted orine, llene este frasco y déselo a la enfermera de guardia.
When you urinate, fill up this bottle and leave it with the head nurse.

llevar a la sala de guardia ◊ *take to emergency*
La ambulancia lo llevó a la sala de guardia.
The ambulance rushed him to emergency.

llevar a urgencias ◊ *take to emergency*
La ambulancia lo llevó a urgencias.
The ambulance rushed him to emergency.

llevar el brazo vendado ◊ *have a bandage on one's arm*
Llevaba el brazo vendado.
He had a bandage on his arm.

llevar un parche en el ojo ◊ *wear an eyepatch*
Llevaba un parche en el ojo.
He wore an eyepatch.

la mató ◊ *she was killed by*
La mató un coche.
She was killed by a car.

lo mató ◊ *he was killed by*
Lo mató un coche.
He was killed by a car.

los cuidados de ◊ *the care of; need a; be taken care of by*
Tu padre necesita los cuidados de una enfermera.
Your father needs a nurse.

Your father needs to be taken care of by a nurse.

los enfermos de ◊ *people who suffer from*
Tienen cien camas para los enfermos de cáncer.
They have one hundred beds for people who suffer from cancer.

lugar seguro ◊ *safe place*
Guarde la medicina en un lugar seguro
Keep the medicine in a safe place.

M

mala memoria ◊ *poor memory*
Si usted tiene mala memoria, su médico puede recetarle una serie de píldoras.
If you have poor memory, your doctor may prescribe a series of pills for you.

mala reacción a ◊ *bad reaction to*
¿Ha tenido una mala reacción a la medicina?
Have you had a bad reaction to the medicine?

mantenerse en ◊ *be kept in*
Debe mantenerse en el refrigerador.
Keep in the refrigerator.

mantener la calma ◊ *keep calm*
Procure mantener la calma.
Try to keep calm.

mantener la rodilla recta ◊ *keep your knee straight*
Usted debe mantener la rodilla recta para que tenga éxito la cirugía.
You must keep your knee straight for the surgery to be successful.

mantenerse muy limpio ◊ keep very clean
Es muy importante mantenerse muy limpio.
It is very important to keep very clean.

más de lo común ◊ *unusually*
¿Ha tenido usted sed, hambre o fatiga más de lo común?
Have you been unusually thirsty, hungry, or fatigued?

más tarde ◊ *later*
Hablaré con usted más tarde.
I'll talk to you later.
Se lo explicaré a su familia más tarde.
I'll explain it to your family later.

matar a golpes ◊ *beat to death*
Casi lo matan a golpes
They almost beat him to death.

Lo mataron a golpes.
They beat him to death.

matarse de un tiro ◊ *shoot oneself*
Se mató de un tiro.
He shot himself.

me está dando ◊ *it's making me*
Me está dando una picazón.
It's making me itch.

me gustaría ◊ *I would like*
Me gustaría tener un hijo.
I would like to have a son.
Me gustaría tener una hija.
I would like to have a daughter.
Me gustaría casarme.
I would like to get married.

medicina que contiene ◊ *medicines that contain*
No dé ninguna medicina que contenga aspirina.
Do not give any medicines that contain aspirin.

médico de cabecera ◊ *attending doctor*
El doctor Jones es el médico de cabecera.
Dr. Jones is the attending doctor.

medio de identificación ◊ *means of identification*
Por favor, muéstreme cualquier medio de identificación que tenga.
Please show me any means of identification you may have.

mesa radiográfica ◊ *X-ray table*
Acuéstese sobre la mesa radiográfica.
Lie down on the X-ray table.

mi vista ◊ *my eyesight*
Mi vista ya no es lo que era.
My eyesight is failing.

miembros más cercanos de la familia ◊ *immediate family*
No puede recibir visitas fuera de los miembros más cercanos de la familia.
No visitors are allowed except the immediate family.

mientras estaba embarazada ◊ *while you were pregnant*
¿Tomó alguna medicina mientras estaba embarazada?
Did you take any medicine while you were pregnant?

mientras que ◊ *while*

Mientras que tiene dolor de cabeza, ¿tiene náuseas?
Do you ever feel nauseated while you have a headache?

mientras tanto ◊ *in the meantime*
Mientras tanto, tiene que descansar.
In the meantime, you must rest.

mirar directo ◊ *look directly*
Mire directo a mi nariz.
Look directly at my nose.

mirar lejos ◊ *look far away*
Por favor, mire lejos.
Please look far away.

mordeduras de insectos ◊ *insect bites*
¿Tiene usted alergia a las mordeduras de insectos?
Are you allergic to insect bites?

morir asesinado ◊ *be murdered*
Ella murió asesinada.
She was murdered.

morir de ◊ *die of*
Murió de cáncer.
He died of cancer.
Su abuelo murió de vejez.
Their grandfather died of old age.
El paciente murió de muerte natural.
The patient died of natural causes.

morir de frío ◊ *freeze to death*
Murieron de frío.
They froze to death.

morir de parto ◊ *die in childbirth*
Murió de parto.
She died in childbirth.

morirse de ◊ *to die of*
Se murió de un infarto.
She died of a heart attack.

mover las piernas ◊ *move your legs*
Por favor, mueva las piernas.
Please move your legs.

mover los dedos ◊ *move your fingers*
Por favor, mueva los dedos.
Please move your fingers.

muchas veces ◊ *often*
Muchas veces tengo catarro.
I often have a cold.

mucho dolor ◊ *much pain*
¿Siente mucho dolor?

Are you in much pain?

muerte muy dolorosa ◊ *very painful death*
Tuvo una muerte muy dolorosa.
He had a very painful death.

muestra de cansancio ◊ *signs of tiredness*
No daba muestra alguna de cansancio.
She was showing no signs of tiredness.

muestra de orina ◊ *urine sample*
Necesito una muestra de orina.
I need a urine sample.

muestra de sangre ◊ *blood sample; blood specimen*
Necesito una muestra de sangre.
I need a blood sample.
Voy a sacarle una muestra de sangre.
I'm going to get a blood sample from you.
Una persona recibirá resultado positivo solamente si cuatro pruebas distintas de la misma muestra de sangre indican positivas.
A person will receive a positive result only if four separate tests on the same blood specimen show positive.

muñeca derecha ◊ *right wrist*
¿Le duele la muñeca derecha?
Does your right wrist hurt?

muñeca izquierda ◊ *left wrist*
No, me duele la muñeca izquierda.
No, my left wrist hurts.

muy propenso a ◊ *very prone to; easily*
Es muy propenso a resfriarse.
He's very prone to colds.
He catches colds easily.

nacer con ◊ *be born with*
¿Nació el bebé con defectos de nacimiento?
Was your baby born with birth defects?
Los gemelos nacieron con defectos de nacimiento.
The twins were born with birth defects.

nacer con cesárea ◊ *be born by cesarean section*
¿Nació su primer hijo con cesárea?
Was your first son born by cesarean section?

nacer muerto ◊ be *stillborn*
El niño nació muerto.
The child was stillborn.

nacer por cesárea ◊ *be born by cesarean section*
Su segunda hija nació por cesárea.
Her second daughter was born by cesarean section.

nariz obstruida ◊ *stuffed nose*
¿Tiene usted la nariz obstruida?
Do you have a stuffed nose?

nariz tapada ◊ *clogged nose*
¿Tiene usted la nariz tapada?
Do you have a clogged nose?

nariz taponada ◊ *clogged nose*
¿Tiene usted la nariz taponada?
Do you have a clogged nose?

nariz tupida ◊ *clogged nose*
¿Tiene usted la nariz tupida?
Do you have a clogged nose?

necesitar ayuda ◊ *be in need of help; need help*
Llame si usted necesita ayuda.
Call if you are in need of help.

necesitar los cuidados de una enfermera ◊ *need a nurse*
Tu mamá necesita los cuidados de una enfermera.
Your mother needs a nurse.

necesitar una receta ◊ *need a prescription*
¿Necesito una receta para comprarlas?
Do I need a prescription to buy them?

ni ... ni ◊ *neither ... nor*
No encuentro ni el pulso de la carótida ni la respiración normal.
I find neither the carotid pulse nor normal breathing.

ningún dolor ◊ *painless*
No causa ningún dolor.
It's painless.

niño o niña ◊ *boy or a girl*
¿Es niño o niña?
Is it a boy or a girl?

niños menores de ◊ *children under*
Las medicinas causan más envenenamientos entre los niños menores de cinco años que cualquier otro producto químico.
Medicines cause more poisoning among children under five than any other product.

no comer ◊ *to not eat*
No coma nada frito.
Don't eat anything fried.

no conduzca ◊ *don't drive*
No conduzca un coche después de tomar esto.
Don't drive a car after taking this.

no deber + infin ◊ *one must not*
No debe comer nada después de la medianoche.
You must not eat anything after midnight.
No debe tomar ningún líquido después de la medianoche.
You must not drink any liquids after midnight.

no dudar que ◊ *not doubt that*
No dudo que ella ha ingresado al hospital.
I don't doubt that she has been admitted to the hospital.

no es más que ◊ *it's just*
No es más que un rasguño.
It's just a scratch.

no guardar ◊ *not keep*
No guardar en el congelador.
Do not keep in the freezer.

no hacer falta ◊ *no need to*
No hace falta que se queden los dos.
There's no need for both of you to stay.

no olvidar ◊ *do not forget to; don't forget to*
No olvide tomar las pastillas.
Don't forget to take your pills.

no poder respirar ◊ *have difficulty breathing*
¿Siente a veces como que no puede respirar?
Do you sometimes have difficulty breathing?

no preocuparse ◊ *to not worry*
No se preocupe. Esta medicina le ayudará.
Don't worry. This medicine will help you.
No se preocupe mucho por la operación.
Don't worry too much about the operation.

no quedar embarazada ◊ *cannot get pregnant*
Fue al médico porque no quedaba embarazada.
She went to the doctor because she couldn't get pregnant.

no saber por qué ◊ *not know why*
No sé por qué está enfermo.
I don't know why you are ill.

no se rasque ◊ *don't scratch*
Sé que le irrita mucho, pero no se rasque.
I know it irritates a lot, but don't scratch.
(The infinitive of **rasque** *is* **rascar**, *an irregular verb)*

no querer comer ◊ *to not want to eat*
Su hija tiene mucha diarrea y no quiere comer.
Your daughter has a bad case of diarrhea, and she doesn't want to eat.

no se permite que ◊ *it is not allowed*
No se permite que los niños visiten al paciente.
Children are not permitted to visit with the patient.
No se permite fumar.
Smoking is not allowed.

no ser más que ◊ *to be just*
No es más que un rasguño.
It's just a scratch.

no ser nada complicada ◊ *not at all complicated*
La recuperación no es nada complicada.
The recuperation is not at all complicated.

no tener cura ◊ *be no cure for*
Esta enfermedad no tiene cura.
There's no cure for this condition.

no tener nunca ◊ *do not ever have*
No tengo nunca catarro.
I do not ever have a cold.

no tomar ◊ *not take; not drink*
No tome las píldoras.
Don't take the pills.
No tome alcohol con esto.
Don't drink alcohol with this.
Se sentía mejor de manera que no tomó las aspirinas.
She felt better so she didn't take the aspirins.

no voltearse ◊ *not turn*
No se voltee sin llamar a la enfermera.
Do not turn without calling the nurse.

nombre de su esposa ◊ *your wife's name*
¿Cuál es el nombre de su esposa?
What is your wife's name?

nombre de su esposo ◊ *your husband's name*
¿Cuál es el nombre de su esposo?
What is your husband's name?

nos explicó ◊ *he/she explained ... to us*
Nos explicó la situación.
He explained the situation to us.
Nos explicó cómo pudo suceder una cosa así.
He explained to us how a situation like this could happen.

O

oído derecho ◊ *right ear*
Hay pus y sangre en el oído derecho.
There's pus and blood in his right ear.

oídos tapados ◊ *blocked ears*
Tengo los oídos tapados.
My ears are blocked.

ojo izquierdo ◊ *left eye*
El ojo izquierdo me duele.
My left eye hurts.
Perdió la visión del ojo izquierdo.
She lost the sight of her left eye.

operar de cataratas ◊ *cataract operation*
Lo operaron de cataratas.
He had a cataract operation.

oprimir el botón ◊ *press the button*
Si usted necesita algo, oprima el botón.
If you need anything, press the button.

P

padecer de ◊ *suffer from; have trouble with*
La mujer padece de hepatitis.
The woman suffers from hepatitis.
Padecía de los nervios.
I had nerve problems.
Su hija padece de paperas.
Your daughter suffers from the mumps.

padecer del corazón ◊ *have heart trouble*
¿Cuánto tiempo hace que padece del corazón?
How long have you had heart trouble?

para ancianos ◊ *for old people*
Este hospital es para ancianos.
This hospital is for old people.

partos múltiples ◊ *multiple births*
¿Ha tenido usted partos múltiples?
Have you had multiple births?

parto normal ◊ *normal delivery*
¿Fue un parto normal o usaron fórceps?
Was it a normal delivery or did they use instruments?

parto prematuro ◊ *premature birth*
¿Fue un parto prematuro?
Was it a premature birth?

pastilla para dormir ◊ *sleeping pill*
¿Necesita usted una pastilla para dormir?
Do you need a sleeping pill?

pedir una cita ◊ *make an appointment*
Llamé al médico para pedir una cita.
I phoned the doctor's to make an appointment.

perder la visión ◊ *lose one's sight*
Perdió la visión del ojo izquierdo.
She lost the sight of her left eye.

perder peso ◊ *lose weight*
Señora Rivera, su hijo necesita perder peso.
Mrs. Rivera, your son needs to lose weight.
Usted tiene que perder mucho peso.
You must lose a lot of weight.
Ha perdido mucho peso.
She's lost a lot of weight.

perder sangre ◊ *lose blood*
El paciente va perdiendo sangre.
The patient is loosing blood.
Ha perdido mucha sangre.
She's lost a lot of blood.

perder un niño ◊ *lose a child; have a miscarriage*
Perdió un niño en el embarazo.
She had a miscarriage.

permanecer en cama ◊ *remain in bed*
Usted debe permanecer en cama hoy.
You are to remain in bed today.

permiso de conducir ◊ *driver's license*
¿Tiene usted permiso de conducir?
Do you have a driver's license?

persona de alto riesgo ◊ *high-risk person*
Un resultado negativo en una persona de alto riesgo no disminuye la importancia de practicar el sexo seguro.
A negative result in a high-risk person doesn't lessen the importance of safer sex guidelines.

peso actual ◊ *present weight*
Es importante mantener su peso actual.
It's important to maintain your present weight.

picaduras de insectos ◊ *insect bites*
¿Tiene usted alergia a las picaduras de insectos?
Are you allergic to insect bites?

pie de la cama ◊ *foot of the bed*
Este botón baja el pie de la cama.
This button lowers the foot of the bed.
El botón levanta el pie de la cama.
The button raises the foot of the bed.

pies cansados ◊ *tired feet*
Tengo los pies cansados.
My feet are tired.

pierna izquierda ◊ *left leg*
Levante usted la pierna izquierda.
Raise your left leg.

pierna derecha ◊ *right leg*
Suba usted la pierna derecha.
Raise your right leg.

pies planos ◊ *flat feet*
Tiene los pies planos.
She has flat feet.

piso bajo ◊ *ground floor*
La cafetería está en el piso bajo.
The cafeteria is on the ground floor.

piso principal ◊ *main floor*
La capilla de los pacientes se halla en el piso
principal.
*The patient's chapel is located on the main
floor.*

planta baja ◊ *ground floor*
La sala de espera está en la planta baja.
The waiting room is on the ground floor.

poco iluminado ◊ *dimmed*
La habitación estará poco iluminada.
The lights will be dimmed.

poder pasar ◊ *may be; can be*
Pueden pasar de dos semanas a seis meses
después de la exposición al virus VIH
antes de que puedan ser detectados los
anticuerpos en la sangre.
*It may be two weeks to six months after
exposure to the HIV virus before antibodies
can be detected in your blood.*

póliza del grupo ◊ *group policy*
¿Cómo se llama el titular de la póliza del
grupo?
What is the name of the group policy holder?

poner a dormir ◊ *put to sleep*
Soy el doctor Smith. Lo voy a poner a dormir
mañana para que los médicos puedan
realizar la operación.
*I am Dr. Smith. I am going to put you to
sleep tomorrow so the doctors can do the
operation.*

poner una almohada ◊ *put a pillow*
Le voy a poner una almohada debajo.
I'm going to put a pillow under you.

poner una sonda ◊ *fit with a catheter*
Le pusieron una sonda.

He was fitted with a catheter.

ponerse + adjective ◊ *to become*
El paciente se pone nervioso en el ascensor.
The patient becomes nervous in the elevator.
El paciente se puso muy delgado.
The patient became very thin.
Cuando la vio se puso muy contento.
He became very happy when he saw her.

ponerse de pie ◊ *stand up*
Por favor, póngase de pie.
Please stand up.
Mañana usted tiene que ponerse de pie.
Tomorrow you have to stand up.

ponerse enfermo ◊ *get ill; get sick*
Se puso enferma.
She got sick.

por aquí ◊ *around here*
La terapia ocupacional está por aquí.
*Occupational therapy is someplace around
here.*

por _____ días ◊ *for _____ days*
He estado enfermo por dos días.
I have been sick for two days.
Ha tenido fiebre por dos días.
He's had a fever for two days.

por el ayudante ◊ *by the orderly*
Usted será llevada allí por el ayudante.
You will be taken there by the orderly.

por hallarse enfermo ◊ *because of illness*
No pudo asistir a la reunión por hallarse
enfermo.
*He was unable to attend the meeting because
of illness.*

por la enfermedad ◊ *because of the illness*
No puede hacerlo por la enfermedad
He can't do it because of the illness.

por la nariz ◊ *through your nose*
Tengo que ponerle este tubo por la nariz
dentro del estómago.
*I have to put this tube through your nose into
your stomach.*

por la noche ◊ *in the night; at night*
¿Se despierta usted por la noche para orinar?
Do you awaken in the night to urinate?
¿Se levanta usted de la cama para orinar por
la noche?
Do you awaken in the night to urinate?

por lo regular ◊ *normally*
¿Cuánto pesa su hijo por lo regular?

How much does your son weigh normally?

por medio de ◊ *by means of; by*
El sida se contrae por medio de las relaciones sexuales.
AIDS is contracted by sexual intercourse.

por muchos años ◊ *for many years*
Padeció de cáncer por muchos años.
She suffered from cancer for many years.

¿por qué trajo...? ◊ *why did you bring...?*
¿Por qué trajo a su niño al hospital?
Why did you bring your child to the hospital?

por razón de la cirugía ◊ *because of the surgery*
Por razón de la cirugía, el tendón que antes doblaba el dedo anular ahora dobla el dedo pulgar.
Because of the surgery, the tendon that used to bend your ring finger now bends your thumb.

por _____ semanas ◊ *for _____ weeks*
Usted tiene que dejarse puesto el yeso por seis semanas.
The cast will remain on for six weeks.

por un rato ◊ *for a while*
Muerda esta gasa por un rato.
Bite on this gauze for a while.

por una semana ◊ *for a week*
Estuvo en la unidad de ciudado intensivo por una semana.
He was in the ICU for a week.

por una semana entera ◊ *for an entire week*
Deje de tomar las píldoras por una semana entera antes de comenzar a tomarlas de nuevo.
Stop taking the pills for an entire week before beginning to take them again.

por unos _____ minutos ◊ *for about _____ minutes*
Usted puede levantarse por unos quince minutos esta tarde.
You may get up for about fifteen minutes this afternoon.

predisposición a ◊ *strain of*
Hay una predisposición a los trastornos nerviosos en la familia.
There's a strain of nervous disorder in the family.

preñada otra vez ◊ *pregnant again*
Estás preñada otra vez.
Your'e pregnant again.

preparar la receta ◊ *fill the prescription*
El farmacéutico le preparará la receta ahora.
The pharmacist will fill your prescription now.

presión alta ◊ *hypertension*
¿Ha tenido presión alta?
Have you ever had hypertension?

primer embarazo ◊ *first pregnancy*
¿Es éste su primer embarazo?
Is this your first pregnancy?

primer hijo ◊ *first son*
Su primer hijo nació por cesárea.
Her first son was born by cesarean section.

primera hija ◊ *first daughter*
Su primera hija nació por cesárea.
Her first son was born by cesarean section.

primeros auxilios ◊ *first aid*
¿Por qué necesita primeros auxilios?
Why do you need first aid?

problema actual ◊ *present illness*
Por favor, describa su problema actual.
Please describe your present illness.

problemas de piel ◊ *skin problems*
¿Ha tenido problemas de piel?
Have you had any skin problems?

problemas de la vista ◊ *problems with your eyesight*
¿Ha tenido problemas de la vista?
Have you had problems with your eyesight?

procurar obtener ◊ *try to get*
Procure usted obtener una ambulancia inmediatamente.
Try to get an ambulance immediately.

propio cuarto ◊ *one's own room*
Cuando vuelva a su propio cuarto, dígale a la enfermera si quiere comer.
When you are back in your own room, tell the nurse if you want to eat.

¿qué clase de ... ◊ *what type of ...?*
¿Qué clase de jabón usa?
What type of soap do you use?

¿qué hace para ...? ◊ *what do you do for ...?*
¿Qué hace para **sus** dolores de cabeza? (m/f)
¿Qué haces para **tus** dolores de cabeza? (m/f/c)
What do you do for headaches?

¿qué le pasó a ...? ◊ *what happened to...?*
¿Qué le pasó a su hijo?
What happened to your son?
¿Qué le pasó al niño?
What happened to the child?

¿qué le van a + infin..? ◊ *what are they going to...?*
¿Qué le van a examinar a usted?
What are they going to examine you for?
¿Qué le van a examinar a su marido?
What are they going to examine your husband for?

qué otros empleos ◊ *what other jobs*
¿Qué otros empleos ha tenido?
What other jobs have you had?

quedarle ... meses de vida ◊ *... months to live*
Le quedaban tres meses de vida.
She had three months to live.

quedar manco ◊ *lose one arm; have no arm*
Es manco de los dos brazos
He has no arms.
Quedó manco del brazo derecho.
He lost his right arm.

quejarse de ◊ *complain of*
Se quejó de dolor de cabeza.
She complained of a headache

quemarse con ◊ *burn oneself with; burn oneself on*
¿Se quemó con la plancha?
Did you burn yourself with the iron?

quemarse fácilmente ◊ *burn easily*
¿Se quema fácilmente?
Do you burn easily?

querer proteger ◊ *want to protect*
Queremos que aquellas personas que lo visiten estén protegidas también.
We want to protect your visitors from possible contact too.

querer ver ◊ *want to see*
El doctor quiere ver cómo le va.
The doctor wants to see how you are getting along.

quisiera consultar con ◊ *I'd like to consult*
Quisiera consultar con mi familia.
I'd like to consult my family.

quitar la sed ◊ *quench one's thirst*
El agua le quitó la sed.
The water quenched his thirst.

quitarse la ropa ◊ *undress*

Favor de quitarse la ropa y de ponerse esta bata.
Please undress and put on this gown.

quizás sienta ◊ *you might feel*
Quizás sienta la sensación de un calor pasajero, dolor de cabeza o náuseas.
You might feel a very brief sensation of warmth, a headache, or nauseated.

R

reacción alérgica ◊ *allergic reaction*
La enfermedad fue causada por una reacción alérgica.
The illness was caused by an allergic reaction.

recetar las píldoras ◊ *prescribe the pills*
El médico le recetará las píldoras ahora.
The doctor will prescribe the pills now.

recibir algún golpe en ◊ *receive a blow to*
¿Ha recibido algún golpe en la cabeza?
Have you received a blow to the head?

reclamar atención ◊ *demand attention*
El enfermo reclamaba constantemente atención.
The patient was constantly demanding attention.

recobrar la respiración ◊ *get one's breath back*
Espera que recobre la respiración.
Let me get my breath back.

reconocimiento físico ◊ *physical examination*
¿Cuándo fue la última vez que tuvo usted un reconocimiento físico?
When was the last time that you had a physical examination?

reconocimiento médico ◊ *medical examination*
¿Cuándo fue la última vez que tuvo usted un reconocimiento médico?
When was the last time that you had a medical examination?

recuento sanguíneo ◊ *blood count*
Para el recuento sanguíneo, voy a pincharle el dedo.
For the blood count, I'm going to prick your finger.

reducir al mínimo el riesgo ◊ *reduce to a minimum the risk*
Con esto se intenta reducir al mínimo el riesgo de infección.

This is intended to reduce to a minimum the risk of infection.

reducir la hinchazón ◊ *reduce the swelling*
Mantenga el brazo lastimado levantado y haga ejercicios con los dedos para reducir la hinchazón.
Keep the injured arm elevated and exercise the fingers to reduce the swelling.

regresar mañana ◊ *return tomorrow*
Si la fiebre no baja, debe regresar mañana.
If the fever doesn't go down, you must return tomorrow.

relaciones sexuales ◊ *(have) intercourse*
El sida se contrae por medio de las relaciones sexuales.
AIDS is contracted by having intercourse.

reponer el sueldo ◊ *recover one's salary*
¿Cómo va a reponer su salario si tiene que ingresar en el hospital?
How will you recover your salary if you have to go to the hospital?

respiración boca a boca ◊ *mouth to mouth resuscitation*
Le hizo respiración boca a boca.
She gave him mouth to mouth resuscitation.

respirar con dificultad ◊ *have trouble breathing*
Respiraba con dificultad.
She was having trouble breathing.

respirar hondo ◊ *take a deep breath*
¡Respire hondo y empuje!
Take a deep breath and push.
Por favor, respire hondo.
Please take a deep breath.

respirar mejor ◊ *breathe easier*
¿Respira usted mejor después de toser?
Do you breathe easier after you cough?

respirar por la nariz ◊ *breathe through the nose*
¿Tiene usted o ha tenido dificultad al respirar por la nariz?
Do you have or have you had trouble breathing through the nose?

respirar profundamente ◊ *take a deep breath*
Respire profundamente y sostenga la respiración.
Take a deep breath and hold it.

resultado del análisis ◊ *results of the test*
El resultado del análisis fue positivo.
The result of the test was positive.

resultado de la prueba ◊ *result of the test; test result*
Los resultados de la prueba se enviarán a su médico.
The results of the test will be sent to your doctor.

revisar el ajuste ◊ *check the fit*
Asegúrese de revisar el ajuste.
Be careful to check the fit.

romperse la pierna ◊ *break one's leg*
Usted se ha roto la pierna.
You have broken your leg.

saber dulce ◊ *taste sweet*
Sabe muy dulce.
It tastes very sweet.

saber el nombre de ◊ *know the name of*
¿Sabe el nombre de la sustancia?
Do you know the name of the substance?

saber mal ◊ *(Food) to disagree; to taste bad*
¿Comió o bebió algo que le ha sabido mal?
Did you eat or drink something that disagreed with you?

sabor agrio ◊ *sour taste*
¿Siente usted un sabor agrio de boca?
Do you have a sour taste in your mouth?

sabor amargo ◊ *bitter taste*
El café me dejó un sabor amargo en la boca.
The coffee left a bitter taste in my mouth.

sacar el apéndice ◊ *remove the appendix*
Vamos a sacarle el apéndice.
We are going to remove your appendix.

sacar la lengua ◊ *stick the tongue out*
Saca la lengua y di "ah."
Stick out your tongue and say "ah."
Por favor, saca la lengua y decir "ah".
Please stick your tongue out and say "ah"

sacar la vesícula biliar ◊ *remove the gall-bladder*
Vamos a sacarle la vesícula biliar.
We are going to take out your gall-bladder.

sacar los cálculos ◊ *remove the gallstones*
Vamos a sacarle los cálculos.
We are going to remove your gallstones.

sacar sangre ◊ *draw blood*
Para el análisis de tiroides voy a sacarle sangre de la vena.

For the thyroid test I'm going to draw blood from the vein.

sacar una radiografía ◊ *take an X-ray; have an X-ray*
Me sacaron una radiografía de tórax.
I had a chest X-ray.

sala de espera ◊ *waiting room*
Hay una sala de espera en el primer piso.
There is a waiting room on the first floor.

sala de operaciones ◊ *operating room*
La sala de operaciones está a la izquierda.
The operating room is to the left.

sala de recuperación ◊ *recovery room*
Después de nacer su niño, se la llevarán a la sala de recuperación.
After the baby is born, you will be taken to the recovery room.

salir de la cama ◊ *get out of bed*
Usted puede salir de la cama, pero no sin ayuda.
You may get out of bed, but not by yourself.

salir después de ◊ *leave after*
El especialista salió después de examinarle.
The specialist left after examining him.

salir los dientes ◊ *be teething; be cutting teeth*
Le están saliendo los dientes.
He is teething.

salir para ◊ *leave for*
Salieron para UCLA Harbor Medical Hospital.
They left for UCLA Harbor Medical Hospital.

salir sangre ◊ *bleed*
Me sale sangre de la nariz.
My nose is bleeding.
Me corté pero no me salió sangre.
I cut myself but I didn't bleed.

salir un salpullido ◊ *break out in a rash; break out in hives*
Le salió un salpullido.
He broke out in a rash.

salir un sarpullido ◊ *break out in a rash; break out in hives*
Le salió un sarpullido.
He broke out in a rash.

salir una ampolla ◊ *have a blister*
Me ha salido una ampolla en el pie.
I have a blister on my foot.

sangre en la orina ◊ *blood in the urine*
¿Tiene usted sangre en la orina?
Do you have blood in your urine?

sano y fuerte ◊ *healthy and strong*
El niño creció sano y fuerte.
The child grew up healthy and strong.

se rompió ◊ *you broke*
Se rompió el brazo.
You broke your arm.
Se rompió la pierna.
You broke your leg.
Se rompió el tobillo.
He broke his ankle.

se quemó ◊ *he/she burned himself/herself*
¿Cómo se quemó?
How did he burn himself?
How did she burn herself?

seguir estas instrucciones ◊ *follow these instructions*
Siga estas instrucciones para acelerar la curación y para prevenir más daño.
Follow these instructions to help healing and prevent further injury.

seguir una dieta ◊ *follow a diet*
Usted tiene que seguir una dieta especial porque tiene la presión alta.
You have to follow a special diet because you have high blood pressure.

según los médicos ◊ *according to the doctors*
Según los médicos, se salvará.
According to the doctors, he will live.

segundo embarazo ◊ *second pregnancy*
¿Es su segundo embarazo?
Is this your second pregnancy?

segundo o tercer día ◊ *second or third day*
Su regla comenzará el segundo o tercer día después de comenzar las píldoras rosadas.
Your period will begin on the second or third day after you begin the pink pills.

segundo piso ◊ *second floor*
Hay una sala de espera en el segundo piso.
There is a waiting room on the second floor.

seguro de salud ◊ *health insurance*
Tengo seguro de salud.
I have health insurance.
No tengo seguro de salud.
I don't have health insurance.

seno derecho ◊ *right breast*
Le extirparon el seno derecho.

She had her right breast removed.

sensación de pesadez ◊ *heavy sensation*
¿Tiene una sensación de pesadez en el pecho?
Do you have a heavy sensation in your chest?

sensación de tristeza ◊ *feeling of sadness*
Lo invadió una sensación de tristeza.
A feeling of sadness came over him.

sensación de calor pasajero ◊ *brief sensation of warmth*
Quizás tenga una sensación de calor pasajero, dolor de cabeza o náuseas.
You might feel a brief sensation of warmth, a headache, or nauseated.

sentarse en la mesa ◊ *sit on the table*
Favor de sentarse en la mesa.
Please sit on the table.

sentir dolor ◊ *feel pain*
¿Le aviso cuando siento dolor?
Should I let you know when I feel pain?
¿Siente usted dolor cuando se pone de pie?
Do you feel pain when you stand?

sentir entumecimiento ◊ *feel numb*
¿Siente entumecimiento en alguna parte?
Do you feel numb anywhere?

sentir hambre ◊ *feel hungry*
Empecé a sentir hambre a eso de la medianoche.
I started to feel hungry around midnight.

sentir mucho ◊ *be very sorry*
Sentí mucho la muerte de tu padre.
I was very sorry to hear about your father's death.
Lo siento mucho.
I'm really sorry.
Sentí mucho no poder ayudarla.
I was very sorry not to be able to help her.

sentir mucho cansancio ◊ *feel very tired*
He estado sintiendo mucho cansancio y debilidad últimamente, doctor.
I've been feeling very tired lately, doctor.

sentir náuseas ◊ *feel nauseated*
Mientras tiene dolor de cabeza, ¿siente náuseas alguna vez?
Do you ever feel nauseated when you have a headache?

sentir un dolor ◊ *feel a pain*
Sentí un dolor en el costado.
I felt a pain in my side.

98   **sentir un tirón** ◊ *feel a tug*

Sentí un tirón en la pierna.
I felt a tug at my leg.

sentir una gran alegría ◊ *be overjoyed*
Sentimos una gran alegría cuando nos enteramos.
We were overjoyed when we found out.

sentirse débil ◊ *feel weak; feel faint*
¿Todavía se siente débil?
Do you still feel weak?
Llame si usted se siente débil.
Call if you feel faint.

sentirse enfermo ◊ *feel ill*
Me siento enfermo.
I feel ill.

sentirse mal ◊ *not feel well*
Me siento mal.
I don't feel well.

sentirse mareado ◊ *feel dizzy*
¿Se siente usted mareado algunas veces? (m)
¿Se siente usted mareada algunas veces? (f)
Do you ever feel dizzy?

sentirse mejor ◊ *feel better*
¿Se siente mejor hoy?
Do you feel better today?
Como se sentía mejor se levantó.
She was feeling better so she got up.

sentirse peor ◊ *feel worse.*
Me siento peor.
I feel worse.

señalar la parte de ◊ *point to the part of*
Señale la parte del cuerpo donde empezó.
Point to the part of your body where it began.

ser alérgico a ◊ *allergic to*
Si usted es alérgico al yodo debe informárselo al médico.
If you are allergic to iodine, you should inform the doctor about it.

ser causado por ◊ *be caused by*
La enfermedad fue causada por una reacción alérgica.
The illness was caused by an allergic reaction.

ser dañino ◊ *be harmful*
A usted le es muy dañino fumar tanto.
It is very harmful for you to smoke so much.
Fumar es dañino para la salud.
Smoking is harmful for one's health.

ser el/la mejor ◊ *be the best*

Es el mejor anestesiólogo del hospital.
He is the best anesthesiologist in the hospital.
Es la mejor doctora del hospital.
She is the best doctor in the hospital.

ser grave ◊ *be serious*
Puede ser grave si su mamá no sigue una
    dieta estricta.
*It can be serious if your mother does not
    follow a strict diet.*

ser picado por ◊ *be stung by*
¿Fue picado por una abeja?
Was he stung by a bee?
¿Fue picado por una avispa?
Was she stung by a wasp?

ser para + infin ◊ *be for*
Es para controlar las barandas de la cama.
It's for controlling the bedrails.
Es para controlar la luz.
It's for controlling the light.
Esta solución es para limpiarlo.
This solution is to cleanse you.

ser susceptible al contagio ◊ *be susceptible to
    other illnesses*
Cuando uno está muy enfermo es muy
    susceptible al contagio, ya que las
    defensas normales del cuerpo están bajas.
*When one is very ill, one is more susceptible
    to other illnesses because your resistance
    is low.*

ser tratado ◊ *be treated*
¿Ha sido tratado en este hospital antes?
Has he been treated in this hospital before?
¿Ha sido tratada en este hospital antes?
Has she been treated in this hospital before?

ser viuda ◊ *be a widow*
¿Es usted viuda?
Are you a widow?

ser viudo ◊ *be a widower*
¿Es usted viudo?
Are you a widower?

servir el almuerzo ◊ *serve lunch*
Se sirve el almuerzo a las once y media.
Lunch is served at 11:30.

servir el desayuno ◊ *serve breakfast*
Se sirve el desayuno a las ocho de la mañana.
Breakfast is served at 8 A.M.

servir la cena ◊ *serve supper*
Se sirve la cena a las cinco de la tarde.
Dinner is served at 5 P.M.

si tiene trabajo ◊ *if you are employed*
Si tiene trabajo, dé la información siguiente:
*If you are employed, give the following
    information:*

silla de ruedas ◊ *wheelchair*
¿Necesita usted una silla de ruedas?
Do you need a wheelchair?
Siéntese usted en la silla de ruedas.
Please sit down on the wheelchair.

sin anestesia ◊ *without an anesthetic*
Sacó la muela sin anestesia.
He took the tooth out without an anesthetic.

sin llamar ◊ *without calling*
No se voltee sin llamar a la enfermera.
Do not turn without calling the nurse.

sin poder ◊ *without being able to*
¿Se despierta en la noche sin poder respirar?
*Do you wake up at night without being able
    to breathe?*

sin respiración ◊ *out of breath*
Llegó sin respiración.
He was out of breath when he arrived.

sobre el lado derecho ◊ *on your right side*
Acuéstese sobre el lado derecho.
Turn on your right side.

sobre el lado izquierdo ◊ *on your left side*
Acuéstese sobre el lado izquierdo.
Turn on your left side.

sobre la mesa ◊ *on the table*
Acuéstese sobre la mesa.
Lie down on the table.
Voy a dejar la cuña sobre la mesa.
I am going to put the bed pan on the table.

soltero o casado ◊ *single or married*
¿Es usted soltero o casado? (male)
¿Es usted soltera o casada? (female)
Are you single or married?

someterse a ◊ *undergo; have*
Tendrá que someterse a un examen médico.
You will have to undergo a medical exam.
Fue sometido a una intervención quirúrgica.
He underwent an operation.
He had an operation.

su hijo ◊ *your son*
¿Cómo está su hijo?
How is your son?

su hija ◊ *your daughter*
¿Cómo está su hija?

How is your daughter?

subir escaleras ◊ *go upstairs*
¿Le duele cuando sube escaleras?
Does it hurt when you go upstairs?
No suba escaleras.
Don't go upstairs.

subirse la manga ◊ *roll up your sleeve*
Favor de subirse la manga.
Please roll up your sleeve.

suele visitar ◊ *usually visits*
Su médico suele visitar a las 8 de la mañana.
*Your doctor usually visits at 8 in the
    morning.*

suero en el brazo ◊ *IV in your arm*
El suero en el brazo es para darle alimento —
    azúcar, sal y agua.
*The IV in your arm is to give you food —
    sugar, salt, and water.*

sufrir de nervios ◊ *suffer from nervousness*
Usted sufre de nervios.
You are suffering from nervousness.

sufrir de tos ◊ *suffer from a cough*
El paciente sufre de tos.
The patient suffers from a cough.

sufrir un colapso ◊ *collapse from*
Sufrió un colapso debido al agotamiento.
She collapsed from exhaustion.

sufrir un encefalocraneano ◊ *suffer head
    injuries*
El paciente sufrió un encefalocraneano.
The patient suffered head injuries.

tablilla para proteger ◊ *splint to protect*
Ésta es una tablilla para proteger la mano.
This is a splint to protect your hand.

tan pronto como ◊ *as soon as*
Use el botón para llamar tan pronto como
    usted haya orinado.
*Use the button to call as soon as you have
    urinated.*

tardarán varios días ◊ *it'll be several days
    before*
Tardarán varios días en darme los resultados.
*It'll be several days before they give me the
    results.*

tarjeta de identificación ◊ *identity card*
¿Tiene usted tarjeta de identificación?

Do you have an identity card?

te han puesto ◊ *they have given you*
¿Te han puesto una inyección?
Have they given you an injection?

temores frecuentes ◊ *recurrent fears*
¿Tiene usted temores frecuentes?
Do you have recurrent fears?

tener aborto ◊ *have an abortion*
¿Ha tenido abortos la joven?
Has the young girl had any abortions?

tener alergia a ◊ *be allergic to*
¿Tiene usted alergia a alguna comida?
Are you allergic to any foods?

tener ardor ◊ *feel a burning sensation*
¿Tiene ardor?
Do you feel a burning sensation?

tener calor ◊ *be hot*
¿Tiene calor?
Are you hot?

tener canas ◊ *have gray hair; go gray*
Ya tiene canas.
She is already beginning to go gray.

tener casa propia ◊ *own one's own home*
¿Alquila usted o tiene casa propia?
Do you rent or own your own home?

tener cuidado ◊ *be careful*
Ten cuidado al bajar las escaleras.
Be careful going down the stairs.
Ten cuidado al levantar pesas después de la
    cirugía.
Be careful lifting weights after surgery.

tener dificultad para respirar ◊ *difficulty in
    breathing*
¿Tiene alguna dificultad para respirar?
Do you have any difficulty in breathing?

tener dolor de cabeza ◊ *have a headache*
El paciente tiene dolor de cabeza.
The patient has a headache.

tener dolor en ◊ *have pain in/on...?/does /do
    your ... hurt?*
¿Tiene dolor en los muslos?
Do you have pain in your thighs?
Do your thighs hurt?
¿Tiene dolor en las rodillas?
Do you have pain in your knees?
Do your knees hurt?
¿Tiene dolor en los tobillos?
Do you have pain in your ankles?

Do your ankles hurt?
¿Tiene dolor en los talones? (**talón** is singular)
Do you have pain in your heels?
Do your heels hurt?

tener el pecho congestionado ◊ *have a chest cold*
Tengo el pecho congestionado.
I've got a chest cold.

tener frío ◊ *be cold*
¿Tiene frío?
Are you cold?

tener ganas de comer ◊ *be hungry; feel like eating*
Tengo ganas de comer.
I'm hungry.
I feel like eating.

tener hemorragia ◊ *have bleeding*
¿Tiene hemorragias que no son regulares?
Do you have any bleeding that is not regular?

tener hijos ◊ *have children*
¿Ha tenido usted hijos?
Have you had any children?
Tengo tres hijos.
I have three children.

tener hambre ◊ *be hungry*
Tengo hambre.
I am hungry.

tener manchas de sangre ◊ *spot*
¿Tiene usted manchas de sangre entre periodos menstruales?
Do you spot between periods?

tener pesadillas ◊ *have nightmares; have bad dreams*
¿Tiene pesadillas frecuentemente?
Do you have nightmares often?

tener piedras en el riñón ◊ *have kidney stones*
Tiene piedras en el riñón.
She has kidney stones.

tener piedras en la vesícula ◊ *have gallstones*
También creo que tengo piedras en la vesícula porque me duele mucho el estómago.
I think I also have gallstones, because my stomach hurts a lot.

tener que ◊ *have to; must*
Tienes que guardar cama.
You have to stay in bed.

tener sarampión ◊ *have the measles*
Su hijo tiene sarampión.
Your son has the measles.

tener secreciones ◊ *have pus; have a discharge*
¿Tiene secreciones en las orejas a veces?
Do you have pus in your ears at times?
Do you have a discharge from the ears at times?

tener sed ◊ *be thirsty*
Tengo mucha sed.
I'm very thirsty.

tener tos ◊ *have a cough*
¿Ha tenido tos con la fiebre?
Has he had a cough with the fever?
Tengo una tos terrible.
I have a terrible cough.

tener trabajo ◊ *be employed*
¿Tiene trabajo?
Are you employed?

tener un hijo ◊ *have a baby*
Voy a tener un hijo.
I'm going to have a baby.

tercer embarazo ◊ *third pregnancy*
¿Es su tercer embarazo?
Is this your third pregnancy?

tener un dolor de cabeza espantoso ◊ *have a splitting headache*
Tengo un dolor de cabeza espantoso.
I have a splitting headache.

tener vértigo ◊ *have dizzy spells*
¿Tiene usted vértigo alguna vez?
Do you ever have dizzy spells?

tercer piso ◊ *third floor*
Hay una sala de espera en el tercer piso.
There is a waiting room on the third floor.

tienda de regalos ◊ *gift shop*
Hay una tienda de regalos en el primer piso.
There is a gift shop on the first floor.

toallas higiénicas ◊ *sanitary pads*
¿Cuántas toallas higiénicas ha usado usted en su última menstruación?
How many sanitary pads did you use during your last menstrual cycle?

tobillos hinchados ◊ *swollen ankles*
¿Tiene usted los tobillos hinchados por la mañana al despertarse?
Are your ankles swollen in the morning when you awaken?

tocar la rodilla ◊ *touch the knee*

Voy a tocarle la rodilla con un instrumento.
I am going to touch your knee with an instrument.

todavía estamos tratando de ◊ *we are still trying to*
Todavía estamos tratando de saber la causa de su enfermedad.
We are still trying to find the cause of your illness.

todavía no saber ◊ *still do not know*
Todavía no sé exactamente lo que usted tiene.
I still don't know exactly what is wrong with you.

todo dolorido, toda dolorida ◊ *aching all over*
Estoy toda dolorida.
I'm aching all over.

todo el tiempo ◊ *at all times*
Usted tiene que mantener la herida limpia todo el tiempo.
You must keep the wound clean at all times.

todo eso ◊ *all that*
Todo eso es necesario.
All that is necessary.

¿toma el bebé el pecho ... ? ◊ *do you breastfeed the baby...?*
¿Toma el bebé el pecho o el biberón?
Do you breastfeed the baby or do you give the bottle to the baby?

tomar drogas ◊ *take drugs*
Dime, ¿cuánto tiempo hace que tomas drogas, Mario?
Tell me, how long have you been taking drugs, Mario?
Creo que mi hija toma drogas.
I think that my daughter is taking drugs.

tomar el pulso ◊ *take the pulse*
Déjeme tomarle el pulso. (adult)
Let me take your pulse.
Déjame tomarte el pulso. (minor)
Let me take your pulse.

tomar la medicina ◊ *take the medicine*
Tome la medicina después de las comidas.
Take the medicine after meals.
Usted va a tener que tomar la medicina.
You are going to have to take the medicine.

tomar leche ◊ *drink milk*
Si no quiere tomar leche, puede comer queso, mantequilla o yogur.

If he doesn't want to drink milk, he can eat cheese, butter or yogurt.

tomar medicina ◊ *take medications*
¿Qué medicinas está tomando ahora?
What medications are you taking at present?

tomar todas las precauciones ◊ *take all precautions*
Se debe tomar todas las precauciones de no infectar a otros o de reinfectarse a sí mismo.
One should, however, take all precautions not to infect others or re-infect oneself.
Su enfermedad se puede transmitir a otras personas y hay que tomar todas las precauciones posibles para evitarlo.
Your illness may be transmitted to others, and all precautions must be taken to avoid this possibility.

tomar un respiro ◊ *take a break; have a rest*
Estoy agotado, voy a tomar un respiro.
I'm exhausted, I'm going to take a break.

tomar una aspirina ◊ *to take an aspirin*
Tome una aspirina y acuéstese.
Take an aspirin and go to bed.

tos ferina ◊ *whooping cough*
¿Está la niña vacunada contra la difteria, la tos ferina y el tétanos?
Is the child vaccinated against diptheria, whooping cough, and tetanus?

tos seca ◊ *dry cough*
¿Es una tos seca?
Is it a dry cough?

tos terrible ◊ *terrible cough*
Tengo una tos terrible.
I have a terrible cough.

transfusión de sangre ◊ *blood transfusion*
Iremos para que usted reciba una transfusión de sangre.
We will go so that you will receive a blood transfusion.
Le hicieron una transfusión de sangre.
They gave him a blood transfusion.

tratar de + infin ◊ *try to*
Trataremos de salvarle el diente.
We'll try to save your tooth.

sufrir un encefalocraneano ◊ *suffer head injuries*
Sufrió un encefalocraneano.
He suffered head injuries.

un poco tristón ◊ *a bit gloomy*
Anda un poco tristón.
He's a bit gloomy.

unas gotas ◊ *some drops*
Voy a poner unas gotas en sus ojos para
dilatar las pupilas.
*I'm going to put some drops in your eyes to
dilate your pupils.*

unos días más ◊ *a few extra days*
Usted tendrá que permanecer en el hospital
unos días más.
*You will have to stay in the hospital a few
extra days.*

unos veinte minutos ◊ *about twenty minutes*
Esto durará unos veinte minutos.
This will last about twenty minutes.

usando jabón en abundancia ◊ *using liberal
amounts of soap*
Tómese una ducha o baño jabonoso caliente
usando jabón en abundancia.
*Take a shower or hot soapy bath using
liberal amounts of soap.*

usar el bacín ◊ *use the bedpan*
¿Tiene que usar el bacín?
Do you have to use the bedpan?

usar muletas ◊ *use crutches*
Usted tendrá que usar muletas por algún
tiempo.
You will have to use crutches for a while.

usted se ve ◊ *you look*
Hoy usted se ve mucho mejor.
You look much better today.

usted tiene que + infin ◊ *you have to; you
must*
Usted tiene que comer mucha carne.
You have to eat a lot of meat.
Usted tiene que tomar vitaminas.
You must take some vitamins.
Usted tiene que tomar mucho jugo.
You must drink a lot of juice.

vacuna para el tétano ◊ *tetanus shot*
¿Cuándo recibió su última vacuna para el
tétano?
When was your last tetanus shot?

vacunar contra ◊ *vaccinate against*

¿Está la niña vacunada contra la difteria, la
tos ferina y el tétanos?
*Is the child vaccinated against diptheria,
whooping cough, and tetanus?*
¿Lo vacunaron contra la viruela?
Were you vaccinated against smallpox?

varón o nena ◊ *boy or a girl*
¿Es varón o nena?
Is it a boy or a girl?

vasos de agua ◊ *glasses of water; water*
¿Cuántos vasos de agua toma al día?
How much water do you drink daily?

vena del brazo ◊ *vein in your arm*
Le inyectarán una solución radiopaca en la
vena del brazo.
*The radiopaque will be injected into a vein in
your arm.*
Le pondrán una inyección en la vena del
brazo.
*You'll be given an injection in the vein of
your arm.*

vendar + body part ◊ *bandage up*
Me vendó el tobillo.
She bandaged up my ankle.

venderse a ◊ *sell for*
Las curitas se venden a 25 centavos la
docena.
The bandages sell for 25 cents a dozen.

ventanas de la nariz ◊ *nasal passages*
Use el atomizador en las ventanas de la nariz
diariamente.
Use the spray in your nasal passages daily.

ver al médico ◊ *see the doctor*
Veía al médico cada día.
I used to see the doctor every day.

vida muy sana ◊ *very healthy life*
Lleva una vida muy sana.
She leads a very healthy life.

visión normal ◊ *normal vision*
¿Tiene su hijo visión normal?
Does your son have normal vision?

vivir en ◊ *live in*
Vivo en el número doce de la calle quince.
I live at 12 Fifteenth street.

volver a la cama ◊ *go back to bed*
Ya es tiempo de volver a la cama.
It's time to go back to bed.

volverse arrogante ◊ *become arrogant*
El paciente se volvió arrogante.

volverse arrogante ◊ *become arrogant*
El paciente se volvió arrogante.
The patient became arrogant.

volverse barrigón/barrigona ◊ *get a bit of a
tummy*
Se está volviendo barrigona.
She's getting a bit of a tummy.

volverse loco ◊ *is mentally ill*
El paciente se volvió loco.
The patient is mentally ill.

voy a dejar ◊ *I am going to put*
Voy a dejar la cuña sobre la mesa.
I am going to put the bedpan on the table.

ya cerca del final ◊ *near the end*
Ya cerca del final, le dirán que orine.
Near the end, you'll be asked to urinate.

ya empezar a + infin ◊ *begin to; start to*
El cirujano ya empieza a operar.
The surgeon is beginning to operate now.

ya es tiempo de + infin ◊ *it's time to*
Ya es tiempo de volver a la cama.
It's time to go back to bed.

ya no ◊ *no longer*
Ya no tomo la medicina.
I no longer take the medicine.

ya yo había ◊ *I had already*
Ya yo había estudiado las radiografías.
I had already studied the X-rays.

ENGLISH-SPANISH
IDIOMS FOR HEALTH CARE

A

a bit gloomy ◊ **un poco tristón**
Anda un poco tristón.
He's a bit gloomy.

a few extra days ◊ **unos días más**
Usted tendrá que permanecer en el hospital
unos días más.
*You will have to stay in the hospital a few
extra days.*

a little high ◊ **estar un poco alto**
La presión está un poco alta.
Your pressure is a little high.

a little low ◊ **estar un poco bajo**
La presión está un poco baja.
Your pressure is a little low.

a while ago ◊ **hacer un rato**
Hace un rato que se fue.
He left a while ago.

about ◊ **acerca de**
¿Tiene usted preguntas acerca de su dieta?
Do you have any questions about your diet?

about _____ minutes ◊ **unos _____ minutos**
Esto durará unos veinte minutos.
This will last about twenty minutes.

accompany your wife ◊ **acompañar a su
esposa**
Usted puede acompañar a su esposa hasta el
cuarto.
You can accompany your wife to the room.

accompany your husband ◊ **acompañar a su
esposo**
Usted puede acompañar a su esposo hasta el
cuarto.
*You can accompany your husband to the
room.*

according to the doctors ◊ **según los médicos**
Según los médicos, se salvará.
According to the doctors, he will live.

aching all over ◊ **todo dolorido**
Estoy toda dolorida.
I'm aching all over.

admittance form ◊ **formulario de entrada**
Tiene que llenar un formulario de entrada.
You have to fill out an admittance form.

advisable ◊ **es aconsejable**
Es aconsejable que usted vaya al especialista.
It is advisable for you to go to the specialist.

affect the liver ◊ **comprometer el hígado**
El cáncer ya le ha comprometido el hígado.
The cancer has already affected the liver.

affect the lung ◊ **comprometer el pulmón**
La puñalada le comprometió el pulmón.
The stab wound affected the lung.

after ◊ **después de + infin**
¿Le duele algunas veces el estómago después
de comer?
*Does your stomach hurt sometimes after
eating?*
¿Ha tenido usted alguna vez ronchas después
de recibir penicilina?
*Have you ever had welts after getting
penicillin?*

after a while ◊ **al poco rato**
Esta sensación desaparecerá al poco rato.
This feeling will go away after a while.

after birth ◊ **después del parto**
En los primeros días después del parto,
saldrá un líquido de los pezones llamado
calostro.
*During the first days after birth, you will
produce colostrum*

after each meal ◊ **después de cada comida**
Tome una píldora después de cada comida.
Take one pill after each meal.

after leaving the hospital ◊ **después de salir
del hospital**
Usted debe descansar por unas doce horas
después de salir del hospital.
*You should rest for about twelve hours after
leaving the hospital.*

after meals ◊ **después de las comidas**
Tome la medicina después de las comidas.
Take the medicine after meals.

after you cough ◊ **después de toser**
¿Respira usted mejor después de toser?
Do you breathe easier after you cough?

all precautions ◊ **todas las precauciones**
Se debe tomar todas las precauciones de no
infectar a otros o de reinfectarse a sí
mismo.
*One should, however, take all precautions
not to infect others or re-infect oneself.*
Su enfermedad se puede transmitir a otras
personas y hay que tomar todas las
precauciones posibles para evitarlo.
*Your illness may be transmitted to others,
and all precautions must be taken to
avoid this possibility.*

all that ◊ **todo eso**

Todo eso es necesario.
All that is necessary.

allergic reaction ◊ **reacción alérgica**
La enfermedad fue causada por una reacción
   alérgica.
*The illness was caused by an allergic
   reaction.*

allergic to ◊ **ser alérgico a**
Si usted es alérgico al yodo debe informárselo
   al médico.
*If you are allergic to iodine, you should
   inform the doctor about it.*

almost two days ◊ **casi dos días**
Tuve fiebre por casi dos días.
I had a fever for almost two days.

amount of salt ◊ **cantidad de sal**
Le aconsejo que elimine o por lo menos
   disminuya la cantidad de sal que usted usa
   en la comida.
*I advise you to eliminate or at least diminish
   the amount of salt you use in your diet.*

answer slowly ◊ **contestar despacio**
Por favor, conteste despacio.
Please answer slowly.

anyone in the family ◊ **alguien de la famila**
¿Ha tenido alguien de la familia algún
   problema con drogas o con alcohol?
*Has anyone in the family had a drug or
   alcohol problem?*

anything else ◊ **algo más**
¿Le duele algo más?
Does anything else hurt you?

are there any ...? ◊ **¿hay algún/alguna ...?**
¿Hay alguna agencia de la ciudad o religiosa
   que le ayuda a usted o a su familia?
*Are there any city or religious agencies
   helping you or your family?*

are there any signs ...? ◊ **¿hay alguna señal
...?**
¿Hay alguna señal antes de que el dolor de
   cabeza empiece?
*Are there any signs before the headache
   starts?*

around here ◊ **por aquí**
La terapia ocupacional está por aquí.
*Occupational therapy is someplace around
   here.*

as soon as ◊ **tan pronto como**
Use el botón para llamar tan pronto como
   usted haya orinado.
*Use the button to call as soon as you have
   urinated.*

at all times ◊ **todo el tiempo**
Usted tiene que mantener la herida limpia
   todo el tiempo.
You must keep the wound clean at all times.

at any pharmacy ◊ **en cualquier farmacia**
La receta se puede preparar en cualquier
   farmacia.
*The prescription can be filled at any
   pharmacy.*

at bedtime ◊ **antes de acostarse**
Tome una píldora antes de acostarse.
Take one pill at bedtime.

at birth ◊ **al nacer**
¿Cuánto pesó el bebé al nacer?
How much did the baby weigh at birth?

at breakfast ◊ **con el desayuno**
Tome una cápsula con el desayuno.
Take one capsule at breakfast.

at his/her bedside ◊ **junto a su cabecera**
Pasaron toda la noche junto a su cabecera.
They sat at his bedside throughout the night.

at ... intervals ◊ **a intervalos de ...**
Le harán una serie de placas a intervalos de
   cinco minutos cada una.
*A series of X-rays will be taken at five-
   minute intervals.*

at the same time ◊ **a la misma hora**
Tome usted la píldora a la misma hora cada
   día.
Take the pill at the same time each day.

at times ◊ **a veces**
¿Tiene doble visión a veces?
Do you have double vision at times?
¿Siente a veces como que no puede respirar,
   como que le falta el aire?
*Do you at times have difficulty in breathing,
   such as gasping for air?*
¿Tiene tos a veces, o está ronco sin estar
   resfriado?
*Do you at times have a cough or are you
   hoarse, without having a cold?*

at what age ...? ◊ **¿a qué edad ...?**
¿A qué edad murió su padre?
At what age did your father die?
¿A qué edad empezaron sus reglas?
At what age did your periods start?
¿A qué edad caminó?
At what age did he walk?

at work ◊ **en el trabajo**
¿Se lastimó en el trabajo?
Were you hurt at work?

¿Lo lastimaron en el trabajo?
Were you hurt at work?

attend school ◊ **asistir a la escuela**
¿Cuántos niños asisten a la escuela?
How many children attend school?

attending doctor ◊ **médico de cabecera**
El doctor Jones es el médico de cabecera.
Dr. Jones is the attending doctor.

away from children ◊ **fuera del alcance de los niños**
Guarde todas las medicinas fuera del alcance de los niños.
Keep all medicines away from children.

away from the heat ◊ **fuera del calor**
Guarde la medicina fuera del calor.
Keep the medicine away from the heat.

bad reaction to ◊ **mala reacción a**
¿Ha tenido una mala reacción a la medicina?
Have you had a bad reaction to the medicine?

bad tooth ◊ **diente picado**
Tengo un diente picado.
I have a bad tooth.

badly scarred ◊ **llena de cicatrices**
Tenía la cara llena de cicatrices.
His face was badly scarred.

bandage up ◊ **vendar** + body part
Me vendó el tobillo.
She bandaged up my ankle.

bang one's forehead ◊ **golpearse la frente**
Se golpeó la frente con el estante.
She banged her forehead on the shelf.

bang one's head (on something) ◊ **darse un golpe en la cabeza**
Se dio un golpe en la cabeza con el estante.
She banged her head on the shelf.
Me di un golpe en la cabeza.
I banged my head.

bathe with ◊ **bañarse con**
Báñese con agua caliente.
Bathe with warm water.

bathroom ◊ **cuarto de baño**
El cuarto de baño está en la segunda planta.
The bathroom is on the second floor.

be a widow ◊ **ser viuda**

¿Es usted viuda?
Are you a widow?

be a widower ◊ **ser viudo**
¿Es usted viudo?
Are you a widower?

be allergic to ◊ **tener alergia a**
¿Tiene usted alergia a alguna comida?
Are you allergic to any foods?

be better ◊ **estar mejor**
El paciente está mejor.
The patient is better.

be born by cesarean section ◊ **nacer con cesárea; nacer por cesárea**
Su segunda hija nació por cesárea.
Her second daughter was born by cesarean section.
¿Nació su primer hijo con cesárea?
Was your first son born by cesarean section?

be born with ◊ **nacer con**
¿Nació el bebé con defectos de nacimiento?
Was your baby born with birth defects?
Los gemelos nacieron con defectos de nacimiento.
The twins were born with birth defects.

be careful ◊ **tener cuidado**
Ten cuidado al bajar las escaleras.
Be careful going down the stairs.
Ten cuidado al levantar pesas después de la cirugía.
Be careful lifting weights after surgery.

be caused by ◊ **ser causado por**
La enfermedad fue causada por una reacción alérgica.
The illness was caused by an allergic reaction.

be cold ◊ **tener frío**
¿Tiene frío?
Are you cold?

be complaining ◊ **estar quejándose**
¿Desde cuándo se está quejando la niña? (girl)
¿Desde cuándo se está quejando el niño? (boy)
How long has the child been complaining?

be cutting teeth ◊ **salir los dientes**
Le están saliendo los dientes.
He is cutting his teeth.

be discharged (from a hospital) ◊ **dar de alta**
A usted le van a dar de alta hoy.
You are going to be discharged today.

be employed ◊ **tener trabajo**
¿Tiene trabajo?
Are you employed?

be for ◊ **ser para** + infin
Es para controlar las barandas de la cama.
It's for controlling the bedrails.
Es para controlar la luz.
It's for controlling the light.
Esta solución es para limpiarlo.
This solution is to cleanse you.

be glad ◊ **alegrarse de**
Me alegro de mejorarme.
I am glad to be better.
Me alegro de que usted se mejore.
I am glad that you are getting better.

be harmful ◊ **ser dañino**
A usted le es muy dañino fumar tanto.
It is very harmful for you to smoke so much.
Fumar es dañino para la salud.
Smoking is harmful for one's health.

be hot ◊ **tener calor**
¿Tiene calor?
Are you hot?

be hungry ◊ **tener hambre**
Tengo hambre.
I am hungry.

be in bed ◊ **estar en cama**
Está en cama con sarampión.
He is in bed with the measles.
No se encuentra bien y está en cama.
She's in bed not feeling well.

be in need of help ◊ **necesitar ayuda**
Llame si usted necesita ayuda.
Call if you are in need of help.

be kept in ◊ **mantenerse en**
Debe mantenerse en el refrigerador.
It must be kept in the refrigerator.

be murdered ◊ **morir asesinado**
Ella murió asesinada.
She was murdered.

be no cure for ◊ **no tener cura**
Esta enfermedad no tiene cura.
There's no cure for this condition.

be overjoyed ◊ **sentir una gran alegría**
Sentimos una gran alegría cuando nos enteramos.
We were overjoyed when we found out.

be released (from a hospital) ◊ **dar de alta**

A usted le van a dar de alta hoy.
You are going to be released today.

be satisfied with ◊ **contentarse con**
Me contento con los resultados dc la prueba.
I'm satisfied with the test results.

be serious ◊ **ser grave**
Puede ser grave si su mamá no sigue una dieta estricta.
It can be serious if your mother does not follow a strict diet.

be stillborn ◊ **nacer muerto**
El niño nació muerto.
The child was stillborn.

be stung by ◊ **ser picado por**
¿Fue picado por una abeja?
Was he stung by a bee?
¿Fue picado por una avispa?
Was she stung by a wasp?

be susceptible to other illnesses ◊ **ser susceptible al contagio**
Cuando uno está muy enfermo es muy susceptible al contagio, ya que las defensas normales del cuerpo están bajas.
When one is very ill, one is more susceptible to other illnesses because your resistance is low.

be the best ◊ **ser el/la mejor**
Es el mejor anestesiólogo del hospital.
He is the best anesthesiologist in the hospital.
Es la mejor doctora del hospital.
She is the best doctor in the hospital.

be thirsty ◊ **tener sed**
Tengo mucha sed.
I'm very thirsty.

be treated ◊ **ser tratado**
¿Ha sido tratado en este hospital antes?
Has he been treated in this hospital before?
¿Ha sido tratada en este hospital antes?
Has she been treated in this hospital before?

be very sorry ◊ **sentir mucho**
Sentí mucho la muerte de tu padre.
I was very sorry to hear about your father's death.
Lo siento mucho.
I'm really sorry.
Sentí mucho no poder ayudarla.
I was very sorry not to be able to help her.

beat to death ◊ **matar a golpes**
Casi lo matan a golpes
They almost beat him to death.
Lo mataron a golpes.

They beat him to death.

because of illness ◊ **por hallarse enfermo**
No pudo asistir a la reunión por hallarse enfermo.
He was unable to attend the meeting because of illness.

because of the illness ◊ **por la enfermedad**
No puede hacerlo por la enfermedad
He can't do it because of the illness.

because of the surgery ◊ **por razón de la cirugía**
Por razón de la cirugía, el tendón que antes doblaba el dedo anular ahora dobla el dedo pulgar.
Because of the surgery, the tendon that used to bend your ring finger now bends your thumb.

become arrogant ◊ **volverse arrogante**
El paciente se volvió arrogante.
The patient became arrogant.

become very weak ◊ **debilitarse mucho**
Se debilitó mucho con la enfermedad.
The illness made him become very weak.

begin to ◊ **ya empezar a** + infin
El cirujano ya empieza a operar.
The surgeon is beginning to operate now.

beds for ◊ **camas para**
Tienen cien camas para los enfermos de cáncer.
They have one hundred beds for people who suffer from cancer.

before ◊ **antes de**
Debe estar aquí antes de las ocho.
You must be here before eight.
Antes de darle el pecho a su niño, lávese las manos con agua y jabón.
Before breast feeding your child, wash your hands with soap and water.
Por favor, tómelas antes de comer.
Please take them before eating.

before eating ◊ **antes de comer**
Tómelas antes de comer.
Take them before eating.

before going to bed ◊ **antes de acostarse**
Tome una píldora antes de acostarse.
Take one pill before going to bed.

before meals ◊ **antes de las comidas**
Tome la medicina antes de las comidas.
Take the medicine before meals.

before use ◊ **antes de usar**

Agítese antes de usar.
Shake well before use.

being seen by a doctor ◊ **a cargo de un médico**
¿Está **el** paciente a cargo de un médico a causa de algún problema médico? (m)
¿Está **la** paciente a cargo de un médico a causa de algún problema médico? (f)
Is the patient currently being seen by a doctor for any medical problem?

between meals ◊ **entre las comidas**
Tome la medicina entre las comidas.
Take the medicine between meals.

between your hands ◊ **entre las manos**
Haga rodar la botella de insulina entre las manos para mezclarla.
Roll the bottle of insulin between your hands in order to mix it.

birth control ◊ **control de la natalidad**
Doctor, estoy interesada en usar la píldora para el control de la natalidad.
Doctor, I'm interested in using the pill for birth control.

birth defects ◊ **defectos de nacimiento**
¿Nació el bebé con defectos de nacimiento?
Was your baby born with birth defects?
Los gemelos nacieron con defectos de nacimiento.
The twins were born with birth defects.

bitter taste ◊ **sabor amargo**
El café me dejó un sabor amargo en la boca.
The coffee left a bitter taste in my mouth.

bleed ◊ **salir sangre**
Tenía una hemorragia interna.
He was bleeding internally.
Me sale sangre de la nariz.
My nose is bleeding.
Me corté pero no me salió sangre.
I cut myself but I didn't bleed.

blocked ears ◊ **oídos tapados**
Tengo los oídos tapados.
My ears are blocked.

blood analysis ◊ **análisis de sangre**
Vamos a hacer un análisis de sangre.
We are going to do a blood analysis.

blood count ◊ **recuento sanguíneo**
Para el recuento sanguíneo, voy a pincharle el dedo.
For the blood count, I'm going to prick your finger.

blood disease ◊ **enfermedades de la sangre**

¿Hay alguna historia en su familia de
    enfermedades de la sangre?
Is there any family history of blood disease?

blood in the urine ◊ **sangre en la orina**
¿Tiene usted sangre en la orina?
Do you have blood in your urine?

blood sample ◊ **muestra de sangre**
Necesito una muestra de sangre.
I need a blood sample.
Voy a sacarle una muestra de sangre.
I'm going to get a blood sample from you.

blood specimen ◊ **muestra de sangre**
Una persona recibirá resultado positivo
    solamente si cuatro pruebas distintas de la
    misma muestra de sangre indican
    positivas.
A person will receive a positive result only if
    four separate tests on the same blood
    specimen show positive.

blood test ◊ **análisis de sangre**
Vamos a hacer un análisis de sangre.
We are going to do a blood analysis.

blood transfusion ◊ **transfusión de sangre**
Le hicieron una transfusión de sangre.
They gave him a blood tranfusion.

blood type ◊ **grupo sanguíneo**
¿A qué grupo sanguíneo pertenece usted?
What is your blood type?

boy or a girl ◊ **niño o niña; varón o nena**
¿Es niño o niña?
Is it a boy or a girl?

brain-damaged ◊ **lesión cerebral**
Nació con una lesión cerebral.
She was born brain-damaged.

break one's leg ◊ **fracturarse la pierna;**
    romperse la pierna
Usted se ha roto la pierna.
You have broken your leg.
Usted se ha fracturado la pierna.
You have broken your leg.

break out in a rash ◊ **salir un sarpullido; salir**
    un salpullido
Le salió un sarpullido.
He broke out in a rash.
Le salió un salpullido.
He broke out in a rash.

break out in hives ◊ **salir un sarpullido, salir**
    un salpullido
Le salió un sarpullido.
He broke out in hives
Le salió un salpullido.

He broke out in hives.

breast cancer ◊ **cáncer de mama**
Tiene cáncer de mama.
She has breast cancer.

breastfeed ◊ **darle el pecho a**
Antes de darle el pecho a su niño, lávese las
    manos con agua y jabón.
Before breast feeding your child, wash your
    hands with soap and water.

breathe easier ◊ **respirar mejor**
¿Respira usted mejor después de toser?
Do you breathe easier after you cough?

breathe through your nose ◊ **respirar por la**
    nariz
¿Tiene usted o ha tenido dificultad al respirar
    por la nariz?
Do you have or have you had trouble
    breathing through your nose?

breathing problems ◊ **dificultades**
    respiratorias
Sufría dificultades respiratorias.
He was suffering from breathing problems.

brief sensation of warmth ◊ **sensación de calor**
    pasajero
Quizás tenga una sensación de calor
    pasajero, dolor de cabeza o náuseas.
You might feel a brief sensation of warmth, a
    headache, or nauseated.

burn easily ◊ **quemarse fácilmente**
¿Se quema fácilmente?
Do you burn easily?

burn oneself on/with ◊ **quemarse con**
¿Se quemó con la plancha?
Did you burn yourself with the iron?

by ◊ **antes de**
Debe estar en hospital antes de las tres.
You must be at the hospital by three.

by; by means of ◊ **por medio de**
El sida se contrae por medio de las relaciones
    sexuales.
AIDS is contracted by sexual intercourse.

by the orderly ◊ **por el ayudante**
Usted será llevada allí por el ayudante.
You will be taken there by the orderly.

call light ◊ **lámpara para llamar a la**
    enfermera

111

call light ◊ **lámpara para llamar a la enfermera**
Ésta es la lámpara para llamar a la enfermera.
This is the call light.

call someone ◊ **llamar a alguien**
Llame a alguien para que le ayude.
Call someone to help you.

call the doctor ◊ **avisar al médico**
Tuvieron que avisar al médico.
They had to call the doctor.

can be ◊ **poder pasar**
Pueden pasar de dos semanas a seis meses después de la exposición al virus VIH antes de que puedan ser detectados los anticuerpos en la sangre.
It can be two weeks to six months after exposure to the HIV virus before antibodies can be detected in your blood.

canned food ◊ **comida de lata**
¿Comió comida de lata?
Did you eat canned food?

cannot get pregnant ◊ **no quedar embarazada**
Fue al médico porque no quedaba embarazada.
She went to the doctor because she couldn't get pregnant.

cataract operation ◊ **operar de cataratas**
Lo operaron de cataratas.
He had a cataract operation.

catch the measles ◊ **coger sarampión**
El niño cogió sarampión.
The child caught the measles.

cause a rash ◊ **causar sarpullido**
Los problemas de la piel quizás podrán causarle sarpullido.
Your skin problems may cause a rash.

cause of death ◊ **causa de la muerte**
Se desconoce la causa de la muerte.
The cause of death is unknown

cause of the illness ◊ **causa de la enfermedad**
Todavía estamos tratando de saber la causa de su enfermedad.
We are still trying to find the cause of your illness.
Pienso que hemos descubierto la causa de su enfermedad.
I think that we have found the cause of your illness.

change clothes ◊ **cambiarse la ropa**
Por favor, cámbiese la ropa.

Please change your clothes.

change jobs ◊ **cambiar de empleo**
¿Por qué cambió usted de empleo?
Why did you change jobs?

change the dressing ◊ **cambiar el vendaje**
Es hora de cambiarle el vendaje.
It's time to change your dressing.

change the sheets ◊ **cambiar las sábanas**
¿Cambio las sábanas?
Shall I change the sheets?
Es hora de cambiar las sábanas.
It's time to change the sheets.

check the fit ◊ **revisar el ajuste**
Asegúrese de revisar el ajuste.
Be careful to check the fit.

childhood disease ◊ **enfermedad infantil**
¿Ha padecido de asma, fiebre de heno o enfermedad infantil en el pasado?
Do you have a history of asthma, hay fever, or childhood disease?

childhood eczema ◊ **eczema infantil**
¿Ha padecido de asma, fiebre de heno o eczema infantil en el pasado?
Do you have a history of asthma, hay fever, or childhood eczema?

children under ◊ **niños menores de**
Las medicinas causan más envenenamientos entre los niños menores de cinco años que cualquier otro producto químico.
Medicines cause more poisoning among children under five than any other product.

choke on ◊ **atragantarse con**
Él se atragantó con la comida.
He choked on the food.

clench your fist ◊ **cerrar el puño**
Cierre el puño.
Clench your fist.
Por favor, cierre el puño.
Please clench your fist.

climb stairs ◊ **subir escaleras**
¿Le duele cuando sube escaleras?
Does it hurt when you climb stairs?
No suba escaleras.
Don't climb stairs

clogged nose ◊ **nariz tapada; nariz taponada; nariz tupida**
¿Tiene usted la nariz taponada?
Do you have a clogged nose?
¿Tiene usted la nariz tapada?
Do you have a clogged nose?

¿Tiene usted la nariz tupida?
Do you have a clogged nose?

collapse from ◊ **sufrir un colapso**
Sufrió un colapso debido al agotamiento.
She collapsed from exhaustion.

come down with the flu ◊ **estar con gripe**
María está con gripe.
Mary came down with the flu.

complain of ◊ **quejarse de**
Se quejó de dolor de cabeza.
She complained of a headache

completely cured ◊ **estar completamente curado**
No tome ninguna bebida alcohólica, hasta estar completamente curada.
Don't drink any alcoholic beverages until you are completely cured.

constipated ◊ **estar estreñido**
El niño está estreñido.
The child is constipated.
¿Está usted estreñido?
Are you constipated?

consult; consult a; consult with ◊ **consultar con**
Quisiera consultar con mi familia.
I'd like to consult my family.
Tendré que consultar con mi esposa.
I'll have to consult my wife about it.
¿Por qué no consulta usted con un especialista?
Why don't you consult a specialist?

cook meals ◊ **cocinar comidas**
Usted tiene que cocinar comidas ricas en minerales.
You have to cook meals rich in minerals.

cough up phlegm ◊ **arrojar flemas**
Al toser, ¿arroja flema?
When you cough, do you cough up phlegm?

coughing fit ◊ **acceso de tos**
Tuvo un acceso de tos.
He had a coughing fit.

crippled for life ◊ **lisiado de por vida**
Quedó lisiado de por vida.
He was crippled for life.

cut one's wrists ◊ **cortarse las venas**
El paciente se cortó las venas.
The patient cut his wrists.

D

daily ◊ **al día**
¿Cuánta mantequilla come usted al día?
How much butter do you eat daily?

date of ◊ **fecha de**
¿Cuál es la fecha de su última menstruación?
What is the date of your last menstruation?

date of birth ◊ **fecha de nacimiento**
¿Cuál es la fecha de nacimiento?
What is the date of birth?

day nurse ◊ **enfermero diurno** (male); **enfermera diurna** (female)
Soy la enfermera diurna.
I am the day nurse.
Soy el enfermero diurno.
I am the day nurse.

decongestant for the nose ◊ **descongestionante para la nariz**
Debemos darle un descongestionante para la nariz.
We'll give him a decongestant for his nose.

demand attention ◊ **reclamar atención**
El enfermo reclamaba constantemente atención.
The patient was constantly demanding attention.

determined to ◊ **estar resuelto a** + infin
Está resuelto a dejar de fumar.
He is determined to stop smoking.

die in ◊ **morir en**
Murió en un accidente.
He died in an accident.

die in childbirth ◊ **morir de parto**
Murió de parto.
She died in childbirth.

die of ◊ **morir de**
Murió de cáncer.
He died of cancer.
Su abuelo murió de vejez.
Their grandfather died of old age.
El paciente murió de muerte natural.
The patient died of natural causes.

difficulty in breathing ◊ **tener dificultad para respirar**
¿Tiene alguna dificultad para respirar?
Do you have any difficulty in breathing?

dimmed ◊ **poco iluminado**
La habitación estará poco iluminada.
The lights will be dimmed.

disagree (Food) ◊ **saber mal**

¿Comió o bebió algo que le ha sabido mal?
Did you eat or drink something that disagreed with you?

do for a living ◊ **ganarse la vida**
¿Cómo se gana usted la vida?
What do you do for a living?

do not ever have ◊ **no tener nunca**
No tengo nunca catarro.
I do not ever have a cold.

do you breastfeed the baby ...? ◊ **¿toma el bebé el pecho ...?**
¿Toma el bebé el pecho o el biberón?
Do you breastfeed the baby or do you give the bottle to the baby?

does it hurt (you) when ...? ◊ **¿le duele cuando ...?**
¿Le duele cuando orina?
Does it hurt when you urinate?
¿Le duele cuando come?
Does it hurt when you eat?

does/do your ... hurt? ◊ **tener dolor en ...**
¿Tiene dolor en los muslos?
Do your thighs hurt?
¿Tiene dolor en las rodillas?
Do your knees hurt?
¿Tiene dolor en los tobillos?
Do your ankles hurt?
¿Tiene dolor en los talones? (**talón** is singular)
Do your heels hurt?

don't drive ◊ **no conduzca**
No conduzca un coche después de tomar esto.
Don't drive a car after taking this.

don't forget to ◊ **no olvidar**
No olvide tomar las pastillas.
Don't forget to take your pills.

don't scratch ◊ **no se rasque**
Sé que le irrita mucho, pero no se rasque.
I know it irritates a lot, but don't scratch.
*(The infinitive of **rasque** is **rascar**, an irregular verb)*

draw blood ◊ **sacar sangre**
Para el análisis de tiroides voy a sacarle sangre de la vena.
For the thyroid test I'm going to draw blood from the vein.

dribbling after urination ◊ **goteo al terminar de orinar**
¿Ha notado goteo al terminar de orinar?
Have you noticed dribbling after urination?

drink a lot of liquids ◊ **beber muchos líquidos**
Usted tiene que beber muchos líquidos.
You have to drink a lot of liquids.

drink milk ◊ **tomar leche**
Si no quiere tomar leche, puede comer queso, mantequilla o yogur.
If he doesn't want to drink milk, he can eat cheese, butter or yogurt.

drinking fountain ◊ **fuente de agua potable**
La fuente de agua potable está a la izquierda.
The drinking fountain is to the left.

drinking water ◊ **agua potable**
Esta no es agua potable.
This is not drinking water.

driver's license ◊ **permiso de conducir**
¿Tiene usted permiso de conducir?
Do you have a driver's license?

dry cough ◊ **tos seca**
¿Es una tos seca?
Is it a dry cough?

dry mouth ◊ **boca seca**
Tenía la boca seca.
He had a dry mouth.

dull pain ◊ **dolor sordo**
Es un dolor sordo pero aumenta durante la noche.
It's a dull pain but it is very strong at night.

during surgery ◊ **durante la cirugía**
Usted se dormirá dentro de poco y estará dormido durante la cirugía.
You will fall asleep soon and be asleep during surgery.

during visiting hours ◊ **durante las horas de visita**
Se admiten visitas solamente durante las horas de visita.
Visitors are only allowed during visiting hours.

dying ◊ **estar muriendo**
Su padre está muriendo.
Your father is dying.

each day ◊ **cada día**
Tome usted la píldora a la misma hora cada día.
Take the pill at the same time each day.

each evening ◊ **cada noche**

Póngase uno de estos supositiorios cada
noche.
Use one of these suppositories each evening.

ear infection ◊ **infección de oído**
Para una infección de oído, el niño tendrá
que seguir un tratamiento con antibióticos
y medicinas para el dolor y la fiebre.
*For an ear infection, the child must undergo
treatment with an antibiotic and
medication for the pain and fever.*
Creo que tiene una infección de oído.
I think he has an ear infection.
Parece tener una infección de oído.
He seems to have an ear infection.

earache ◊ **dolor de oído**
Llevo toda la mañana con dolor de oído.
I've had an earache all morning.

earn a living ◊ **ganarse la vida**
¿Cómo se gana usted la vida?
How do you earn a living?

element of risk ◊ **componente de riesgo**
En cualquier operación hay un componente
de riesgo.
There's an element of risk in any operation.

enter through ◊ **entrar por**
Entre por esta puerta.
Enter through this door.

ever ◊ **alguna vez**
¿Ha tenido usted alguna vez comezón
después de recibir penicilina?
*Have you ever had itching after getting
penicillin?*
Mientras tiene dolor de cabeza, ¿siente
náuseas alguna vez?
*Do you ever feel nauseated while you have a
headache?*
¿Ha estado embarazada alguna vez?
Have you ever been pregnant?

every evening ◊ **cada noche**
Póngase uno de estos supositiorios cada
noche.
Use one of these suppositories every evening.

every hour ◊ **cada hora**
Póngase usted una compresa caliente y
húmeda cada hora.
Apply a hot and wet compress every hour.

examine your eyes ◊ **examinarle los ojos**
Voy a examinarle los ojos.
I'm going to examine your eyes.

examine your head ◊ **examinarle la cabeza**
Voy a examinarle la cabeza.
I am going to examine your head.

exercise ◊ **hacer ejercicios**
Mantenga el brazo lastimado levantado y
haga ejercicios con los dedos para reducir
la hinchazón.
*Keep the injured arm elevated and exercise
the fingers to reduce the swelling.*

exhausted; be exhausted ◊ **estar agotado**
Estoy agotado, voy a tomar un respiro.
I'm exhausted, I'm going to take a break.

explain briefly ◊ **explicar brevemente**
Brevemente explique la manera en que su
empleo causó esta incapacidad.
*Briefly explain in what way your condition
was caused by employment.*

eyes ◊ **ojos**
Tiene los ojos azules.
He has blue eyes.

eyes get tired ◊ **cansarse la vista**
Se le cansa la vista.
Her eyes get tired.

fairly easy to ◊ **bastante fácil de**
Lo que tienes es bastante fácil de curar.
What you have is fairly easy to cure.

fall over ◊ **caerse al suelo**
Tropezó y se cayó al suelo.
She tripped and fell over.

fatty foods ◊ **comida grasosa**
No coma comida grasosa.
Don't eat fatty foods.

feel a burning sensation ◊ **tener ardor**
¿Tiene ardor?
Do you feel a burning sensation?

feel a pain ◊ **sentir un dolor**
Sentí un dolor en el costado.
I felt a pain in my side.

feel a tug ◊ **sentir un tirón**
Sentí un tirón en la pierna.
I felt a tug at my leg.

feel better ◊ **sentirse mejor**
¿Se siente mejor hoy?
Do you feel better today?
Como se sentía mejor se levantó.
She was feeling better so she got up.

feel depressed ◊ **estar deprimido**
He estado deprimido. (male)
I have been depressed.

He estado deprimida. *(female)*
I have been depressed.

feel dizzy ◊ **sentirse mareado**
¿Se siente usted mareado algunas veces? (m)
¿Se siente usted mareada algunas veces? (f)
Do you ever feel dizzy?

feel faint ◊ **sentirse débil**
Llame si usted se siente débil.
Call if you feel faint.

feel hungry ◊ **sentir hambre**
Empecé a sentir hambre a eso de la
medianoche.
I started to feel hungry around midnight.

feel ill ◊ **sentirse enfermo**
Me siento enfermo.
I feel ill.

feel like eating ◊ **tener ganas de comer**
Tengo ganas de comer.
I feel like eating.

feel nauseated ◊ **sentir náuseas**
Mientras tiene dolor de cabeza, ¿siente
náuseas alguna vez?
*Do you ever feel nauseated when you have a
headache?*

feel numb ◊ **sentir entumecimiento**
¿Siente entumecimiento en alguna parte?
Do you feel numb anywhere?

feel pain ◊ **sentir dolor**
¿Le aviso cuando siento dolor?
Should I let you know when I feel pain?
¿Siente usted dolor cuando se pone de pie?
Do you feel pain when you stand?

feel very tired ◊ **sentir mucho cansancio**
He estado sintiendo mucho cansancio y
debilidad últimamente, doctor.
I've been feeling very tired lately, doctor.

feel weak ◊ **sentirse débil**
¿Todavía se siente débil?
Do you still feel weak?
Llame si usted se siente débil.
Call if you feel weak.

feel worse ◊ **sentirse peor**
Me siento peor.
I feel worse.

feeling of sadness ◊ **sensación de tristeza**
Lo invadió una sensación de tristeza.
A feeling of sadness came over him.

fill out the form ◊ **llenar el formulario**

Ahora usted tiene que llenar el formulario y
firmar aquí.
*Now you must fill out the form and sign
here.*
Tiene que llenar un formulario de entrada.
You have to fill out an admittance form.

fill the prescription ◊ **preparar la receta**
El farmacéutico le preparará la receta ahora.
*The pharmacist will fill your prescription
now.*

fill this prescription ◊ **dar esta receta**
¿Pudiera usted darme esta receta?
Could you fill this prescription?

fill up this bottle ◊ **llenar este frasco**
Cuando usted orine, llene este frasco y déselo
a la enfermera de guardia.
*When you urinate, fill up this bottle and
leave it with the head nurse.*

financial assistance ◊ **ayuda financiera**
¿Necesita usted ayuda financiera?
Do you need financial assistance?

first aid ◊ **primeros auxilios**
¿Por qué necesita primeros auxilios?
Why do you need first aid?

first daughter ◊ **primera hija**
Su primera hija nació por cesárea.
*Her first daughter was born by cesarean
section.*

first pregnancy ◊ **primer embarazo**
¿Es éste su primer embarazo?
Is this your first pregnancy?

first son ◊ **primer hijo**
Su primer hijo nació por cesárea.
Her first son was born by cesarean section.

fit with a catheter ◊ **poner una sonda**
Le pusieron una sonda.
He was fitted with a catheter.

flat feet ◊ **pies planos**
Tiene los pies planos.
She has flat feet.

follow a diet ◊ **seguir una dieta**
Usted tiene que seguir una dieta especial
porque tiene la presión alta.
*You have to follow a special diet because you
have high blood pressure.*

follow these instructions ◊ **seguir estas
instrucciones**
Siga estas instrucciones para acelerar la
curación y para prevenir más daño.

Follow these instructions to help healing and prevent further injury.

foot ◊ **pie**
Mide seis pies.
He is six feet tall.

foot of the bed ◊ **pie de la cama**
Este botón baja el pie de la cama.
This button lowers the foot of the bed.
El botón levanta el pie de la cama.
The button raises the foot of the bed.

for a week ◊ **por una semana**
Estuvo en la unidad de ciudado intensivo por una semana.
He was in the ICU for a week.

for a while ◊ **por un rato**
Muerda esta gasa por un rato.
Bite on this gauze for a while.

for about _____ minutes ◊ **por unos _____ minutos**
Usted puede levantarse por unos quince minutos esta tarde.
You may get up for about fifteen minutes this afternoon.

for an entire week ◊ **por una semana entera**
Deje de tomar las píldoras por una semana entera antes de comenzar a tomarlas de nuevo.
Stop taking the pills for an entire week before beginning to take them again.

for_____ days ◊ **por _____ días**
He estado enfermo por dos días.
I have been sick for two days.
Ha tenido fiebre por dos días.
He's had a fever for two days.

for many years ◊ **por muchos años**
Padeció de cáncer por muchos años.
She suffered from cancer for many years.

for old people ◊ **para ancianos**
Este hospital es para ancianos.
This hospital is for old people.

for _____ weeks ◊ **por _____ semanas**
Usted tiene que dejarse puesto el yeso por seis semanas.
The cast will remain on for six weeks.

for some days now ◊ **hace días que**
Hace días que ando mal del estómago.
I've been having trouble with my stomach for some days now.

four months pregnant ◊ **embarazada de cuatro meses**
Usted está embarazada de cuatro meses.
You are four months pregnant.

freeze to death ◊ **morir de frío**
Murieron de frío.
They froze to death.

frequently ◊ **a menudo**
¿Está usted ronco a menudo?
Are you frequently hoarse?

frequently ◊ **con (mucha) frecuencia**
¿Ocurre esto con frecuencia?
Does this occur frequently?
¿Le molesta el estómago con frecuencia?
Does your stomach bother you frequently?
¿Está orinando con mucha frecuencia?
Are you urinating frequently?

friend of mine ◊ **amigo mío, amiga mía**
La paciente es amiga mía.
The patient is a friend of mine.

from birth ◊ **de nacimiento**
Es sorda de nacimiento.
She's been deaf from birth.
Es ciego de nacimiento.
He's been blind from birth.

from + country or *city* ◊ **de + country** *or* **city**
Soy de México.
I'm from Mexico.
Es de Los Ángeles.
He's from Los Angeles.

fractured fibula ◊ **fractura de peroné**
Sufrió fractura de peroné.
He has a fractured fibula.

gasp for air ◊ **faltarle a uno el aire**
¿Siente a veces como que no puede respirar, como que le falta el aire?
Do you sometimes have difficulty in breathing, such as gasping for air?

get a bit of a tummy ◊ **volverse barrigón/barrigona**
Se está volviendo barrigona.
She's getting a bit of a tummy.

get a cramp in one's leg ◊ **acalambrarse la pierna**
Se me ha acalambrado la pierna.
I've got a cramp in my leg.
¿Se te ha acalambrado la pierna?
Do you have a cramp in your leg?

get ill ◊ **ponerse enfermo**

Se puso enferma.
She got ill.

get one's breath back ◊ **recobrar la respiración**
Espera que recobre la respiración.
Let me get my breath back.

get out of bed ◊ **salir de la cama**
Usted puede salir de la cama, pero no sin ayuda.
You may get out of bed, but not by yourself.

get sick ◊ **ponerse enfermo**
Se puso enferma.
She got sick.

get the measles ◊ **coger sarampión**
El niño cogió sarampión.
The child got the measles.

get worse ◊ **ir empeorando**
La paciente va empeorando.
The patient is getting worse.

gift shop ◊ **tienda de regalos**
Hay una tienda de regalos en el primer piso.
There is a gift shop on the first floor.

give a back rub ◊ **frotar la espalda**
Voy a frotarle la espalda.
I'm going to give you a back rub.

give a prescription ◊ **dar una receta**
La doctora le dará una receta.
The doctor will give you a prescription.

give birth ◊ **dar a luz**
Usted dio a luz a gemelos.
You gave birth to twins.
Dio a luz a una hermosa niña.
She gave birth to a beautiful girl.

give the following information ◊ **dar la información siguiente**
Si tiene trabajo, dé la información siguiente:
If you are employed, give the following information:

glasses of water; water ◊ **vasos de agua**
¿Cuántos vasos de agua toma al día?
How much water do you drink daily?

go back to bed ◊ **volver a la cama**
Ya es tiempo de volver a la cama.
It's time to go back to bed.

go gray ◊ **tener canas**
Ya tiene canas.
She is already beginning to go gray.

go to the bathroom ◊ **ir al cuarto de baño**

Llame cuando tenga que ir al cuarto de baño.
Call when you have to go to the toilet.

go to the delivery room ◊ **ir a la sala de partos**
Van a la sala de partos.
They are going to the delivery room.

go to the doctor ◊ **ir al médico**
Fue al médico porque no quedaba embarazada.
She went to the doctor because she couldn't get pregnant.
Tengo que hacer una cita para ir al médico.
I have to make an appointment to go to the doctor.

go to the toilet ◊ **ir al inodoro; ir al servicio**
Llame cuando tenga que ir al inodoro.
Call when you have to go to the toilet.
Llame cuando tenga que ir al servicio.
Call when you have to go to the toilet.

go upstairs ◊ **subir escaleras**
¿Le duele cuando sube escaleras?
Does it hurt when you go upstairs?
No suba escaleras.
Don't go upstairs.

ground floor ◊ **piso bajo; planta baja**
La cafetería está en el piso bajo.
The cafeteria is on the ground floor.
La sala de espera está en la planta baja.
The waiting room is on the ground floor.

group policy ◊ **póliza del grupo**
¿Cómo se llama el titular de la póliza del grupo?
What is the name of the group policy holder?

happy with ◊ **estar contento con**
¿Está usted contenta con su esposo?
Are you happy with your husband?
¿Está usted contento con su esposa?
Are you happy with your wife?

hard choices ◊ **decisiones difíciles**
Los médicos a veces tienen que tomar decisiones difíciles.
Doctors have to make hard choices sometimes.

has arrived ◊ **ha llegado**
La ambulancia ha llegado.
The ambulance has arrived.
La ambulancia no ha llegado.
The ambulance has not arrived.

have a baby ◊ **tener un hijo**
Voy a tener un hijo.
I'm going to have a baby.

have a bandage on one's arm ◊ **llevar el brazo vendado**
Llevaba el brazo vendado.
He had a bandage on his arm.

have a bellyache ◊ **doler la pancita**
Le duele la pancita.
She has a bellyache.

have a blister ◊ **salir una ampolla**
Me ha salido una ampolla en el pie.
I have a blister on my foot.

have a bowel movement ◊ **evacuar el vientre**
¿Ha habido sangre alguna vez cuando evacuó el vientre?
Has there ever been blood when you had a bowel movement?

have a cesarean ◊ **hacer una cesárea**
Le tuvieron que hacer una cesárea.
She had to have a cesarean.

have a chest cold ◊ **tener el pecho congestionado**
Tengo el pecho congestionado.
I've got a chest cold.

have a child ◊ **esperar un niño**
Espero un niño para mayo.
I'm having a baby in May.

have a cough ◊ **tener tos**
¿Ha tenido tos con la fiebre?
Has he had a cough with the fever?
Tengo una tos terrible.
I have a terrible cough.

have a discharge ◊ **tener secreciones**
¿Tiene secreciones en las orejas a veces?
Do you have a discharge from the ears at times?

have a headache ◊ **tener dolor de cabeza**
El paciente tiene dolor de cabeza.
The patient has a headache.

have a pain ◊ **doler**
Me duele la pierna.
I've got a pain in my leg.

have a splitting headache ◊ **tener un dolor de cabeza espantoso**
Tengo un dolor de cabeza espantoso.
I have a splitting headache.

have a tummyache ◊ **doler la pancita**
Le duele la pancita.
She has a tummyache.

have any abortions ◊ **tener abortos**
¿Ha tenido abortos la joven?
Has the young girl had any abortions?

have bleeding ◊ **tener hemorragia**
¿Tiene hemorragias que no son regulares?
Do you have any bleeding that is not regular?

have children ◊ **tener hijos**
¿Ha tenido usted hijos?
Have you had any children?
Tengo tres hijos.
I have three children.

have cravings for ◊ **antojarse + me/te/le/ etc.**
Cuando estaba embarazada se le antojaban las cosas más extrañas.
When she was pregnant, she had cravings for the strangest things.

have difficulty breathing ◊ **no poder respirar**
¿Siente a veces como que no puede respirar?
Do you sometimes have difficulty breathing?

have dizzy spells ◊ **tener vértigo**
¿Tiene usted vértigo alguna vez?
Do you ever have dizzy spells?

have gallstones ◊ **tener piedras en la vesícula**
También creo que tengo piedras en la vesícula porque me duele mucho el estómago.
I think I also have gallstones, because my stomach hurts a lot.

have gray hair ◊ **tener canas**
Ya tiene canas.
She already has gray hair.

have heart trouble ◊ **padecer del corazón**
¿Cuánto tiempo hace que padece del corazón?
How long have you had heart trouble?

have just ◊ **acabar de + infin**
Acabo de examinar a su hijo.
I have just examined your son.
Acabo de hablar con tu hermano.
I've just talked to your brother

have kidney stones ◊ **tener piedras en el riñón**
Tiene piedras en el riñón.
She has kidney stones.

have pain in/on ◊ **tener dolor en**
¿Tiene dolor en los muslos?
Do you have pain in your thighs?
¿Tiene dolor en las rodillas?
Do you have pain in your knees?

¿Tiene dolor en los tobillos?
Do you have pain in your ankles?
¿Tiene dolor en los talones? (**talón** is singular)
Do you have pain in your heels?

have pus ◊ **tener secreciones**
¿Tiene secreciones en las orejas a veces?
Do you have pus in your ears at times?

have swelling of ◊ **tener hinchazón de**
¿Ha tenido hinchazón de los tobillos?
Have you had swelling of the ankles?

have the flu ◊ **estar con gripe; estar engripado**
Mi hijo está engripado.
My son has the flu.
María está con gripe.
Mary has the flu.
Mary came down with the flu.

have to ◊ **tener que**
Tienes que guardar cama.
You have to stay in bed.

have trouble breathing ◊ **respirar con dificultad**
Respiraba con dificultad.
She was having trouble breathing.

have the measles ◊ **tener sarampión**
Su hijo tiene sarampión.
Your son has the measles.

have trouble with the stomach ◊ **andar mal del estómago**
Hace días que ando mal del estómago.
I've been having trouble with my stomach for some days now.

have you ever lost ...? ◊ **¿ha perdido alguna vez ...?**
¿Ha perdido alguna vez el conocimiento?
Have you ever lost consciousness?

hay fever ◊ **fiebre del heno**
¿Ha tenido fiebre del heno?
Have you ever had hay fever?

he/she burned himself/herself ◊ **se quemó**
¿Cómo se quemó?
How did he burn himself?
How did she burn herself?

he/she explained ... to us ◊ **nos explicó**
Nos explicó la situación.
He explained the situation to us.
Nos explicó cómo pudo suceder una cosa así.
He explained to us how a situation like this could happen.

120

he was killed by ◊ **lo mató**
Lo mató un coche.
He was killed by a car.

head of the bed ◊ **cabecera de la cama**
Es para controlar la cabecera de la cama.
It's for controlling the head of the bed.

headache ◊ **dolor de cabeza**
¿Cuánto tiempo ha tenido este dolor de cabeza?
How long has he had this headache?
¿Tiene usted dolores de cabeza?
Do you have headaches?
Mientras tiene dolor de cabeza, ¿siente náuseas alguna vez?
Do you ever feel nauseated while you have a headache?

heal up well ◊ **cicatrizar muy bien**
La herida le ha cicatrizado muy bien.
The wound has healed up well.

health ◊ **salud**
Es bueno para la salud.
It's good for your health.
Está preocupado por su salud.
He's worried about his health.

healthy and strong ◊ **sano y fuerte**
El niño creció sano y fuerte.
The child grew up healthy and strong.

health insurance ◊ **seguro de salud**
Tengo seguro de salud.
I have health insurance.
No tengo seguro de salud.
I don't have health insurance.

heavy sensation ◊ **sensación de pesadez**
¿Tiene una sensación de pesadez en el pecho?
Do you have a heavy sensation in your chest?

here is; here are ◊ **aquí tiene**
Aquí tiene para enjuagarse la boca.
Here is some mouthwash.

her/hers ◊ **de ella**
Tengo las gotas de ella
I have her drops.

high blood pressure ◊ **alta presión sanguínea**
¿Cuánto tiempo ha tenido alta presión sanguínea?
How long has he had high blood pressure?

high-risk person ◊ **persona de alto riesgo**
Un resultado negativo en una persona de alto riesgo no disminuye la importancia de practicar el sexo seguro.

*A negative result in a high-risk person
doesn't lessen the importance of safer sex
guidelines.*

his ◊ **de él**
Tengo las gotas de él.
I have his drops.

hoarse; be hoarse ◊ **ronco; estar ronco**
¿Tiene tos a veces, o está ronco sin estar
resfriado?
*Do you sometimes have a cough or are you
hoarse, without having a cold?*
¿Está usted ronco a menudo?
Are you frequently hoarse?

hope that ◊ **esperar que**
Espero que duerma bien esta noche.
I hope that you sleep well tonight.

hospital ◊ **hospital; ingresar**
Está en el hospital.
He's in the hospital.
Lo van a tener que ingresar.
He's going to have to go into the hospital.

hospital gown ◊ **bata del hospital**
Llevará solamente la bata del hospital.
You'll wear only the hospital gown.

hot soapy bath ◊ **baño jabonoso caliente**
Tómese una ducha o baño jabonoso caliente
usando jabón en abundancia.
*Take a shower or hot soapy bath using
liberal amounts of soap.*

how are ...? ◊ **¿cómo están ...?**
¿Cómo están sus hijos?
How are your children?

how can I ...? ◊ **¿en qué puedo ...?**
¿En qué puedo servirle?
How can I help you?

how deep ...? ◊ **¿cuánto de profundo ...?**
¿Cuánto de profundo es el tajo?
How deep is the cut?

how frequently ...? ◊ **¿con qué frecuencia ...?**
¿Con qué frecuencia se baña?
How frequently do you bathe?
¿Con qué frecuencia se ducha?
How frequently do you shower?

how high ◊ **cuán alto**
Vamos a ver cuán alta tiene la presión
sanguínea.
Let's see how high your blood pressure is.
Vamos a ver cuán alta tiene la tensión
arterial.
Let's see how high your blood pressure is.

how is ...? ◊ **¿cómo está ...?**
¿Cómo está su hijo?
How is your son?

how long ...? ◊ **¿cuánto tiempo ...?**
¿Cuánto tiempo ha vivido en Nueva York?
How long have you lived in New York?
¿Cuánto tiempo le dura el mareo? (m/f)
¿Cuánto tiempo te dura el mareo? (m/f/c)
How long have you felt dizzy?

how long ...? ◊ **¿cuánto tiempo hace que ...?**
¿Cuánto tiempo hace que tiene estos
síntomas?
How long have you had these symptoms?
¿Cuánto tiempo hace que tiene estos dolores?
How long have you had these pains?

how long ...? ◊ **¿desde cuándo ...?**
¿Desde cuándo tiene este salpullido?
How long have you had this rash?
¿Desde cuándo tiene este bulto?
How long have you had this growth?

how long have you had ...? ◊ **¿cuánto tiempo
ha tenido ...?**
¿Cuánto tiempo ha tenido este dolor?
How long have you had this pain?
¿Cuánto tiempo ha tenido este dolor de
cabeza?
How long has he had this headache?

how low ◊ **cuán bajo**
Vamos a ver cuán baja tiene la presión
sanguínea.
Let's see how low your blood pressure is.

how many days ...? ◊ **¿cuántos días ...?**
¿Cuántos días le duran?
How many days does it last?

how many weeks ...? ◊ **¿cuántas semanas ...?**
¿Cuántas semanas de embarazo tenía su hija
cuando tuvo el aborto inducido?
*How many weeks pregnant was your
daughter when she had the abortion?*

how often ...? ◊ **¿cada cuánto ...?**
¿Cada cuánto evacúa el vientre?
How often do you have a bowel movement?

how wide ...? ◊ **¿cuánto de ancho ...?**
¿Cuánto de ancho es el quiste?
How wide is the cyst?

hurt ◊ **hacer daño**
No voy a hacerle daño.
I will not hurt you.
Me he hecho daño en la espalda.
I've hurt my back.

hurt oneself ◊ **darse un golpe**
Te vas a dar un golpe.
You'll hurt yourself.

hypertension ◊ **presión alta**
¿Ha tenido presión alta?
Have you ever had hypertension?

I

I am going to leave ◊ **voy a dejar**
Voy a dejar la cuña sobre la mesa.
I am going to put the bedpan on the table.

I had already ◊ **ya yo había**
Ya yo había estudiado las radiografías.
I had already studied the X-rays.

I would like ◊ **me gustaría**
Me gustaría tener un hijo.
I would like to have a son.
Me gustaría tener una hija.
I would like to have a daughter.
Me gustaría casarme.
I would like to get married.

I'd like to consult ◊ **quisiera consultar con**
Quisiera consultar con mi familia.
I'd like to consult my family.

identity card ◊ **tarjeta de identificación**
¿Tiene usted tarjeta de identificación?
Do you have an identity card?

if you are employed ◊ **si tiene trabajo**
Si tiene trabajo, dé la información siguiente:
*If you are employed, give the following
   information.*

immediate family ◊ **miembros más cercanos
   de la familia**
No puede recibir visitas fuera de los miembros más cercanos de la familia.
*No visitors are allowed except the immediate
   family.*

implant a pacemaker ◊ **colocar un
   marcapasos**
Le colocaron un marcapasos.
They implanted a pacemaker in him.

improving ◊ **estar mejorando**
Usted tiene un poco de fiebre, pero está
mejorando.
*You have a little fever, but you are
   improving.*

in a few days ◊ **dentro de unos días**
El tubo se lo quitaremos dentro de unos días.
The tube will come out in a few days.

in any operation ◊ **en cualquier operación**
En cualquier operación hay un componente
   de riesgo.
There's an element of risk in any operation.

in case of emergency ◊ **en caso de emergencia**
Necesitamos alguna información en caso de
   emergencia.
*We need some information from you in case
   of emergency.*
A quién avisamos en caso de emergencia?
Whom do we notify in case of emergency?

in good health ◊ **gozar de buena salud**
¿Gozan de buena salud sus hijos?
Are your children in good health?

in one place ◊ **en un sólo lugar**
¿Se queda el dolor en un sólo lugar?
Does the pain stay in one place?

in the freezer ◊ **en el congelador**
No lo/los/la/las guarde en el congelador.
Do not keep in the freezer.

in the fridge; in the refrigerator ◊ **en la
   nevera**
Guarde la medicina en la nevera.
Keep the medicine in the fridge.

in the hospital ◊ **del hospital**
Es el mejor anestesiólogo del hospital.
He is the best anesthesiologist in the hospital.

in the meantime ◊ **mientras tanto**
Mientras tanto, tiene que descansar.
In the meantime, you must rest.

in the night ◊ **por la noche**
¿Se despierta usted por la noche para orinar?
Do you awaken in the night to urinate?
¿Se levanta usted de la cama para orinar por
   la noche?
Do you awaken in the night to urinate?

in two weeks ◊ **dentro de quince días; en
   quince días**
Haga usted una cita en la clínica para verme
   en quince días.
*Make an appointment to come back to the
   clinic to see me in two weeks.*
Regrese dentro de quince días.
Come back in two weeks.

indicate where it hurts you ◊ **indicar dónde le
   duele**
Por favor, indique dónde le duele.
Please indicate where it hurts you.

insect bites ◊ **picaduras de insectos**

¿Tiene usted alergia a las picaduras de insectos?
Are you allergic to insect bites?

insect bites ◊ **mordeduras de insectos**
¿Tiene usted alergia a las mordeduras de insectos?
Are you allergic to insect bites?

insulin injection; insulin shot ◊ **inyección de insulina**
Le puso una inyección de insulina.
She gave him an insulin injection.

intensive care ◊ **cuidado intensivo**
Por algún tiempo en el pasado, ¿ha estado enfermo o ha requerido cuidado intensivo?
Have you been ill or required intensive care for any amount of time in the past?

intercourse (have) ◊ **relaciones sexuales**
El sida se contrae por medio de las relaciones sexuales.
AIDS is contracted by having intercourse.

interested in ◊ **estar interesado en**
Doctor, estoy interesada en usar la píldora para control de la natalidad.
Doctor, I'm interested in using the pill for birth control.

is there anyone ... ?; is anybody ...? ◊ **¿hay alguien ...?**
¿Hay alguien en la familia con los mismos problemas?
Is there anyone in the family with the same problems?
¿Hay alguien más en la familia que esté afectado?
Is anybody else in the family affected?
¿Hay alguien más en la famlia que tenga picazón?
Is anybody else in the family itchy?

is mentally ill ◊ **volverse loco**
El paciente se volvió loco.
The patient is mentally ill.

it's just ◊ **no es más que**
No es más que un rasguño.
It's just a scratch.

it is necessary for/to ◊ **es necesario que + subj**
Es necerio que su hijo vaya al hospital.
It is necessary for your son to go to the hospital.

it is necessary to ◊ **es necesario + infin**
Es necesario ir al hospital.
It is necesary to go to the hospital.

it is not allowed ◊ **no se permite (que)**

No se permite que los niños visiten al paciente.
Children are not permitted to visit with the patient.
No se permite fumar.
Smoking is not allowed.

it will be a while yet ◊ **aún tardará**
Aún tardará en llegar.
It will be a while yet before he gets here.

it'll be several days before ◊ **tardarán varios días**
Tardarán varios días en darle los resultados.
It'll be several days before they give you the results.

it's making me ◊ **me está dando**
Me está dando una picazón.
It's making me itch.

it's time to ◊ **ya es tiempo de + infin**
Ya es tiempo de volver a la cama.
It's time to go back to bed.

IV in your arm ◊ **suero en el brazo**
El suero en el brazo es para darle alimento — azúcar, sal y agua.
The IV in your arm is to give you food — sugar, salt, and water.

junk food ◊ **comida basura**
No coma comida basura.
Don't eat junk food.

keep calm ◊ **mantener la calma**
Procure mantener la calma.
Try to keep calm.

keep the medicine ◊ **guardar las medicinas**
Siempre guarde las medicinas bajo llave.
Always keep the medicines locked away.

keep your knee straight ◊ **mantener la rodilla recta**
Usted debe mantener la rodilla recta para que tenga éxito la cirugía.
You must keep your knee straight for the surgery to be successful.

keep very clean ◊ **mantenerse muy limpio**
Es muy importante mantenerse muy limpio.
It is very important to keep very clean.

kidney infection ◊ **infección en los riñones**
Tengo una infección en los riñones

I have a kidney infection.

kidney stones ◊ **cálculos renales**
¿Ha tenido alguna vez cálculos renales?
Have you ever had kidney stones?

know the name of ◊ **saber el nombre de**
¿Sabe el nombre de la sustancia?
Do you know the name of the substance?

labor pains ◊ **dolores de parto**
Ya estaba con dolores de parto.
She was already having labor pains.

lack of ◊ **falta de**
Anuria es la falta de formación de orina por
   los riñones.
*Anuria is the lack of urine formation by the
   kidneys.*

last night ◊ **anoche**
Anoche volvió a casa muy tarde.
Last night she returned home very late.

later ◊ **más tarde**
Hablaré con usted más tarde.
I'll talk to you later.
Se lo explicaré a su familia más tarde.
I'll explain it to your family later.

learn how to ◊ **aprender a**
Usted tiene que aprender a enfrentar el estrés.
You must learn how to cope with stress.
Usted tiene que aprender a enfrentar las
   tensiones.
You must learn how to cope with stress.

leave a scar ◊ **dejar una cicatriz**
La herida le dejó una cicatriz.
The wound left her with a scar.

leave after ◊ **salir después de**
El especialista salió después de examinarle.
The specialist left after examining him

leave for ◊ **salir para**
Salieron para UCLA Harbor Medical
   Hospital.
*They left for UCLA Harbor Medical
   Hospital.*

left eye ◊ **ojo izquierdo**
El ojo izquierdo me duele.
My left eye hurts.
Perdió la visión del ojo izquierdo.
She lost the sight of her left eye.

left leg ◊ **pierna izquierda**

Levante usted la pierna izquierda.
Raise your left leg.

left side ◊ **lado izquierdo**
Favor de voltearse al lado izquierdo.
Please turn over on your left side.

left wrist ◊ **muñeca izquierda**
No, me duele la muñeca izquierda.
No, my left wrist hurts.

let me know when ◊ **avíseme cuando**
Avíseme cuando sienta dolor.
Let me know when you feel pain?

liberal amounts of soap ◊ **jabón en
   abundancia**
Tómese una ducha o baño jabonoso caliente
   usando jabón en abundancia.
*Take a shower or hot soapy bath using
   liberal amounts of soap.*

like (person); to like ◊ **caer bien**
Me cae bien la enfermera de guardia.
I like the nurse on duty.

live in ◊ **vivir en**
Vivo en el número doce de la calle quince.
I live at 12 Fifteenth street.

located on; be located in ◊ **hallarse en**
La capilla de los pacientes se halla en el piso
   principal.
*The patient's chapel is located on the main
   floor.*

locked away ◊ **bajo llave**
Siempre guarde las medicinas bajo llave.
Always keep the medicines locked away.

long period of rest ◊ **largo periodo de
   descanso**
Necesitas un largo periodo de descanso para
   recuperarte.
You need a long period of rest to convalesce.

look directly ◊ **mirar directo**
Mire directo a mi nariz.
Look directly at my nose.

look far away ◊ **mirar lejos**
Por favor, mire lejos.
Please look far away.

lose a child; have a miscarriage ◊ **perder un
   niño**
Perdió un niño en el embarazo.
She had a miscarriage.

lose blood ◊ **perder sangre**
El paciente va perdiendo sangre.
The patient is loosing blood.

Ha perdido mucha sangre.
She's lost a lot of blood.

lose one arm; have no arm ◊ **quedar manco**
Es manco de los dos brazos
He has no arms.
Quedó manco del brazo derecho.
He lost his right arm.

lose one's sight ◊ **perder la visión**
Perdió la visión del ojo izquierdo.
She lost the sight of her left eye.

lose weight ◊ **perder peso; bajar de peso**
Señora Rivera, su hijo necesita perder peso.
Mrs. Rivera, your son needs to lose weight.
Usted tiene que perder mucho peso.
You must lose a lot of weight.
Ha perdido mucho peso.
She's lost a lot of weight.
Tiene que bajar de peso porque la obesidad
  es peligrosa.
*He has to lose weight because obesity is
  dangerous.*

low back pain ◊ **dolores de la cintura**
¿Suele usted tener dolores de la cintura?
Do you ever have low back pain?

low blood pressure ◊ **baja presión sanguínea**
¿Cuánto tiempo ha tenido baja presión
  sanguínea?
How long has he had low blood pressure?

lower the bed ◊ **bajar la cama**
Este botón baja la cama.
This button lowers the bed.
¿Bajo la cama?
Shall I lower the bed?

lukewarm water ◊ **agua tibia**
Para cuidarla, lávela con agua tibia.
To care for it, wash it in lukewarm water.

lung cancer ◊ **cáncer de pulmón**
Tiene cáncer de pulmón.
She has lung cancer.

main floor ◊ **piso principal**
La capilla de los pacientes se halla en el piso
  principal.
*The patient's chapel is located on the main
  floor.*

make a fist ◊ **cerrar el puño**
Cierre el puño.
Make a fist.

Por favor, cierre el puño.
Please make a fist.

make an appointment ◊ **pedir una cita**
Llamé al médico para pedir una cita.
*I phoned the doctor to make an
  appointment.*

make someone pregnant ◊ **embarazar a
alguien**
¿Sabe si su marido embarazó a alguien antes
  de casarse con usted?
*Do you know if your husband made
  someone pregnant before marrying you?*

make the bed ◊ **arreglar la cama**
Voy a arreglarle la cama.
I'm going to make the bed.

marital status ◊ **estado civil**
¿Cuál es su estado civil?
What is your marital status?

married ◊ **estar casado**
¿Había estado casado su marido antes de
  casarse con usted?
*Was your husband married before marrying
  you?*

may be ◊ **poder pasar**
Pueden pasar de dos semanas a seis meses
  después de la exposición al virus VIH
  antes de que puedan ser detectados los
  anticuerpos en la sangre.
*It may be two weeks to six months after
  exposure to the HIV virus before antibodies
  can be detected in your blood.*

means of identification ◊ **medio de identificación**
Por favor, muéstreme cualquier medio de
  identificación que tenga.
*Please show me any means of identification
  you may have.*

medical examination ◊ **reconocimiento
médico; examen médico**
¿Cuándo fue la última vez que tuvo usted un
  reconocimiento médico?
*When was the last time that you had a
  medical examination?*
Se sometió a un examen médico.
He had a medical exam.

medicines that contain ◊ **medicina que
contiene**
No dé ninguna medicina que contenga
  aspirina.
*Do not give any medicines that contain
  aspirin.*

mental illness ◊ **enfermedad mental**

125

¿Alguna vez ha tenido una enfermedad mental algún miembro de la familia **del** paciente? (m)
¿Alguna vez ha tenido una enfermedad mental algún miembro de la familia de **la** paciente? (f)
Has anyone in the patient's family ever had a mental illness?

miscarriage ◊ **aborto espóntaneo**
¿Ha tenido usted algún aborto espóntaneo?
Have you had any miscarriages?

months to live ◊ **quedarle ... meses de vida**
Le quedaban tres meses de vida.
She had three months to live.

mouth to mouth resuscitation ◊ **respiración boca a boca**
Le hizo respiración boca a boca.
She gave him mouth to mouth resuscitation.

move your fingers ◊ **mover los dedos**
Por favor, mueva los dedos.
Please move your fingers.

move your legs ◊ **mover las piernas**
Por favor, mueva las piernas.
Please move your legs.

much pain ◊ **mucho dolor**
¿Siente mucho dolor?
Are you in much pain?

multiple births ◊ **partos múltiples**
¿Ha tenido usted partos múltiples?
Have you had multiple births?

must undergo ◊ **deber someterse a**
Debe someterse a un examen físico completo.
You must undergo a thorough physical exam.

my eyesight ◊ **mi vista**
Mi vista ya no es lo que era.
My eyesight is failing.

nasal passages ◊ **ventanas de la nariz**
Use el atomizador en las ventanas de la nariz diariamente.
Use the spray in your nasal passages daily.

near the end ◊ **ya cerca del final**
Ya cerca del final, le dirán que orine.
Near the end, you'll be asked to urinate.

necessary attention ◊ **cuidados necesarios**
UCLA Harbor es el hospital donde recibió los cuidados necesarios.

UCLA Harbor is the hospital where she received the necessary attention.

need ◊ **faltarle a uno**
Al doctor Pérez le falta el termómetro.
Dr. Pérez needs a thermometer.

need a nurse ◊ **necesitar los cuidados de una enfermera**
Tu mamá necesita los cuidados de una enfermera.
Your mother needs a nurse.

need a prescription ◊ **necesitar una receta**
¿Necesito una receta para comprarlas?
Do I need a prescription to buy them?

need help ◊ **necesitar ayuda**
Llame si usted necesita ayuda.
Call if you need help.

need to ◊ **hacer falta**
Le hace falta descansar.
He needs to rest.

neither ... nor ◊ **ni ... ni**
No encuentro ni el pulso de la carótida ni la respiración normal.
I find neither the carotid pulse nor normal breathing.

next week ◊ **la semana que viene**
Le haremos unos análisis la semana que viene.
We are taking some tests next week.
Usted tiene que regresar la semana que viene.
You have to return next week.

no longer ◊ **ya no**
Ya no tomo la medicina.
I no longer take the medicine.

no need to ◊ **no hacer falta**
No hace falta que se queden los dos.
There's no need for both of you to stay.

normal delivery ◊ **parto normal**
¿Fue un parto normal o usaron fórceps?
Was it a normal delivery or did they use instruments?

normal vision ◊ **visión normal**
¿Tiene su hijo visión normal?
Does your son have normal vision?

normally ◊ **por lo regular**
¿Cuánto pesa su hijo por lo regular?
How much does your son weigh normally?

not at all complicated ◊ **no ser nada complicada**
La recuperación no es nada complicada.

The recuperation is not at all complicated.

not doubt that ◊ **no dudar que**
No dudo que ella ha ingresado al hospital.
I don't doubt that she has been admitted to the hospital.

not eat ◊ **no comer**
No coma nada frito.
Don't eat anything fried.

not feel well ◊ **sentirse mal**
Me siento mal.
I don't feel well.

not keep ◊ **no guardar**
No guardar en el congelador.
Do not keep in the freezer.

not know why ◊ **no saber por qué**
No sé por qué está enfermo.
I don't know why you are ill.

not take; not drink ◊ **no tomar**
No tome las píldoras.
Don't take the pills.
No tome alcohol con esto.
Don't drink alcohol with this.
Se sentía mejor de manera que no tomó las aspirinas.
She felt better so she didn't take the aspirins.

not turn ◊ **no voltearse**
No se voltee sin llamar a la enfermera.
Do not turn without calling the nurse.

not want to eat ◊ **no querer comer**
Su hija tiene mucha diarrea y no quiere comer.
Your daughter has a bad case of diarrhea, and she doesn't want to eat.

not worry ◊ **no preocuparse**
No se preocupe. Esta medicina le ayudará.
Don't worry. This medicine will help you.
No se preocupe mucho por la operación.
Don't worry too much about the operation.

notify immediately ◊ **avisar enseguida**
Avíseme usted enseguida si hay un cambio en el color de la piel de los dedos.
Notify me immediately if there is a change in the skin color of the fingers.

numbness of ◊ **adormecimiento de**
¿Ha tenido adormecimiento de los miembros?
Have you had numbness in your arms or legs?

nurse on duty ◊ **enfermera de guardia**
Me cae bien la enfermera de guardia.

I like the nurse on duty.

often ◊ **muchas veces**
Muchas veces tengo catarro.
I often have a cold.

on admission ◊ **al ingresar**
¿Cuál fue el diagnóstico al ingresar?
What was the diagnosis on admission?

on his/her face ◊ **en la cara**
Tiene varios cortes en la cara.
He has several cuts on his face.

on one's stomach; face down ◊ **boca abajo**
Por favor, acuéstese boca abajo.
Please lie on your stomach.
Duerme boca abajo.
He sleeps on his stomach.
Échate boca abajo.
Lie on your stomach.
Póngase usted boca abajo, por favor.
Please turn face down.

on one's back; face up ◊ **boca arriba**
Duerme boca arriba.
He sleeps on his back.
Póngase usted boca arriba, por favor.
Please turn face up.

on the date that ◊ **en la fecha en que**
Un resultado negativo es válido solamente en la fecha en que la muestra fue obtenida.
A negative test result is negative only on the date that the blood specimen was obtained.

on the table ◊ **sobre la mesa**
Acuéstese sobre la mesa.
Lie down on the table.
Voy a dejar la cuña sobre la mesa.
I am going to put the bed pan on the table.

on the way out ◊ **a la salida**
A la salida coje un folleto.
Pick up a leaflet on the way out.

on your left side ◊ **sobre el lado izquierdo**
Acuéstese sobre el lado izquierdo.
Turn on your left side.

on your right side ◊ **sobre el lado derecho**
Acuéstese sobre el lado derecho.
Turn on your right side.

one hundred two degrees (102°) ◊ **ciento dos grados**
La fiebre del niño está a ciento dos grados.

The child's fever is 102°.

one must not ◊ **no deber** + infin
No debe comer nada después de la
  medianoche.
You must not eat anything after midnight.
No debe tomar ningún líquido después de la
  medianoche.
*You must not drink any liquids after
  midnight.*

one's own room ◊ **propio cuarto**
Cuando vuelva a su propio cuarto, dígale a
  la enfermera si quiere comer.
*When you are back in your own room, tell
  the nurse if you want to eat.*

open the window ◊ **abrir la ventana**
¿Abro la ventana?
Shall I open the window?
La enfermera abrirá la ventana ahora.
The nurse will open the window now.

open your mouth ◊ **abrir la boca**
Abra la boca bien grande, por favor.
Open your mouth wide, please.

operating room ◊ **sala de operaciones**
La sala de operaciones está a la izquierda.
The operating room is to the left.

operation ◊ **intervención quirúrgica**
Fue sometido a una intervención quirúrgica.
He underwent an operation.
He had an operation.

out of breath ◊ **sin respiración**
Llegó sin respiración.
He was out of breath when he arrived.

over the last few days ◊ **durante los últimos
  días**
Su condición ha empeorado durante los
  últimos días.
*His condition has worsened over the last few
  days.*

own one's own home ◊ **tener casa propia**
¿Alquila usted o tiene casa propia?
Do you rent or own your own home?

painless ◊ **ningún dolor**
No causa ningún dolor.
It's painless.

pains in your chest ◊ **dolores en el pecho**
¿Tiene usted dolores en el pecho?
Do you have pains in your chest?

Parkinson's disease ◊ **enfermedad de
  Parkinson**
¿Ha padecido usted alguna vez de la
  enfermedad de Parkinson?
Have you ever had Parkinson's disease?

people who suffer from ◊ **los enfermos de**
Tienen cien camas para los enfermos de
  cáncer.
*They have one hundred beds for people who
  suffer from cancer.*

perfectly still ◊ **completamente inmóvil**
Quédese completamente inmóvil.
Remain perfectly still.

permanent address ◊ **dirección permanente**
¿Es ésta su dirección permanente?
Is this your permanent address?

physical examination ◊ **reconocimiento físico**
¿Cuándo fue la última vez que tuvo usted un
  reconocimiento físico?
*When was the last time that you had a
  physical examination?*

physical exercise ◊ **ejercicios físicos**
Evite ejercicios físicos.
Avoid physical exercise.

pick up a leaflet ◊ **coger un folleto**
A la salida coja un folleto.
Pick up a leaflet on the way out.

point to the part of ◊ **señalar la parte de**
Señale la parte del cuerpo donde empezó.
*Point to the part of your body where it
  began.*

policy holder ◊ **dueño de la póliza**
¿Cuál es el nombre completo del dueño de la
  póliza?
*What is the complete name of the policy
  holder?*

poor memory ◊ **mala memoria**
Si usted tiene mala memoria, su médico
  puede recetarle una serie de píldoras.
*If you have poor memory, your doctor may
  prescribe a series of pills for you.*

pregnancy and delivery ◊ **embarazo y parto**
¿Cómo fue su embarazo y parto?
How was your pregnancy and delivery?

pregnant ◊ **estar embarazada**
Usted está embarazada de 4 meses.
You are 4 months pregnant.

pregnant; be pregnant ◊ **estar encinta**
La joven fue violada y ahora está encinta.

128

The young girl was raped and now she is pregnant.

pregnant again ◊ **preñada otra vez**
Estás preñada otra vez
Your'e pregnant again.

pregnant with; she was expecting ◊ **estar embarazada de**
Estaba embarazada de su segundo hijo.
She was pregnant with her second child.
She was expecting her second child.

premature birth ◊ **parto prematuro**
¿Fue un parto prematuro?
Was it a premature birth?

prescribe the pills ◊ **recetar las píldoras**
El médico le recetará las píldoras ahora.
The doctor will prescribe the pills now.

prescribed drugs ◊ **drogas recetadas**
¿Usa el paciente drogas no recetadas por el médico?
Does the patient use any drugs not prescribed by the doctor?

present illness ◊ **problema actual**
Por favor, describa su problema actual.
Please describe your present illness.

present weight ◊ **peso actual**
Es importante mantener su peso actual.
It's important to maintain your present weight.

press the button ◊ **oprimir el botón**
Si usted necesita algo, oprima el botón.
If you need anything, press the button.

problems with your eyesight ◊ **problemas de la vista**
¿Ha tenido problemas de la vista?
Have you had problems with your eyesight?

public health nurse ◊ **enfermera de salud pública**
Soy la enfermera de salud pública.
I'm the public health nurse.

puff and pant ◊ **dar resoplidos**
El paciente llegó dando resoplidos.
The patient arrived puffing and panting.

pump (someone's) stomach ◊ **hacer un lavado de estómago; lavar el estómago**
No hay nadie que le haga un lavado de estómago.
There is no one who will pump his stomach.
Le lavaron el estómago.
He had his stomach pumped.

put a pillow ◊ **poner una almohada**
Le voy a poner una almohada debajo.
I'm going to put a pillow under you.

put a splint on; put in a splint ◊ **entablillar +** body part
Le entablillaron la pierna.
They put a splint on his leg.

put to sleep ◊ **poner a dormir**
Soy el doctor Smith. Lo voy a poner a dormir mañana para que los médicos puedan realizar la operación.
I am Dr. Smith. I am going to put you to sleep tomorrow so the doctors can do the operation.

put your gum to sleep ◊ **anestesiar la encía**
Voy a ponerle una inyección para anestesiar la encía.
I am going to give you a shot to put your gum to sleep.

quench one's thirst ◊ **quitar la sed**
El agua le quitó la sed.
The water quenched his thirst.

quite high ◊ **bastante alto**
Su presión arterial está bastante alta.
Your blood pressure is quite high

raise one's hips ◊ **levantar las caderas**
Levante las caderas, por favor.
Please raise your hips.

raise the bed ◊ **levantar la cama**
Este botón levanta la cama.
This button raises the bed.
¿Levanto la cama?
Shall I raise the bed?

rash on your face ◊ **erupción en la cara**
¿Desde cuándo tienes esta erupción en la cara?
How long have you had this rash on your face?

reach ◊ **alcanzar con las manos**
¿Alcanza con las manos algún objeto?
Does he reach for objects?

receive a blow to ◊ **recibir algún golpe en**
¿Ha recibido algún golpe en la cabeza?
Have you received a blow to the head?

129

recover one's salary ◊ **reponer el sueldo**

¿Cómo va a reponer su salario si tiene que ingresar en el hospital?
How will you recover your salary if you have to go to the hospital?

recovery room ◊ **sala de recuperación**
Después de nacer su niño, se la llevarán a la sala de recuperación.
After the baby is born, you will be taken to the recovery room.

recurrent fears ◊ **temores frecuentes**
¿Tiene usted temores frecuentes?
Do you have recurrent fears?

reduce the swelling ◊ **reducir la hinchazón**
Mantenga el brazo lastimado levantado y haga ejercicios con los dedos para reducir la hinchazón.
Keep the injured arm elevated and exercise the fingers to reduce the swelling.

reduce to a minimum the risk ◊ **reducir al mínimo el riesgo**
Con esto se intenta reducir al mínimo el riesgo de infección.
This is intended to reduce to a minimum the risk of infection.

refrain from handling ◊ **evitar tocar**
En todo momento los visitantes deben evitar tocar los objetos en su cuarto.
Your visitors should refrain from handling things in your room.

remain in bed ◊ **permanecer en cama; guardar cama**
Usted debe permanecer en cama hoy.
You are to remain in bed today.
remain in bed ◊
Usted debe guardar cama hoy.
You are to remain in bed today.
Tienes que guardar cama.
You have to stay in bed.
El médico le mandó guardar cama.
The doctor told her to stay in bed.

remove the appendix ◊ **extirpar el apéndice; sacar el apéndice**
Le extirparon el apéndice.
She had her appendix removed.
Vamos a sacarle el apéndice.
We are going to remove your appendix.

remove the gall-bladder ◊ **sacar la vesícula biliar**
Vamos a sacarle la vesícula biliar.
We are going to take out your gall-bladder.

remove the gallstones ◊ **sacar los cálculos**
Vamos a sacarle los cálculos.
We are going to remove your gallstones.

remove the left breast ◊ **extirpar el seno izquierdo**
Le extirparon el seno izquierdo.
She had her left breast removed.

respiratory complaint ◊ **insuficiencia respiratoria**
Sufre de insuficiencia respiratoria.
He has a respiratory complaint.

rest more ◊ **descansar más**
Es necesario descansar más.
It is necessary to rest more.

rest one's chin ◊ **apoyar el mentón**
Apoye el mentón aquí.
Rest your chin here.

results of the test ◊ **resultado de la prueba**
Los resultados de la prueba se enviarán a su médico.
The results of the test will be sent to your doctor.

return tomorrow ◊ **regresar mañana**
Si la fiebre no baja, debe regresar mañana.
If the fever doesn't go down, you must return tomorrow.

Rh blood factor ◊ **factor Rh**
¿Cuál es el factor Rh suyo?
What is your Rh blood factor?

right breast ◊ **seno derecho**
Le extirparon el seno derecho.
She had her right breast removed.

right ear ◊ **oído derecho**
Hay pus y sangre en el oído derecho.
There's pus and blood in his right ear.

right leg ◊ **pierna derecha**
Suba usted la pierna derecha.
Raise your right leg.

right now ◊ **ahora mismo**
El médico está examinando a su hija ahora mismo.
The doctor is examining your daughter right now.

right side ◊ **lado derecho**
Favor de voltearse al lado derecho.
Please turn over on your right side.

right wrist ◊ **muñeca derecha**
¿Le duele la muñeca derecha?
Does your right wrist hurt?

roll up your sleeve ◊ **subirse la manga**
Favor de subirse la manga.
Please roll up your sleeve.

rub oneself with ◊ **frotarse con**
Frótese con alcohol.
Rub yourself with alcohol.

runny nose ◊ **escurrimiento de la nariz**
Y también ha tenido escurrimiento de la
    nariz.
And he has also had a runny nose

sanitary pads ◊ **toallas higiénicas**
¿Cuántas toallas higiénicas ha usado usted en
    su última menstruación?
*How many sanitary pads did you use during
    your last menstrual cycle?*

say "ah" ◊ **decir "ah"**
Favor de sacar la lengua y decir "ah".
Please stick your tongue out and say "ah"

scarlet fever ◊ **fiebre escarlatina**
¿Ha tenido fiebre escarlatina?
Have you ever had scarlet fever?

second floor ◊ **segundo piso**
Hay una sala de espera en el segundo piso.
There is a waiting room on the second floor.

second or third day ◊ **segundo o tercer día**
Su regla comenzará el segundo o tercer día
    después de comenzar las píldoras rosadas.
*Your period will begin on the second or third
    day after you begin the pink pills.*

second pregnancy ◊ **segundo embarazo**
¿Es su segundo embarazo?
Is this your second pregnancy?

see the doctor ◊ **ir al médico; ver al médico**
Veía al médico cada día.
I used to see the doctor every day.
Fue al médico porque no quedaba
    embarazada.
*She saw the doctor because she couldn't get
    pregnant.*
Tengo que hacer una cita para ir al médico.
*I have to make an appointment to see the
    doctor.*

sell for ◊ **venderse a**
Las curitas se venden a 25 centavos la
    docena.
The bandages sell for 25 cents a dozen.

seriously ill ◊ **gravemente enfermo**
Está gravemente enfermo.
He is seriously ill.

serve breakfast ◊ **servir el desayuno**
Se sirve el desayuno a las ocho de la mañana.

Breakfast is served at 8 A.M.

serve lunch ◊ **servir el almuerzo**
Se sirve el almuerzo a las once y media.
Lunch is served at 11:30.

serve supper ◊ **servir la cena**
Se sirve la cena a las cinco de la tarde.
Dinner is served at 5 P.M.

severe menstrual cramps ◊ **dolores fuertes del
    periodo**
¿Sufre usted de dolores fuertes del periodo?
Do you have severe menstrual cramps?

shake the bottle ◊ **agitar la botella**
Es importante no agitar la botella.
It's important not to shake the bottle.
No agite la botella.
Do not shake the bottle.

she was killed by ◊ **la mató**
La mató un coche.
She was killed by a car.

shine a light in your eyes ◊ **iluminarle los
    ojos**
Voy a iluminarle los ojos con una lámpara.
*I'm going to shine a light in your eyes with a
    lamp.*

shoot oneself ◊ **matarse de un tiro**
Se mató de un tiro.
He shot himself.

short of breath ◊ **faltar el aire**
¿Le falta el aire?
Are you short of breath?

shortly ◊ **dentro de unos minutos**
Le atenderemos dentro de unos minutos.
We'll be with you shortly.

should subside rapidly ◊ **deber pasar pronto**
El dolor de su herida debe pasar pronto.
*The pain of your injury should subside
    rapidly.*

should undergo ◊ **deber someterse a**
Debe someterse a un examen físico completo.
*You should undergo a thorough physical
    exam.*

sick; be ill; suffer with; have trouble ◊ **estar
    enfermo**
No sé por qué está enfermo.
I don't know why you are sick.
Está enferma de los nervios.
She suffers with her nerves.

side rails ◊ **barandillas laterales**
La cama no tiene barandillas laterales.

The bed does not have side rails.

signs of tiredness ◊ **muestra de cansancio**
No daba muestra alguna de cansancio.
She was showing no signs of tiredness.

since birth ◊ **de nacimiento**
Es sorda de nacimiento.
She's been deaf since birth.
Es ciego de nacimiento.
He's been blind since birth.

since I was a child ◊ **desde niño**
La conozco desde niño.
I've known her since I was a child.

since last night ◊ **desde anoche**
No he comido nada desde anoche.
I haven't eaten anything since last night.

since when ...? ◊ **¿desde cuándo ...?**
¿Desde cuándo tiene este salpullido?
Since when have you had this rash?
¿Desde cuándo tiene este bulto?
Since when have you had this growth?

single or married ◊ **soltero o casado**
¿Es usted soltero o casado? (male)
¿Es usted soltera o casada? (female)
Are you single or married?

situated in; be located in ◊ **hallarse situado en**
El hospital se halla situado en las afueras de la ciudad.
The hospital is located on the outskirts of the city.

skin cancer ◊ **cáncer de piel**
¿Hay alguien en su familia que padezca de cáncer de piel?
Does anyone in your family have skin cancer?

skin problems ◊ **problemas de piel**
¿Ha tenido problemas de piel?
Have you had any skin problems?

slash one's wrists ◊ **cortarse las venas**
El paciente se cortó las venas.
The patient cut his wrists.

sleep; fall asleep; go to sleep ◊ **dormir; dormirse**
Usted se dormirá dentro de poco y estará dormido durante la cirugía.
You will fall asleep soon and be asleep during surgery.
Se durmió hacia las tres de la madrugada.
She went to sleep at about three in the morning.
No dormí nada.

I didn't sleep a wink.
Trata de dormir un poco.
Try to get some sleep.
Necesito dormir por lo menos ocho horas.
I need at least eight hours sleep.

sleeping ◊ **estar durmiendo**
Su hijo está durmiendo.
Your son is sleeping.

sleeping pill ◊ **pastilla para dormir**
¿Necesita usted una pastilla para dormir?
Do you need a sleeping pill?

so ◊ **de manera que**
Se sentía mejor de manera que no tomó las aspirinas.
She felt better so she didn't take the aspirins.

some discomfort ◊ **alguna molestia**
Le advirtieron que sentiría alguna molestia después de la operación.
He was told to expect some discomfort after the operation.

some drops ◊ **unas gotas**
Voy a poner unas gotas en sus ojos para dilatar las pupilas.
I'm going to put some drops in your eyes to dilate your pupils.

someone can ◊ **alguien puede**
Creo que alguien puede ayudarme.
I believe someone can help me.

sometimes ◊ **algunas veces**
¿Siente a veces como que no puede respirar, como que le falta el aire?
Do you sometimes have difficulty in breathing, such as gasping for air?
¿Tiene tos a veces, o está ronco sin estar resfriado?
Do you sometimes have a cough or are you hoarse, without having a cold?
¿Le duele algunas veces el estómago después de comer?
Does your stomach hurt sometimes after eating?

somewhat difficult; rather difficult ◊ **algo difícil**
La operación es algo difícil.
The operation is rather difficult.

soon; shortly ◊ **dentro de poco**
El médico llegará dentro de poco.
The doctor will arrive soon.
La enfermera le llamará dentro de poco.
The nurse will call you shortly.

sore arm ◊ **brazo dolorido**
Tengo el brazo muy dolorido.

I've got a very sore arm.

sour taste ◊ **sabor agrio**
¿Siente usted un sabor agrio de boca?
Do you have a sour taste in your mouth?

spit blood; spit up blood ◊ **escupir sangre**
¿Escupe el niño sangre?
Does the child spit blood?
¿Escupe usted sangre?
Do you spit up blood?

splint to protect ◊ **tablilla para proteger** ≈
Ésta es una tablilla para proteger la mano.
This is a splint to protect your hand.

spread to the liver ◊ **comprometer el hígado**
El cáncer ya le ha comprometido el hígado.
The cancer has spread to the liver.

stand up ◊ **ponerse de pie**
Por favor, póngase de pie.
Please stand up.
Mañana usted tiene que ponerse de pie.
Tomorrow you have to stand up.

start to ◊ **ya empezar a** + infin
El cirujano ya empieza a operar.
The surgeon is starting to operate now.

stick the tongue out ◊ **sacar la lengua**
Saca la lengua y dí "ah."
Stick out your tongue and say "ah."
Por favor, saca la lengua y decir "ah".
Please stick your tongue out and say "ah"

still do not know ◊ **todavía no saber**
Todavía no sé exactamente lo que usted tiene.
I still don't know exactly what is wrong with you.

stop breastfeeding ◊ **dejar de tomar el pecho**
¿A qué edad dejó de tomar el pecho?
At what age did he/she stop breastfeeding?

stop smoking; quit smoking ◊ **dejar de fumar**
Usted tiene que dejar de fumar.
You have to stop smoking.

stop; quit ◊ **dejar de** + infin
Deje de tomar las píldoras por una semana entera antes de comenzar a tomarlas de nuevo.
Stop taking the pills for an entire week before beginning to take them again.
Está resuelto a dejar de fumar.
He is determined to stop smoking.

strain of ◊ **predisposición a**

Hay una predisposición a los trastornos nerviosos en la familia.
There's a strain of nervous disorder in the family.

strain the eyes ◊ **cansarse la vista**
Se le cansa la vista.
It strains her eyes.

strep throat ◊ **inflamación de garganta**
¿Ha tenido alguna vez una inflamación de garganta?
Have you ever had strep throat?

stuffed nose ◊ **nariz obstruida**
¿Tiene usted la nariz obstruida?
Do you have a stuffed nose?

suffer from; have trouble with ◊ **padecer de**
La mujer padece de hepatitis.
The woman suffers from hepatitis.
Padecía de los nervios.
I had nerve problems.
Su hija padece de paperas.
Your daughter suffers from the mumps.

suffer from a cough ◊ **sufrir de tos**
El paciente sufre de tos.
The patient suffers from a cough.

suffer from nervousness ◊ **sufrir de nervios**
Usted sufre de nervios.
You are suffering from nervousness.

suffer head injuries ◊ **sufrir un encefalocraneano**
El paciente sufrió un encefalocraneano.
The patient suffered head injuries.

sunscreen ◊ **filtro solar**
¿Usa filtro solar regularmente?
Do you wear sunscreen regurlarly?

swollen ankles ◊ **tobillos hinchados**
¿Tiene usted los tobillos hinchados por la mañana al despertarse?
Are your ankles swollen in the morning when you awaken?

take a break; have a rest ◊ **tomar un respiro**
Estoy agotado, voy a tomar un respiro.
I'm exhausted, I'm going to take a break.

take deep breath ◊ **respirar hondo; respirar profundamente;**
Por favor, respire hondo
Please take a deep breath.

Respire profundamente y sostenga la respiración.
Take a deep breath and hold it.

take a test (of) ◊ **hacer una prueba de**
También vamos a hacer una prueba de tuberculosis.
We are also going to take a tuberculin test.

take a tub bath ◊ **bañarse en la bañadera**
¿Le gustaría bañarse en la bañadera?
Would you like to take a tub bath?

take all precautions ◊ **tomar todas la precauciones**
Se debe tomar todas la precauciones de no infectar a otros o de reinfectarse a sí mismo.
One should, however, take all precautions not to infect others or re-infect oneself.
Su enfermedad se puede transmitir a otras personas y hay que tomar todas las precauciones posibles para evitarlo.
Your illness may be transmitted to others, and all precautions will be taken to avoid this possibility.

take an X-ray; have an X-ray ◊ **sacar una radiografía; hacer una radiografía**
Voy a tener que hacerle una radiografía.
I will have to take an X-ray.
Me sacaron una radiografía de tórax.
I had a chest X-ray.

take drugs ◊ **tomar drogas**
Dime, ¿cuánto tiempo hace que tomas drogas, Mario?
Tell me, how long have you been taking drugs, Mario?
Creo que mi hija toma drogas.
I think that my daughter is taking drugs.

take effect ◊ **hacer efecto**
Tendrá que esperar dos o tres horas para que la inyección haga efecto.
You will have to wait from two to three hours for the injection to take effect.

take medication ◊ **tomar medicina**
¿Qué medicinas está tomando ahora?
What medications are you taking at present?

take the medicine ◊ **tomar la medicina**
Tome la medicina después de las comidas.
Take the medicine after meals.
Usted va a tener que tomar la medicina.
You are going to have to take the medicine.

take the pulse ◊ **tomar el pulso**
Déjeme tomarle el pulso. (adult)
Let me take your pulse.
Déjame tomarte el pulso. (minor)

134

Let me take your pulse.

take to emergency ◊ **llevar a la sala de guardia; llevar a urgencias**
La ambulancia lo llevó a la sala de guardia.
The ambulance rushed him to emergency.
La ambulancia lo llevó a urgencias.
The ambulance rushed him to emergency.

talk to; talk with ◊ **hablar con; consultar con**
La doctora está hablando con tu tía.
The doctor is talking to your aunt.
Acabo de hablar con tu hermana.
I've just talked to your sister.
Quisiera consultar con mi familia.
I'd like to talk to my family.
Tendré que consultar con mi esposa.
I'll have to talk with my wife about it.
¿Por qué no consulta usted con un especialista?
Why don't you talk to a specialist?

taste sweet ◊ **saber dulce**
Sabe muy dulce.
It tastes very sweet.

teething ◊ **salir los dientes**
Le están saliendo los dientes.
He is teething.

tell me which ◊ **dígame cuál**
Dígame cuál de las manos se está moviendo.
Tell me which one of my hands is moving.

terminate the pregnancy ◊ **interrumpir el embarazo**
Decidió interrumpir el embarazo.
She decided to terminate the pregnancy.

terrible cough ◊ **tos terrible**
Tengo una tos terrible.
I have a terrible cough.

test result ◊ **resultado del análisis; resultado de la prueba**
El resultado del análisis fue positivo.
The result of the test was positive.
Los resultados de la prueba se enviarán a su médico.
The test result will be sent to your doctor.

tetanus shot ◊ **vacuna para el tétano**
¿Cuándo recibió su última vacuna para el tétano?
When was your last tetanus shot?

than usual ◊ **de lo ordinario**
¿Sangró usted más de lo ordinario?
Did you bleed more than usual?

the care of; need a; be taken care of by ◊ **los cuidados de**
Tu padre necesita los cuidados de una enfermera.
Your father needs a nurse.
Your father needs to be taken care of by a nurse.

the pulse becomes irregular ◊ **alterar el pulso**
Se le alteró el pulso.
The pulse became irregular.

there are pills to ◊ **hay pastillas para**
Hay pastillas para detener la picazón.
There are pills to stop the itching.

there is little chance of ◊ **es poco el riesgo de que**
La prueba es muy exacta y es poco el riesgo de que haya un resultado positivo falso.
The test is extremely accurate and there is little chance of a false-positive test result.

these symptoms ◊ **estos síntomas**
¿Cuánto tiempo hace que tiene estos síntomas?
How long have you had these symptoms?

they have given; they have given … to ◊ **le han puesto**
Le han puesto una inyección a su hijo.
They have given your son an injection.
They have given an injection to your son.

they have given you ◊ **te han puesto**
¿Te han puesto una inyección?
Have they given you an injection?

third floor ◊ **tercer piso**
Hay una sala de espera en el tercer piso.
There is a waiting room on the third floor.

touch the knee ◊ **tocar la rodilla**
Voy a tocarle la rodilla con un instrumento.
I am going to touch your knee with an instrument.

third pregnancy ◊ **tercer embarazo**
¿Es su tercer embarazo?
Is this your third pregnancy?

this afternoon ◊ **esta tarde**
Usted puede levantarse por unos diez minutos esta tarde.
You may get up for about ten minutes this afternoon.

this year ◊ **este año**
¿Cómo está su salud este año?
How is your health this year?

this will last; this will take ◊ **esto durará**
Esto durará unos diez minutos.

This will last about ten minutes.

thorough medical examination ◊ **examinado a fondo**
Será examinado a fondo por el médico.
He will undergo a thorough medical examination.

through your nose ◊ **por la nariz**
Tengo que ponerle este tubo por la nariz dentro del estómago.
I have to put this tube through your nose into your stomach.

thyroid test ◊ **análisis de tiroides**
Para el análisis de tiroides voy a sacarle sangre de la vena.
For the thyroid test I'm going to draw blood from the vein.

tightly ◊ **con fuerza**
Apriete usted mis manos con fuerza.
Grip my hands tightly.

tired feet ◊ **pies cansados**
Tengo los pies cansados.
My feet are tired.

to be just ◊ **no ser más que**
No es más que un rasguño.
It's just a scratch.

to be well ◊ **andar bien de salud**
No anda muy bien de salud.
He's not doing very well.

to become ◊ **llegar a ser**
Mi hijo llegó a ser médico.
My son became a doctor.
Por fin llegó a ser el director del hospital.
He finally became the director of the hospital.

to become ◊ **Ponerse + adjective**
El paciente se pone nervioso en el ascensor.
The patient becomes nervous in the elevator.
El paciente se puso muy delgado.
The patient became very thin.
Cuando la vio se puso muy contento.
He became very happy when he saw her.

to die of ◊ **morirse de**
Se murió de un infarto.
She died of a heart attack.

to take an aspirin ◊ **tomar una aspirina**
Tome una aspirina y acuéstese.
Take an aspirin and go to bed.

to the left ◊ **a la izquierda**
El ascensor está a la izquierda.
The elevator is to the left.

135

to the right ◊ **a la derecha**
La fuente de agua potable está a la derecha.
The drinking fountain is to the right.

to your pharmacist ◊ **a su farmacéutico**
Lleve esta receta a su farmacéutico.
Take the prescription to your pharmacist.

toe ◊ **dedo del pie**
Se rompió un dedo del pie.
He broke a toe.

too high ◊ **demasiado alto**
Su presión arterial es demasiado alta.
Your blood pressure is too high.

too many visitors ◊ **demasiadas visitas**
Hay demasiadas visitas en el cuarto.
There are too many visitors in the room.

tooth that hurts you ◊ **diente que le duele**
Indique cuál es el diente que le duele.
Point to the tooth that hurts you.

total rest ◊ **descanso total**
El médico recomienda descanso total.
The doctor recommends complete rest.

treated ◊ **estar en tratamiento**
Está en tratamiento por una úlcera.
She's being treated for an ulcer.

try to ◊ **tratar de** + infin
Trataremos de salvarle el diente.
We'll try to save your tooth.

try to get ◊ **procurar obtener**
Procure usted obtener una ambulancia inmediatamente.
Try to get an ambulance immediately.

turn off the light ◊ **apagar la luz**
¿Apago la luz?
Shall I turn off the light?

turn on the light ◊ **encender la luz**
¿Enciendo la luz?
Shall I turn on the light?

twice daily ◊ **dos veces al día**
El médico me deja tomarlas dos veces al día.
The doctor lets me take them twice daily.

under; below ◊ **debajo de**
¿Tiene usted o ha tenido dolor debajo de los ojos?
136 *Do you have or have you ever had pain under your eyes?*

under an anesthetic ◊ **con anestesia**
Lo operaron con anestesia.
He was operated under an anesthetic.

under great stress ◊ **estar muy estresado**
Su esposa está muy estresada.
Your wife is under great stress.

under intensive care ◊ **bajo cuidado intensivo**
Su padre está bajo cuidado intensivo.
Your father is under intensive care.

under lock and key ◊ **bajo llave**
Siempre guarde las medicinas bajo llave.
Always keep the medicines under lock and key.

undergo; have ◊ **someterse a**
Tendrá que someterse a un examen médico.
You will have to undergo a medical exam.
Fue sometido a una intervención quirúrgica.
He underwent an operation.
He had an operation.

undress ◊ **quitarse la ropa**
Favor de quitarse la ropa y de ponerse esta bata.
Please undress and put on this gown.

until ◊ **hasta que**
Por favor, espere aquí hasta que lo llamemos.
Please wait here until we call you.
Apriete el émbolo suavemente hasta que se haya terminado toda la insulina de la jeringuilla.
Push the plunger slowly until all the insulin is gone from the syringe.
Espere aquí hasta que oiga su nombre.
Wait here until you hear your name.

unusual expenses ◊ **gastos extraordinarios**
¿Tiene usted gastos extraordinarios?
Do you have any unusual expenses?

unusally ◊ **más de lo común**
¿Ha tenido usted sed, hambre o fatiga más de lo común?
Have you been unusually thirsty, hungry, or fatigued?

up to now ◊ **hasta ahora**
¿Han sido regulares sus reglas hasta ahora?
Have your periods been regular up to now?

upon coughing; when you cough ◊ **al toser**
¿Le duele al toser?
Does it hurt you when you cough?
Al toser, ¿arroja usted sangre?
Do you cough up blood?

upset the patient ◊ **alterar al paciente**

Traten de no alterar al paciente.
Try not to upset the patient.

urine analysis; urine test ◊ **análisis de orina**
Voy a hacer el análisis de orina.
I am going to do a urine analysis.

urinary infection ◊ **infección urinaria**
Tengo una infección urinaria.
I have a urinary infection.

urine sample ◊ **muestra de orina**
Necesito una muestra de orina.
I need a urine sample.

U.S. citizen ◊ **ciudadano de Estados Unidos**
¿Es usted ciudadano de Estados Unidos?
Are you a U.S. citizen?

use crutches ◊ **usar muletas**
Usted tendrá que usar muletas por algún tiempo.
You will have to use crutches for a while.

use the bedpan ◊ **usar el bacín**
¿Tiene que usar el bacín?
Do you have to use the bedpan?

using liberal amounts of soap ◊ **usando jabón en abundancia**
Tómese una ducha o baño jabonoso caliente usando jabón en abundancia.
Take a shower or hot soapy bath using liberal amounts of soap.

usually visits ◊ **suele visitar**
Su médico suele visitar a las 8 de la mañana.
Your doctor usually visits at 8 in the morning.

vaccinate against ◊ **vacunar contra**
¿Está la niña vacunada contra la difteria, la tos ferina y el tétanos?
Is the child vaccinated against diptheria, whooping cough, and tetanus?
¿Lo vacunaron contra la viruela?
Were you vaccinated against smallpox?

vein in your arm ◊ **vena del brazo**
Le inyectarán una solución radiopaca en la vena del brazo.
The radiopaque will be injected into a vein in your arm.
Le pondrán una inyección en la vena del brazo.
You'll be given an injection in the vein of your arm.

veneral disease ◊ **enfermedad venérea**

Me gustaría hablar con un médico porque creo que tengo una enfermedad venérea.
I would like to speak with a doctor because I think I have a venereal disease.

very healthy life ◊ **vida muy sana**
Lleva una vida muy sana.
She leads a very healthy life.

very painful death ◊ **muerte muy dolorosa**
Tuvo una muerte muy dolorosa.
He had a very painful death.

very prone to; easily ◊ **muy propenso a**
Es muy propenso a resfriarse.
He's very prone to colds.
He catches colds easily.

visiting hours ◊ **horas de visita**
Las horas de visita son de seis a ocho.
The visiting hours are from 6 to 8.
Se admiten visitantes solamente durante las horas de visita.
Visitors are only allowed during visiting hours.

visiting nurse ◊ **enfermera ambulante**
Soy la enfermera ambulante.
I'm the visiting nurse.

wait here ◊ **esperar aquí**
Tú y él pueden esperar aquí.
You and he can wait here.
Espere aquí hasta que oiga su nombre.
Wait here until you hear your name.

waiting room ◊ **sala de espera**
Hay una sala de espera en el primer piso.
There is a waiting room on the first floor.

wake up with ◊ **amanecer con**
¿Amaneció con fiebre?
Did he wake up with a fever?

walk in the hall ◊ **caminar en el pasillo**
¿Quiere caminar en el pasillo?
Do you want to go for a walk in the hall?

walk with difficulty ◊ **andar con dificultad**
Andaba con dificultad.
She was walking with difficulty.

want to protect ◊ **querer proteger**
Queremos que aquellas personas que lo visiten estén protegidas también.
We want to protect your visitors from possible contact too.

want to see ◊ **querer ver**
El doctor quiere ver cómo le va.
The doctor wants to see how you are getting along.

warm water ◊ **agua caliente**
Báñese con agua caliente.
Bathe with warm water.

wash one's hair ◊ **lavarse el pelo; lavarse la cabeza**
Tengo que lavarme el pelo.
I have to wash my hair.
Tengo que lavarme la cabeza.
I have to wash my hair.

wash one's hands ◊ **lavarse las manos**
Lávese las manos.
Wash your hands.
Antes de darle el pecho a su niño, lávese las manos con agua y jabón.
Before breast feeding your child, wash your hands with soap and water.

water; amniotic fluid ◊ **bolsa de aguas**
Rompió la bolsa de aguas.
Her water broke.

we are still trying to ◊ **todavía estamos tratando de**
Todavía estamos tratando de saber la causa de su enfermedad.
We are still trying to find the cause of your illness.

wear an eyepatch ◊ **llevar un parche en el ojo**
Llevaba un parche en el ojo.
He wore an eyepatch.

well ◊ **estar bien**
Mi mamá está bien pero mi padre no.
My mother is well but my father isn't.

well enough ◊ **bastante fuerte**
Usted no está bastante fuerte todavía para levantarse.
You are not well enough yet to get out of bed.

what ...? ◊ **¿de qué ...?**
¿De qué enfermedades padece?
What diseases do you have?
¿De qué color es la flema?
What color is the phlegm?
¿De qué color es la orina?
What color is your urine?

what are they going to ...? ◊ **¿qué le van a +
infin ..?**
¿Qué le van a examinar a usted?
What are they going to examine you for?

¿Qué le van a examinar a su marido?
What are they going to examine your husband for?

what do you do for ...? ◊ **¿qué hace para ...?**
¿Qué hace para **sus** dolores de cabeza? (adult)
¿Qué haces para **tus** dolores de cabeza? (child)
What do you do for headaches?

what happened to ...? ◊ **¿qué le pasó a ...?**
¿Qué le pasó a su hijo?
What happened to your son?
¿Qué le pasó al niño?
What happened to the child?

what is ...? ◊ **¿cuál es ...?**
¿Cuál es su nombre?
What is your name?
¿Cuál es su dirección?
What is your address?
¿Cuál es el factor Rh suyo?
What is your Rh blood factor?
¿Cuál es su número de teléfono?
What is your telephone number?

what other jobs ◊ **qué otros empleos**
¿Qué otros empleos ha tenido?
What other jobs have you had?

what type of ...? ◊ **¿qué clase de ...**
¿Qué clase de jabón usa?
What type of soap do you use?

wheelchair ◊ **silla de ruedas**
¿Necesita usted una silla de ruedas?
Do you need a wheelchair?
Siéntese usted en la silla de ruedas.
Please sit down on the wheelchair.

when do you get ...? ◊ **¿cuándo te dan ...?**
¿Cuándo te dan los resultados?
When do you get the results?

when I/he/she was ◊ **cuando era**
Cuando era niña, sufría de asma.
When she was a child, she suffered from asthma.

when the bell rings ◊ **cuando suene el timbre**
Cuando suene el timbre tiene que salir. (one person)
Cuando suene el timbre tienen que salir. (more than one person)
Cuando suene el timbre tienes que salir. (to a child)
When the bell rings you have to leave.

when you are resting ◊ **al descansar**
¿Le falta la respiración al descansar?

Are you short of breath when you are resting?

when you have pain ◊ **cuando tenga dolor**
Tome la medicina cuando tenga dolor.
Take the medicine when you have pain.

when you stand ◊ **cuando se pone de pie**
¿Siente usted dolor cuando se pone de pie?
Do you feel pain when you stand?

where ...? ◊ **¿en qué lugar ...?**
¿En qué lugar ocurrió la herida?
Where did the injury occur?

where ... from? ◊ **¿de dónde ...?**
¿De dónde es usted?
Where are you from?

where you work ◊ **lugar donde trabaja**
¿Cuál es el número de teléfono del lugar donde trabaja?
What is the telephone number where you work?

while ◊ **mientras que**
Mientras que tiene dolor de cabeza, ¿tiene náuseas?
Do you ever feel nauseated while you have a headache?

while exercising; when exercising ◊ **al hacer ejercicios**
¿Le falta la respiración al hacer ejercicios?
Are you short of breath while exercising?

while you were pregnant ◊ **mientras estaba embarazada**
¿Tomó alguna medicina mientras estaba embarazada?
Did you take any medicine while you were pregnant?

whooping cough ◊ **tos ferina**
¿Está la niña vacunada contra la difteria, la tos ferina y el tétanos?
Is the child vaccinated against diptheria, whooping cough, and tetanus?

why did you bring ...? ◊ **¿por qué trajo ...?**
¿Por qué trajo a su niño al hospital?
Why did you bring your child to the hospital?

wipe off the top ◊ **limpiar la tapa**
Limpie la tapa de la botella con algodón mojado en alcohol.
Wipe off the top of the bottle with alcohol and cotton.

wipe one's hands ◊ **limpiarse las manos**
Me limpié las manos en un trapo.

I wiped my hands on a cloth.

wipe one's nose ◊ **limpiar la nariz**
Le tuve que limpiar la nariz.
I had to wipe his nose.

with breakfast ◊ **con el desayuno**
Tome una cápsula con el desayuno.
Take one capsule with breakfast.

with the measles ◊ **con sarampión**
Está en cama con sarampión.
He is in bed with the measles.

with this ◊ **con esto**
No tome alcohol con esto.
Don't drink alcohol with this.

with your legs hanging ◊ **con las piernas colgando**
Siéntese en esta mesa con las piernas colgando.
Sit on this table with your legs hanging on the side.

with water ◊ **con agua**
Tome la medicina con agua.
Take the medicine with water.

with whom ◊ **con quien**
Necesitamos saber el nombre y la dirección del hombre con quien tuvo relaciones sexuales.
We need to know the name and address of the man with whom you had sex.

with your palms facing out ◊ **con las palmas hacia afuera**
Ponga las manos en la cadera con las palmas hacia afuera.
Put your hands on your hips with palms facing out.

within the last five years ◊ **durante los últimos cinco años**
¿Ha estado usted hospitalizado por cualquier razón durante los últimos cinco años?
Have you been hospitalized for any reason within the last five years?

without an anesthetic ◊ **sin anestesia**
Sacó la muela sin anestesia.
He took the tooth out without an anesthetic.

without being able to ◊ **sin poder**
¿Se despierta en la noche sin poder respirar?
Do you wake up at night without being able to breathe?

without calling ◊ **sin llamar**
No se voltee sin llamar a la enfermera.
Do not turn without calling the nurse.

139

X-ray room ◊ **cuatro de rayos X**
Alguien le llevará al cuarto de rayos X.
Someone will come to take you to the X-ray room.

X-ray table ◊ **mesa radiográfica**
Acuéstese sobre la mesa radiográfica.
Lie down on the X-ray table.

you broke ◊ **se rompió**
Se rompió el brazo.
You broke your arm.
Se rompió la pierna.
You broke your leg.
Se rompió el tobillo.
He broke his ankle.

you have to; you must ◊ **usted tiene que +
infin**
Usted tiene que comer mucha carne.
You have to eat a lot of meat.
Usted tiene que tomar vitaminas.
You must take some vitamins.
Usted tiene que tomar mucho jugo.
You must drink a lot of juice.

you look ◊ **usted se ve**
Hoy usted se ve mucho mejor.
You look much better today.

you might feel ◊ **quizás sienta**
Quizás sienta la sensación de un calor
pasajero, dolor de cabeza o náuseas.
*You might feel a very brief sensation of
warmth, a headache, or nauseated.*

you'll be asked to ◊ **le dirán que**
Ya cerca del final le dirán que orine.
Near the end, you will be asked to urinate.

your ◊ **de usted**
Tengo las gotas de usted.
I have your drops.

your ◊ **de ustedes**
Tengo las gotas de ustedes.
I have your drops.

your daughter ◊ **su hija**
¿Cómo está su hija?
How is your daughter?

your husband's name ◊ **nombre de su esposo**
¿Cuál es el nombre de su esposo?

140

What is your husband's name?

your leg needs to be ◊ **la pierna tiene que
estar**
La pierna tiene que estar levantada con
almohadas para ayudarle con la circulación.
*Your leg needs to be elevated on pillows to
help your circulation.*

your son ◊ **su hijo**
¿Cómo está su hijo?
How is your son?

your wife's name ◊ **nombre de su esposa**
¿Cuál es el nombre de su esposa?
What is your wife's name?

FOCUSED CARE DIALOGUES

ADDICTION · NEWBORN

ESPAÑOL

ENGLISH

1. ¿Tomó drogas o bebidas alcohólicas durante su embarazo?

2. ¿Qué tipo de droga tomó?

   ¿Drogas duras? ¿Drogas blandas?

   ¿Use más de una droga al mismo tiempo?

3. ¿Qué a menudo la usaba?

4. ¿Cuándo fue la última vez que tomó la droga?

5. ¿Fumó Usted durante el embarazo?

6. ¿Cuántos cigarillos al día?

7. ¿Su bebé ...

   está tomando bien el biberón?

   vomita o tiene diarrea?

   está inquieto?

   está muy irritable o duerme demasiado?

   está ganando peso bien?

8. ¿Ha tenido convulsiones su bebé?

9. Su bebé tendrá que ser ingresado en el hospital para observalo.

---

1. *Did you use drugs or alcohol during your pregnancy?*

2. *What drug did you use?*

   Hard drugs? Soft Drugs?

   Did you take more than one drug at the same time?

3. *How often did you take it?*

4. *When was the last time you took it?*

5. *Did you smoke during your pregnancy?*

6. *How many cigarettes a day?*

7. *Is your baby ...*

   taking the bottle well?

   vomiting or having diarhhea?

   jittery?

   very fussy or sleeping too much?

   gaining weight well?

8. *Has your baby had convulsions?*

9. *Your baby will need to be hospitalized for observation.*

AIDS

1. ¿Qué es el sida?

2. El sida significa síndrome de inmunodeficiencia adquirida.

3. Es una enfermedad en la cual el sistema de inmunidad del cuerpo (el sistema de defensa contra las enfermedades) deja de funcionar.

4. Cuando el sistema falla, una persona con sida típicamente desarrolla una variedad de enfermedades que ponen en peligro su vida.

5. ¿Qué es el VIH?

6. El VIH significa Virus de Inmuno-deficiencia Humano.

7. Es el virus que causa el sida.

8. ¿Puedo contagiarme si alguien en mi escuela tiene sida?

9. No, el VIH es transmitido por la introducción del virus en el sistema sanguíneo a través de contacto sexual, intercambio de agujas o sangre infectada.

10. Las personas infectadas con el VIH no pueden transmitir el virus a otras personas a través de las actividades diarias de los niños y jóvenes en las escuelas.

11. ¿Puedo infectarme con el VIH por medio de besos apasionados con una persona infectada?

---

1. What is AIDS?

2. AIDS stands for Acquired Immune Deficiency Syndrome.

3. It is an illness in which the body's immune system (the body's defense system against illness) stops functioning correctly.

4. Typically, a person with AIDS develops a variety of life-threatening illnesses.

5. What is HIV?

6. HIV stands for Human Immunodeficiency Virus.

7. It is the Virus that causes AIDS.

8. Can I become infected if someone in my school has AIDS?

9. No, HIV is transmitted by the introduction of the virus through sexual contact, sharing needles with an infected person, or by contact with infected blood.

10. An infected person will not transmit the virus through the normal daily activities of children in school.

11. Can I become infected with HIV by passionate kissing with an infected person?

AIDS

ESPAÑOL	ENGLISH

12. Probablemente no. A veces el VIH se encuentra en la saliva pero en muy pocas cantidades.

13. Los científicos creen que es imposible transmitir el virus por medio de besos apasionados.

14. ¿Puedo infectarme con el VIH por contacto sexual oral con una persona infectada?

15. Sí, es posible. Durante el contacto oral, a menudo hay intercambio de semen, secreciones vaginales o sangre: secreciones que contienen el VIH.

16. Durante el contacto oral el virus puede entrar en la sangre a través de pequeñas lesiones o cortaduras en la boca.

17. ¿Es verdad que si uso un condón durante el acto sexual, no puedo contagiarme?

18. Se ha demostrado que los condones ayudan en la prevención de infección por VIH y otras enfermedades sexualmente transmitidas, pero los condones no son totalmente seguros.

19. Los condones pueden romperse durante el acto sexual.

20. ¿Es posible infectarme con el VIH al donar sangre?

21. No.

---

12. *Probably not. Sometimes HIV is found in saliva, but in very small amounts.*

13. *Scientists think that it is impossible to transmit the virus through passionate kissing.*

14. *Can I become infected with HIV through oral sex with an infected person?*

15. *Yes, it is possible during oral sex there is often an exchange of semen, vaginal fluids, or blood: secretions that contain HIV.*

16. *During oral sex the virus can enter the bloodstream via small lesions or cuts in the mouth.*

17. *Is it true that if I use a condom during the sexual act, I cannot become infected?*

18. *Condoms have been demonstrated to help in the prevention of HIV and other sexually transmitted diseases, but they are not totally effective.*

19. *Condoms can break during the sexual act.*

20. *Is it possible to become infected with HIV by donating blood?*

21. *No.*

ANESTHESIA

ESPAÑOL	**ENGLISH**

1. Soy el doctor Smith. Soy el anestesista.

2. Le voy anestesiar para que los médicos puedan operarlo.

3. ¿Ha tenido alguna operación antes? ¿Para qué y cuándo?

4. ¿Está usted medicado? ¿Qué es?

5. ¿Tiene problemas al tomar las medicinas?

6. ¿Tiene alergias?

7. ¿Hay alguien en su familia que haya tenido problemas con la anestesia o que haya tenido hemorragias?

8. ¿Ha tomado usted esteroides en el pasado — cortisona o prednisona?

9. ¿Tiene dientes flojos, coronas o dientes astillados (rotos), o problemas al abrir la quijada (mandíbula)?

10. ¿Fuma usted? ¿Cuántos cigarrillos?

11. ¿Tiene problemas respiratorios, tos, o asma?

12. ¿Padece del corazón?

13. ¿Tiene dolor de pecho al hacer ejercicio?

14. ¿Tiene problemas al respirar en la noche?

15. ¿Toma pastillas para el corazón? ¿Para la presión alta?

---

1. *I am Dr. Smith. I am the anesthetist.*

2. *I am going to put you to sleep so the doctors can do the operation.*

3. *Have you had any operations before? What and when?*

4. *Are you on any medication? What?*

5. *Do you have trouble taking medicines?*

6. *Do you have allergies?*

7. *Has anyone in your family had problems with anesthesia or bleeding?*

8. *Have you taken steroids in the past—cortisone or prednisone?*

9. *Do you have any loose teeth, capped teeth, or chipped teeth, or trouble opening your jaw?*

10. *Do you smoke? How many cigarettes?*

11. *Do you have a weak chest: coughing, or asthma.*

12. *Do you have any heart trouble?*

13. *Do you have pain in the chest when you exercise?*

14. *Do you have trouble breathing at night?*

15. *Do you take pills for your heart? For high blood pressure?*

ANESTHESIA

ESPAÑOL	ENGLISH
16. ¿Sufre del hígado? ¿Sufre una hepatitis? ¿Ha tenido ictericia?	16. *Do you have any liver problems? hepatitis? jaundice?*
17. ¿Padece del riñón?	17. *Do you have any kidney problems?*
18. ¿Cuándo fue la última vez que comió?	18. *When did you eat last?*
19. Usted no debe comer ni beber nada después de la medianoche. Esto es muy importante.	19. *You must not eat or drink anything after midnight tonight. This is very important.*
20. Cuando venga a la sala de operaciones le daré una medicina para que usted se duerma.	20. *When you come to the operating room, I will give you some medicine so you will go to sleep.*
21. Usted sentirá un pinchacito ahora. Es el suero.	21. *You will feel a small needle prick now. This is your IV.*
22. Aspire profundamente de este oxígeno. Le hará bien.	22. *Take a deep breath of this oxygen. It is good for you.*
23. Usted tendrá sueño pronto.	23. *You will feel sleepy soon.*
24. Abra los ojos. Respire profundamente.	24. *Open your eyes. Take a deep breath.*
25. Se terminó su operación. Todo salió bien.	25. *Your operation is over, and everything went fine.*
26. Vamos a la sala de recuperación para que usted pueda despertarse.	26. *We are going to the recovery room now, so that you can wake up.*
27. Esta es la sala de recuperación.	27. *This is the recovery room.*

BREAST EXAM

ESPAÑOL	ENGLISH
D: ¿Tiene algún problema en los senos? ¿Cuál es el problema?	D: *Do you have any problems with your breasts? What's wrong?*
P: Se sienten tirantes e hinchados. Se sienten doloridos.	P: *They feel tight and swollen. They hurt.*
D: ¿Tiene una bolita? ¿Tiene bultos?	D: *Do you have a lump? Do you have bumps?*
P: Sí, tengo una bolita pequeña. También me sale algo del pezón.	P: *Yes, I have a small lump. I also secrete something from the nipple.*
D: ¿Se examina los senos con frecuencia? ¿Cada cuánto se examina los senos?	D: *Do you examine your breasts regularly? How often to you examine them?*
P: Todos los días. Los examino cada vez que me baño.	P: *Every day. I examine them when I take a bath.*
D: ¿Cuándo fue la última vez que se examinó los senos?	D: *When was the last time you examined your breasts?*
P: Hoy.	P: *Today.*
D: ¿Notó algo anormal?	D: *Did you notice anything abnormal?*
P: Nada.	P: *Nothing.*
D: ¿Tiene usted dolor en los senos?	D: *Do you have pain in your breasts?*
P: No.	P: *No.*
D: ¿Ha tenido alguna vez un examen de los senos por un médico o una enfermera?	D: *Have you ever had a breast exam by a doctor or a nurse?*
P: Sí.	P: *Yes.*

CARDIOLOGY

ESPAÑOL	**ENGLISH**

D: ¿Le ha dicho su médico que usted tiene problemas con el corazón?

D: *Has your doctor told you that you have problems with your heart?*

P: No, pero tengo algunos síntomas que podrían indicar un problema, y mi médico me dijo que viniera a verlo a usted.

P: *No, but I have some symptoms which could indicate a problem, and my doctor told me to come to see you.*

D: ¿Ha tenido alguna vez fiebre reumática o temblores en las extremidades?

D: *Have you ever had rheumatic fever or twitching of the limbs?*

P: No, nunca.

P: *No, never.*

D: ¿Le duele el pecho o siente alguna opresión cuando hace ejercicios?

D: *Does your chest hurt, or do you feel any tightness when you excercise?*

P: Sí, a veces tengo dolor y me falta el aire ... cuando subo escaleras, por ejemplo.

P: *Yes, sometimes I have pain and shortness of breath ... when I climb the stairs, for instance.*

D: ¿Es un dolor sordo o agudo?

D: *Is it a dull pain or a sharp one?*

P: Es un dolor agudo.

P: *It's a sharp one.*

D: ¿Le late el corazón muy rápidamente a veces?

D: *Does your heart beat very fast sometimes?*

P: Sí, cuando corro.

P: *Yes, when I run.*

D: ¿Tiene a veces sudor frío después de un ejercicio violento?

D: *Do you sometimes break out in a cold sweat after a strenuous exercise?*

P: No.

P: *No.*

CARDIOLOGY

D: ¿Algún pariente cercano suyo ha tenido alguna vez un ataque al corazón antes de los sesenta años?

P: Bueno, un hermano de mi mamá murió de un ataque al corazón a los cincuenta años.

D: Tiene calambres en las piernas cuando camina varias cuadras?

P: Bueno, si yo caminara, tal vez tendría calambres, pero casi nunca camino.

D: ¿Le han encontrado el ácido úrico elevado en la sangre alguna vez?

P: No.

D: Le voy a colocar en el pecho, debajo de la piel, una caja pequeña que contiene baterías.

P: ¿Eso me va a mejorar?

D: Sí, con el marcapasos, su corazón va a latir mejor.

P: ¿Voy a estar despierto cuando me lo haga?

D: No, va a estar dormido.

P: ¿Cuánto tiempo me va a durar el marcapasos?

D: Le va a durar dos años.

D: *Has any blood relative of yours ever had a heart attack before sixty?*

P: *Well, a brother of my mother's died of a heart attack at fifty.*

D: *Do you get any cramps in your legs when you walk several blocks?*

P: *Well, if I walked, perhaps I would have cramps, but I hardly ever walk.*

D: *Have they ever found elevated uric acid in your blood?*

P: *No.*

D: *I'm going to place in your chest, under the skin, a small box which contains batteries.*

P: *Is that going to help me?*

D: *Yes, with the pacemaker, your heart is going to beat better.*

P: *Am I going to be awake when you insert it in me?*

D: *No, you're going to be asleep.*

P: *How long is the pacemaker going to last me?*

D: *It's going to last you two years.*

CHILD ABUSE

ESPAÑOL	ENGLISH
1. ¿Qué te pasó?	1. *What happened to you?*
2. ¿Te lastimó alguien?	2. *Did someone hurt you?*
3. ¿Te tocó alguien de una manera que te asustó o incomodó?	3. *Did someone touch you in a way that was scary or uncomfortable?*
4. ¿Quién fue?	4. *Who was it?*
5. ¿Con qué te tocó él?	5. *What did he touch you with?*
6. ¿Con qué te tocó ella?	6. *What did she touch you with?*
7. ¿Te dolió eso?	7. *Did that hurt?*
8. ¿Había sangre?	8. *Was there any blood?*
9. ¿Cuántas veces te tocó/lastimó él/ella?	9. *How many times did he/she touch/hurt you?*
10. ¿Cómo llamas la parte del cuerpo cerca de donde orinas (donde haces pipí, tu parte privada)?	10. *What do you call the part of your body near where you urinate ("where you go pee," "your private area")?*
11. ¿Te duele allí ahora?	11. *Does it hurt there now?*
12. ¿Te ha dolido alguna vez allí?	12. *Has it ever hurt there?*
13. ¿Te ha dolido alguna vez cuando orinas (haces pipí)?	13. *Does it ever hurt there when you go pee pee?*
14. ¿Te tocó allí él/ella?	14. *Did he/she ever touch you there?*
15. ¿Te dolió allí cuando él/ella te tocó?	15. *Did it hurt there when he/she touched you there?*
16 ¿Te dolió cuando usaste el baño después de que él/ella te tocó allí?	16. *Did it hurt when you went poo after he/she touched you there?*

CHILD ABUSE

ESPAÑOL	ENGLISH
17. ¿Cómo llamas la parte del cuerpo por donde (evacuas) haces caca?	17. *What do you call the part of your body where you (have a bowel movement) go poo?*
18. ¿Te duele allí ahora?	18. *Does it hurt there now?*
19. ¿Te ha dolido alguna vez allí?	19. *Has it ever hurt there?*
20. ¿Te duele allí cuando haces caca?	20. *Does it hurt there when you poo?*
21. ¿Ha habido sangre alguna vez cuando hiciste caca? ¿en el excremento? (caca)? ¿en el papel higiénico?	21. *Was there ever blood when you went poo? In the excrement? On the toilet paper?*
22. ¿Te tocó él/ella allí alguna vez?	22. *Did he/she touch you there?*
23. ¿Te dolió allí cuando hiciste caca después de que él/ella te tocó allí?	23. *Did it hurt there when he/she touched you there?*
24. ¿Te dolió cuando hiciste caca después de que él/ella te tocó allí?	24. *Did it hurt when you went to the bathroom after he/she touched you there?*
25. ¿Ha habido sangre en la ropa interior?	25. *Was there ever blood in your underpants?*

COLOSTOMY

ESPAÑOL

1. ¿Una colostomía es una incisión en el colon (intestino grueso) para crear una abertura artificial.

2. Esta abertura sirve de substituto al ano para evacuar el contenido.

3. La colostomía evacua el excremento del intestino que generalmente sale por el recto.

4. Hay muchos productos disponibles para el cuidado de una colostomía. Se le darán instrucciones precisas sobre el cuidado de una colostomía antes del alta del hospital. Muchas estomas son temporales y posteriormente pueden ser cerradas.

5. ¿Qué es una bolsa? Una bolsa es un objeto de plástico que cabe bien ajustado sobre su estoma.

6. ¿Las heces caen dentro de una bolsa de recolección.

7. ¿El personal de enfermeras de colostomía le enseñarán el cuidado de la piel y cómo cambiar la bolsa.

8. La bolsa se vacía en el baño.

9. ¿Habrá excremento todo el tiempo? Al principio puede ocurrir a menudo y ser delgado. Pero cuando esté comiendo mejor, fiuncionará sólo una o dos veces al día como antes de tener la colostomía.

ENGLISH

1. A colostomy is an incision in the colon (large intestine to create an artificial opening.

2. This opening serves as a substitute for the anus.

3. It empties the stool from the intestine that normally comes out your rectum.

4. There are many products available for the care of a colostomy. You will be given prcise instructions on the care of a colostomy before you are released from the hospital. Many colostomies are temporary and can be closed subsequently.

5. What is a pouch? A pouch is a plastic bag that fits snugly (closely) over your stoma.

6. The excrement falls inside a collection pouch.

7. The team of nurses will teacb you how to care for your skin and how to change the pouch.

8. Empty the pouch in the bathroom.

9. Will stool be in there all the time? At first it may be often and thin. But when you are eating more normally, it will probably work just once or twice a day like before you had the colostomy.

DERMATOLOGY

ESPAÑOL	ENGLISH
1. ¿Desde cuándo tiene este crecimiento?	1. *How long have you had this growth?*
2. ¿Desde cuándo tiene este sarpullido (also salpullido)?	2. *How long have you had this rash?*
3. ¿Desde cuándo tiene este bulto?	3. *How long have you had this lump?*
4. ¿Le pica?	4. *Does it itch?*
5. ¿Toma el sol muy a menudo?	5. *Do you you sunbathe often?*
6. ¿Usa filtro solar regularmente?	6. *Do you wear sunscreen regularly?*
7. ¿Se quema fácilmente?	7. *Do you burn easily?*
8. ¿Ha padecido de asma, fiebre del heno o eczema de la niñez en el pasado?	8. *Do you have a history of asthma, hay fever, or childhood eczema?*
9. ¿Qué tipo de .... usa? jabón champú maquillaje detergente crema hidratante/humectante	9. *What type of .... do you use?* *soap* *shampoo* *make-up* *detergent* *moisturizer*
10. ¿Con qué frecuencia se baña?	10. *How frequently do you bathe?*
11. ¿Con qué frecuencia se ducha?	11. *How frequently do you shower?*
12. ¿Hay alguien más en la familia que esté afectado?	12. *Is anybody else in the family affected?*
13. ¿Hay alguien más en la familia que tenga picazón?	13. *Is anybody else in the family itchy?*
14. ¿Cuándo le pica más?	14. *When does it itch most?*
15. ¿Dónde empezó el sarpullido? (also: salpullido)	15. *Where did the rash first start?*
16. ¿Le duele?	16. *Is it painful?*
17. ¿Qué tipo de tratamiento está recibiendo actualmente?	17. *What type of treatment are you currently receiving?*
18. ¿Qué tipo de medicina sin receta está usando?	18. *What type of over the counter medicine are you using?*
19. ¿Ha tenido hemorragia recientemente?	19. *Have you been hemmorhaging recently?*
20. ¿Qué medicinas está tomando?	20. *What medicines are you taking?*
21. ¿es alérgico {male} es alérgica {female} eres alérgico {male child} eres alérgica {female child}	21. *{same in English}*
22. ¿Tiene algún otro problema médico?{adult}	22. *Do you have any allergies to medicines?*
23. ¿Tienes algún otro problema médico?{child}	23. *Do you have any other medical problems?*
24. ¿Hay algo más en que pueda ayudarle?{adult}	24. *Is there anything else that I can help you with?*
25. ¿Hay algo más en que pueda ayudarte?{child}	

DETERMINING
THE PATIENT'S NEEDS

ESPAÑOL

1. ¿Puedo ayudarle?
2. ¿Se siente mejor hoy?
3. ¿Durmió bien?
4. ¿Tiene usted sueño?
5. El (La) doctor(a) le examinará ahora.
6. Usted debe guardar cama hoy.
7. Queremos que se levante ahora.
8. Puede bañarse.
9. Puede tomar una ducha.
10. Le voy a dar un baño de esponja ahora.
11. ¿Ha notado hemorragia ...

    del recto?
    de la vagina?
    de la boca?
12. Debo revisar si está sangrando.
13. ¿Todavía siente adormecimiento?
14. Esta inyección le hará dormir.
15. ¿Tiene dolor de oído?
16. ¿Tiene dolor de garganta?
17. ¿Tiene tos?
18. ¿Tiene dolor de pecho?
19. ¿Tiene dolor de cabeza?
20. ¿Tiene dolor de espalda?
21. ¿Es usted alérgico(a) a alguna medicina?
22. ¿Orina con demasiada frecuencia?
23. ¿Siente ardor al orinar?
24. Su infección está bajando rápidamente.
25. Quiero ver su vendaje.
26. Necesito cambiar su vendaje.
27. ¿Qué medicinas está tomando ahora?
28. El nivel de su colesterol es alto.
29. El nivel de su triglicérido es alto.
30. Debe seguir una dieta para perder peso.
31. ¿Necesita el bacín (la chata)?
32. Voy a poner el bacín sobra la cama.
33. ¿Necesita papel higiénico?
34. ¿Está usted estreñido(a)?
35. ¿Necesita una pastilla para dormir?
36. ¿Necesita un laxante/purgante?

ENGLISH

1. *May I help you?*
2. *Do you feel better today?*
3. *Did you sleep well?*
4. *Are you sleepy?*
5. *The doctor will examine you now.*
6. *You should remain in bed today.*
7. *We want to get you up now.*
8. *You may take a bath.*
9. *You may take a shower.*
10. *I am going to give you a sponge bath now.*
11. *Have you noticed any bleeding from...*
    the rectum?
    the vagina?
    the mouth?
12. *I must check for bleeding.*
13. *Do you still have any numbness?*
14. *This shot will make you sleep.*
15. *Do you have an earache?*
16. *Do you have a sore throat?*
17. *Do you have a cough?*
18. *Do you have chest pain?*
19. *Do you have a headache?*
20. *Do you have a backache?*
21. *Do you have any drug allergies?*
22. *Do you urinate too frequently?*
23. *Do you have burning when you urinate?*
24. *Your infection is clearing up nicely.*
25. *I want to see your dressing.*
26. *I need to change your dressing.*
27. *What medications are you taking now?*
28. *Your cholesterol level is high.*
29. *Your triglyceride level is high.*
30. *You must follow a diet to lose weight.*
31. *Do you need a bed pan?*
32. *I'm going to put the bedpan on the bed.*
33. *Do you need toilet paper?*
34. *Are you constipated?*
35. *Do you need a sleeping pill?*
36. *Do you need a laxative?*

DIET AND NUTRITION

ESPAÑOL	ENGLISH
1. Cada día debe comer algo de cada uno de los cuatro grupos generales de alimentos.	1. Each day you should eat something from each one of the four general food groups.
2. Los cuatro grupos generales de alimentos son lácteos, carnes, legumbres y verduras y cereales.	2. The four general food groups are the milk group, the meats, the vegetables, and the cereals.
3. En el grupo de lácteos puede usted elegir entre leche, helado, budín, queso y caldos que tengan leche.	3. In the milk group you may choose from milk, ice cream, pudding, cheese and soups that have milk in them.
4. En el grupo de carnes puede elegir entre carnes de res, carne de ave, pescado, huevos, queso y nueces.	4. In the meat group you may choose from animal meat, poultry, fish, eggs, cheese and nuts.
5. En el grupo de legumbres y verduras están los vegetales y las frutas frescas.	5. The vegetable group includes vegetables and fresh fruits.
6. En el grupo de cereales puede elegir entre pan, tortillas, todo aquello que venga en granos, harina y pastas como el macarrón y los tallarines.	6. In the cereal group you may choose from bread, tortillas, any grain, flour and the macaroni and noodle family.
7. Tome seis a ocho vasos de agua por día.	7. Drink from six to eight glasses of water daily.
8. No coma mucha sal, comidas muy grasosas, aderezos o salsas con muchas especias.	8. Don't eat a lot of salt, greasy food, dressings or highly seasoned sauces.

DIZZINESS

ESPAÑOL	ENGLISH
9. ¿Se siente mareado/a cuando se levanta?	9. *Are you dizzy when you get up?*
10. ¿Se siente mareado/a cuando se para?	10. *Are you dizzy when you stand up?*
11. ¿Son los mareos mejores desde que empezaron?	11. *Is the dizziness better since it started?*
12. ¿Son los mareos peores desde que empezaron?	12. *Is the dizziness worse since it started?*
13. ¿Son los mareos iguales desde que empezaron?	13. *Is the dizziness the same since it started?*
14. ¿Recientemente ha tenido usted un resfriado?	14. *Have you had a cold recently?*
15. ¿Recientemente se golpeó la cabeza?	15. *Did you hit your head recently?*
16. ¿Sufre usted de ...	16. *Do you have ...*
alta presión sanguínea?	*high blood pressure?*
diabetes?	*diabetes?*
enfermedades del corazón?	*heart disease?*
17. ¿Toma algún medicamento?	17. *Are you taking any medication?*
18. ¿Qué toma?	18. *What are you taking?*
19. Vamos a hacerle un electrocardiograma.	19. *We are going to do an EKG.*
20. Vamos a hacerle un análisis de sangre.	20. *We are going to do some blood tests.*
21. Usted necesita una tomografía de la cabeza.	21. *You need a CT scan of your head.*
22. Voy a tomarle la presión.	22. *I am going to take your blood pressure.*
23. Necesito hacerle un examen del recto.	23. *I need to do a rectal exam.*
24. Regrese al hospital (a la clínica) si ...	24. *Return to the hospital (clinic) if ...*
sus mareos empeoran.	*your dizziness is worse.*
tiene vómitos.	*you have vomiting.*
siente entumecidos o débiles los brazos o las piernas.	*you feel numbness or weakness in your arms or legs.*

EMERGENCY ROOM

ESPAÑOL

ENGLISH

1. ¿Quién es el paciente?
2. ¿Cuál es el problema? ¿Qué le pasa?
3. ¿Dónde siente el dolor? ¿Desde cuándo lo tiene? ¿Ha tenido este dolor antes?
4. ¿Cómo sucedió el accidente?
5. ¿Cómo sucedió esto? ¿Cuánto tiempo hace?
6. ¿Se lastimó?
7. ¿Sabe dónde se encuentra usted?
8. ¿Tiene la identificación para registrarse/firmar?
9. ¿Ha estado aquí antes?
10. ¿Todavía vive en esta dirección?
11. ¿Cuál es su número de teléfono?
12. ¿Dónde trabaja? ¿Cuál es su profesión o trabajo? ¿Qué hace usted?
13. ¿Tiene algún doctor (médico) particular que debamos llamar?
14. ¿Ha visto a algún otro(a) médico/a por este problema?
15. ¿Qué medicinas está usted tomando ahora?
16. ¿Padece de diabetes?
17. ¿Tiene la presión alta?
18. ¿Ha recibido una inyección para el tétano en los últimos cinco años?
19. ¿Cuándo recibió su última inyección para el tétano?
20. ¿Tiene alergias a algunas medicinas?
21. ¿Perdió el conocimiento? ¿Por cuánto tiempo?
22. ¿Le duele algo? ¿Le duele mucho?
23. ¿Dónde? Enséñeme.
24. ¿Le duele cuando le aprieto aquí?
25. ¿Cuándo le duele más—por la mañana o por la noche?
26. ¿Alguna vez se ha lastimado un pie?
27. ¿Siente cuando lo (la) toco aquí?
28. Dígame, cuándo lo (la) toco, ¿es una sensación aguda o sorda?
29. ¿Puede mover los brazos? ¿Piernas? ¿Dedos? ¿Dedos del pie?
30. ¿Le duele al respirar?
31. ¿Le duele al moverse?
32. Es necesario inyectarle anestesia para dormirle la parte afectada. Usted estará bien.
33. Usted necesita llamar a este número para pedir una cita en la clínica.

1. Who is the patient?
2. What is wrong?
3. Where is the pain? How long have you had it? Have you had it before?
4. How did the accident happen?
5. How did this happen? How long ago?
6. Did you injure yourself?
7. Do you know where you are?
8. Do you have identification to get yourself registered/signed in?
9. Have you been here before?
10. Are you still living at this address?
11. What is your phone number?
12. Where do you work? What do you do?
13. Do you have a private doctor we should call?
14. Have you seen another doctor about this problem?
15. What medicines are you taking now?
16. Do you have diabetes?
17. Do you have high blood pressure?
18. Have you had a tetanus shot in the last five years?
19. When was your last tetanus shot?
20. Do you have allergies to any medicines?
21. Did you lose consciousness? For how long?
22. Does anything hurt? Does it hurt much?
23. Where? Show me.
24. Does it hurt when I press here?
25. When does it hurt more—during the morning or evening?
26. Have you ever injured a foot?
27. Can you feel me touching you here?
28. Tell me, when I touch you, is it sharp or dull?
29. Can you move your arms? Legs? Fingers? Toes?
30. Does it hurt when you breathe?
31. Does it hurt when you move?
32. It is necessary to inject anesthetic to make the area numb. You will be OK.
33. You need to call this number for an appointment in the clinic.

EYES AND EARS

ESPAÑOL	ENGLISH
1. ¿Tiene usted alguna vez infecciones del oído medio?	1. *Do you ever have middle ear infections? (Do you ever have inner ear infections?)*
2. ¿Tiene usted falta de oído musical?	2. *Are you tone deaf?*
3. ¿Es usted sordo? {m}	3. *Are you deaf?*
4. ¿Es usted sorda? {f}	4. *Are you deaf?*
5. ¿Se le hace difícil oír?	5. *Are you hard of hearing?*
6. ¿Tiene usted buen oído?	6. *Do you have good hearing?*
7. ¿Tiene usted mal oído?	7. *Do you have bad hearing?*
8. ¿Tiene usted problemas auditivos?	8. *Do you have hearing difficulties?*
9. ¿Tiene usted problemas de audición?	9. *Do you have any hearing difficulties?*
10. ¿Padece usted de defectos de la audición?	10. *Do you have any hearing problems?*
11. ¿Le supuran los oídos?	11. *Do you have a discharge in your ears?*
12. ¿Le supura el oído izquierdo?	12. *Do you have a discharge in your left ear?*
13. ¿Le supura el oído derecho?	13. *Do you have a discharge in your right ear?*
14. ¿Le duelen con frecuencia los oídos?	14. *Do you usually get earaches?*
15. ¿Siente usted los oídos taponados?	15. *Are your ears clogged?*
16. ¿Siente usted un tintín en los oídos?	16. *Do your ears ring?*
17. ¿Le zumban a usted los oídos?	17. *Do you have a buzzing in your ears?*
18. ¿Le zumba el oído izquierdo?	18. *Do you have a ringing in your left ear?*
19. ¿Le zumba el oído derecho?	19. *Do you have a ringing in your right ear?*
20. ¿Tiene usted vértigo alguna vez?	20. *Do you ever have dizzy spells?*
21. ¿Suele usted tener mareos?	21. *Do you ever have dizzy spells?*
22. ¿Tiene usted episodios de mareos?	22. *Do you ever have dizzy spells?*
23. ¿Tiene usted mareos al levantarse de la cama rápido?	23. *Do you ever get dizzy on getting up quickly from bed?*

EYE EXAM

ESPAÑOL	ENGLISH
1. ¿Usa usted anteojos?	1. *Do you wear glasses?*
2. ¿Usa usted anteojos para ver de cerca?	2. *Do you wear glasses for close up?*
3. ¿Usa usted anteojos para ver de lejos?	3. *Do you wear glasses for distance?*
4. ¿Usa usted anteojos para leer?	4. *Do you wear glasses for reading?*
5. ¿Usa usted anteojos todo el tiempo?	5. *Do you wear glasses all the time?*
6. ¿Usa usted lentes de contacto?	6. *Do you wear contact lenses?*
7. ¿Ve usted doble alguna vez?	7. *Do you sometimes see things double?*
8. ¿Ve usted borroso?	8. *Do you have blurred vision?*
9. ¿Le arden los ojos?	9. *Do your eyes burn?*
10. ¿Le lagrimean mucho los ojos?	10. *Do your eyes water a lot?*
11. Sus ojos parecen inflamados.	11. *Your eyes seem inflamed.*
12. Sus ojos parecen rojos.	12. *Your eyes seem red.*
13. ¿Sufre usted de dolores de ojos?	13. *Do you have eyeaches?*
14. ¿Le duele a usted el ojo derecho?	14. *Does your right eye hurt?*
15. ¿Le duele a usted el ojo izquierdo?	15. *Does your left eye hurt?*
16. ¿Le duelen a usted los dos ojos?	16. *Do both your eyes hurt?*
17. ¿Tiene usted picazón en los ojos?	17. *Do your eyes itch?*
18. ¿Le supuran los ojos?	18. *Do you have a discharge from your eyes?*
19. ¿Tenía los ojos pegados cuando se despertó usted esta mañana?	19. *Were your eyes stuck together when you awoke this morning?*
20. ¿Siente el ojo hinchado?	20. *Does your eye feel swollen?*
21. ¿Desde cuándo tiene usted los párpados hinchados?	21. *How long have your eyelids been swollen?*
22. ¿Cuándo empezaron sus ojos a tener este color amarillo?	22. *When did your eyes begin to look yellow?*
23. ¿Ha tenido alguna vez dificultades con su vista?	23. *Have you ever had trouble with your vision?*
24. ¿Ha tenido alguna vez dificultades con su visión?	24. *Have you ever had trouble with your eyesight?*
25. ¿Le entró algo en el ojo?	25. *Did anything get into your eyes?*

EYE EXAM

ESPAÑOL	ENGLISH
Dr.: Buenas tardes, señor Gómez. Siéntese por favor.	*Dr.: Hello, Mr. Gómez, please sit down.*
Sr. G: Gracias doctor.	*Mr. G: Thank you, Doctor.*
Dr.: Vamos a ver, ¿cuál parece ser la molestia?	*Dr.: Let's see, what seems to be your trouble?*
Sr. G: Me duelen los ojos.	*Mr. G: My eyes hurt.*
Dr.: ¿Cuánto tiempo hace que se examinó los ojos?	*Dr.: When were your eyes last examined?*
Sr. G: Hace tres años, más o menos.	*Mr. G: It's been about three years.*
Dr.: ¿Ha tenido alguna vez dificultades con su vista?	*Dr.: Did you ever have trouble with your vision?*
Sr. G: Sí, tenía astigmatismo en el ojo izqurdo y me dieron una receta para anteojos.	*Mr. G: Yes, I has astigmatism in the left eye and they gave me a prescription for glasses.*
Dr.: ¿Todavía lleva los anteojos?	*Dr.: Do you still wear glasses now?*
Sr. G: No, no los llevo porque se me perdieron el año pasado y no tuve bastante dinero para comprar otros nuevos.	*Mr. G: No, I don't wear them because I lost my glasses last year and I didn't have enough money to buy new ones.*
Dr.: ¿Siente dolor en el ojo derecho?	*Dr.: Do you feel pain in your right eye?*
Sr. G: No, pero me duele el ojo iz-quierdo, y muchas veces tengo horribles dolores de cabeza.	*Mr. G: No, but my left eye hurts me, and I often have bad headaches.*
Dr.: ¿De veras? ¿Sufre de dolores de ojos también?	*Dr.: Really? Do you ever have eyeaches too?*

FEEDING AND DIGESTION — INFANT

ESPAÑOL	ENGLISH

1. ¿Tuvo el niño cólicos severos o algún trastorno inusual para alimentarse en los primeros 3 meses?

2. ¿Es el apetito de su niño general-mente bueno?

3. ¿Tiene buen apetito ahora?

4. ¿Ha tenido su niño cambios de ape-tito recientemente?

5. ¿Hay algunas comidas que no pueda comer?

6. ¿Tiene su niño diarrea frecuente-mente?

7. ¿El estreñimiento ha sido un problema para su niño?

8. ¿Toma él ...
    vitaminas?
    hierro?
    fluoruro?
    otra medicina?

---

1. *Was there severe colic or any unusual feeding problem the first 3 months?*

2. *Is your child's appetite usually good?*

3. *Is the appetite good now?*

4. *Has there been any change in your child's appetite recently?*

5. *Are there any foods he cannot eat?*

6. *Does your child often have diarrhea?*

7. *Has constipation been much of a problem?*

8. *Does he take ...*
    vitamins?
    iron?
    fluoride?
    other medicine?

GASTROINTESTINAL

ESPAÑOL	ENGLISH
1. ¿Come usted algo entre comidas?	1. *Do you eat between meals?*
2. ¿Toma usted muchos líquidos?	2. *Do you drink a lot of liquids?*
3. ¿Bebe usted leche?	3. *Do you drink milk?*
4. ¿Toma usted bebidas alcohólicas?	4. *Do you drink alcoholic beverages?*
5. ¿Cuánto bebe usted?	5. *How much do you drink?*
6. ¿Qué clase de bebida alcohólica toma usted?	6. *What kind of alcoholic beverage do you drink?*
7. ¿Qué tipo de bebida alcohólica toma usted?	7. *What type of alcoholic beverage do you drink?*
8. ¿Bebe usted café?	8. *Do you drink coffee?*
9. ¿Cuántas tazas de café bebe usted?	9. *How many cups of coffee do you drink?*
10. ¿Qué clase de café toma usted?	10. *What kind of coffee do you drink?*
11. ¿Toma usted café regular o descafeinado?	11. *Do you drink regular or decaffeinated coffee?*
12. ¿Cuántos vasos de agua bebe usted diariamente?	12. *How much water do you drink daily.*
13. ¿Cuántas bebidas gaseosas toma usted diariamente?	13. *How much pop do you drink?*
14. ¿Qué alimentos le caen mal?	14. *What food disagrees with you?*
15. ¿Qué alimentos le gustan?	15. *What food do you like?*
16. ¿Suele usted tener gases?	16. *Do you get gas pains?*
17. ¿Eructa usted mucho?	17. *Do you belch {burp} a lot?*
18. ¿Padece usted de indigestión?	18. *Do you suffer from indigestion?*
19. ¿Suele tener ardor de estómago?	19. *Do you get heartburn?*
20. ¿Suele tener acidez en el esófago?	20. *Do you usually get heartburn?*

GASTROINTESTINAL

ESPAÑOL	ENGLISH

Dr. Jones: ¿Qué le sucede a usted, señorita Pérez?

Dr. Jones: What is your problem, Miss Pérez?

Srta. P: Me molesta mucho el estómago con frecuencia.

Miss Pérez: My stomach bothers me frequently.

Dr. P: ¿Cuántas comidas come usted al día?

Dr. J: How many meals a day do you normally eat?

Srta. P: Pues, siempre me desayuno bien. Jugo de naranja, dos huevos, jamón, unas tostadas y café.

Miss P: Well, I always eat a good breakfast. Orange juice, two eggs, ham, some toast and coffee.

Dr. J: ¿Almuerza usted?

Dr. J: Do you eat lunch?

Srta P: Generalmente bebo café negro todo el día.

Miss P: Usually I just drink black coffee all day.

Dr. J: ¿Y para la cena?

Dr. J: What about supper?

Srta. P: Con frecuencia estoy tan cansada que no tengo ganas de cocinar. Generalmente compro una hamburguesa y papas fritas y una Coca, o pollo frito con papas fritas.

Miss P: I am generally too tired to cook, so I have a hamburger and french fries, and a coke, or else fried chicken and french fries.

Dr. J: ¿Se siente descompuesta del estómago después de comer tal cena?

Dr. J: Do you have an upset stomach after eating such a supper?

GASTROINTESTINAL

ESPAÑOL	ENGLISH

EL SISTEMA GASTRO-INTESTINAL

1. ¿Tiene con frecuencia ...
    dolor de estómago?
    hinchazón?
    vómitos?
    eructos?

2. ¿Ha tenido...
    estreñimiento?
    diarrea?
    cólicos?

3. ¿Ha notado cambios en la consistencia de su excremento? ¿Es ...
    duro?
    suave?
    mucoso?

4. ¿Siente usted ...
    hinchazón?
    gases?
    acidez después de comer?

5. ¿Ha cambiado el color del excremento? ¿Es ...
    negro?
    claro?
    sanguinolento?

6. ¿Le han diagnosticado ...

    úlcera?
    infección de la vesícula biliar?
    cáncer de colon?
    pus en la orina?
    sangre en la orina?

THE GASTROINTESTINAL SYSTEM

1. Do you often have ...
    a stomachache?
    swelling?
    vomiting?
    belching?

2. Have you had ...
    constipation?
    diarrhea?
    abdominal cramps?

3. Have you noticed changes in the consistency of your stools? Is your stool ...
    hard?
    soft?
    full of mucus?

4. Do you feel...
    swollen?
    bloated?
    heartburn after eating?

5. Has your stool changed in color? Is it ...
    black?
    pale?
    bloody?

6. Have you ever been diagnosed as having...
    ulcers?
    gallbladder infection?
    cancer of the colon?
    pus in your urine?
    blood in your urine?

GENERAL INFORMATION

ESPAÑOL	ENGLISH
1. ¿A qué grupo sanguíneo pertenece usted?	1. What is your blood group?
2. ¿Pertenece usted al grupo... A?, B?, O?, AB?	2. Do you belong to group... A?, B?, O?, AB?
3. ¿Cuál es el factor RH suyo?	3. What is your RH blood factor?
4. ¿Es positivo? ¿Es negativo?	4. Is it positive? Is it negative?
5. ¿Sabe?	5. Do you know?
6. ¿Cómo se lesionó usted?	6. How were you injured?
7. ¿Se cayó?	7. Did you fall?
8. ¿Le dio un mareo?	8. Did you become dizzy?
9. ¿Se cortó?	9. Did you cut yourself?
10. ¿Se quemó?	10. Did you burn yourself?
11. ¿Tiene contusiones?	11. Do you have bruises?
12. ¿Tiene quemaduras?	12. Do you have burns?
13. ¿Tiene cortaduras?	13. Do you have cuts?
14. ¿Tiene una dislocación?	14. Do you have a dislocation?
15. ¿Tiene una fractura?	15. Do you have a fracture?
16. ¿Tiene laceraciones?	16. Do you have lacerations?
17. ¿Tiene perforaciones?	17. Do you have punctures?
18. ¿Tiene rasguños?	18. Do you have scrapes?
19. ¿Tiene una torcedura?	19. Do you have a sprain?
20. ¿Dónde se lesionó?	20. Where were you injured?
21. ¿Se lesionó en el trabajo?	21. Were you injured at work?
22. ¿Se lesionó en casa?	22. Were you injured at home?

GENERAL INFORMATION

ESPAÑOL	ENGLISH

21. ¿Se lesionó
     en casa?
     en el trabajo?
     en la escuela?
     en un accidente?

22. ¿De qué enfermedades padece o padecía su papá/mamá?

23. ¿Padece o padecía ...
     de diabetes?
     del corazón?
     de alta presión?
     de los riñones?
     de hemorragias?
     un ataque de apoplejía?

24. ¿Tiene o ha tenido usted ...

     algún problema cardíaco?
     dolor en el pecho?

25. ¿Cuándo le empezó?

26. ¿Con qué frecuencia lo siente?

27. ¿Es un dolor ...
     fuerte?
     sordo?
     con ardor?

28. ¿Se le extiende el dolor ...
     a uno de los brazos?
     a la espalda?
     al cuello?
     a los hombros?

29. ¿Tiene sensación de pesadez en el pecho?

30. ¿Siente entumecimiento en alguna parte?

31. ¿Le falta el aire?

32. ¿Escupe usted sangre?

33. ¿Tiene náuseas?

34. ¿Vomita mucho?

---

21. Were you injured
     at home?
     at work?
     at school?
     in an accident?

22. What disease does or did your father/mother have?

23. Does he/she have or had ...
     diabetes?
     heart trouble?
     high blood pressure?
     kidney problems?
     bleeding disorders?
     a stroke?

24. Do you have or have you ever had ...

     any heart problems?
     any pain in the chest?

25. When did it start?

26. How frequent is it?

27. Is it a ... pain?
     sharp
     dull
     burning

28. Does the pain radiate ...
     to either of your arms?
     to your back?
     to the neck?
     to the shoulders?

29. Do you have a heavy sensation in your chest?

30. Do you feel numb anywhere?

31. Are you short of breath?

32. Do you spit up blood?

33. Do you feel nauseous?

34. Are you vomiting much?

GENERAL INFORMATION

ESPAÑOL

ENGLISH

1. Por favor, muéstreme cualquier medio de identificación que tenga.

2. ¿Tiene usted ...
   tarjeta de identificación?
   permiso de conducir?
   tarjeta de seguro o Medicare?
   tarjeta del Seguro Social?

3. Si no tiene ninguna, no se preocupe. Cálmese.

4. ¿Quién es su médico? Por favor, escriba su nombre, dirección y número de teléfono.

5. ¿A quién quiere usted que notifiquemos? Favor de escribir su nombre, dirección y número de teléfono.

6. ¿Qué parentesco tiene esa persona con usted? ¿Es su ...
   esposo?
   esposa?
   mamá?
   papá?
   suegra?
   suegro?
   hijo?
   hija?
   hermano?
   hermana?
   patrón? } both are employer in English
   patrona? }
   amigo? } both are friend in English
   amiga? }

7. ¿Cómo se siente usted?

8. ¿ Se siente usted ...
   bien?
   más o menos?
   muy mal?

9. Por favor, indíqueme dónde le duele.

10. ¿Le duele ...
    la cabeza?
    el pecho?
    el costado?
    la espalda?

11. ¿Tiene dolor en algún otro lugar?

12. ¿Cómo le duele?

13. Le duele ...
    ligeramente?
    moderadamente?
    mucho?
    poco?

14. ¿Todavía le duele?

1. Please show me any means of identification you may have.

2. Do you have ...
   an identity card?
   a driver's license?
   an insurance or Medicare card?
   a Social Security card?

3. If you don't have any, don't worry. Just relax.

4. Who is your doctor? Please write his name, address, and telephone number.

5. Whom do you want us to notify? Please write the name, address, and telephone number.

6. What relation is this person to you? Is He/she your ...
   husband?
   wife?
   mother?
   father?
   mother-in-law?
   father-in-law?
   your son?
   your daughter?
   brother?
   sister?

   employer?

   friend?

7. How do you feel?

8. Do you feel ...
   fine?
   so-so?
   very bad?

9. Please point to where it hurts.

10. Does it hurt ...
    in the head?
    in the chest?
    on the side?
    in the back?

11. Do you hurt in any other place?

12. How does it hurt you?

13. Does it hurt you ...
    slightly?
    moderately?
    very much?
    a little?

14. Does it still hurt you?

GENERAL INFORMATION

ESPAÑOL	ENGLISH
1. ¿Cuál es su nombre?	1. *What is your name?*
2. ¿Cuál es su dirección?	2. *What is your address?*
3. ¿Cuál es su número de teléfono?	3. *What is your telephone number?*
4. ¿Cuánto pesa actualmente?	4. *How much do you currently weigh?*
5. ¿Es su peso normal?	5. *Is it your normal weight?*
6. ¿Ha bajado usted de peso recientemente?	6. *Have you lost any weight lately?*
7. ¿Qué enfermedades o síntomas tiene, que sepa usted?	7. *What illnesses or medical conditions do you have that you know about?*
8. ¿Ninguno?	8. *None?*
9. ¿Tiene una afección cardíaca?	9. *Do you have a heart condition?*
10. Padece usted de ...	10. *Do you have ...*
diabetes?	*diabetes?*
de los pulmones?	*lung problems?*
de los riñones?	*kidney problems?*
de presión alta?	*high blood pressure?*
de úlcera gástrica?	*stomach ulcers?*
11. ¿Cuándo era joven, ¿tuvo usted ...	11. *When you were young, did you have ...*
sarampión?	*measles?*
paperas?	*mumps?*
ictericia?	*jaundice?*
tos ferina?	*whooping cough?*
varicela?	*chickenpox?*

GENERAL INFORMATION

ESPAÑOL	ENGLISH
1. ¿Ha tenido usted hijos?	1. Have you had any children?
2. ¿Los tuvo normalmente o por cesárea?	2. Were they born naturally, or by cesarean?
3. ¿A qué edad le comenzó la menstruación?	3. At what age did you begin to menstruate?
4. ¿Se hace usted la prueba del Papanicolao todos los años?	4. Do you have a Pap smear every year?
5. ¿Practica usted control de la natalidad?	5. Do you practice birth control?
6. ¿Qué usa usted?	6. What do you use?
7. ¿Usa usted la píldora?	7. Do you use pills?
8. ¿Es usted regular en sus periodos?	8. Are your menstrual periods regular?
9. ¿Cuántos días le duran?	9. How many days do they last?
10. ¿Cuándo tuvo el periodo la última vez?	10. When did you last menstruate?
11. ¿Le pareció a usted que fue normal?	11. Did the flow seem normal?
12. ¿Tuvo dolor?	12. Was it painful?
13. ¿Tuvo alguna secreción de color amarillo o blanco?	13. Was there any yellow or white discharge?
14. ¿Ha tenido usted secreciones vaginales entre un periodo y otro?	14. Have you had vaginal discharge between menstrual periods?
15. ¿Cuándo fue la última vez que tuvo contacto sexual?	15. When did you last have sexual intercourse?

GENERAL INFORMATION

ESPAÑOL	ENGLISH
Q. Necesitamos alguna información en caso de emergencia.	Q. *We need some information from you in case of emergency.*
A. Bueno.	A. *OK.*
Q. ¿Cuántos años tiene usted?	Q. *How old are you?*
A. Tengo treinta y dos años.	A. *I am thirty two years old.*
Q. ¿De dónde es usted?	Q. *Where are you from?*
A. Soy de México.	A. *I am from Mexico.*
Q. ¿En qué trabaja usted?	Q. *What work do you do?*
A. Soy jardinero.	A. *I am a gardener.*
Q. ¿Está usted casado?	Q. *Are you married?*
A. Sí, estoy casado.	A. *Yes, I'm married.*
Q. ¿Trabaja su esposa?	Q. *Does your wife work?*
A. Sí, ella trabaja en McDonald's.	A. *Yes, she works at McDonald's.*
Q. ¿Tiene usted hijos?	Q. *Do you have any children?*
A. Sí, tengo dos; un hijo y una hija.	A. *Yes, I have two; a son and a daughter.*
Q. ¿Cuántos años tienen ellos?	Q. *How old are they?*
A. El muchacho tiene siete y la muchacha tiene cuatro.	A. *The boy is seven and the girl is four.*
Q. ¿A quién avisamos en caso de emergencia?	Q. *Whom do we notify in case of emergency?*
A. Tienen que avisar a mis padres porque mi esposa trabaja. Su número de teléfono es _____.	A. *You have to notify my parents because my wife works. Their telephone number is _____.*
Muy bien. Ahora usted tiene que llenar el formulario y firmar aquí.	*Very well. Now you must fill out the form and sign here.*

170

GENERAL INFORMATION

ESPAÑOL	ENGLISH
Q: ¿Cuándo es su cita con el especialista?	Q: *When is your appointment with the specialist?*
A: Es el martes a las dos de la tarde pero tengo que cambiar el día.	A: *It's on Tuesday at two in the afternoon but I have to change the day.*
Q: ¿Por qué?	Q: *Why?*
A: Porque el martes voy a trabajar hasta las cuatro y media.	A: *Because on Tuesday I have to work until four thirty.*
Q: ¿Es conveniente el jueves a las cinco?	Q: *Is Thursday at five convenient?*
A: Sí. Muchas gracias.	A: *Yes, thank you very much.*

GENERAL INFORMATION

ESPAÑOL	ENGLISH
Q: Buenos días. Hoy se ve mucho mejor. ¿Cómo durmió anoche?	Q: *Good morning. You look much better today. How did you sleep last night?*
A: Dormí mejor con las pastillas que me dio el médico.	A: *I slept better with the tablets that the doctor gave me.*
Q: Sí, eran calmantes. ¿Le duele el brazo donde le pusieron sangre?	Q: *Yes, they were tranquilizers. Does your arm hurt where they gave you the blood transfusion?*
A: No. Pero tengo unos moretones alrededor de la vena. ¿Cuándo me va a quitar el suero?	A: *No. But I have some bruises around the vein. When are you going to take out the I.V.?*
Q: Voy a quitárselo ahora mismo. Pero antes voy a tomarle el pulso y la temperatura. Por favor, póngase el termómetro debajo de la lengua.	Q: *I'm going to take it out right now. But first I'm going to take your pulse and temperature. Please put the thermometer under your tongue.*

GENITOURINARY

ESPAÑOL	ENGLISH

EL SISTEMA GENITO-URINARIO

1. Cuando orina, ¿tiene...
   dolor?
   ardor?
   dificultad al empezar o al
      terminar?

2. ¿Ha cambiado recientemente el
   color de su orina? ¿Es...
   oscura?
   turbia?
   anaranjada?
   sanguinolenta?

3. ¿Orina mucho o poco?

4. ¿Cuántas veces se levanta a orinar
   por las noches?

5. ¿Ha tenido un análisis de sangre
   positivo por ...
   sífilis?
   gonorrea?
   sida?

6. ¿Sufre de ...
   glándulas inflamadas en la
      ingle?
   secreción de los órganos
      genitales?
   dolor en los genitales?

7. ¿Ha tenido...
   pus en la orina?
   sangre en la orina?
   azúcar en la orina?

8. ¿Le han diagnosticado una
   infección ...
   de la vejiga?
   de los riñones?

THE GENITOURINARY SYSTEM

1. *When you urinate do you have...*
   pain?
   burning?
   difficulty when starting or
      finishing?

2. *Has the color of your urine changed*
   recently? Is it...
   dark?
   cloudy?
   orange-colored?
   bloody?

3. *Do you urinate a lot or a little?*

4. *How many times do you get up at*
   night to urinate?

5. *Have you had a positive blood test*
   for ...
   syphillis?
   gonorrhea?
   AIDS?

6. *Do you suffer from...*
   swelling of the glands in the
      groin?
   discharge from your genitalia?

   pain in your genitals?

7. *Have you had...*
   pus in the urine?
   blood in the urine?
   sugar in the urine?

8. *Have you ever been diagnosed as*
   having an infection ...
   of the bladder?
   of the kidneys?

GENITOURINARY

ESPAÑOL	ENGLISH
1. ¿Puede usted orinar?	1. Can you urinate?
2. Al orinar, ¿ha notado usted una demora en comenzar a orinar?	2. When you urinate do you notice a delay in beginning?
3. ¿Tiene usted pérdidas involuntarias de orina?	3. Are you unable to control your urine?
4. ¿Desde cuándo no orina usted?	4. How long has it been since you have urinated?
5. ¿Tiene usted ganas de orinar constantemente?	5. Do you feel like urinating constantly?
6. ¿Se le sale la orina involuntariamente cuando ... se ríe? estornuda? tose?	6. Have you ever passed urine involuntarily when you ... laugh? sneeze? cough?
7. ¿Con qué frecuencia orina usted?	7. How frequently do you urinate?
8. ¿Cuánto orina usted?	8. How much do you urinate?
9. Al orinar, ¿pasa mucha o poca orina?	9. When you urinate do you pass a lot or a little urine?
10. ¿Se despierta usted por la noche para orinar?	10. Do you awaken in the night to urinate?
10a. ¿Se levanta usted de la cama para orinar por la noche?	10a. Do you get out of bed to urinate during the night.
11. ¿Cuántas veces?	11. How often?
12. ¿Orinó usted?; ¿Hizo pipí? (slang)	12. Did you urinate? Did you pee? (Slang)
13. ¿Tiene usted o ha tenido dolor de riñones o de vejiga?	13. Do you have or have you ever had pain from your kidneys or bladder?
14. ¿Dónde le duele (dolía)?	14. Where is (was) the pain?
15. ¿Cuánto tiempo hace (hacía) que usted tiene (tenía) el dolor?	15. How long have (did) you had (have) the pain?
16. ¿Cuánto tiempo le dura (duraba)?	16. How long does (did) it last?
17. ¿Con qué frecuencia lo tiene (tenía)?	17. How often do (did) you have it?
18. ¿Cómo es el dolor?	18. What is the pain like?
19. ¿Siente dolor al empezar a orinar?	19. Is it pain when you begin to urinate?
20. ¿Siente dolor durante todo el tiempo que orina?	20. Is it pain the entire time you urinate?
21. ¿Siente dolor al terminar de orinar?	21. Is it pain at the end of urination?
22. ¿Le duele cuando orina usted?	22. Does it hurt when you urinate?
23. ¿Siente un ardor (quemazón) al orinar?	23. Is there a burning sensation when you urinate?
24. ¿Siente usted una urgencia para orinar?	24. Do you have a feeling of urgency to urinate?
25. ¿Hay alguna dificultad para empezar a orinar?	25. Is there any difficulty starting to urinate?
26. ¿Hay un chorro interrumpido de orina?	26. Is there an interrupted flow of urine?
27. ¿Ha notado goteo al terminar de orinar?	27. Do you notice dribbling after urination?
28. ¿Ha disminuido la fuerza del chorro de orina?	28. Is there a decrease in the force of flow of urine?
29. ¿Orina usted con arenilla?	29. Are there small stones in your urine?
30. ¿Ha tenido alguna vez cálculos renales?	30. Have you ever had kidney stones?
31. ¿Suele usted tener dolores de espalda?	31. Do you usually get backaches?

GYNECOLOGY

ESPAÑOL	ENGLISH
1. ¿Cuándo fue su última menstruación? ¿Cuándo fue su último periodo? ¿Cuándo fue su última regla?	1. When was your last menstrual period?
2. ¿Cuánto tiempo le duró?	2. How long did it last?
3. ¿Cada cuándo menstrúa usted?	3. How often do you get your periods?
4. ¿Cuántos días le dura?	4. How many days does it last?
5. ¿La tiene ahora?	5. Do you have it now?
6. ¿Sale poca (mucha) sangre?	6. Do you have a light (heavy) flow?
7. ¿A qué edad tuvo su primera menstruación?	7. How old were you when you first began to menstruate?
8. ¿Han sido regulares sus reglas hasta ahora?	8. Have your periods always been regular up to now?
9. ¿Ha tenido alguna vez desórdenes menstruales?	9. Have you ever had menstrual problems?
10. ¿Ha tenido dolor con ella?	10. Do you have pain with it?
11. ¿Suele usted tener dolor con su regla?	11. Do you usually have pain with your periods?
12. ¿Fue más fuerte esta vez?	12. Was it worse this time?
13. ¿Sangró usted más de lo ordinario?	13. Was there more bleeding than usual?
14. ¿Cómo es su estado de ánimo durante la menstruación?	14. How is your mood during your period?
15. Describa usted su hemorragia menstrual.	15. Describe your menstrual flow.
16. ¿Tiene usted manchas de sangre entre periodos menstruales?	16. Do you spot between periods?
17. ¿Está sangrando mucho?	17. Are you bleeding heavily?
18. ¿Cuántas toallas higiénicas ha usado usted en su última menstruación?	18. How many sanitary pads or tampons did you use during your last menstrual cycle?
19. ¿Aumenta usted de peso durante su periodo?	19. Do you gain weight during your period?

GYNECOLOGY

ESPAÑOL	ENGLISH
20. ¿Sufre usted de dolores fuertes del periodo?	20. Do you have severe menstrual cramps?
21. Con su periodo, ¿le duelen los senos?	21. Are your breasts tender during your period?
22. ¿Tiene usted secreciones vaginales?	22. Do you have vaginal secretions?
23. ¿Son acuosas?	23. Are they watery?
24. ¿Son espesas y amarillas?	24. Are they thick and yellow?
25. ¿Son espesas y blancas?	25. Are they thick and white?
26. ¿Son espumosas y verdosas?	26. Are they frothy and greenish?
27. ¿Tiene usted comezón en la vagina?	27. Is your vagina itchy?
28. ¿La ha tenido antes?	28. Have you had it before?
29. ¿Cuánto tiempo hace que le sale esta descarga?	29. How long has the discharge been there?
30. ¿Ha tenido una enfermedad venérca?	30. Have you ever had venereal disease?
31. ¿Está circuncidado su esposo?	31. Is your husband circumcised?
32. ¿Padece usted de prolapso uterino?	32. Do you suffer from prolapse of the uterus?
33. ¿Cuándo se le hizo su último Papanicolau?	33. When was your last Pap Smear?
34. ¿Fueron normales los resultados?	34. Were the results normal?
35. ¿Fueron anormales los resultados?	35. Were the results abnormal?

GYNECOLOGY

ESPAÑOL	ENGLISH

1. ¿Cuántos hijos ha tenido usted?

2. ¿Cuántas veces ha estado embarazada?

3. ¿Cuándo espera dar a luz?

4. ¿Ha tenido algún aborto espontáneo?

5. ¿A qué hora le empezaron las contracciones?

6. ¿Cuánto le dura cada contracción?

7. ¿Con qué frecuencia tiene las contracciones?

8. ¿Ya se le rompió la bolsa? ¿Cuándo?

9. ¿Qué color y olor tenía el líquido?

10. ¿Cuál es la cantidad y el color del flujo vaginal?

11. ¿Cuándo fue la última vez que comió o bebió algo? ¿Qué fue y cuánto?

12. ¿Tiene dolores?

13. Indíqueme dónde.

14. ¿Necesita tomar una pastilla para calmar el dolor?

15. ¿Necesita una inyección para calmar el dolor?

16. ¿Le duelen los pechos o los siente llenos?

17. Esta pastilla es para sacarle la leche.

18. Todavía no es hora de tomar la pastilla.

19. ¿Tiene mareos?

20. ¿Ha evacuado el intestino? ¿Cuándo?

21. ¿Ha orinado?

22. Queremos tomarle una muestra de orina.

---

1. How many children have you had?

2. How many times have you been pregnant?

3. What is your due date?

4. Have you had any stillborn births?

5. What time did the contractions begin?

6. How long is each contraction?

7. How far apart are the contractions?

8. Have the membranes ruptured? When?

9. What was the color and odor of the fluid?

10. What is the color and amount of vaginal drainage?

11. When was the last time you ate or drank anything? What was it and how much?

12. Do you have pain?

13. Show me where.

14. Do you need a pain pill?

15. Do you need a pain shot?

16. Are your breasts sore or filling up?

17. This pill is to dry up your breasts.

18. It isn't time for your pain pill yet.

19. Do you feel dizzy?

20. Have you moved your bowels? When?

21. Have you urinated?

22. We need a urine specimen from you.

GYNECOLOGY

ESPAÑOL	ENGLISH

1. **ABORTO:** expulsión del feto antes del tiempo normal.

1. *ABORTION: expulsion of the fetus before normal time.*

2. **AMENORREA:** cese anormal de la menstruación.

2. *AMENORRHEA: abnormal cessation of menstruation.*

3. **PARTO:** nacimiento de una criatura.

3. *DELIVERY: birth of a child.*

4. **TROMPAS DE FALOPIO:** conductos que unen los ovarios con el útero.

4. *FALLOPIAN TUBES: tubes connecting the ovaries with the uterus.*

5. **FETO:** embrión después del tercer mes.

5. *FETUS: embryo after the third month.*

6. **OVARIOS:** las dos glándulas sexuales femeninas que producen los óvulos.

6. *OVARIES: the two female sex glands that produce the eggs (ovum).*

7. **EPISIOTOMÍA:** incisión en la pared vaginal para facilitar el parto y evitar el desgarro del perineo.

7. *EPISIOTOMY: incision of the vaginal wall to facilitate delivery and prevent perineal tears.*

8. **MASTITIS:** inflamación del seno por alguna infección.

8. *MASTITIS: inflamation of the breast due to infection.*

9. **MENSTRUACIÓN:** flujo mensual de sangre del útero.

9. *MENSTRUATION: monthly flow of blood from the uterus.*

10. **PRIMÍPARA:** mujer en estado por primera vez.

10. *PRIMIPARA: woman who is pregnant for the first time.*

HEADACHES

ESPAÑOL	ENGLISH
1. ¿Tiene usted dolores de cabeza?	1. *Do you have headaches?*
2. ¿Tiene usted jaquecas?	2. *Do you have headaches?*
3. ¿Tiene usted migrañas?	3. *Do you have migraines?*
4. ¿Se siente usted mareado algunas veces? (male)	4. *Do you ever feel dizzy?*
5. ¿Se siente usted mareada algunas veces? (female)	5. *Do you ever feel dizzy?*
6. ¿Te sientes mareado algunas veces? (male child)	6. *Do you ever feel dizzy?*
7. ¿Te sientes mareada algunas veces? (female child)	7. *Do you ever feel dizzy?*
8. ¿Cuánto tiempo le dura el mareo? (male/female)	8. *How long do you feel dizzy?*
9. ¿Cuánto tiempo te dura el mareo? (male/female/child)	9. *How long do you feel dizzy?*
10. ¿Cuánto tiempo le duran los dolores de cabeza?	10. *How long do your headaches usually last?*
11. Mientras tiene dolor de cabeza, ¿siente náuseas alguna vez? {male/female}	11. *Do you ever feel nauseated while you have a headache?*
12. Mientras tienes dolor de cabeza, ¿sientes náuseas alguna vez? {male/female/child}	12. *Do you ever feel nauseated while you have a headache?*
13. ¿Qué hace para sus dolores de cabeza? (adult)	13. *What do you do for headaches?*
14. ¿Qué haces para tus dolores de cabeza? (child)	14. *What do you do for headaches?*
15. ¿Cuánto hace que tiene estos dolores de cabeza? (adult)	15. *How long have you had these headaches?*
16. ¿Cuánto hace que tienes estos dolores de cabeza? (child)	16. *How long have you had these headaches?*
17. ¿Dónde le duele, exactamente? (male/female adult)	17. *Where is the pain exactly?*
18. ¿Dónde te duele, exactamente? (male/female child)	18. *Where is the pain exactly?*
19. ¿Siempre tiene (tienes) el dolor de cabeza en el mismo sitio?	19. *Is the headache in the same place each time?*
20. ¿Qué le (te) causa los dolores de cabeza?	20. *What causes the headaches?*

HEADACHES

21. ¿Ha tenido dolores de cabeza con vómitos? (male/female/adult)

21. *Have the headaches occured with vomiting?*

22. ¿Has tenido dolores de cabeza con vómitos? (male/female/child)

22. *Have the headaches occured with vomiting?*

23. ¿Ha (has) tenido recientemente trauma en la cabeza?

23. *Have you had recent head trauma?*

24. ¿Tiene la presión alta?

24. *Do you have high blood pressure?*

25. ¿Tiene la tensión alta?

25. *Do you have high blood pressure?*

26. ¿Hay algunos cambios en su vista?

26. *Are there any changes in your vision?*

27. ¿Dónde siente {sientes} el dolor de cabeza?

27. *Where do you feel the headache?*

28. ¿Hacia dónde se irradia?

28. *Where does it radiate?*

29. ¿Su (tu) dolor de cabeza ocurrió de repente o gradualmente?

29. *Did the headache occur suddenly or gradually?*

30. ¿Cuándo ocurren sus (tus) dolores de cabeza?

30. *When do the headaches occur?*

31. ¿Con qué frecuencia ocurren?

31. *How often do they occur?*

32. ¿Son continuos o intermitentes?

32. *Are they continuous or intermittent?*

33. ¿Puede (puedes) describir el dolor de cabeza?

33. *Can you describe the pain?*

34. ¿El dolor de cabeza lo (la) despierta?

34. *Does the headache awaken you from sleep?*

35. ¿El dolor de cabeza te despierta? (male/female/child)

35. *Does the headache awaken you from sleep?*

HIV TESTING

ESPAÑOL

1. Esta no es una prueba de sida, sino para el anticuerpo del virus VIH.

2. Este anticuerpo es fabricado por el cuerpo después de tener exposición al virus y no parece que este anticuerpo proteja el cuerpo contra el virus.

3. La infección por el virus puede causar el sida, una condición relacionada con el sida (una enfermedad menos grave con las glándulas hinchadas), o ningún síntoma.

4. Pueden pasar de dos semanas a seis meses después de la exposición al virus VIH antes de que puedan ser detectados los anticuerpos en la sangre.

5. La prueba es muy exacta y es poco el riesgo de obtener un resultado positivo falso.

6. Un resultado positivo falso quiere decir que la prueba indica una infección del virus cuando no ha habido contacto con él.

7. Una persona recibe resultado positivo solamente si cuatro pruebas distintas de la misma muestra de sangre dan positivo.

8. Un resultado positivo no quiere decir que una persona desarrollará el sida.

9. Se deben tomar todas las precauciones de no infectar a otros o de reinfectarse a sí mismo.

10. La prueba es exacta y es poco el riesgo de un resultado negativo falso.

11. Un resultado negativo falso quiere decir que la prueba indica que no hay infección cuando sí la hay, pero ahora, no hay bastante anticuerpo en la sangre para que la prueba pueda indicar una infección.

12. Un resultado negativo es válido solamente en la fecha en que la muestra fue obtenida.

13. Un resultado negativo es válido solamente si no ha sido expuesto/a al virus dentro de los seis meses anteriores a la fecha de la prueba.

14. Un resultado negativo en una persona de alto riesgo no disminuye la importancia de tener relaciones sexuales con protección.

ENGLISH

1. *This is not a test for AIDS, but for the HIV virus.*

2. *These antibodies are made by the body following exposure to the virus and do not seem to protect the body against the virus.*

3. *Infection with the virus may cause AIDS, an AIDS-related illness (a less severe illness with swollen glands), or no symptomatic illness.*

4. *It may be two weeks to six months after exposure to the HIV virus before antibodies can be detected in your blood.*

5. *The test is extremely accurate and there is little chance of a false-positive test result.*

6. *A false-positive means a test result that shows positive when no infection with the virus has occurred.*

7. *A person will receive a positive result only if four separate tests on the same blood specimen show positive.*

8. *A positive result does not mean a person will develop AIDS.*

9. *One should, however, take all precautions not to infect others or re-infect oneself.*

10. *The test is accurate and there is little chance of a false-negative test result.*

11. *A false-negative means a test result that shows negative when there actually was exposure to the virus, but not enough antibody has developed to be detected in your blood at this time.*

12. *A negative test result is negative only on the date the blood specimen was obtained.*

13. *A negative blood test result is valid only if you have had no additional exposure to the virus within six months prior to the test date.*

14. *A negative result in a high-risk person doesn't lessen the importance of safer sex guidelines.*

HOME SERVICES

ESPAÑOL

ENGLISH

AYUDANTES Y SERVICIO CASERO

AIDES AND HOMEMAKER SERVICE

1. ¿Quisiera ayuda para bañarse?

1. *Would you like help with a bath?*

2. ¿Quisiera algo de comer?
Quisiera ...
    el desayuno?
    el almuerzo?
    una merienda
    un bocadito?

2. *Would you like something to eat?*
Would you like ...
    breakfast?
    lunch?
    a snack?
    a snack?

3. ¿Quisiera algo de beber?
¿Quisiera ...
    agua?
    jugo de naranja?
    jugo de piña?
    jugo de toronja?
    jugo de ciruela?
    jugo de arándano?
    jugo de manzana?

3. *Would you like something to drink?*
Would you like ...
    water?
    orange juice?
    pineapple juice?
    grapefruit juice?
    prune juice?
    cranberry juice?
    apple juice?

4. ¿Puedo prepararle una comida hoy para que usted pueda comerla mañana?

4. *Can I make a meal today for you to eat tomorrow?*

5. ¿Puedo lavar su ropa?

5. *May I do your laundry?*

6. ¿Tiene calor/frío?

6. *Do you feel hot/cold?*

7. ¿Está usted cómodo/a?

7. *Are you comfortable?*

HOME SERVICES

ESPAÑOL	ENGLISH
EL DIETISTA/LA DIETISTA	*DIETITIAN*
1. Yo soy su dietista.	1. I am your dietitian.
2. ¿Tiene problemas al mascar (masticar)?	2. Do you have any problems chewing?
3. ¿Tiene alergias a ciertos alimentos?	3. Do you have any food allergies?
4. ¿Usa dentadura postiza?	4. Do you wear dentures?
5. ¿La siente bien?	5. Do they fit properly?
6. ¿Necesita comida mecánicamente ablandada o en puré?	6. Do you need your food mechanically softened or pureed?
7. ¿Tiene su menú listo para manaña?	7. Do you have your menu filled out for tomorrow?
8. ¿Necesita ayuda con el menú?	8. Do you need help with your menu?
9. ¿Sigue una dieta en casa?	9. Do you follow a diet at home?
10. ¿Cocina para usted mismo/a?	10. Do you cook for yourself?
11. ¿Ha tenido problemas de peso casi toda su vida?	11. Have you had a weight problem most of your life?
12. ¿Ha ganado o perdido peso en los últimos seis meses?	12. Have you gained or lost any weight in the past six months?
13. ¿Sabe cuál es su dieta actual y por qué está en esa dieta?	13. Do you know what your present diet is, and why you are on that diet?
14. ¿Lo/La visitará hoy algún miembro de su familia que hable inglés?	14. Is a family member who speaks English coming to visit you today?
15. ¿Cómo está la comida?	15. How is the food?
16. ¿Le gusta comer algo fuera de las horas de comidas?	16. Do you like to snack between meals?
17. Durante los siguientes tres días se le contarán las calorías (análisis nutricional) para ver cuántas calorías consume.	17. For the next three days you will be on a calorie count (nutritional analysis) to see how many calories you are eating.
18. Beba ocho vasos de agua por día.	18. Drink eight glasses of water each day.
19. ¿Tiene hambre?	19. Are you hungry?
20. ¿Está satisfecho/a?	20. Are you full?
21. ¿Hay algo que le podamos traer?	21. Is there something we can bring you?

HYGEINE

ESPAÑOL	ENGLISH
1. Usted puede bañarse.	1. You may take a bath.
2. Usted puede darse una ducha.	2. You may take a shower.
3. Usted puede ducharse.	3. You may take a shower.
4. Usted puede darse una regadera. {Mexican}	4. You may take a shower.
5. Usted puede darse un baño de asiento.	5. You may take a sitz bath.
6. Tome un baño de asiento caliente cada cuatro horas.	6. Take a hot sitz bath every four hours.
7. Usted puede usar la chata (el bacín/el pato).	7. You may use the bedpan.
8. Usted puede usar el lavamanos.	8. You may use the washbowl.
9. Usted puede usar la jofaina.	9. You may use the washbowl.
10. Vamos a darle un baño.	10. We are going to give you a bath.
11. ¿Quiere usted que yo lo bañe? (male)	11. Do you want me to wash you?
12. ¿Quiere usted que yo la bañe? (female)	12. Do you want me to wash you?
13. ¿Quiere usted que yo lo lave? (male)	13. Do you want me to wash you?
14. ¿Quiere usted que yo la lave? (female)	14. Do you want me to wash you?
15. Lávese los órganos genitales.	15. Wash your genitals.
16. ¿Puede bañarse sin ayuda?	16. Can you take a bath without help?
17. ¿Puede peinarse sin ayuda?	17. Can you comb yourself without help?
18. ¿Puede afeitarse sin ayuda?	18. Can you shave yourself without help?
19. ¿Quiere que yo lo/la peine?	19. Do you want me to comb you?
20. ¿Quiere que yo lo/la afeite?	20. Do you want me to shave you?

HYGIENE

ESPAÑOL	**ENGLISH**
21. Trate de hacerlo por sí mismo. {male}	*21. Try to do it yourself.*
22. Trate de hacerlo por sí misma. {female}	*22. Try to do it yourself.*
23. Llame cuando tenga que ir al inodoro.	*23. Call when you have to go to the toilet.*
24. Llame cuando tenga que ir al servicio.	*24. Call when you have to go to the toilet.*
25. Llame cuando tenga que ir al cuarto de baño.	*25. Call when you have to go to the toilet.*
26. ¿Quiere ir al inodoro?	*26. Do you want to go to the toilet?*
27. ¿Quiere ir al servicio?	*27. Do you want to go to the toilet?*
28. ¿Quiere ir al cuarto de baño?	*28. Do you want to go to the toilet?*
29. ¿Necesita usted la cuña (el bacín, el pato)?	*29. Do you need the bed pan?*

INJURIES

ESPAÑOL	ENGLISH
Violación	*Rape/Sexual Assault*

1. ¿A qué hora ocurrió?	1. *What time did it happen?*
2. ¿Cuándo ocurrió?	2. *When did it happen?*
3. ¿Hubo penetración de la vagina?	3. *Was there vaginal penetration?*
4. ¿Hubo penetración por el recto?	4. *Was there rectal penetration?*
5. ¿Hubo penetración oral?	5. *Was there oral penetration?*
6. ¿Usó él objetos extraños?	6. *Did he use any foreign objects?*
7. ¿Está herida?	7. *Are you hurt?*
8. ¿Está lastimada?	8. *Are you hurt?*
9. ¿Dónde está ahora?	9. *Where are you now?*
10. ¿Está usted en un lugar seguro?	10. *Are you in a safe place?*
11. ¿Está usted sola?	11. *Are you alone?*
12. ¿Cómo se siente?	12. *How do you feel?*
13. ¿Tiene miedo de embarazarse?	13. *Are you afraid of getting pregnant?*
14. ¿Cuándo fue su última regla (menstruación)?	14. *When did you last menstruate?*
15. ¿Cuando fue la última vez que tuvo relaciones sexuales?	15. *When was the last time that you had sexual relations?*
16. No es su culpa que fuera violada.	16. *It is not your fault you were raped.*
17. Necesitamos esta información con propósitos médicos, no porque seamos curiosos.	17. *We need this information for medical purposes, not because we are curious.*
18. Usted está segura ahora. Necesitamos llevarla al hospital.	18. *You are safe now. We need to take you to the hospital.*
19. ¿Quiere que yo llame a un(una) amigo(a) o pariente?	19. *Do you want me to call a friend or relative for you?*
20. ¿Quiere que yo llame a alguien del "Rape Crisis Center" para que esté con usted?	20. *Do you want me to call someone from the Rape Crisis Center to be with you?*
21. ¿Sabe usted quién lo hizo?	21. *Do you know who did it?*
22. Yo sé que es vergonzoso que usted me dé toda la información.	22. *I know it is embarrassing to give me all of the information.*
23. Algunas pruebas que le vamos a hacer posiblemente le van a doler.	23. *Some of the tests we are going to run might hurt.*

185

INJURIES

ESPAÑOL	ENGLISH

HERIDAS, CORTADURAS

1. Usted se ha
   a. herido.
   b. cortado.

2. Usted tiene una
   a. laceración.
   b. cuchillada.
   c. herida punzante.

3. Usted no necesitará puntos (suturas).

4. Le voy a aplicar medicina para quitarle el dolor.

5. No le va a doler.

6. Necesita puntos para su cortadura.

7. Debe mantener los puntos secos.

8. Regrese en unos días para que le quiten los puntos.

9. No se moje la venda.

10. Regrese enseguida si la herida le duele, o si se le enrojece o se le hincha.

WOUNDS, CUTS

1. *You have been*
   a. *wounded.*
   b. *cut.*

2. *You have a*
   a. *laceration.*
   b. *gash.*
   c. *puncture wound*

3. *You won't need stitches.*

4. *I will apply medicine to make the pain go away.*

5. *It will not hurt.*

6. *You will need stitches for your cut.*

7. *You must keep the stitches dry.*

8. *Return in a few days to have the stitches removed.*

9. *Do not get the bandage wet.*

10. *Return at once if the wound becomes painful, red, or swollen.*

INJURIES

ESPAÑOL	ENGLISH

FRACTURAS

1. Usted se ha quebrado/roto un hueso.

2. Usted se ha fracturado un hueso.

3. Usted se ha dislocado una coyuntura (una articulación).

4. Usted se ha distendido un músculo.

5. Usted se ha torcido un músculo.

   Usted se ha torcido un ligamento.

6. Necesitará un yeso para su brazo quebrado.

7. Regrese enseguida si los dedos (los dedos del pie) se le entumecen, se le azulan o si no puede moverlos.

SPRAINS

1. You have broken a bone.

2. You have fractured a bone.

3. You have dislocated a joint.

4. You have pulled a muscle.

5. You have twisted (sprained) a muscle.
   You have twisted (sprained) a ligament.

6. You will need a cast for your broken arm.

7. Return at once if your fingers (toes) become numb or blue or if you cannot move them.

INJUItES

ESPAÑOL	**ENGLISH**

EL PACIENTE INCONSCIENTE

UNCONSCIOUS PATIENT

1. ¿Qué le pasó?

2. ¿Qué le sucedió?

3. ¿Se ha desmayado? (male/female)

4. Él(Ella) se quejó de dolor y se cayó al suelo.

5. Él(Ella) se atragantó con la comida.

6. Se emborrachó.

7. ¿Padece ...
   del corazón?
   de diabetes?
   de enfisema? del asma?
   de bronquitis?
   de problemas respiratorios?

8. ¿Está tomando alguna medicina? ¿De qué clase?
   ¿Para el corazón?
   ¿Para los pulmones?
   ¿Insulina?

9. ¿Puede traerme las medicinas que él(ella) toma?

10. ¿Ha sufrido recientemente una lesión/herida en la cabeza?

11. ¿Ha vomitado?

12. ¿Ha sido tratado en este hospital antes?

13. ¿Ha estado enfermo/a antes?

14. ¿ Está embarazada?

15. ¿Tiene alergias?

16. ¿Ha sido picado/a ...
    por una abeja?
    por una avispa?
    por una araña?

17. ¿Fue mordido/a por una culebra?

18. ¿De qué clase?

---

1. *What happened to him(her)?*

2. *What happened to him(her)?*

3. *Has he(she) fainted?*

4. *He(She) complained of pain and fell to the floor.*

5. *He(She) choked on food.*

6. *He(She) got drunk.*

7. *Does he(she) have ...*
   heart disease?
   diabetes?
   emphysema? asthma?
   bronchitis?
   breathing problems?

8. *Is he(she) taking any medications? What kind?*
   For the heart?
   For the lungs?
   Insulin?

9. *Can you bring me the medicines he(she) takes?*

10. *Has he(she) had a recent head injury?*

11. *Has he(she) vomited?*

12. *Has he(she) been treated in this hospital before?*

13. *Has he(she) been ill before?*

14. *Is she pregnant?*

15. *Does he(she) have allergies?*

16. *Has he(she) been stung ...*
    by a bee?
    by wasp?
    by a spider?

17. *Was he(she) bitten by a snake?*

18. *What kind?*

INSULIN SELF-INJECTION

ESPAÑOL	ENGLISH
1. Es muy importante mantenerse muy limpio.	1. *It is very important to keep very clean.*
2. Lávese las manos.	2. *Wash your hands.*
3. Haga rodar la botella de insulina entre las manos para mezclarla.	3. *Roll the bottle of insulin between your hands in order to mix.*
4. Es importante no agitar la botella. No agite la botella.	4. *It's important not to shake the bottle. Do not shake the bottle.*
5. Limpie la tapa de la botella con algodón mojado en alcohol.	5. *Wipe off the top of the bottle with alcohol and cotton.*
6. Mantenga la aguja esterilizada.	6. *Keep the needle sterile.*
7. Mueva el émbolo hasta la marca que corresponde a la dosis.	7. *Set the plunger at the mark showing your dosage.*
8. Después inserte la aguja por la tapa de goma de la botella e inyecte el aire de la jeringuilla dentro de la botella.	8. *Then push the needle through the rubber top of the bottle and inject the air from the syringe into the bottle.*
9. Invierta la botella.	9. *Invert the bottle.*
10. Mantenga la aguja bajo la superficie de la solución.	10. *Keep the needle below the surface of the solution.*
11. Extraiga la dosis de insulina dentro de la jeringuilla.	11. *Draw out your dosage of insulin into the syringe.*
12. Saque el aire de la jeringuilla.	12. *Push out the air bubbles from the syringe.*

INSULIN SELF-INJECTION

ESPAÑOL	ENGLISH
13. Ponga la jeringuilla sobre la caja del frasco.	*13. Place the syringe on the boxtop.*
14. No permita que la aguja toque nada.	*14. Keep the needle from touching anything.*
15. Limpie o frote la piel con algodón mojado en alcohol en el sitio de la inyección.	*15. Wipe the skin with alcohol at the place of the injection.*
16. Pellizque la piel con los dedos puestos a unas tres pulgadas para hacer un pliegue.	*16. Pinch the skin up with the fingers spread at about three inches apart, to make a fold.*
17. Inserte la aguja rápidamente bajo la piel en la parte de arriba del pliegue.	*17. Insert the needle quickly under the skin into the top of the fold.*
18. Apriete el émbolo suavemente hasta que se haya terminado toda la insulina en la jeringuilla.	*18. Push the plunger slowly until all the insulin is gone from the syringe.*
19. Ponga algodón con alcohol sobre el sitio, apriete la piel ligeramente y extraiga la aguja.	*19. Place cotton with alcohol over the spot, press slightly, and pull out the needle.*
20. Póngase la insulina a la misma hora todos los días, o según se lo indique el médico.	*20. Take your insulin at the same time every day or as the doctor orders.*
21. Conserve su insulina en el refrigerador o según se lo indique el médico.	*21. Keep your insulin in the refrigerator or where the doctor recommends.*
22. Deseche la aguja en una lata de café vacía o en otro envase cerrado antes de ponerla en la basura.	*22. Dispose of the needle in an empty coffee can or another safe, sealed container before placing it in the garbage.*

LABOR AND DELIVERY

ESPAÑOL	ENGLISH
1. ¿Se le rompió la bolsa de aguas? ¿Cuándo?	1. *Has your water broken? When?*
2. ¿Cuándo le comenzaron los dolores?	2. *When did your pains begin?*
3. ¿Cuántos minutos pasan entre un dolor y otro?	3. *How many minutes apart are they now?*
4. ¿Tiene usted mucho dolor?	4. *Do you have a lot of pain?*
5. Abra la boca y respire. No empuje.	5. *Open your mouth and breathe. Do not push.*
6. Cuando le venga el dolor, empuje.	6. *Every time the pain comes, push.*
7. Necesito hacerle un examen interno.	7. *I need to examine you internally.*
8. Tengo que examinarla vaginalmente.	8. *I have to examine you vaginally.*
9. Ponga los pies en estos estribos.	9. *Put your feet in these stirrups.*
10. Abra las rodillas y las piernas.	10. *Spread your knees and legs apart.*
11. No es posible que su bebé nazca por la vagina; por eso vamos a hacerle una cesárea. ¿Entiende?	11. *It is not possible for your baby to be born vaginally; we are going to do a cesarean section. Do you understand?*
12. Su bebé está en posición de nalgas y es mejor que hagamos una cesárea.	12. *Your baby is in a difficult breech position, and it is safer to have your baby with a cesarean section.*
13. Empuje.	13. *Push.*
14. No empuje.	14. *Don't push.*

LABOR AND DELIVERY

ESPAÑOL

ENGLISH

15. Una operación cesárea (cirugía de parto) es una operación en la que nace su bebé cuando hacemos una incisión en el abdomen.

15. *A cesarean section is an operation in which your baby is born via an incision made abdominally.*

16. Hay dos tipos de anestesia que se pueden usar.

16. *There are two possible types of anesthesia.*

17. Con la epidural usted está despierta y puede ver al (a la) bebé inmediatamente pero no podrá sentir la incisión.

17. *With an epidural, you will be awake and can see your baby right away, but you won't be able to feel the incision.*

18. Con la anestesia general podrá ver al (a la) bebé cuando usted salga de la sala de recuperación.

18. *With full anesthesia you will be able to see your baby when you come out of the recovery room.*

19. Voy a escuchar los latidos del corazón del (de la) bebé.

19. *I'm going to listen to the baby's heartbeat.*

20. Éste es un monitor del feto que nos ayuda a revisar el latido del corazón del (de la) bebé.

20. *This is a fetal monitor which enables us to check the baby's heartbeat continually.*

21. Tenemos que ponerle un catéter.

21. *We have to catheterize you.*

22. Le será un poco incómodo.

22. *It will be a little uncomfortable.*

23. Tenemos que ponerle un suero en el brazo.

23. *We have to start an IV in your arm.*

24. Ayudará a mantenerle los fluidos.

24. *It will help keep fluids in you.*

25. Le voy a dar una medicina que le producirá dolores más fuertes— Pitocin (oxytocin).

25. *I'm going to give you some medication to make your pains stronger—Pitocin (oxytocin).*

26. Le voy a dar una medicina para el dolor a través del suero.

26. *I am going to give you some medication for the pain through your IV.*

27. Póngase de lado. (Voltéese.)

27. *Roll over on your side.*

28. Agárrese las rodillas y empuje.

28. *Grab your knees and push.*

29. Felicidades, usted tiene un(a) niño(a) sano(a).

29. *Congratulations, you have a healthy baby boy (girl).*

30. Su bebé tiene algunos problemas médicos.

30. *Your baby has some medical problems.*

31. Llamaremos a un(a) intérprete para que se los explique.

31. *We will call an interpreter so that he/she will explain the problems to you.*

MEDICAL SOCIAL WORKER

ESPAÑOL

ENGLISH

1. Soy uno/a de los/las trabajadores sociales del hospital. ¿Usted quería verme?

1. *I am one of the hospital social workers. You asked to see me?*

2. ¿En qué puedo ayudarle?

2. *How can I help you?*

3. Soy el/la trabajador/a social ...
   en este piso.
   en este servicio.
   en esta unidad.
   que va a trabajar con usted y con el equipo de rehabilitación.

3. *I am the social worker ...*
   on this floor.
   on this service.
   on this unit.
   who will be working with you and the rehabilitation team.

4. Su médico me ha pedido que le vea para hablar ...
   sobre sus planes para cuando salga de aquí.
   sobre sus problemas.
   sobre su situación en casa.

4. *Your doctor has asked me to see you ...*
   about your plans for discharge.

   about your concerns.
   about your home situation.

5. ¿Vive solo/a? ¿Habrá alguien disponible para ayudarle? ¿Miembros de la familia?

5. *Do you live alone? Will someone be available to help you? Family members?*

6. ¿Prefiere hablar en español o en inglés?

6. *Would you prefer to speak in English or Spanish?*

7. Favor de repetir eso. No entiendo.

7. *Please repeat that, I don't quite understand.*

8. ¿Sabe dónde está usted?

8. *Do you know where you are?*

9. ¿Sabe que usted está en un hospital?

9. *Do you know that you are in a hospital?*

10. ¿Sabe por qué está aquí?

10. *Do you know why you are here?*

11. ¿Sabe su familia que usted está aquí?

11. *Does your family know you are here?*

12. ¿Quiere ponerse en contacto con alguien?

12. *Do you want to contact anyone?*

MEDICAL SOCIAL WORKER

ESPAÑOL

ENGLISH

13. ¿Dónde vivía usted antes de que viniera al hospital?

13. *Where were you living before you came into the hospital?*

14. ¿Podrá usted regresar allí?

14. *Will you be able to return there?*

15. ¿Por qué no puede regresar allí?

15. *Why can't you return there?*

16. ¿Hay alguien que pueda traerle a sus citas? ¿Llevarle a casa?

16. *Is there someone who can transport you (bring you) to your appointments? Take you home?*

17. ¿Va a necesitar ayuda en casa?

17. *Will you need help at home?*

18. Su médico(a) cree que sería mejor tener un(a) enfermero(a) visitante (enfermero(a) de salud pública) que venga a verle para asegurar que usted se maneja bien.

18. *Your doctor believes it would be best to have a visiting nurse (public health nurse) come by and see you to make sure you are managing all right.*

19. ¿Entiende qué actividades usted debe evitar?

19. *Do you understand what activities you are to avoid?*

20. ¿Entiende lo que puede hacer?

20. *Do you understand what you are able to do?*

21. ¿Tiene un/a trabajador/a social de la comunidad?

21. *Do you have a community social worker?*

22. ¿Cree que el alcohol ha sido un problema mayor para usted?

22. *Do you think alcohol has been a major problem for you?*

23. ¿Ha ido alguna vez a una casa de recuperación del alcoholismo?

23. *Have you ever been to an alcohol recovery facility?*

24. ¿Ha visto a un/a psiquiatra antes?

24. *Have you seen a psychiatrist before?*

25. ¿Ha estado alguna vez en una unidad psiquiátrica?

25. *Have you ever been in a psychiatric facility?*

MENTAL HEALTH

ESPAÑOL

1. ¿Cómo se llama usted?

2. ¿Cuántos años tiene usted?

3. ¿Cómo cree usted que yo puedo ayudarle hoy?

4. ¿Qué estaba haciendo usted cuando se sintió mal?

5. ¿Qué enfermedades ha tenido en el pasado?

6. ¿Usa drogas o medicamentos en la actualidad?

7. ¿Ha tenido periodos difíciles en que se ha sentido muy mal emocionalmente?

8. ¿Ha consultado a un psicólogo, psiquiatra o consejero antes?

9. ¿Ha habido en su familia alguna persona con ...
   depresión?
   ansiedad?
   psicosis?
   alcoholismo?

10. ¿Cómo son sus relaciones con su familia?

11. Recibe usted ayuda moral de ...
    sus padres?
    sus hermanos?
    sus parientes?

12. Le ayudan emocionalmente ...
    sus amigos?
    la iglesia?

ENGLISH

1. *What's your name?*

2. *How old are you?*

3. *How do you think I can be of help to you today?*

4. *What were you doing when you felt sick?*

5. *What illness have you had in the past?*

6. *Do you use drugs or medicines at the present time?*

7. *Have you had difficult periods in which you have felt emotionally upset?*

8. *Have you ever seen a psychologist, a psychiatrist, or a counselor?*

9. *Has there ever been anyone in your family with ...*
   depression?
   anxiety?
   psychosis?
   alcoholism?

10. *How are your personal relationships with your family?*

11. *Do you get moral support from ...*
    your parents.
    your siblings?
    your relatives?

12. *Do you get emotional support ...*
    from your friends?
    from your church?

MENTAL HEALTH

ESPAÑOL	**ENGLISH**
13. ¿Cuándo nació usted?	13. *When were you born?*
14. ¿Dónde está usted ahora?	14. *Where are you now?*
15. ¿Por qué está usted aquí?	15. *Why are you here?*
16. ¿Quién soy yo?	16. *Who am I?*
17. ¿Qué día es hoy?	17. *What day is it today?*
18. ¿En qué año estamos?	18. *What year is this?*
19. Debe ser terrible sentirse tan solo.	19. *It must be terrible to feel so lonely.*
20. Puedo imaginarme su dolor al sentirse tan abandonado.	20. *I can imagine your pain at feeling so abandoned.*
21. Como es sólo una sala de emergencia, yo necesito su ayuda para continuar su cuidado médico.	21. *Since this is only an emergency room, I need your help to continue your medical care.*
22. ¿Me puede dar un poco de información?	22. *Can you give me some information?*
23. ¿Ve usted a un consejero o psicólogo?	23. *Are you seeing a counselor or psychologist?*
24. Tiene que hacer una cita para ver al médico quien le puede ayudar más.	24. *You have to make an appointment with the physician who can help you more.*

M.R.I. SCANNING

ESPAÑOL

1. La imagen por resonancia magnética es una técnica por medio de la cual se obtienen excelentes imágenes de la estructura interna del cuerpo sin usar rayos X o inyecciones con agentes para dar contraste. Para su información:

2. Le pedirán que llene un formulario dando detalles médicos, si usted es un paciente externo.

3. Le deberá informar al doctor si usted tiene algún implante metálico, si tiene frenos en los dientes o un marcapasos.

4. Tendrá que quitarse los anillos, todo tipo de joyas, relojes, ganchos y tarjetas de crédito o del banco.

5. Tendrá que ponerse una bata del hospital y probablemente tenga que pasar por un detector de metales.

6. Le dirán que se acueste por varios minutos boca arriba, o boca abajo, en una cama tipo sofá la cual se irá moviendo hacia el interior de un anillo magnético.

7. Le pedirán que aguante la respiración y que no se mueva. Después podrá respirar normalmente de nuevo.

8. No sentirá dolor ni incomodidad, ni habrá ningún efecto secundario ni calor. Estará en contacto con el técnico a través de un sistema de intercomunicación.

9. Una vez terminada la prueba se podrá cambiar de ropa.

ENGLISH

1. This diagnostic technique provides superior pictures of the body's internal structures without the use of radiation or injection with a contrasting agent. For your information:

2. You'll be asked to fill out a medical information sheet if you are an out-patient.

3. You must inform the doctor if you have any metal implants, dental braces or a pacemaker.

4. You must remove all rings, jewelry, watches, hairpins, and credit or bank cards.

5. You'll have to wear a hospital gown. You may also have to go through a metal detector.

6. You'll be asked to lie for several minutes on your back, or on your stomach, on a couch-type bed that will be moved into a ring magnet.

7. You'll be asked to hold your breath and not move; then you may breathe normally again.

8. You'll feel no pain, discomfort, side effects, or any heat; and you will be in communication with the technician through an intercom system.

9. After the test is over, you may change your clothes.

M.R.I. SCANNING

ESPAÑOL	ENGLISH

<table>
<tr><td>PREGUNTAS ANTES DE LA EXPLORACIÓN</td><td>QUESTIONS BEFORE THE M.R.I. SCAN</td></tr>
<tr><td>1. ¿Tiene usted puesto un marcapasos?</td><td>1. Do you wear a pacemaker?</td></tr>
<tr><td>2. ¿Tiene puesto un neuroestimulador?</td><td>2. Do you wear a stimulator (tens unit)?</td></tr>
<tr><td>3. ¿Tiene presillas quirúrgicas de metal? ¿Dónde?</td><td>3. Do you have any surgical clips? Where?</td></tr>
<tr><td>4. ¿Tiene frenos o aritos en los dientes?</td><td>4. Do you have braces?</td></tr>
<tr><td>5. ¿Tiene algún pedazo de metal en los dientes? ¿Se lo puede quitar?</td><td>5. Do you have any metal dental work? Can it be removed?</td></tr>
<tr><td>6. ¿Tiene algún pedazo de metal suelto (metralla, bala) en el cuerpo?</td><td>6. Do you have any loose metal (shrapnel) in your body?</td></tr>
<tr><td>7. ¿Tiene alguna derivación en la cabeza?</td><td>7. Do you have a shunt (bypass) in your head?</td></tr>
<tr><td>8. ¿Tiene la presión alta? ¿Desde cuándo?</td><td>8. Do you have high blood pressure? Since when?</td></tr>
<tr><td>9. ¿Tiene diabetes? ¿Desde cuándo?</td><td>9. Do you have diabetes? Since when?</td></tr>
<tr><td>10. ¿Tiene cáncer? ¿Desde cuándo?</td><td>10. Do you have any kind of cancer? Since when?</td></tr>
<tr><td>11. ¿Tiene algún mal de los riñones? ¿Desde cuándo?</td><td>11. Do you have any kidney disease? Since when?</td></tr>
<tr><td>12. ¿Le han operado alguna vez? ¿Dónde? ¿Por qué? ¿Cuándo?</td><td>12. Have you had any surgery? Where? Why? When?</td></tr>
<tr><td>13. ¿Tiene algún dolor? ¿Dónde? ¿Desde cuándo?</td><td>13. Do you have pain? Where? Since when?</td></tr>
</table>

M.R.I. SCANNING

ESPAÑOL	ENGLISH
14. ¿Tiene problemas con la vista?	14. *Do you have vision problems?*
15. ¿Tiene dolores de cabeza? ¿Desde cuándo?	15. *Do you have headaches? Since when?*
16. ¿Tiene mareos? ¿Desde cuándo?	16. *Do you have dizziness? Since when?*
17. ¿Tiene ataques apopléticos o epilépticos? ¿Desde cuándo?	17. *Do you have seizures? Since when?*
18. ¿Tiene debilidad muscular? ¿Dónde? ¿Desde cuándo?	18. *Do you have muscle weakness? Where? Since when?*
19. ¿Tiene sensación de entumecimiento/hormigueo? ¿Dónde? ¿Desde cuándo?	19. *Do you have numbness/tingling? Where? Since when?*
20. ¿Tiene pérdida de memoria?	20. *Do you have memory loss?*
21. ¿Está tomando algunas medicinas? ¿De qué clase?	21. *Do you take any medicines? What kind?*
22. ¿Cuándo le empezó su problema actual?	22. *When did your current problem start?*
23. ¿Está mejorando o empeorando?	23. *Is it getting better, or worse?*
24. ¿Ha tenido algún trauma o accidente?	24. *Have you had any trauma (accidents)?*

NEUROLOGY

ESPAÑOL	ENGLISH
1. Cierre los ojos.	1. *Close your eyes.*
2. Cierre la ventanilla izquierda (derecha) con el dedo.	2. *Hold your left (right) nostril shut with your finger.*
3. ¿Puede oler algo?	3. *Can you smell anything?*
4. ¿Qué huele usted?	4. *What do you smell?*
5. Mire derecho a mi nariz.	5. *Look straight at my nose.*
6. Dígame dónde puede ver movimiento.	6. *Tell me where you see movement.*
7. Por favor, siga mi dedo con su mirada, sin mover la cabeza.	7. *Please follow my finger with your eyes, without moving your head.*
8. Apriete los dientes.	8. *Clench your teeth.*
9. Cierre los ojos.	9. *Close your eyes.*
10. Dígame si siente esto puntiagudo o sin punta.	10. *Tell me whether this feels sharp or dull.*
11. Dígame si siente esto caliente o frío.	11. *Tell me whether this feels hot or cold.*
12. Dígame cuando usted sienta algo en la piel.	12. *Tell me when you feel a touch on your skin.*
13. Por favor, mire arriba y a la izquierda, y no deje de mirar allá hasta que yo le diga.	13. *Please look up and to your left, and keep looking there until I tell you.*
14. Levante las cejas (así).	14. *Raise your eyebrows (like this).*
15. Frunza el ceño.	15. *Frown.*
16. Cierre los ojos bien apretados; no me deje que yo los abra.	16. *Close your eyes tightly; do not let me open them.*
17. Muéstreme los dientes.	17. *Show me your teeth.*
18. Sonría.	18. *Smile.*
19. Infle los cachetes.	19. *Puff out your cheeks.*
20. ¿Oye este sonido más fuerte en un lado?	20. *Do you hear this sound louder on one side?*

NEUROLOGY

ESPAÑOL	ENGLISH
21. ¿De qué lado?	21. *Which side?*
22. Dígame cuando ya no oiga el sonido.	22. *Tell me as soon as you cannot hear the sound anymore.*
23. ¿Lo oye ahora?	23. *Can you hear it now?*
24. Abra la boca bien abierta. Diga "ah".	24. *Open your mouth wide. Say "ah."*
25. Encoja los hombros (o trate de levantar mis manos con sus hombros).	25. *Shrug your shoulders (or try to lift my hands up with your shoulders).*
26. Ponga la cabeza contra mi mano; haga fuerza en contra de mi mano.	26. *Put your head against my hand; try to resist my hand.*
27. Saque la lengua.	27. *Stick out your tongue.*
28. Mueva la lengua de un lado al otro.	28. *Move your tongue from side to side.*
29. Por favor, camine a través del cuarto.	29. *Please walk across the room.*
30. Por favor, camine poniendo el talón en la punta del otro pie (así).	30. *Please walk heel-to-toe (like this).*
31. Camine de puntillas.	31. *Walk on tiptoes.*
32. Camine sobre los talones.	32. *Walk on your heels.*
33. Por favor, párese con los pies juntos.	33. *Please stand with your feet together.*
34. Cierre los ojos y quédese quieto por un momento.	34. *Close your eyes and stand still for a moment.*
35. Por favor, salte en el mismo lugar sobre el pie izquierdo (derecho).	35. *Please hop in place on your left (right) foot.*
36. Por favor, relájese, y permítame mo-verle los músculos mientras están relajados.	36. *Please relax, and let me move your muscles while they are relaxed.*

201

NEUROLOGY

ESPAÑOL	ENGLISH

1. El encéfalo es el centro de la conciencia, el pensamiento, la razón, el juicio y las emociones.

2. Incluye el cerebro, el cerebelo, la protuberancia, o pons, y la médula oblongada.

3. El cerebro es la parte más voluminosa y visible del encéfalo. Comprende las siete octavas partes del peso total del mismo).

4. Incluye los dos hemisferios cerebrales que están unidos entre sí por bandas de tejido nervioso.

5. Cada hemisferio tiene sus correspondientes lóbulos (frontal, parietal, temporal, occipital y central), cuya responsabilidad es controlar las facultades mentales.

6. La parte exterior del cerebro está cubierta por una capa gris de células nerviosas que tiene más o menos un octavo de pulgada (0,32 cm.) de espesor.

7. Se le conoce por el nombre de corteza cerebral, o materia gris.

8. Debajo de la corteza cerebral hay una masa de tejidos blancos constituida mayormente por axones y dendritas, responsables de la conducción de los impulsos aferentes y eferentes.

9. El cerebelo, en la parte posterior del encéfalo y directamente debajo de los dos hemisferios cerebrales, también está dividido en dos hemisferios, afectando cada uno el lado opuesto del cuerpo (al igual que los hemisferios cerebrales).

10. El cerebelo controla el equilibrio y tiene que ver también con el control de la actividad muscular voluntaria, por ejemplo cuando una persona toca un instrumento musical, escribe a máquina o martilla.

---

1. *The brain (encephalon) is the center of consciousness, thought, reason, judgment, and emotions.*

2. *It includes the cerebrum, the cerebellum, the brain stem, and the medulla oblongata.*

3. *The cerebrum is the largest and most conspicuous part of the brain. It representing seven eighths of the total weight of the brain.*

4. *It includes the two cerebral hemispheres connected by bands of nerve tissue (commissures).*

5. *Each hemisphere has its corresponding lobes (frontal, parietal, temporal, occipital, and the central), which are responsible for the control of the mental functions.*

6. *The exterior part of the cerebrum has a grayish layer of nerve cells about one eighth of an inch (0.32 cm) thick.*

7. *It is known as the cerebral cortex, or gray matter.*

8. *Under the cortex there is a mass of white tissue formed mainly by axons and dendrites responsible for the afferent and efferent impulses.*

9. *The cerebellum, in the back part of the brain and directly under the two cerebral hemispheres, is also divided into two hemispheres, each affecting the opposite side of the body (as is also the case with the cerebral counterparts).*

10. *The cerebellum controls balance and is also concerned with the control of voluntary muscular activity, such as when a person is playing an instrument, typing, or hammering.*

NEUROLOGY

11. La médula espinal es la continuación de la médula oblongada dentro del canal vertebral.

12. Actúa como centro para los reflejos simples así como también de vía para los impulsos que van al cerebro y los que provienen del mismo.

13. Es una masa de tejido blanco en el exterior con una masa gris en el centro; tiene unos tres cuartos de pulgada de grueso (unos 2 cm.), unas 17 pulgadas de largo (43 cm.) y un peso aproximado de 1,5 onzas (unos 43 g.)

14. Todas las funciones del cuerpo humano dependen de esta masa de tejido relativamente pequeña protegida por las meninges.

15. Todos los nervios espinales entran o salen de la espina dorsal por un orificio al lado de cada vértebra, menos los doce pares de nervios craneanos que están conectados directamente al cerebro.

16. Los mensajes enviados por el cerebro pasan por la médula espinal en ruta hacia los nervios periféricos.

17. Los nervios periféricos trasmiten las señales que van hacia partes específicas del cuerpo, o que vienen de ellas, tales como los nervios del cuello y los brazos, que salen de la región cervical.

18. El sistema nervioso periférico es la vasta red de nervios que se extiende por todo el cuerpo, menos el encéfalo, la médula espinal y los doce pares de nervios craneanos que salen de la parte inferior del encéfalo.

19. Este sistema tiene control de todos los impulsos conscientes y afecta algunos de los inconscientes también, tales como el ritmo cardíaco y las funciones de los intestinos.

20. El sistema nervioso autónomo se divide en simpático y parasimpático. Está constituido por fibras y células nerviosas agrupadas en ganglios, los cuales intervienen en la regulación del funcionamiento de los órganos de la digestión, los de la circulación y los de la respiración, así como de las glándulas exocrinas, del movimiento pupilar y de otras actividades.

---

11. *The spinal cord is the continuation of the medulla oblongata in the vertebral canal.*

12. *It acts as the center for simple reflexes as well as a conducting path for impulses to and from the brain.*

13. *It is a mass of cord tissue, white outside with a gray mass in the center; it is about three quarters of an inch thick (about 2 cm), about 17 inches long (43 cm), and it weighs approximately 1.5 ounces (about 43 gm).*

14. *All the functions of the body depend upon this relatively small mass of cord tissue protected by the meninges.*

15. *All the spinal nerves enter or leave the spine through a gap in the vertebrae, except the twelve pairs of cranial nerves, which are connected directly to the brain.*

16. *Nerve signals from the brain travel to the spinal cord on their way to the peripheral nerves.*

17. *The peripheral nerves transmit or relay the signals to and from specific parts of the body, such as those serving the neck and arms, which emerge from the cervical region.*

18. *The peripheral nervous system is an extensive network of nerves throughout the body with the exception of the brain, the spinal cord, and the twelve pairs of cranial nerves, which emerge from the lower part of the brain.*

19. *This system controls all the conscious activities and affects some of the unconscious processes such as the heart rate and bowel functions.*

20. *The autonomic nervous system is divided into the sympathetic and the parasympathetic nerves. It is made up of fibers and nerve cells clustered into ganglia, which stimulate the activities of the digestive, circulatory, and respiratory organs, as well as the exocrine glands, pupillary movement, and other activities.*

NEUROLOGY

ESPAÑOL	ENGLISH
1. ¿Se siente débil?	1. *Do you feel weak?*
2. ¿Se siente mareado(a)?	2. *Do you feel dizzy?*
3. ¿Tiene desmayos?	3. *Do you have fainting spells?*
4. ¿Sabe si usted nació de parto normal o de nalgas?	4. *Do you know whether you were a normal birth or a breech birth?*
5. ¿Ha tenido alguna vez fiebre alta?	5. *Have you ever had a high fever?*
6. ¿Ha sufrido alguna vez un golpe fuerte en la cabeza?	6. *Have you ever had a head injury?*
7. ¿Ha tenido alguna vez un accidente en su motocicleta?	7. *Have you ever had a motorcycle accident?*
8. ¿Ha sufrido alguna vez un golpe fuerte practicando deportes?	8. *Have you ever had a sports injury?*
9. ¿Tiene convulsiones?	9. *Do you have convulsions?*
10. ¿Ve usted doble?	10. *Do you see double?*
11. ¿Tiene la vista borrosa?	11. *Do you have blurred vision?*
12. ¿Tiene hormigueos?	12. *Do you have tingling sensations?*
13. ¿Siente entumecidas las manos, los brazos o los pies?	13. *Do you have numbness in your hands, arms, or feet?*
14. ¿Perdió alguna vez el conocimiento? ¿Por cuánto tiempo?	14. *Have you ever lost consciousness? For how long?*
15. ¿Con qué frecuencia ocurre esto?	15. *How frequently does this happen?*
16. ¿Ha tenido alguna vez un electromiograma?	16. *Have you ever had an electromyogram?*
17. ¿Siente tintineo en los oídos? ¿En el derecho, en el izquierdo o en los dos?	17. *Do you get a ringing in your ears? Right, left, or both?*
18. Relájese. Repita las palabras que le voy a decir.	18. *Relax. Repeat the words I am going to say.*
19. Cierre los ojos.	19. *Close your eyes.*
20. Mueva la cabeza hacia la derecha, hacia la izquierda, hacia atrás y hacia adelante, así.	20. *Move your head to your right, to the left, back and forward, like this.*
21. Camine hacia la puerta.	21. *Walk toward the door.*
22. Ahora camine hacia mí.	22. *Now walk to me.*
23. Camine en una línea recta, poniendo un pie directamente enfrente del otro, así.	23. *Walk in a straight line, putting one foot directly in front of the other like this.*
24. Brinque en un pie, ahora en el otro.	24. *Hop on one foot; now the other one.*

NEUROLOGY

ESPAÑOL	ENGLISH

25. Párese con los pies juntos y los brazos extendidos enfrente, las palmas arriba así, y cierre los ojos.

25. *Stand with your feet together and your arms extended in front of you, palms up like this, and close your eyes.*

26. Mantenga los brazos extendidos.

26. *Keep your arms extended.*

27. Jale contra mi mano.

27. *Pull against my hand.*

28. Empuje contra mi mano. Más fuerte.

28. *Push against my hand. Harder.*

29. Flexione la muñeca contra mi mano.

29. *Flex your wrist against my hand.*

30. Levante los brazos contra mis manos.

30. *Raise your arms against my hand.*

31. Levante la pierna y no me deje bajarla.

31. *Lift up your leg and don't let me push it down.*

32. Extienda la pierna contra mi mano.

32. *Extend your leg against my hand.*

33. Jálela hacia atrás.

33. *Pull it back.*

34. Empuje los pies contra mis manos.

34. *Push your feet against my hands.*

35. Flexione los pies hacia arriba.

35. *Bend your feet at the ankle upward.*

36. Tóquese la nariz con el dedo y entonces toque mi dedo.

36. *Touch your nose with your finger and then touch my finger.*

37. Siga tocando la nariz y mi dedo, uno y otro, rápido.

37. *Keep on touching your nose and my finger, back and forth, rapidly.*

38. Toque la rodilla con el talón de la otra pierna.

38. *Touch your knee with the heel of your other leg.*

39. ¿Puede sentir cuando le toco con este algodón?

39. *Can you feel it when I touch you with this piece of cotton?*

40. Voy a usar este alfiler para revisar sus sensaciones.

40. *I am going to use this pin to test your sensations.*

41. Este es agudo.

41. *This is sharp.*

42. Este es sordo.

42. *This is dull.*

43. Cierre los ojos y dígame si siente agudo o sordo cada vez que le toco.

43. *Close your eyes and tell me if you feel it sharp or dull each time I touch you.*

44. Voy a revisar sus reflejos.

44. *I am going to check your reflexes.*

45. Apriete mis dedos en su mano lo más fuerte que pueda.

45. *Squeeze my fingers in your hand as hard as you can.*

46. Suba el brazo hacia el hombro.

46. *Pull your arm toward your shoulder.*

47. Diga "sí" cuando sienta que algo le toca.

47. *Say "yes" when you feel something touching you.*

48. ¿Está frío o caliente esto?

48. *Is this hot or cold?*

49. ¿Siente las vibraciones?

49. *Do you feel the vibrations?*

50. Junte los pies.

50. *Put your feet together.*

51. ¿Le estoy pinchando con la punta o con la cabeza del alfiler?

51. *Am I sticking you with the point or the head of the pin?*

52. ¿Le estoy pinchando con dos puntas o con una?

52. *Am I sticking you with two points or with one?*

53. ¿Lo siente más en un lado que en el otro?

53. *Do you feel it more on one side than on the other?*

NOSE AND EARS

ESPAÑOL	ENGLISH
1. ¿Tiene usted ronquera a menudo?	1. *Are you frequently hoarse?*
2. ¿Está usted ronco (ronca) con frecuencia?	2. *Are you frequently hoarse?*
3. ¿Siente la lengua hinchada, gruesa o dura?	3. *Does your tongue feel swollen, thick, or rough?*
4. ¿Está su lengua con costra?	4. *Does your tongue feel furry?*
5. ¿Se forman incrustaciones en su lengua?	5. *Does your tongue feel furry?*
6. ¿Desde cuándo tiene la lengua de ese color?	6. *How long has your tongue been that color?*
7. ¿Le arde la lengua?	7. *Does your tongue burn?*
8. ¿Puede usted sentir sabores?	8. *Can you taste anything?*
9. ¿Siente usted un sabor agrio en la boca?	9. *Do you have a sour taste in your mouth?*
10. ¿Tiene usted un sabor ácido en la boca?	10. *Do you have a sour taste in your mouth?*
11. ¿Suele usted tener la garganta dolorida?	11. *Do you have a sore throat?*
12. ¿Le duele la garganta con frecuencia?	12. *Do you have a sore throat?*
13. ¿Le duele la garganta cuando traga?	13. *Does your throat hurt when you swallow?*
14. ¿Tiene usted dolores o dificultades al tragar?	14. *Does your throat hurt when you swallow?*
15. ¿Está rascosa (rasposa)?	15. *Is it just scratchy?*
16. ¿Tiene catarro también?	16. *Do you also have a cold?*
17. ¿Tiene usted la lengua dolorida?	17. *Does your tongue feel sore?*
18. ¿Le sangran las encías frecuentemente?	18. *Do your gums bleed frequently?*
19. ¿Tiene usted infecciones de las encías?	19. *Do you have infections of the gums?*
20. ¿Tiene usted dolor de muelas?	20. *Do you have a toothache?*
21. ¿Cuál de los dientes le duele?	21. *Which tooth hurts?*
22. Señale usted, por favor.	22. *Please point.*

NUCLEAR MEDICINE

ESPAÑOL	ENGLISH
1. Regrese mañana a esta hora.	1. *Return at this time tomorrow.*
2. Le vamos a sacar unas radiografías de su cerebro/hígado/riñón.	2. *We are going to take some pictures of your brain/liver/kidney.*
3. Este examen (esta prueba) dura dos días.	3. *This test takes two days.*
4. Tome esta cápsula ahora.	4. *Take this capsule now.*
5. Regrese mañana a esta hora.	5. *Come back tomorrow at this time.*
6. No hay preparativos para esta prueba.	6. *There is no preparation for this test.*
7. Puede tomar o comer lo que quiera antes de la prueba.	7. *You may have anything to eat or drink before this test.*
8. Guarde toda su orina durante un periodo de veinticuatro horas para una prueba de Schilling.	8. *Save all your urine for twenty-four hours for a Schilling test.*
9. El(la) doctor(a) quiere examinarle el cuello.	9. *The doctor wants to examine your neck.*
10. ¿Está agrandado su cuello?	10. *Is your neck enlarged?*
11. ¿Siente alguna masa (bolita) en el cuello?	11. *Can you feel any lumps in your neck?*
12. ¿Puede tragar y respirar sin dolor?	12. *Can you swallow and breathe without pain?*
13. ¿Ha perdido o ha ganado peso?	13. *Have you lost or gained weight?*
14. ¿Cuánto y en cuánto tiempo?	14. *How much and in what period of time?*
15. ¿Se le cae el pelo?	15. *Is your hair falling out?*
16. ¿Le molesta cuando hace calor o cuando hace frío?	16. *Does the hot or cold weather bother you?*
17. ¿Cómo es su apetito?	17. *How is your appetite?*
18. ¿Es usted una persona nerviosa?	18. *Are you a nervous person?*
19. ¿Está seca su piel?	19. *Is your skin dry?*
20. ¿Se le quiebran las uñas con facilidad?	20. *Do your nails break easily?*
21. ¿Suda usted mucho?	21. *Do you perspire very much?*
22. ¿Le han sacado rayos X durante los últimos seis meses?	22. *Have you had an X-ray in the past six months?*
23. ¿Toma usted alguna medicina?	23. *Do you take any medications?*

NUCLEAR MEDICINE

ESPAÑOL

PREGUNTAS PARA PACIENTES MUJERES

1. Si la paciente es una mujer, se le deben hacer las siguientes preguntas antes de administrarle núclidos radioactivos.

2. ¿Ha terminado la menopausia?

3. ¿Ha tenido una histerectomía?

4. ¿Cuál es la fecha de su último periodo?

5. ¿Toma usted píldoras anticonceptivas?

6. ¿Usa usted un aparato intrauterino?

7. ¿Está usted embarazada (encinta)?

8. ¿Hay alguna posibilidad de embarazo?

ENGLISH

QUESTIONS FOR FEMALE PATIENTS

1. *If the patient is female, the following questions should be asked prior to any administration of radioactive nuclides.*

2. *Have you completed menopause?*

3. *Have you had a hysterectomy?*

4. *What is the date of your last menstrual period?*

5. *Are you taking birth control pills?*

6. *Do you have an IUD?*

7. *Are you pregnant?*

8. *Is there any possibility of pregnancy?*

PEDIATRICS

ESPAÑOL	ENGLISH

1. La Prueba de Binet-Simon es un examen que se hace para determinar el desarrollo de la inteligencia en los niños de acuerdo con su edad.

2. La varicela es una enfermedad infecciosa de origen viral que se caracteriza por la aparición de ampollas.

3. Crup es la inflamación de la garganta con dificultad para respirar y tos espasmódica. Se debe generalmente a una infección viral.

4. La difteria es una enfermedad muy infecciosa acompañada de un estado febril, caracterizada por la formación de placas en la garganta.

5. Disnea es la falta de aire que hace difícil la respiración. Va acompañada generalmente de dolor.

6. El sarampión alemán o rubeola es una enfermedad aguda y contagiosa parecida al sarampión, pero de corta duración.

7. El sarampión o rubeola es una enfermedad muy contagiosa que ocurre mayormente en los niños en forma de erupción por todo el cuerpo.

1. *The Binet-Simon-Test is a test given to determine the development of the intelligence of children in relation to their age.*

2. *Chickenpox is an infectious viral disease with blister formations.*

3. *Croup is the inflammation of the throat, with difficult breathing and cough spasms. It is generally due to viral infection.*

4. *Diphtheria is a febrile, extremely infectious disease characterized by the formation of a false membrane on the throat.*

5. *Dyspnea is the shortness of breath making breathing difficult. It is usually accompanied by pain.*

6. *German measles or rubella is an acute, contagious disease resembling measles, but of a shorter duration.*

7. *Measles or rubeola is a highly infectious disease occurring mostly in children in the form of a rash all over the body.*

PEDIATRICS

ESPAÑOL	ENGLISH
8. La fiebre del heno es una condición alérgica de los conductos de la nariz y de los conductos superiores, acompañada de síntomas catarrales.	8. *Hay fever is an allergic condition of mucus passages of the nose and the upper air passages, accompanied by the symptoms of a cold.*
9. Es causada generalmente por polen ambiental.	9. *It is caused by exposure to pollen.*
10. Ictericia es una condición anormal que se caracteriza por el color amarillento de la piel y de la parte blanca de los ojos.	10. *Jaundice is an abnormal body condition characterized by yellowness of the skin and the whites of the eyes*
11. Se debe a depósitos pigmentosos de bilis en la sangre, por exceso de bilirrubina.	11. *It is due to deposits of bile pigment in the blood, resulting from an excess of bilirubin.*
12. La meningitis es la inflamación de las membranas del cerebro o de la médula espinal.	12. *Meningitis is the inflammation of the membranes of the brain or spinal cord.*
13. El mongolismo es la condición anormal de un niño que ha nacido con retardo mental.	13. *Mongolism or down's syndrome is a congenital condition characterized by mental retardation.*
14. La poliomielitis es la inflamación de la materia gris de la médula espinal.	14. *Polio is the inflammation of the gray matter of the spinal cord.*
15. El raquitismo o raquitis es la condición por la cual los huesos no se endurecen normalmente, debido a insuficiencia de calcio.	15. *Rickets or rachitis a condition in which the bones do not harden normally, due to insufficient calcium.*
16. La fiebre reumática es una enfermedad grave que se caracteriza por la presencia de fiebre, hinchazón y dolor en las coyunturas y dolor de garganta. Va generalmente seguida de algún mal cardíaco grave.	16. *Rheumatic fever is a serious disease characterized by fever, swelling, pain in the joints, and a sore throat, usually followed by serious heart disease.*

PEDIATRICS

ESPAÑOL	ENGLISH

1. ¿Estaba completamente bien el niño antes?

1. Was the child completely well before?

2. ¿Cuándo comenzaron los primeros síntomas?

2. When did the first signs, or symptoms, appear?

3. ¿Se han empeorado los síntomas, o no ha habido ningún cambio?

3. Have the symptoms gotten worse, or have they remained the same?

4. ¿Le empezó de pronto este problema, o le fue aumentando progresivamente?

4. Did this problem start suddenly, or progressively?

5. ¿Estaba el niño tomando alguna medicina?

5. Was the child taking any medication?

6. ¿Tiene vómitos?

6. Is there any vomiting?

7. ¿Con qué frecuencia?

7. How often?

8. ¿Cuándo fue la última vez que vomitó?

8. When was the last time?

9. ¿Puede usted decirme cómo era el vómito?

9. Can you tell me the characteristics of the vomiting?

10. ¿Tiene tos?

10. Is there any coughing?

11. ¿De qué tipo es y con qué frecuencia tose?

11. What type and how often?

12. ¿Es una tos seca?

12. Is it a dry cough?

13. Si tiene flema, ¿cómo es?

13. Describe the phlegm, if any.

14. ¿Tiene congestión nasal?

14. Does the patient have nasal congestion?

15. ¿Tiene alguna segregación? ¿Es ...
    clara?
    amarilla?
    verde?
    con sangre?

15. Any discharge? Is it ...
    clear?
    yellow?
    green?
    bloody?

PEDIATRICS

ESPAÑOL	ENGLISH
16. ¿Está evacuando bien?	16. *Is he voiding well?*
17. ¿Cuándo fue la última vez?	17. *When was the last time?*
18. ¿Notó usted algo anormal?	18. *Anything abnormal?*
19. ¿Necesita todavía ayuda de alguien para ir al baño?	19. *Is he independent in toileting?*
20. ¿Se orina en la cama?	20. *Does he wet the bed?*
21. ¿Ha notado usted alguna segregación genital?	21. *Have you noticed any discharge from genitalia?*
22. ¿Duerme la siesta?	22. *Does he take a nap?*
23. ¿A qué hora se acuesta generalmente?	23. *What is his usual bedtime hour?*
24. ¿Come y bebe bien?	24. *Is he eating and drinking well?*
25. ¿Le falta apetito en general, o es que no tiene deseos de comer ciertos alimentos o a ciertas horas?	25. *Is there a general lack of appetite, or is it only for certain things or at certain times?*
26. Cuando el niño está bien, ¿qué alimentos le gustan más y cuáles menos?	26. *When the child is well, which foods does he like or dislike the most?*
27. ¿Come algo entre las comidas?	27. *Does he eat between meals?*
28. ¿Tiene usted que forzarlo a comer?	28. *Do you have to force him to eat?*
29. ¿Necesita que lo ayuden para comer?	29. *Does he need help to eat?*
30. ¿Cuándo le ocurrió la lesión o la mordida?	30. *When did the injury or bite occur?*
31. ¿Cuándo le pusieron la última inyección antitetánica?	31. *When did he have the last tetanus booster shot?*
32. ¿Cuándo le ocurrió la lesión?	32. *When did the injury occur?*
33. ¿Perdió el conocimiento?	33. *Did he lose consciousness?*
34. ¿Por cuánto tiempo?	34. *For how long?*

PEDIATRICS

ESPAÑOL	ENGLISH
1. ¿Cómo se llama el niño/la niña?	1. What is the child's name?
2. ¿Cuántos años tiene?	2. How old is he/she?
3. ¿Por qué trajo al niño a la clínica?(male child)	3. Why did you bring your child to the clinic?
4. ¿Por qué trajo a la niña a la clínica? (female child)	4. Why did you bring your child to the clinic?
5. ¿Cuánto tiempo hace que está enfermo/a?	5. How long has he/she been sick?
6. ¿Cuáles son sus síntomas ahora?	6. What are his/her symptoms now?
7. ¿Cómo fue su embarazo y parto?	7. How was your pregnancy and delivery?
8. ¿Cuánto pesó el niño/la niña al nacer?	8. How much did he/she weigh at birth?
9. ¿Cómo fue su desarrollo?	9. How was his/her development?
10. ¿Cuándo le salieron los dientes?	10. When did her/his teeth come out?
11. ¿A qué edad caminó?	11. At what age did she/he walk?
12. ¿Cuándo empezó a hablar?	12. When did he/she start to speak?
13. ¿Puede orinar y evacuar solo/a?	13. Can he/she urinate and defecate by himself/herself?
14. ¿Ha estado alguna vez en el hospital?	14. Has he/she ever been hospitalized?
15. ¿Qué enfermedades de la infancia ha tenido?	15. What childhood diseases has he/she had?
16. ¿Ha tenido ... varicela? tos ferina? difteria? sarampión? meningitis?	16. Has he/she had ... chickenpox? whooping cough? diphtheria? measles? meningitis?
17. ¿Ha tenido otras enfermedades? asma bronquitis infección del oído convulsiones fiebre reumática fiebre escarlatina	17. Has he/she had other sicknesses? asthma bronchitis ear infection convulsions rheumatic fever scarlet fever
18. ¿Ha recibido vacunas o inmunizaciones contra ... la poliomielitis (polio)? DPT (difteria, pertusis, tétano)? la viruela? el sarampión? las paperas?	18. Has he/she received vaccinations or immunizations against ... poliomyelitis (polio)? DPT (diphtheria, pertussis, tetanus)? smallpox? measles? mumps?

213

PEDIATRICS

ESPAÑOL	ENGLISH
18. ¿Ha recibido la tuberculina?	18. *Has he/she received the TB test?*
19. ¿Tiene alergias?	19. *Does he/she have allergies?*
20. ¿Cómo es la salud de la mamá?	20. *How is the mother's health?*
21. ¿Cómo es la salud del padre?	21. *How is the father's health?*
22. ¿Hay alguien en la familia con los mismos problemas?	22. *Is there anyone in the family with the same problems?*
23. ¿Hay alguien en la familia con ... diabetes? hemofilia? sida? asma? enfermedad del corazón? cáncer?	23. *Is there anyone in the family with ...* *diabetes?* *hemophilia?* *AIDS?* *asthma?* *heart problems?* *cancer?*
24. ¿Cuál es la ocupación del padre?	24. *What's the father's occupation?*
25. ¿Cuál es la ocupación de la mamá?	25. *What's the mother's occupation?*
26. ¿Cómo es la casa donde vive el niño?	26. *What's the house like where the child lives?*
27. ¿Cuántas personas viven en la casa?	27. *How many people live in the house?*
28. ¿Va el niño a la escuela?	28. *Does the child go to school?*
29. ¿Con quién vive el niño, con la mamá, con el padre o con ambos?	29. *With whom does the child live, the mother, the father, or both?*
30. ¿Toma el bebé el pecho o el biberón?	30. *Do you breastfeed the baby or do you give the bottle to the baby?*
31. ¿A qué edad dejó de tomar el pecho?	31. *At what age did he/she stop breastfeeding?*
32. ¿Come algunas comidas blandas?	32. *Does he/she eat any soft foods?*
33. ¿Toma algunas vitaminas?	33. *Does he/she take any vitamins?*
34. ¿Tiene alergias a algunas comidas o a la leche?	34. *Is he/she allergic to any foods or milk?*

PELVIC EXAM

ESPAÑOL	ENGLISH
Dr.: ¿Qué la trae a mi oficina, señora Sánchez?	Dr.: What brings you to my office today, Mrs. Sánchez?
Sra.: Tengo muchos problemas. He perdido el apetito y estoy bajando mucho de peso.	Mrs.: I have many problems. I have lost my appetite and I am losing a lot of weight.
Dr.: ¿Pesa menos que el año pasado, entonces?	Dr.: Do you weigh less than last year, then?
Sra.: ¡Oh sí! mucho menos. Antes pesaba 140 libras y ahora sólo peso 90.	Mrs.: Oh yes, much less. I used to weigh 140 pounds and now I only weigh 90 pounds.
Dr.: ¿Qué otros síntomas tiene?	Dr.: What other symptoms do you have?
Sra.: Estoy muy preocupada, porque mis reglas no están normales. Ya van seis meses que tengo muchos coágulos y dolor en el vientre.	Mrs.: I am very worried because my periods are not normal. I have been passing blood clots and have had pain in my womb for six months already.
Dr.: ¿Toma las pastillas anticonceptivas?	Dr.: Are you taking contraceptive pills?
Sra.: No, no me gustan. Me ligaron las trompas... pero ahora me duele mucho aquí abajo.	Mrs.: No, I don't like them. I have had a tubal ligation but now it hurts me a lot, down here.
Dr.: Voy a examinarla por dentro y le haré un Papanicolau también.	Dr.: I'm going to examine you internally and I will also do a Pap smear.
Sra.: Está bien, doctor. ¿Es muy grave esto?	Mrs.: All right, Doctor. Is this very serious?
Dr.: No sé todavía.	Dr.: I don't know yet.

PHYSICAL THERAPY

ESPAÑOL	ENGLISH

1. Voltéese y siéntese sobre el borde de la cama.
2. Párese despacio.
3. Ponga peso sobre la pierna derecha.
4. Mueva el bastón, luego dé un paso con la otra pierna.
5. Mueva el andador primero, y dé un paso con la pierna derecha, luego con la pierna izquierda.
6. Ponga más peso en las manos.
7. Pase por aquí con el talón.
8. Levante la cabeza.
9. Dé un paso al lado.
10. Dé un paso hacia atrás hasta que sienta la silla de ruedas detrás de las piernas.
11. Alcance hacia atrás y siéntese.
12. Doble a la izquierda.
13. Doble a la derecha.
14. ¿Se le corre el dolor a la pierna izquierda?
15. Levante la pierna. No me deje movérsela hacia abajo.
16. Párese y camine.
17. Enderece la pierna.
18. Doble la rodilla.
19. Mueva el andador hacia adelante.

1. Roll over and sit up over the edge of the bed.
2. Stand up slowly.
3. Put weight only on your right foot.
4. Move the cane, then step with the opposite leg.
5. Move the walker first, then take a step with your right foot, then with your left foot.
6. Put more weight on your hands.
7. Step through with the heel.
8. Lift your head up.
9. Take a step to the side.
10. Step back until you feel the wheelchair at the back of your legs.
11. Reach back and sit down.
12. Turn to your left.
13. Turn to your right.
14. Does the pain radiate to your left leg?
15. Hold your leg up. Don't let me push it down.
16. Stand up and walk.
17. Straighten your leg.
18. Bend your knee.
19. Move the walker forward.

PHYSICAL THERAPY

ESPAÑOL

1. Copie este diseño.
2. Esta tablilla le ayudará a estirar los músculos.
3. Es importante usarla.
4. Hágalo usted mismo.
5. Hágalo usted misma.
6. Use usted las dos manos.
7. Use la mano derecha.
8. Use la mano izquierda.
9. Ponga ...
  la pierna derecha primero.
  la pierna izquierda primero.
  el brazo derecho primero.
  el brazo izquierdo primero.
10. Mueva la silla de ruedas cerca de la cama.
11. Ponga los frenos.
12. Muévase hacia adelante.
13. Alcance el timbre.
14. Párese y vuélvase.
15. Alcance por detrás el brazo de la silla.
16. Siéntese.
17. Esto le ayudará a fortificar los músculos.
18. Esto le ayudará a ver mejor.
19. Empújese hacia arriba en la cama.
20. Empújese e incorpórese.
21. Levante las caderas.
22. Ponga éstos en orden.
23. Cálmese.
24. Levante el brazo.
25. ¿Entiende?
26. Deje las manos quietas.

ENGLISH

1. Copy this design.
2. This splint will help stretch your muscles out.
3. It is important to wear it.
4. Do it yourself. (male)
5. Do it yourself. (female)
6. Use both hands.
7. Use your right hand.
8. Use your left hand.
9. Put ...
  your right leg in first.
  your left leg in first.
  your right arm in first.
  your left arm in first.
10. Move the wheelchair close to the bed.
11. Lock your brakes.
12. Scoot forward.
13. Reach for the bell.
14. Stand up and turn.
15. Reach behind you for the arm of the chair.
16. Sit down.
17. This will help you to strengthen your muscles.
18. This will help you to see things better.
19. Push yourself up in bed.
20. Push yourself up to a sitting position.
21. Lift up your hips.
22. Put these in order.
23. Calm down.
24. Raise your arm.
25. Do you understand?
26. Don't move your hands.

PHYSICAL THERAPY

ESPAÑOL	ENGLISH
26. Ponga peso sólo en la pierna derecha.	26. *Put weight only on your right foot.*
27. Ponga peso sólo en la pierna izquierda.	27. *Put weight only on your left foot.*
28. Mueva el bastón, luego dé un paso con la otra pierna.	28. *Move the cane, then step with the opposite leg.*
29. Mueva el andador primero, y dé un paso con la pierna derecha, luego con la pierna izquierda.	29. *Move the walker first, then take a step with your right foot, then with your left.*
30. Ponga más peso en las manos.	30. *Put more weight on your hands.*
31. Pase por aquí con el talón.	31. *Step through with the heel.*
32. Levante la cabeza.	32. *Lift your head.*
33. Dé un paso al lado.	33. *Take a step to the side.*
34. Dé un paso hacia atrás hasta que sienta la silla de ruedas detrás de las piernas.	34. *Step back until you feel the wheelchair at the back of your legs.*
35. Alcance hacia atrás y siéntese.	35. *Reach back and sit down.*
36. Doble a la izquierda.	36. *Turn to your left.*
37. Doble a la derecha.	37. *Turn to your right.*
38. ¿Se le corre el dolor a la pierna izquierda?	38. *Does the pain radiate to your left leg?*
39. Levante la pierna.	39. *Hold your leg up.*
40. No me deje movérsela hacia abajo.	40. *Don't let me push it down.*
41. Párese y camine.	41. *Stand up and walk.*
42. Enderece la pierna.	42. *Straighten your leg.*
43. Doble la rodilla.	43. *Bend your knee.*
44. Mueva el andador hacia adelante.	44. *Move the walker forward.*

PHYSICAL THERAPY

ESPAÑOL	ENGLISH
1. Levántese, por favor.	1. *Please stand up.*
2. Siéntese, por favor.	2. *Please sit down.*
3. Camine, un poco.	3. *Walk a little.*
4. Vuelva, por favor.	4. *Come back, please.*
5. Regrese, por favor.	5. *Return, please.*
6. Camine hacia atrás.	6. *Walk backwards.*
7. Camine sobre los dedos.	7. *Walk on your toes.*
8. Camine sobre los talones.	8. *Walk on your heels.*
9. Dóblese hacia adelante.	9. *Bend over.*
10. Dóblese hacia atrás.	10. *Bend backwards.*
11. Doble el tronco hacia adelante tanto como pueda.	11. *Bend your trunk forward as far as you can.*
12. Cierre la mano.	12. *Close your hand.*
13. Ábrala por favor.	13. *Open it, please.*
14. Cierre el puño.	14. *Close your fist.*
15. Ábralo por favor.	15. *Open it, please.*
16. Apriete mis manos con fuerza.	16. *Grip my hands tightly.*
17. Empuje mi mano tan fuerte como pueda.	17. *Push against my hand as hard as you can.*
18. Levante los brazos completamente.	18. *Raise your arms all the way up.*
19. Suba los brazos completamente.	19. *Lift your arms all the way up.*
20. Más bajo.	20. *Lower.*
21. Levante la pierna derecha.	21. *Raise your right leg.*
22. Levante la pierna izquierda.	22. *Raise your left leg.*
23. ¿Puede levantar ese brazo?	23. *Can you move that arm?*
24. ¿Puede mover esa pierna?	24. *Can you move that leg?*

POISON CONTROL

ESPAÑOL	ENGLISH
1. ¿Qué pasó?	1. What happened?
2. ¿Dónde pasó?	2. Where did it happen?
3. ¿Cuándo pasó?	3. When did it happen?
4. ¿Con quién pasó?	4. With whom did it happen?
5. ¿Cómo pasó?	5. How did it happen?
6. ¿Cree que fue expuesto a sustancias químicas?	6.⎫
6a. ¿Cree que fue expuesta a sustancias químicas?	6a.⎬ Do you think that you were exposed to dangerous
6b. ¿Cree que fueron expuestos a sustancias químicas?	6b.⎭ chemicals or poisons?
7. ¿Sabe el nombre de la sustancia?	7. Do you know the name of the substance?
8. ¿Estaba solo cuando vino en contacto con la sustancia?	8. Were you alone at the time of the exposure?
8a. ¿Estaba sola cuando vino en contacto con la sustancia?	8a. Were you alone at the time of the exposure?
9. ¿Estaba con otros cuando vino en contacto con la sustancia?	9. Were you with someone else at the time of the exposure?
10. ¿Inhaló el gas de la sustancia?	10. Did you breathe the vapors of the substance?
11. ¿Tragó la sustancia?	11. Did you swallow the substance?
12. Hubo contacto con la sustancia en la piel?	12. Did the substance get on your skin?
13. ¿Entró la sustancia en los ojos?	13. Did the substance get in your eyes?
14. ¿Tiene náuseas?	14. Do you feel nauseated?
15. ¿Está mareado? (m/s)	15. Do you feel dizzy?
15a. ¿Está mareada? (f/s)	15a. Do you feel dizzy?
15b. ¿Están mareados? (pl)	15b. Do you feel dizzy?

PRE-SURGERY

ESPAÑOL	ENGLISH

1. La hora de ingreso al hospital es de acuerdo con las instrucciones del médico.

2. El médico ha dejado suficiente tiempo para preparar todo.

3. El médico ha dejado tiempo para que usted vaya familiarizándose con la rutina del hospital y con el personal que lo va a atender.

4. Después de estar en su cuarto es posible que un interno lo visite.

5. Va a hacerle un reconocimiento físico.

6. Le tomarán muestras de orina y de sangre para analizarlas.

7. La parte específica del cuerpo donde le van a hacer la operación será afeitada.

8. Luego se la lavarán con agua y un jabón especial.

9. El anestesista le hará una visita para familiziarse con su problema.

10. El anestesista decidirá el tipo de anestesia que va a usar, si va a ser local o general.

11. Le darán medicamento para que le ayude a dormir bien la noche antes de la operación.

12. Usted, o la persona autorizada, firmará un formulario consintiendo en que se lleve a cabo la operación.

13. No podrá comer ni beber nada después de la medianoche antes de la operación.

14. Por la mañana se podrá cepillar los dientes y lavarse la cara.

15. Llevará solamente la bata del hospital.

---

1. *The time for your admission to the hospital was set by your doctor.*

2. *The doctor allowed sufficient time for thorough preparation.*

3. *The doctor allowed time for you to become acquainted with the hospital routine and the personnel that will be attending you.*

4. *Following your admission to your room, you may be visited by an intern.*

5. *He will give you a routine physical examination and take your medical history.*

6. *Specimens of urine and blood will be taken for lab tests.*

7. *The skin area specific to your operation will be shaved.*

8. *Then it will be washed with water and a special soap.*

9. *The anesthetist will visit you to familiarize himself with your problem.*

10. *The anesthetist will decide on the type of anesthesia he is going to use, which may be either local or general.*

11. *You'll receive medication to help you sleep well the night before the operation.*

12. *You, or someone legally authorized, will have to sign an authorization of consent for the operation.*

13. *No food or fluids are allowed after midnight on the night before the operation.*

14. *In the morning you may brush your teeth and wash up.*

15. *You'll wear only the hospital gown to the operating room.*

PRE-SURGERY

ESPAÑOL

16. Antes de la operación tendrá que quitarse lo siguiente:
    la dentura postiza o los puentes.
    los ganchos del pelo u otros adornos similares.
    el esmalte de uñas.
    el lápiz de labios.
    el reloj y los anillos.
    todas las cosas de valor, las cuales guardará el enfermero bajo llave.

17. Para su identificación le pondrán una cinta plástica en la muñeca.

18. Antes de la operación le pondrán un tubito plástico, un catéter, hasta la vejiga para que drene la orina, siempre que esto sea necesario.

19. A su debido tiempo le pondrán una inyección o le darán algo para relajarlo y prepararlo para la anestesia.

20. Cerca de media hora antes de la operación lo llevarán en una camilla al quirófano. Allí será atendido por el personal.

21. Después de la operación lo llevarán al salón de recuperación.

22. Allí será atendido hasta que vuelva de la anestesia.

23. Los médicos y enfermeros llevarán traje quirúrgico.

24. Aunque lo observen, no hablarán con usted.

25. Así puede surtir efecto el medicamento.

26. Es posible que le pongan electrodos sobre el pecho para observar el latido del corazón.

27. Le va a invadir el sopor a medida que la anestesia surta efecto.

28. Es importante calmarse en este momento.

ENGLISH

16. *The following should be removed before surgery:*
    dentures or partial plates.
    bobby pins and other hair decorations.
    nail polish.
    lipstick.
    watch and rings.
    all valubles, which the nurse will keep in a secure place.

17. *For identification purposes, a plastic band will be attached to your wrist.*

18. *Just before surgery, a small plastic tube or catheter, will be inserted into your bladder for drainage of urine, if and when necessary.*

19. *At a specific time, you'll be given an injection and other medication to help you relax and to prepare you for the anesthetic.*

20. *About half an hour before surgery, you'll be taken on a gurney to the operating room. There you'll be cared for by the surgery personnel.*

21. *After the operation, you'll be taken to a recovery room.*

22. *There you will be carefully observed until you've recovered from the anesthesia.*

23. *The doctors and nurses will be wearing surgical clothing.*

24. *Although they'll be observing you closely, they won't talk to you.*

25. *This will allow the medication to take effect.*

26. *They may put electrodes on your chest to monitor your heart rate.*

27. *You will feel a drowsy sensation as the medication takes effect.*

28. *It's important to relax at this time.*

PRE-SURGERY

ESPAÑOL	ENGLISH
1. Buenos días, Señor Ramos.	1. *Good morning, Mr. Ramos.*
2. ¿Sigue sintiendo los mismos dolores?	2. *Do you still feel the same pains?*
3. No se preocupe, con la operación se le quitarán todos estos dolores.	3. *Don't worry, all these pains will go away with the operation.*
4. No tenga miedo, usted no va a sentir nada mientras lo estén operando.	4. *Don't be afraid, you will not feel anything while they are operating on you.*
5. Después de la operación no sentirá sino la pequeña molestia de los puntos de la herida.	5. *After the operation you will not feel anything but a little discomfort from the stitches.*
6. Los peores momentos los está pasando ahora.	6. *Now you are going through the worst moments.*
7. Ya verá qué aliviado se va a sentir cuando despierte después de la operación.	7. *You will see how much better you'll feel when you wake up after the operation.*
8. Hoy no le han dado desayuno porque dentro de poco tiempo lo van a llevar a la sala de rayos equis para sacarle más placas.	8. *Today they didn't give you breakfast because they are going to take you to the x-ray room in a little while to take more x-rays.*

PRE-SURGERY

ESPAÑOL

ENGLISH

9. Después de que le saquen las placas lo traerán de vuelta para acá y le servirán un poco de almuerzo.

9. *After they take the x-rays they will bring you back here and serve you a small lunch.*

10. Después de la operación podrá comer de todo y se sentirá mejor.

10. *After the operation you will be able to eat everything and you will feel better than ever.*

11. Estará unas cuatro horas en la sala de operaciones. Después lo pasarán a otra sala hasta que despierte.

11. *You will be in the operation room about four hours. Then they will take you to another room until you wake up.*

12. Siempre habrá una enfermera cuidándole.

12. *There always will be a nurse taking care of you.*

13. No se sorprenda si al despertar encuentra una aguja en uno de los brazos.

13. *Don't be surprised if you find a needle in one of your arms when you wake up.*

14. Esa aguja es para ponerle sangre o para ponerle alimento en la sangre.

14. *This needle is for giving you blood or putting food into your blood.*

15. Tal vez encuentre algunos instrumentos raros alrededor de su cama después de la operación.

15. *Perhaps you will find some odd instruments around your bed after the operation.*

16. Esos instrumentos son para ayudarle a respirar

16. *Those instruments are to help with your breathing.*

17. No hay ningún peligro

17. *There is no danger.*

PREGNANCY

ESPAÑOL	ENGLISH
1. ¿Ha estado embarazada alguna vez? ¿Ha estado encinta alguna vez?	1. Have you ever been pregnant?
2. ¿Cuántos embarazos ha tenido usted?	2. How many times have you been pregnant?
3. ¿Fueron todos sus embarazos normales?	3. Were all your pregnancies normal?
4. ¿Fue el parto natural o provocado?	4. Was the birth natural or induced?
5. ¿Fue un parto natural o usaron tenazas (fórceps)?	5. Was the delivery normal or did they use instruments?
6. ¿Fue el parto por operación cesárea?	6. Was the delivery by caesarean section?
7. ¿Cuántos hijos tiene usted?	7. How many children do you have?
8. ¿Cuántos años tiene el (la) mayor?	8. How old is your oldest child?
9. ¿Cuántos años tiene el (la) menor?	9. How young is your youngest child?
10. ¿Ha tenido alguna vez un aborto inducido o un aborto espontáneo?	10. Have you ever had an abortion or a miscarriage?
11. ¿Cuántos?	11. How many?
12. ¿Cuántas semanas de embarazo tenía usted cuando tuvo el aborto inducido?	12. How many weeks pregnant were you when you had the abortion?
13. ¿Ha tenido alguna vez algún niño que haya muerto poco después de nacer?	13. Have you ever had a baby who died at birth?
14. ¿Cuántos?	14. How many?
15. ¿Ha tenido alguna vez un niño que haya nacido muerto?	15. Have you ever had a stillborn child?
16. ¿Ha tenido alguna vez un niño que haya nacido con el cordón umbilical alrededor del cuello?	16. Have you ever had a child who was born with the cord wrapped around the neck?

225

PREGNANCY

ESPAÑOL	ENGLISH
17. Ha tenido alguna vez problema con la placenta previa?	17. *Have you ever had placenta previa?*
18. Ha tenido alguna vez hemorragia después del parto?	18. *Have you ever had postpartum hemorrhage?*
19. ¿Cuánto tiempo duró su parto con ... su primer hijo? sus otros hijos?	19. *How long was your labor with ...* *your first child?* *your other children?*
20. ¿Cuál fue la fecha de su última regla?	20. *What was the date of your last period?*
21. ¿Está usted embarazada en este momento?	21. *Are you pregnant now?*
22. ¿Cuántos meses?	22. *How many months?*
23. ¿Se planeó este embarazo?	23. *Was this a planned pregnancy?*
24. ¿Cuándo va a dar a luz?	24. *When are you going to give birth?*
25. ¿Cuándo va a nacer el niño?	25. *When is your baby due?*
26. ¿Ha tenido usted rubéola durante este embarazo?	26. *Have you had German measles during this pregnancy?*
27. ¿Sufre usted de alguna enfermedad hereditaria?	27. *Do you have any hereditary diseases?*
28. ¿Sufre usted de diabetes?	28. *Do you have diabetes?*
29. ¿Sufre usted de presión arterial?	29. *Do you have high blood pressure?*
30. ¿Ha tomado algunas medicinas?	30. *Have you been using any medications?*
31. ¿Qué clase?	31. *What type?*
32. ¿Cómo se llama la medicina?	32. *What is the name of the medicine?*
33. ¿Ha estado tomando drogas durante este embarazo?	33. *Have you been taking narcotics during this pregnancy?*
34. ¿Ha tomado alcohol durante este embarazo todos los días?	34. *Have you been drinking daily during this pregnancy?*

SCABIES

ESPAÑOL	ENGLISH

1. Su enfermedad cutánea es causada por un pequeño parásito.

2. Puede pasar de una persona a otra por contacto.

3. Todos los miembros de la familia pueden estar afectados.

4. El tratamiento debe realizarse cuidadosamente, en la forma siguiente:

5. Para sarna:

   A. Tome una ducha o baño jabonoso caliente usando una cantidad abundante de jabón.

   B. Después de secar la piel, apliquese la crema o loción Kwell a las áreas afectadas, incluyendo la piel que las rodea.

   C. No deje de cubrir ninguna porción de la superficie de la piel.

   D. Déjese la crema o loción en la piel durante doce horas.

   E. Después lávese enteramente y póngase ropa limpia o lavada en seco en la lavanderías.

   F. El tratamiento se ha terminado.

   G. Si es necesario puede emplearse una segunda o tercera aplicación en intervalos de una semana.

---

1. *Your skin condition is caused by a small parasite.*

2. *It can be transferred from one person to another by contact.*

3. *Any or all members of your family may be affected.*

4. *Carry out treatment carefully as follows:*

5. *For scabies:*

   A. *Take a hot, soapy bath or shower using liberal amounts of soap.*

   B. *Dry your skin and apply a thin layer of Kwell cream or lotion to affected areas as well as surrounding skin.*

   C. *Do not miss a single portion of the skin surface.*

   D. *Leave medication on skin up to twelve hours.*

   E. *Wash thoroughly, then put on freshly laundered or dry-cleaned clothing.*

   F. *The treatment is finished.*

   G. *If necessary, a second or third application may be made at weekly intervals.*

SCROTAL PAIN

ESPAÑOL	ENGLISH
1. ¿Cuándo empezó el dolor?	1. When did the pain start?
2. ¿En cuál testículo tiene el dolor?	2. In which testicle do you have the pain?
3. ¿Ha tenido dolor similar en el pasado?	3. Have you had a similar pain in the past?
4. ¿Cuándo?	4. When?
5. ¿Tiene hinchazón en el testículo?	5. Do you have swelling in the testicle?
6. ¿Recibió un golpe en el testículo?	6. Did you receive a blow to the testicle?
7. ¿Levantó algo pesado?	7. Did you lift anything heavy?
8. ¿Tiene descarga del pene?	8. Do you have a discharge from the penis?
9. ¿Siente ardor al orinar?	9. Does it burn when you urinate?
10. ¿Tiene fiebre?	10. Do you have a fever?
11. ¿Tiene dolor abdominal?	11. Do you have abdominal pain?
12. ¿Tiene náusea o vómito?	12. Do you have nausea or vomiting?
13. ¿Con cuántas personas tiene sexo?	13. With how many people do you have sex?
14. ¿Usa condones? (preservativos) ... siempre? a veces? nunca?	14. Do you use condoms ... always? sometimes? never?
15. ¿Ha tenido enfermedades venéreas en el pasado?	15. Have you had venereal diseases in the past?
16. ¿Ha tenido ... gonorrea? sífilis? herpes?	16. Have you had ... gonorrhea? syphilis? herpes?

UNCONSCIOUS PATIENT

ESPAÑOL	ENGLISH

1. ¿Qué le pasó?

1. *What happened to him/her?*

2. ¿Qué le sucedió?

2. *What happened to him/her?*

3. ¿Él(Ella) se ha desmayado?

3. *Has he/she fainted?*

4. Él(Ella) se quejó de dolor y se cayó al suelo.

4. *He/She complained of pain and fell to the floor.*

5. El(Ella) se atragantó con la comida.

5. *He/She choked on food.*

6. Se emborrachó.

6. *He/She got drunk.*

7. ¿Padece ...
    del corazón?
    de diabetes?
    de enfisema?
    de asma?
    de bronquitis?
    de problemas al respirar?

7. *Does he/she have ...*
    heart disease?
    diabetes?
    emphysema?
    asthma?
    bronchitis?
    breathing problems?

8. ¿Está tomando algunas medicinas?

8. *Is he/she taking any medications?*

9. ¿De qué clase? ¿Para ...
    el corazón?
    los pulmones?

9. *What kind? For ...*
    the heart?
    the lungs?

10. ¿Puede traerme las medicinas que él(ella) toma?

10. *Can you bring me the medicines he/she takes?*

11. ¿Ha sufrido recientemente un golpe en la cabeza?

11. *Has he/she had a recent head injury?*

12. ¿Ha vomitado?

12. *Has he/she vomited?*

13. ¿Ha sido tratado en este hospital antes?

13. *Has he/she been treated in this hospital before?*

14. ¿Ha estado enfermo(a) antes?

14. *Has he/she been ill before?*

15. ¿ Está embarazada?

15. *Is she pregnant?*

16. ¿Tiene alergias?

16. *Does he/she have allergies?*

17. ¿Ha sido picado(a) por una abeja/avispa?

17. *Has he/she been stung by a bee/wasp?*

18. ¿Fue mordido(a) por una culebra?

18. *Was he/she bitten by a snake?*

19. ¿De qué clase?

19. *What kind?*

URINARY RETENTION

ESPAÑOL

1. ¿Cuándo fue la última vez que orinó?

2. ¿Tiene dolor abdominal?

3. ¿Se le ha recrecido el abdomen?

4. ¿Tiene fiebre?

5. ¿Tiene náusea o vómito?

6. ¿Tiene problemas al empezar a orinar?

7. ¿Gotea al terminar de orinar?

8. ¿Tiene ardor al orinar?

9. ¿Ha notado sangre en la orina?

10. ¿Ha tenido problemas con la próstata?

11. ¿Ha tenido enfermedades venéreas?

12. Usted necesita una sonda en la vejiga.

13. Necesito examinarle la próstata.

14. La próstata está muy grande.

15. Usted tiene una infección del tracto urinario.

16. Usted tiene una infección de la próstata.

17. Necesita ver a un especialista.

18. Tome su medicina.

19. Deje la sonda en la vejiga hasta que vea al especialista.

20. Regrese al hospital si ...
    tiene fiebre o vómitos.
    tiene dolor abdominal.
    si la sonda está tapada.
    si la sonda se sale.

ENGLISH

1. When was the last time you urinated?

2. Do you have abdominal pain?

3. Is your abdomen getting bigger?

4. Do you have fever?

5. Do you have nausea or vomiting?

6. Do you have problems starting to urinate?

7. Do you dribble when you finish urinating?

8. Does it burn when you urinate?

9. Have you noticed blood in your urine?

10. Have you had problems with your prostate?

11. Have you had venereal diseases?

12. You need a catheter in your bladder.

13. I need to examine your prostate.

14. Your prostate is very big.

15. You have a urinary tract infection.

16. You have a prostate infection.

17. You need to see a specialist.

18. Take your medicine.

19. Leave the catheter in your bladder until you see the specialist.

20. Return to the hospital if ...
    you have fever or vomiting.
    you have abdominal pain.
    if the catheter is blocked.
    if the catheter falls out.

VISITING HOURS

ESPAÑOL	ENGLISH
1. Se permiten visitas.	1. *Visitors are allowed.*
2. No se permiten visitas.	2. *Visitors are not allowed.*
3. Se admiten visitas solamente durante las horas de visita.	3. *Visitors are only allowed during visiting hours.*
4. Las horas de visitas son desde las seis hasta las ocho de la noche.	4. *Visiting hours are from six to eight.*
5. Los visitantes deben obtener un pase en la mesa de información del vestíbulo.	5. *Visitors must obtain a pass from the information desk in the lobby.*
6. Sólo dos visitantes al mismo tiempo.	6. *No more than two visitors at a time.*
7. Solamente se permiten dos visitantes por paciente.	7. *Only two visitors per patient are allowed.*
8. Favor de devolver los pases cuando usted salga.	8. *Please return the passes when you leave. (addressing one person)*
9. Favor de devolver los pases cuando ustedes salgan.	9. *Please return the passes when you leave. (addressing more than one person)*
10. Hay demasiados visitantes en el cuarto.	10. *There are too many visitors in the room.*
11. Favor de no fumar en los cuartos de los pacientes.	11. *Please do not smoke in the patient's room.*
12. Se permite fumar solamente en la sala de espera.	12. *Smoking is only allowed in the waiting room.*
13. Los niños que no tienen doce años no pueden visitar a los pacientes.	13. *Children under 12 are not able to visit patients.*
14. A los niños de menores de doce años, no se les permite visitar a los pacientes.	14. *Children under 12 are not allowed to visit patients.*
15. Los visitantes entre la edad de doce y dieciséis años tienen que ser acompañados por un adulto.	15. *Children between the ages of 12 and 16 must be accompanied by an adult.*
16. No se debe dejar solos en la sala de espera a los niños que acompañan a los visitantes.	16. *Children accompanying visitors should not be left unattended in the lobby.*